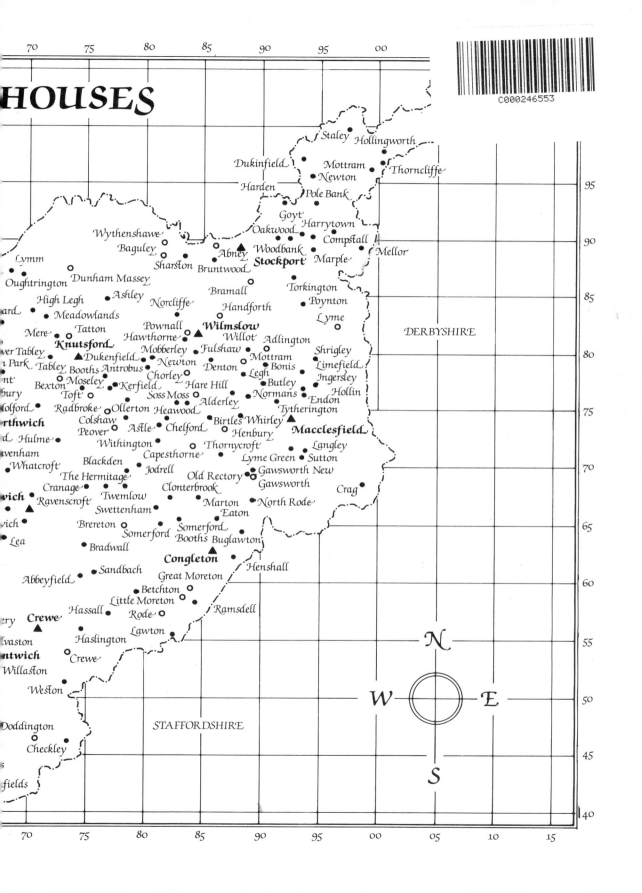

HOUSES

CHESHIRE
COUNTRY HOUSES

The front door, Pownall Hall.

English Country Houses Series   *General Editor:* **Nicholas Kingsley**

CHESHIRE
COUNTRY HOUSES

Peter de Figueiredo
and Julian Treuherz

Phillimore

1988

Published   by
PHILLIMORE & CO. LTD.
Shopwyke Manor Barn, Chichester, Sussex

ISBN 0 85033 655 4

Printed and bound in Great Britain by
Butler & Tanner Ltd, Frome and London

CONTENTS

LIST OF ILLUSTRATIONS

Frontispiece: The front door, Pownall Hall

Colour Plates

List of Plans

ILLUSTRATION ACKNOWLEDGEMENTS

The authors are grateful to the following for permission to reproduce photographs: Airviews (Manchester) Ltd., 87; Architectural Press Ltd., 63, 86, 103; Anthony Barbour, 21-4; Julian Bicknell, 74; Trustees of the British Museum, 69; Sir Walter and Lady Bromley Davenport, 25, 32-3; Cheshire County Council, 112, 128; Cheshire Libraries, 59, 168-9, 178; *Cheshire Life*, 19; Cheshire Record Office, 129-30, 165, 176, 178; *Congleton Chronicle*, 160; Conway Library, Courtauld Institute of Art, 48, 85, 94-5 (photographs by Fred H. Crossley, copyright Maurice H. Ridgway); *Country Life*, 8, 9, 30, 35-7, 46-7, 50, 53, 65, 79, 82, 83, 89-90, 104-5, 108, 110-11, 113-19, 124-6, 135-6, 151, 183, colour plate VIII; English Life Publications Ltd., Derby, 67; Sebastian de Ferranti, 73, colour plate V (photograph by Peter Jenion); Graham Holland, 132; I.C.I. Mond Division, 131, 134, 137; Ian Laurie, 1; Mayotte Magnus, 52, colour plate I; Manchester City Art Galleries, 13, 17, 99, 140-1, 177; Manchester Public Libraries, 27, 29, 40, 54, 58, 146, 148, 153, 181, 188, 196 – also 16 & 199 (photographs by T. Baddeley) and 5, 11, 38, 45, 71, 152, 159, 164, 179 (photographs by James Watts); National Trust, 2, 55-7 – also 78 (photograph by Molyneux), 80 (photograph by A. F. Kersting), 81 & 84 (photographs by John Bethell), colour plate VI (photograph by Jeremy Whitaker); Photographic Records Ltd., 49, 191, colour plate III; Private collection, 44, 72, 186; Timothy Richards, 24, 66, 197; Royal Commission on the Historical Manuscripts of England, 14 & 15 (copyright Lady Ashbrook), 20, 41-3, 142, 143 (copyright N. J. Moore), 145 (copyright Gervase Jackson Stops), 162-3, 192 – also 75-7, 120, 157 (photographs by Bedford Lemere); Walter Scott (Bradford) Ltd., 60, 62; Paul Sherratt, Brampton Photographers, 92; Peter Sisam, colour plate X; Stockport M.B.C., Museum and Art Gallery Service, 25, 28; John Tebbit, 10, 98, 154, 156, 161, 184-5, 193, colour plates II, IV, VII, IX; Tirley Garth, 123; Lord Tollemache, 139; Basil Luis Thomson, 4, 6 (photographs by James Watts); Trustees of the Victoria and Albert Museum, 61; His Grace the Duke of Westminster, 3; Michael Wisehall, 127; Thomas Worthington & Sons, 100. All other photographs are by Peter de Figueiredo and the maps and plans were drawn by Peter de Figueiredo.

FOREWORD

Sotheby's and Strutt & Parker are delighted to be associated with the publication of *Cheshire Country Houses*. Besides the well-known stately homes open to the public, the county has many attractive manor houses and smaller homes. For those of us who live and work in Cheshire, the history of these houses, their estates, their contents and the story of the patrons and architects who created them, is of enormous interest.

There has not been a book on the country houses of Cheshire for over a century and it has hitherto been very difficult to find out the simplest facts about who built them and when. The authors of this book are to be congratulated for their careful research which has brought to light a wealth of fascinating documentation, much of which has previously been unrecorded. The collection of illustrations, many of them rare archive photographs, make the book a pleasure to read as well as an important work of reference.

It is appropriate that Sotheby's and Strutt & Parker should be sponsoring this book. Both companies have offices in Chester, and a long tradition of advising clients in the ownership of works of art, and country houses and estates. There is a greater awareness than ever before for conservation of fine architecture, local and domestic history, and we are keen to encourage the public to appreciate the outstanding beauty of the county. We are sure this book will give both enjoyment and instruction to all those who read it.

Richard Allen
Sotheby's, Chester

Jonathan Major
Strutt & Parker, Chester

SOTHEBY'S
FOUNDED 1744

Booth Mansion
28-30 Watergate Street
Chester CH1 2NA
Telephone: (0244) 315531

STRUTT &
PARKER

19 Grosvenor Street
Chester CH1 2DD
Telephone (0244) 310274

PREFACE AND ACKNOWLEDGEMENTS

This book is divided into two parts. The first consists of a description of 45 country houses selected as the most interesting and representative in the county. These are treated in some detail. This is followed by a gazetteer with briefer entries on all other architecturally significant country houses in Cheshire. The area covered is the historical county of Cheshire before the boundaries were changed in 1974. By a country house, we mean a house at the centre of an historic manor, or with a supporting agricultural estate. Town houses, suburban residences and villas without land have been excluded, although the distinction becomes a little blurred in the 19th century, when industrialists built medium-sized houses in the country. We have left out a few minor country houses which are of little architectural interest or about which nothing is known, and we have included a few lesser houses within the entry on a nearby major house. The more interesting demolished houses have also been described.

Nearly all the houses in the book are private property and we would ask readers to respect this. When a house or garden is open to the public, this is indicated at the head of the entry, and readers are referred to the current yearbooks for up-to-date information on opening times. A number of gardens are also opened on an occasional basis under the National Gardens Scheme and details of these are published in the Scheme's annual booklet. But for private houses we must emphasise that architectural enthusiasm is no excuse for trespass.

We would like to thank all the owners and custodians of the houses for their unfailing generosity and hospitality. In order to preserve their privacy, we have not named individual owners, but we are deeply indebted to them all. Though we have visited all the major houses and many of the lesser ones, we have not been able to inspect every house. For some, we have relied on secondary sources and we apologise for any errors or omissions.

Besides the owners, we would like to thank the many other people who have assisted us. Graham Holland lent us his second-best copy of Ormerod, and helped us on several houses with which he has been associated. Rick Turner, Cheshire County Archaeologist, generously shared with us a great deal of information and research. He and Michael Bellamy, former DoE Listing Inspector, read our first draft and made many helpful comments on it. We have received a great deal of assistance from the many librarians and archivists we consulted, and would particularly like to thank David Taylor of the Local History Department at the Manchester Central Reference Library, Glenyse Matheson of the John Rylands Library, and Ian Dunn at the Cheshire County Record Office, and their staff. We would also like to thank the following: R. Ashton, John Banks, H. N. B. Barrett, Geoffrey Beard, Oliver Beck, Julian Bicknell, Oliver Bott, Martin Boyatt, Linda Briggs, Tim Brinton, Randal Brooks, Kathleen Bryan, Geoff Buchan, Donald Buttress, Maurice Clegg, Peter Cormack, John Cornforth, Belinda Cousens, Stuart Evans, Rev. Alan Fell, Charles Foster, Kath Goodchild, Andor Gomme, John Hardy, John Harris, Edward Hubbard, Mr. & Mrs. Philip Hunter, Mr. & Mrs. David Johnson, Frank Latham, Claire Latimer, Ian Laurie, E. G. M. Leycester-Roxby, Alice Lock, Helen Lowenthal, Clive Luhrs, David Lyle, Laurie McKenna,

John Martin Robinson, W. J. Smith, Colin Stansfield, John Tebbit, N. R. Thompson, Dinah Lady Tollemache, Clive Wainwright, Alan Waterworth, Jim Wigan, W. K. Williams, and Gerald Willis.

Finally, we wish to express our thanks to our editor Noel Osborne, and to George Bailey and Richard Allen of Sotheby's Chester and Jonathan Major of Strutt & Parker for their generous sponsorship, without which this book could not have been published.

BIBLIOGRAPHY AND ABBREVIATIONS

The bibliographies for each house are not intended to be exhaustive; works are cited only where they have been particularly useful, either for text or illustrations. In every case, references have been given to two standard works on Cheshire, Ormerod's magisterial *History of Cheshire* in Helsby's revised edition, and Twycross's *Mansions of Cheshire*, the only previous book on the country houses of the county. Ormerod incorporates earlier histories including William Webb's *Itinerary* of Cheshire *c.* 1623, from Daniel King's *The Vale Royal of England*, 1656, and also Sir Peter Leycester's *Historical Antiquities*, 1673; these works have not been cited separately and page numbers are given for the material from them in Ormerod. Nor have individual references been given to two particularly useful modern works, H. M. Colvin's *A Biographical Dictionary of British Architects*, 1978, and the Cheshire volume of *The Buildings of England* by Nikolaus Pevsner and Edward Hubbard, 1971. These have been used as sources for so many houses that repeated citation would be unnecessarily laborious and, unlike Ormerod or Twycross, they are so arranged that individual houses can be easily found in them. A detailed bibliography on all aspects of Cheshire history is available in *The History of the County Palatine of Chester, A Short Bibliography and Guide to Sources*, edited by Brian Harris, 1983. For a list of published illustrations of country houses 1715-1872 the reader is referred to *A Country House Index* by John Harris, 1979. Some views not recorded elsewhere are contained in two extra-illustrated copies of King's *Vale Royal* compiled by John Broster in the early 19th century, and here referred to as the Broster albums, one at Tatton and the other in a private collection. The National Monuments Record and the Manchester Central Reference Library (Local History Department) have good collections of photographic views.

In the bibliographies given after each entry, printed sources are listed first in chronological order, and then manuscript sources. The most frequently cited works and the principal archive collections are abbreviated as follows:

Aikin	J. Aikin, *A description of the Country from 30 to 40 Miles round Manchester*, 1795
AMS	*Transactions of the Ancient Monuments Society*
APSD	*The Dictionary of Architecture*, ed. Wyatt Papworth for The Architectural Publication Society, 8 vols., 1852-92
AR	*Architectural Review*
B	*The Builder*
BA	*The British Architect*
BM	British Museum
BN	*Building News*
Ches Life	*Cheshire Life*
CL	*Country Life*
Country Heritage	H. R. Shaw, *Country Heritage*, Liverpool Daily Post and Echo, 1951
CRO	Cheshire Record Office (Cheshire County Council)
CCRO	Chester City Record Office (Chester City Council)
Douglas	John Douglas, *The Abbey Square Sketchbook*, 2 vols., 1872
FM	Fletcher Moss, *Pilgrimages to Old Homes*, 7 vols., 1902-20
Franklin	Jill Franklin, *The Gentleman's Country House and its Plan*, 1981
Girouard	Mark Girouard, *The Victorian Country House*, 1971

Hanshall	J. H. Hanshall, *The History of the County Palatine of Chester*, 1817-23
Harris	John Harris, *The Artist and the Country House*, 1979
Heginbotham	H. Heginbotham, *Stockport Ancient and Modern*, 2 vols., 1882, 1892
ILN	*Illustrated London News*
Irvine	W. F. Irvine, *Notes on the Old Halls of Wirral*, 1903
JCAS	*Journal of the Chester Archaeological Society*
JRL	John Rylands Library, University of Manchester
Leland	*Leland's Itinerary*, ed. L. T. Smith, 5 vols., 1964
Lysons	D. & S. Lysons, *Magna Britannia*, vol. ii, part ii, *The County Palatine of Chester*, 1810
Macartney	M. Macartney, *Recent English Domestic Architecture*, 5 vols., 1908-13
Massey	Isaac Massey & Sons, List of Works, *c.* 1929
Mercer	Eric Mercer, *English Vernacular Houses*, 1975
MCRL	Manchester Central Reference Library
Mortimer	W. W. Mortimer, *A History of the Hundred of Wirral*, 1847
Neale	J. P. Neale, *Views of the Seats of Noblemen and Gentlemen in England, Wales, Scotland and Ireland*, vol. v (2nd series), 1829
NMR	National Monuments Record
O	George Ormerod, *The History of the County Palatine and City of Chester*, 3 vols., (1819), 2nd edition revised and enlarged by Thomas Helsby, 1882
Oswald	Arthur Oswald, 'William Baker of Audlem, Architect', *Collections for a History of Staffordshire* (Staffordshire Record Society), 1950-1 (1954)
P & O	J. Parkinson & E. S. Ould, *Old Cottages, Farmhouses and Other Half-Timber Buildings in Shropshire, Herefordshire and Cheshire*, 1904
Pike 1904	W. T. Pike & R. Head, *Cheshire at the Opening of the Twentieth Century*, 1904
Pike 1911	W. T. Pike & R. Head, *Liverpool and Birkenhead in the Twentieth Century*, 1911
RCHM	Royal Commission on Historical Monuments
RIBA	Royal Institute of British Architects Drawings Collection
Robinson	J. M. Robinson, *The Wyatts*, 1979
RSLC	Record Society of Lancashire and Cheshire
Taylor	Henry Taylor, *Old Halls in Lancashire and Cheshire*, 1884
T	E. Twycross, *The Mansions of the County Palatine of Chester*, 2 vols., 1850
Torrington	*The Torrington Diaries* ed. L. B. Andrews, 4 vols., 1935
THSLC	*Transactions of the Historic Society of Lancashire and Cheshire*
TLCAS	*Transactions of the Lancashire and Cheshire Antiquarian Society*
V & A	Victoria and Albert Museum
VCH	*The Victoria County History of Cheshire*, 2 vols., 1979-80

INTRODUCTION

Cheshire is a county of many manors and few mansions; it has an exceptionally large number of seats for its area.[1] Though many of these are substantial, there is no concentration of great houses such as is found in the Dukeries, no prodigy houses like Burghley or palaces on the scale of Chatsworth or Blenheim, which rivalled the court in their conspicuous display of wealth, influence and taste. Only 17th-century Crewe Hall and 19th-century Eaton come into this opulent category. More typical of Cheshire and much better known are Little Moreton Hall, endearingly crooked in pretty black and white, and Tatton Park, sleekly Grecian, fashionable without being startlingly innovatory. But even more common is another class of seat, the small manor house. Some scarcely more than enlarged farmhouses, they have been built by the gentry all over the county since the Middle Ages. Many survive almost unnoticed behind 19th- or 20th-century fronts, with only a mullioned window or a fragment of timber framing to betray their antiquity.

The history of the houses is closely linked to the history of the families which built and improved them, and a surprising number have been resident on their present estates since the Middle Ages: the Cholmondeleys of Cholmondeley, the Delves of Doddington, the Dods of Edge, the Grosvenors of Eaton, the Lancelyns of Poulton, the Leghs of Adlington and the Warburtons of Arley. Families intermarried, sometimes adopting double-barrelled names; when the direct line failed, the indirect heir would take the old name in order to inherit. Some families disappeared, others multiplied into different parts of the county: 'As many Leghs as fleas; Massies as asses; Crewes as crows; and Davenports as dogs' tails'.[2] Old estates were broken up; others were sold and improved. The purchase of an estate, a marriage or the succession of an heir was frequently an occasion for rebuilding.

The proliferation of county families and houses was noted early in Cheshire's history. After the Conquest, because of the county's distance from London and its position on the turbulent Welsh border, Cheshire was made a County Palatine, ruled by the powerful Earls of Chester and a small number of barons. (In 1237 the Earldom passed to the crown.) By 1536, when the palatinate ended, and the county's administration ceased to be separate from the rest of the country, Wales had long been subdued and the castles built for defence had fallen into disrepair. The Dissolution of the monasteries brought the gentry more land to farm and the county families flourished; in the early 17th century the county was described as a 'seedplot of gentilitie'.[3] Agriculture was the main source of wealth in Cheshire until the industrial revolution, and remained of great importance even after it. Cheshire never had an agricultural boom such as produced the wool churches and wealthy houses of East Anglia, but the land remained constantly and quietly profitable over a long period. Cheese was the most famous product of Cheshire from the 16th century. Office holding at court and political jobbery did not lead to the building of big houses in Cheshire as it did in areas closer to London; Cheshire families lived and farmed on their lands, their town houses were in Chester or Nantwich, and they improved their estates conservatively.

There is a striking continuity between medieval moated sites, Elizabethan manor houses and early 19th-century seats. Many Elizabethan houses were built on moated sites, and between 1580 and 1820 only about 36 new sites were established as the centres of estates. On the other hand, over the same period around 130 houses declined into farmhouses

1

1. The landscape park at Birtles.

2. The Cheshire Hunt painted by Henry Calvert, 1839, showing members of all the leading county families.

or disappeared altogether, indicating that the 16th century was the first high water mark of the Cheshire country house.[4] The decline after this period is not solely attributable to the Civil War; most of the old Cheshire families which had suffered fines and confiscation reappeared at the Restoration, and though much land changed hands during the Interregnum, and some houses were damaged, the decline in numbers was part of a wider change caused by the breakdown of the manorial system.[5] While some of the smaller estates contracted, the larger ones grew. The 18th century saw an increase in the enclosure of common land. This and the introduction of improved methods of agriculture enabled landowners to consolidate their estates, to indulge in large scale landscaping of their parks and ,to rebuild their houses in more up-to-date styles. Later in the century a new development arising from the industrialisation of the towns contributed to the revitalisation of the old estates. Urban fortunes made in Manchester and Liverpool financed the aspirations of a new breed of country landowners. But whether their money came from the slave trade, cotton or property, the Liverpool gentlemen and Manchester men who moved out of the cities adopted the style of the established country gentry; they improved and consolidated their estates, rode with the Cheshire hunt, dined with the Tarporley Hunt Club, supported the Cheshire Yeomanry, became High Sheriffs of the county and married their children off into neighbouring families. They built new houses, like Great Moreton and Birtles, both of which replaced old halls, or they bought and preserved existing ones like Brereton and Bolesworth, and soon they were indistinguishable from the county establishment.

A new type of house emerged in the course of the 19th century, the country mansions of urban businessmen. These houses tended to be smaller than traditional seats and were within reach of the counting houses and mills of the cities. Like older country houses, they were set up with parks, farms and lodges, but their owners were actively involved in business, manufacture or the professions and wished to be country gentlemen only in their spare time. Some of these houses were within the boundaries of Liverpool and Manchester and so fall outside the scope of this book; examples are Grove House, Allerton, and The Towers, Didsbury, which was published in *The British Architect* as one of 'the country mansions of Manchester'.[6] But many were built in Cheshire particularly on its north-eastern and north-western fringes, and they were considered by contemporaries to be country houses. Two especially luxurious examples are Abney Hall and the demolished Claughton Manor. Thus the second high water mark of the country house in Cheshire was the early and middle years of the 19th century. Many of the new houses were described and illustrated in Edward Twycross's volumes on *The Mansions of the County Palatine of Chester* of 1850; but the boom continued for many years after. At the same time, the established large seats were being rebuilt or extended to meet the needs of Victorian country house life with its regiments of servants and gardeners, its estate farms and villages, vast domestic wings and stable blocks.

In the 20th century war, taxation, agricultural change and new social attitudes affected the survival of the great country houses and brought to a virtual standstill the building of new ones. The two biggest Victorian houses were Eaton and Peckforton; their symbolic roles had ceased and both had become impractical as family homes. Eaton was demolished in 1969 and a new smaller house built on the same site. Peckforton has stood empty for decades. Other houses are schools, offices and religious establishments and some have survived this institutionalisation remarkably well, above all Tirley Garth, which is maintained with the style and dignity of a private house. Several houses taken over by big companies are engulfed by car parks and office blocks or even, in the case of Winnington, by factories. Houses have suffered amputation in order to survive; this has been done sensitively at Adlington and brutally at Arley. A few have been preserved as

3. The demolition of Eaton Hall, Chester, 1963.

country house museums and some private homes are opened to the public. Too many have been demolished altogether. The site of High Legh is covered in executive-style homes, whilst cattle graze at Somerford; walkers follow nature trails at Marbury, racing cars roar round the circuit at Oulton, and the stables at Eaton-by-Congleton teeter on the edge of a sand quarry. Yet many of the small and middle-sized houses survive in private hands, new or old, and though land has had to be sold for housing, outbuildings pruned and gardens rationalised, a combination of sensible management and a little loving care has seen them through.

*   *   *

The look of Cheshire houses comes from the use of local materials, red or buff sandstone, brick and timber. Most characteristic is timber framing. In 1819 the great Cheshire historian George Ormerod recorded over seventy halls of 'timber and plaister' either in existence or recently demolished.[7] Just over thirty stand today, of which many have been mutilated, partially rebuilt or over-restored. Little Moreton Hall is the only complete example of the traditional courtyard house. The 14th-century Baguley, miraculously preserved in the middle of a housing estate, is the earliest extant timber-framed Hall, and Moss Hall, Audlem, dated 1616, one of the latest. For barns and cottages the technique lasted longer but the 16th century was its heyday. An unusually well preserved example of a small timber-framed house is Churche's Mansion, Nantwich; as this is a town house it is not described in this book but it is similar in plan, scale and structure to a small manor house.

The earliest houses have simple square framing, sometimes with diagonal bracing, but carpenters of the mid- and later 16th century revelled in creating busy and elaborate patterns with quatrefoils, balusters, herringbone designs and crossed clubs, and in jettying out the upper floors. A peculiarity of Cheshire and South Lancashire is the rounded form of the coving beneath the jetties. In the greater houses, the love of decoration was also expressed in the variety of shapes and designs of the small leaded window panes.

4

The infill between timbers was originally of wattle and daub, but in the 15th century lath and lime plaster replaced it. The patterns of the framing were in the 19th century often emphasised by whitening the plaster and by coating the timbers with opaque pitch or tar; the Victorians went so far as to paint fake black and white designs on blank coving and even on stone walls. In the 16th century timbers probably looked more natural in weathered silvery or brownish colours with warmer cream or ochre plaster infill.

Although many half-timbered buildings had brick chimneys, houses of brick such as Brereton and Peover were the exception in the 16th century. Brick became more popular in the 17th century as timber became more expensive; brick was often used to replace plaster infilling when timber-framed houses were being repaired or rebuilt. During the 17th century houses entirely of brick with dressings of stone became the norm. The gabled vernacular of small manor houses like Willaston, Wirral of about 1615, in brick with stone copings, quoins and mullions, is common throughout the county and lasted until well after the Restoration in the case of outbuildings such as the stables at Swettenham, dated 1696. Another type of brick house, such as Bexton Hall, near Knutsford, has wooden cross windows and sometimes a cupola, reflecting the Restoration fashion. In the 18th century classical houses such as Oulton and Tabley successfully combined brick walls with stone basements, columns and architraves. However, the sophisticated brick detailing found in the south and east was never a feature in Cheshire.

Stone was an essential component of both timber-framed and brick houses. Half-timbered buildings were always set on a stone plinth, often of the red or pink sandstone from the western part of the county, and they were roofed in heavy buff-coloured stone slabs from Kerridge or Mow Cop, carefully graded in size. Houses solely of stone were less frequent except where it was handy or where it was used because of special circumstances, as in the case of the tower houses at Brimstage or Doddington, built for defence. The medieval halls at Chorley and Storeton were both conveniently sited next to quarries. Chorley is near Alderley Edge, the source of crow's feet stone with its distinctive markings; the Storeton quarry produced a fierce dark red stone. Grand houses tended to be of stone for reasons of prestige, as at Saighton, the country house of the wealthy abbots of Chester, and at the great Elizabethan houses of Rocksavage and Lyme. Leoni's monumental classical front to Lyme of the 1720s was also of stone but this was the last time it was used on such a scale in the county until the Neo-classical houses of the Wyatts and the castles of the early 19th century. By then changing techniques and improved transport had led to the availability of a greater variety of non-local stone besides new materials such as stucco, Coadestone and, later still, terracotta.

In reaction to this came the vernacular revival of the late 19th century, which in Cheshire meant a self-conscious return to timber framing. The revival was anticipated by the antiquarian-trained architect Edward Blore, not in his Cheshire houses, but on estate buildings at Worsley in Lancasire in the 1840s; it was first seen in Cheshire in Chester itself in the 1850s. At nearby Eaton Hall in the 1870s the architects Alfred Waterhouse and John Douglas used timber framing in the gables of the stable block and in many lesser buildings on the estate. Douglas, born in the county, was one of the leaders of the Cheshire vernacular revival. In his wake applied half timbering became a cliché of late Victorian and Edwardian houses; in contrast is Hill Bark (Bidston Court) by Douglas's pupil Edward Ould, which displays a scholarly understanding of construction combined with a real feeling for the texture and natural irregularities of the material. Ould also recorded the vanishing half-timbered buildings of the region in his book of 1904, illustrated by his own sketches and the sensitive collotype photographs of James Parkinson. Lesser houses of the Arts and Crafts movement such as Inglewood, Ledsham, in beautifully detailed red sandstone, diapered brick and half timbering, demonstrate that the late 19th and early 20th century was a golden age of craftsmanship, when architects were brought up with a deep knowledge of and respect for traditional local techniques. Neither the skills nor many of the materials are available today; the most recent house described in this book employs ornament cast in reconstituted stone, and where real stone is used most of it comes from France.

*   *   *

The stylistic development of Cheshire country houses is closely linked to that of the English country house in general. It is however marked by two phases. Up to the late 18th century most Cheshire houses were old-fashioned. The county was far from the orbit of the Office of Works architects and the London Guilds of tradesmen, and there was not the pressure to keep up with London fashion that existed in the south of England. Cheshire was not only conservative, it could be provincial; the ill-educated Elizabethan frontispiece to a great house like Lyme and the inept late Baroque mural paintings at Adlington show that some Cheshire patrons lacked discrimination. Things began to change in the mid- to late 18th century with improvements in communications, the rise of the professional architect and the growing wealth of the greater landowners. Palladianism was late in coming to Cheshire, but the Wyatt brand of Neo-classicism achieved rapid success. After this, the county was more up-to-date and occasionally in the van of fashion, adopting with enthusiasm the full gamut of styles and revivals of the 19th century and beyond.

The persistence of half-timbered architecture went against the gradual adoption of greater discipline and symmetry seen in Elizabethan and Jacobean houses elsewhere in the country. Little Moreton Hall of the mid-16th century was planned not as a whole, like a classical building, but was added to in a more or less *ad hoc* fashion. It shows a naive taste for all-over surface pattern and its courtyard plan is basically medieval, with the Great Hall asymmetrically placed and entered at one side, not in the centre. Bramall was rebuilt in the 1590s along similar lines. The picture in Cheshire is obscured by the lack of knowledge of contemporary stone or brick houses. The remains of Ridley and Rocksavage indicate quite grand houses, probably, like the surviving Brereton, symmetrical but not very classical. The fragments of the old Woodhey and Tilstone Halls which survive include classical columns and entablatures. Grafton was symmetrical on an E plan, but plain, as was Dorfold. Only Crewe, which 'brought London into Cheshire',[8] is comparable with the Elizabethan prodigy houses; it has a sophisticated frontage and ornate plasterwork, but is a late flowering of the Jacobean style.

From the age of Charles I there are instances of Artisan Mannerism: the demolished Wettenhall Hall of 1635, and Peel Hall, Ashton of 1637, now only a tantalising fragment, but showing a centralised plan of an advanced type. There is also a record of an intriguing meeting between backwoods Cheshire and the new connoisseurship. Peter Moreton, a younger son of the Little Moreton Hall family, travelled to Italy with Nicholas Lanier, who was on his way to arrange the purchase of the Duke of Mantua's pictures for Charles I.[9] Were the Moretons ever tempted to modernise or rebuild? It is fortunate for us that they did not. But the world of Inigo Jones and Palladio did come to Cheshire in the strikingly pure classicism of the chapel at Over Peover church, built in 1648 to receive the tomb of Philip Mainwaring, whose uncle was a member of the court circle of Charles I. The house, however, remained old-fashioned, and the new stable block of 1654 built, like the chapel, by Philip's widow was still essentially Jacobean in its decoration. The Jacobean style persisted in Cheshire in small manor houses such as Shotwick of 1662 and Nether Tabley of 1671, rebuilt for the scholarly Sir Peter Leycester, learned in history, but not in architecture.

All the major Restoration houses of Cheshire have been demolished. William Samwell's Eaton was as modern a house as could be desired for the date, 1675, though dependent on the work of another of Wren's contemporaries Sir Roger Pratt. Less up-to-date was the sumptuously rebuilt Aston, and the creditable effort by the amateur architect Lady Elizabeth Wilbraham at Woodhey. The Samwell type, a central block with two matching detached wings, was used as late as 1732 by Francis Smith at the old Capesthorne, but the only house of the type to survive is Mottram, of the 1750s, with attached rather than separate wings. Of Baroque houses with a giant order, Oulton and old Cholmondeley have gone, leaving only the very provincial Hockenhull as an example; Leoni's south front at Lyme is in a class apart, a learned and monumental design in the grand manner such as only a European could devise.

Leoni's achievement was all the more remarkable because Lyme was not a new house but a recasing, and he had to wrestle with an old-fashioned courtyard plan, a screens passage and inconvenient sets of apartments with no corridors or piano nobile. Vanbrugh faced similar problems at Cholmondeley, where he was called in because of dissatisfaction with the Smiths. The timber-framed Arley was being recased in the 1750s, and Combermere even after 1815. But in general, by the 1760s architects were no longer being asked to make the best of an old house. At Tabley Sir Peter Byrne Leicester, though bound by the terms of his inheritance to keep up the old Hall, decided to build a completely new house on a better site; in the 1770s Samuel Wyatt did the same for the Delves Broughtons at Doddington and the Stanleys at Hooton. At last Cheshire families were breaking free of tradition and wholeheartedly embracing the new style.

Tabley, designed by Carr of York, is the only Cheshire example of Lord Burlington's chaste Palladianism; it came at the very tail end of the movement. On the other hand Belmont Hall of 1755, though a late work by Gibbs and provincial in execution, was part of the fashionable revival of the villa form in the 1750s. But from the 1770s classical architecture in Cheshire meant the Wyatts, two generations of whom dominated the Cheshire country house scene for 60 years, James, his brother Samuel and their nephew Lewis. James worked at only one house in the county, Norton Priory, but the practices of Samuel and Lewis were extensive. Samuel's first complete house, Doddington, of 1776, was novel and original and would have looked startling anywhere, not just in Cheshire, but thereafter his work slipped into an easy elegance.

At Tatton, Lewis continued his uncle's work in this vein, but introduced his own more stylish manner in the interior. It was however the style of Samuel which permeated Cheshire through the work of Wyatt-trained craftsmen such as Lawrence Robinson, who designed additions to Somerford Hall, or Thomas Lee, who made an unexecuted design for Eaton-by-Congleton. Excellent plasterwork in the Wyatt style was at Capesthorne before the fire of 1861, and can still be seen at Mottram, Davenham and Poole.

The latter two houses were examples of Neo-classical villas, country houses more modest than the grand mansions of the Wyatts. The rooms are arranged around a top-lit staircase hall, as in a Palladian villa. The type is at its purest and most Grecian in the work of Thomas Harrison of Chester. At his Woodbank and Tilstone Lodge proportion is all and decoration minimal. The type begat countless plain brick boxes erected as if to a formula, with a single storey porch with columns and perhaps a bow on the garden front. These are found particularly on the fringes of the cotton towns of Stockport and Stalybridge; Twycross illustrates many but credits only one to an architect, Green Hill (now Compstall Hall) by the obscure John Day and Goldsmith. The type was elaborated in the mid-century into the *nouveau riche* Italianate villas of Charles Reed and John Cunningham, with showy belvederes and conservatories.

In his later houses Lewis Wyatt showed an eclectic interest in historical styles. At Lyme he created a Restoration-style dining room and prettied up some of the Elizabethan rooms into rich 'olden time' interiors. His use of Elizabethan on the exteriors of Cranage and Eaton-by-Congleton was by contrast somewhat vapid, but dating from 1828 and 1829 they are the earliest examples of a style which became very popular. Usually mixing Elizabethan with Jacobean motifs, it was called 'Queen Elizabethan' by its chief exponent in Cheshire, George Latham of Nantwich, who used it at Willington in 1829 and from 1833 at Arley. It is seen in less scholarly hands at Mere New Hall by Thomas Johnson and later at Backford by John Cunningham. Also common in the 1830s and '40s was a thin, spiky mixture of Tudor and Gothic as used at Norley and Arrowe.

Lewis Wyatt never used Gothic for a country house, though he restored St Mary's church, Stockport, in the Perpendicular style. The first instance in Chesire of the lacy, decorative style of James Wyatt's Gothick houses was by one of his pupils, William Porden, who began remodelling Eaton Hall, Chester, in 1804. It was a spectacular display of applied pointed ornament, much criticised by fascinated visitors. Eaton was extended in the 1820s but its excesses were toned down in the 1840s by William Burn, for in the meantime a heavier castellated medieval style had become the vogue, exemplified in Cheshire by Cholmondeley, Bolesworth and Great Moreton, big stone sham castles, all massive towers and battlements on the outside and conventionally planned libraries and drawing rooms within. Cholmondeley was begun in 1801 as a small Gothick villa, thus slightly preceding Eaton, but neither it nor Bolesworth made any attempt at scholarly detail. Blore's Great Moreton of 1841 was more ambitious; it contains a vast Great Hall with an elaborate hammerbeam roof, but the detail is hard and mechanical and the house is planned like a Palladian villa.

With Anthony Salvin's Peckforton Castle of 1844-50 the medieval style came of age. It is an astonishing *tour de force*, a romantic Victorian castle convincingly medieval in both appearance and plan, and not just a piece of scenery. It perches on a hilltop looking across at the genuinely medieval Beeston Castle and it is quite equal to its neighbour. But by the time it was completed, castles were out of fashion. Salvin adopted the style of a 17th-century French château for his next big Cheshire house, Marbury, but most architects were turning to the serious Gothic revival. Arderne by J. S. Crowther, an architect known principally for his churches, was designed on Puginian lines. Abney Hall has gorgeous High Victorian interiors in the Pugin manner but they were designed after Pugin's death by his associate J. G. Crace. Victorian Gothic in Cheshire means Waterhouse's Eaton Hall, the biggest and most lavish of all Victorian country houses. Like Peckforton, this was an architectural statement of the power of the landowner and not a house for comfortable living. But Eaton belongs to the late Victorian phase of Gothic, influenced by the Loire style and anticipating the informality of the domestic revival in the private wing and in the free grouping of the stables and estate buildings. Many of these are by John Douglas who, like Waterhouse, started as a High Victorian. Douglas's country houses can be disappointing but at The Paddocks, Eccleston, and the demolished Barrowmore his work shows a strong feeling for picturesque composition.

The interiors at Eaton, with painted rooms by Stacy Marks, stylised aesthetic patterns and much carving and inlay, look forward to the artistic styles of the 1880s. Pownall Hall, Wilmslow, of 1887, is filled with quaint woodcarvings and mottoes, stained glass and inglenooks, but there is also unexpectedly *avant-garde* work by A. H. Mackmurdo and the Century Guild; here in the remarkable metalwork can be seen the beginnings of Art Nouveau. More frequently to be found in Cheshire houses of the 1880s are the conventionally busy Queen Anne interiors of George Faulkner Armitage of Altrincham. The Queen Anne style at its prettiest can be seen in the outbuildings at Haughton Hall, the work of J. F. Doyle, a Liverpool follower of Norman Shaw. In contrast, Shaw's own Dawpool, now demolished, showed him at his most grim and stark.

Cheshire boasts a number of distinguished Arts and Crafts houses. Ould's Hill Bark is rivalled by W. E. Tower's Portal, with its Old English garden, and by C. E. Mallows's masterpiece Tirley Garth where house and garden are sensitively interwoven. Also rewarding are lesser Arts and Crafts houses in the local vernacular such as Manley Knoll. It is significant, however, that two of the principal Arts and Crafts architects to work in the county, Voysey and Baillie Scott, designed not country but suburban houses: Voysey extended a Victorian villa in Alderley Edge and Baillie Scott built a house in Knutsford published in the *Studio* as 'an ideal suburban house'.[10] Wealth and taste were now as likely to be found in the suburbs as on the country estates. A Manchester architect who designed a number of Arts and Crafts suburban residences was Sir Percy Worthington; he also built two country houses proper, Kerfield House, a neo-Georgian remodelling of a Victorian house, and Radbroke Hall. Like Lutyens, with whom his brother Hubert Worthington had worked, Percy moved towards 17th-century classicism and Radbroke, in suave white Portland stone with Wren-style panelled interiors, has both solidity and sophistication. Built between 1913 and 1918 it was the last great Cheshire house.

The inter-war period saw the truncation of Adlington Hall and the destruction of many other important houses – Alderley, Delamere, Hooton, Norton, Oulton and Somerford. Only Delamere was replaced, and not by a house of great distinction. On the positive side, a small group of houses was remodelled with freshness and individuality: Rode and Winnington by Darcy Braddell, Bolesworth by Clough Williams-Ellis and Birtles by James Henry Sellers. These were imaginative commissions. But since the war there has been further truncation, demolition and institutionalisation. Only the new Villa Rotonda at Henbury, a bold and ambitious project, keeps the tradition alive.

1. *CL* cxxxiii, 846; Lysons, 335.
2. F. H. Crossley, *Cheshire*, 1948, 82.
3. John Speed, *Theatre of the Empire of Great Britaine*, 1611.
4. *The Historical Atlas of Cheshire*, ed. D. Sylvester and R. Nulty, 1958, 30-3.
5. R. N. Dore, *The Civil Wars in Cheshire*, 1966, 97.
6. *BA* 2 January 1874, 8.
7. Crossley *op. cit.*, 140.
8. Thomas Fuller, *The Worthies of England*, ed. J. Freeman, 1952, 77.
9. *Little Moreton Hall* guidebook, 1984, 35.
10. *Woodbrook* by Voysey, Drawings at RIBA; *Bexton Croft* by Baillie Scott, *Studio*, iv, 127.

4. The drawing room, Abney Hall, *c*.1900.

Part One

ABNEY HALL, *Cheadle*

860 893 *Park open to the public. (Stockport Borough Council)*

Abney Hall is the best surviving example of a type of house once common in the environs of Manchester and Liverpool, the country mansion of the successful Victorian businessman. Built with the trappings of a country estate, its glossy opulence proclaimed new money. In 1847 Alfred Orrell, a prominent cotton spinner, married and began to build a house at Cheadle, now a suburb, but then a village between Stockport and Manchester. Originally called The Grove, it was an undistinguished villa in the neo-Tudor style, with one idiosyncrasy, a Norman doorway with mechanical zig-zag mouldings and nook shafts.

Orrell died 14 months later, before his house was ready, and in 1849 it was bought by James Watts, partner with his father and uncle in the largest wholesale drapery business in Manchester. Watts was a classic type of Manchester entrepreneur, a free trader and a dissenter. As a mark of his religious views he changed the name of his house to Abney Hall after his namesake, the non-conformist hymn writer Isaac Watts, who lived at Abney Park near London, as guest of his patron Sir Thomas Abney. James Watts, the son of a self-made man, began to climb the social ladder. In 1849 he had become a City Councillor; he was to be twice Lord Mayor of Manchester and later High Sheriff of Lancaster. The Abney Hall visitors' book records the names of Gladstone, Disraeli, Lord Derby and many bishops, peers and notabilities. Watts's big moment came in 1857 when he entertained Prince Albert, for which he was later knighted by the Queen. Albert came to open the great Manchester Art Treasures exhibition and stayed at Abney in a bedroom luxuriously appointed for the purpose. Watts used to point proudly to the verse from *Proverbs* on his library ceiling (the house is full of mottoes), 'Seest thou a man diligent in his business, He shall stand before kings', and then recount how he had sat not stood under it whilst speaking to Prince Albert.

Watts had Abney remodelled by the architects Travis and Mangnall, who in 1850 were to build the S. & J. Watts warehouse, the most grandiose in Manchester. The alterations at Abney were, on the outside at least, less spectacular. The Norman doorway was preserved, but the house was enlarged with lavish reception rooms and a grand staircase. The new work was carried out in brick and stone to match the old, but the more generous proportions, the Gothic ornaments and the pinnacled and gabled skyline gave a sense of amplitude and parade lacking from the former villa.

Nevertheless, the true spectacle at Abney was inside. Watts commissioned the interiors from J. G. Crace & Son, a well-known firm of London decorators. Crace had worked a great deal with the Gothic Revival architect A. W. N. Pugin, the great pioneer of the polychromatic medieval interior. The two had been closely associated over the decoration of the House of Lords, and the Medieval Court at the Great Exhibition. Crace's firm used many of Pugin's designs, and Crace's own style was infected with Pugin's love of gorgeous colours and strong all-over patterning. Pugin provided Crace with drawings for Abney in February 1852 (now in the Victoria and Albert Museum). Mainly pattern designs, they are very sketchy and are among the last he ever drew. 'I have done my best and am nearly done myself', he wrote to Crace just before his fatal illness. After Pugin's death later in 1852 Crace completed the decorations alone, using Pugin's favoured team of manufacturers, Minton for tiles, Hardman for metalwork and Myers for carving.

The commission at Abney may have resulted from a visit by Watts to the Medieval Court at the 1851 Exhibition, for the cabinet from Abney now at Salford Art Gallery (or one very like it) was shown there. In the Victoria and Albert Museum is an inlaid octagonal table from Abney similar to those designed by Pugin for the House of Lords, and photographs of the Abney dining room show a set of sturdy oak chairs with leather upholstery, a standard Westminster type. But there is only one piece still at Abney, a massive oak sideboard with a mirror and a tall coved and crested canopy lettered 'In vino veritas'. Originally in the dining room, it now stands inappropriately in the drawing room. Most of the furniture was dispersed at a sale in 1958 following the death of James Watt M.P., grandson of Sir James. The house was bought privately but sold to the local authority for use as Cheadle Town Hall. The successor council, Stockport, left the Hall in 1974 and leased it to commercial tenants, but retained the furniture then still in the house for use elsewhere; there are pieces at Lyme, Bramall and Stockport Town Hall.

From the front door a small lobby leads through a glazed Gothic screen into a broad corridor floored in Minton tiles. A glittering brass gasolier hangs from the ceiling, which is divided by heavy ribs and bosses. These and the elaborate crestings over the doors are all made of *carton pierre*, a kind of papier maché which Crace used despite Pugin's belief in truth to materials. On the left is the staircase hall and on the right the principal rooms, dining room, library and drawing room. Now almost empty, the dining room and library were originally very sumptuous, with lettered friezes and decorated ceilings and walls. Over the dining room fireplace hung *The Englishman in the Gypsy Quarter at Seville*, a painting by John Phillip whose flashy style was fashionable amongst High Victorian millionaires. It was exhibited at the Royal Academy in 1853 and so was bought new for the house with works by other modern British artists, all now dispersed.

But the spirit of the 1850s still lives on in the drawing room where the dazzling wall and ceiling decoration remains, filling the room despite the lack of furnishings. The walls are covered in a green silk damask, based on a 16th-century Italian design. At intervals are broad vertical bands stencilled in a bold pattern of rich colours. Above, the wide frieze is emblazoned with coats of arms and diagonally placed mottoes in Gothic lettering. Around the top of the walls runs a long quotation on friendship, a homely message amidst all the finery. On the ceiling, the star-shaped rib patterns and the pendants are picked out with gilding and in the centre is a magnificent brass gasolier decorated with spiky Gothic ivy leaves, enamelled coats of arms and plenty of glass buttons to provide sparkling reflections of the gas jets. Pier glasses and an overmantel mirror give further glitter. The bees on the frieze and coats of arms are Watts heraldry, but are also the emblem of Manchester itself and signify industry.

The staircase hall has lost most of its stencilling but is still spatially dramatic, approached through three pointed arches and ascending in a central flight dividing into two at the first landing. It is lit from an enormous stained glass window, and from above by an octagonal lantern like that in the central lobby at the Palace of Westminster, itself inspired by the octagon at Ely Cathedral. Upstairs are the principal bedrooms, now empty. Prince Albert's had rich Pugin wallpaper and furniture, and a heavy marble washbasin with handles for hot and cold water supplied from above, a novel luxury for the time.

Sir James Watts died in 1878; in 1893-4 his son, James Watts jnr., employed George Faulkner Armitage to extend the house in his quaint, exaggerated but mechanical Arts and Crafts manner. Typical of his style are heavy oak beams, enormous inglenooks, hooded fireplaces, twirly copper

5. The garden front, Abney Hall, *c*.1900, showing Armitage's additions.

6. The music room, Abney Hall, *c*.1900.

and wrought ironwork, leaded lights and heraldic glass. Armitage enlarged the conservatory, which had been added by John Shaw in the 1860s, creating the top-lit terrace room, leading through Crace's former breakfast.room to the new east wing containing morning, music and billiard rooms.

The music room, panelled in oak with a half-timbered frieze, is pleasantly low and irregular in plan, the main space flowing into smaller areas, with alcoves, window bays and changes of level. Off the principal inglenook, a small doorway leads to a darkroom. James Watts jnr. was a passionate amateur photographer, the 'X' who accompanied Fletcher Moss on his *Pilgrimages to Old Homes*. Some of his photographs have been used to illustrate this book. Watts jnr. was also a magpie collector and antiquarian, cramming both the Crace and the Armitage rooms with quaint old oak, carved and turned chairs, gate-leg tables, spinning wheels, old musical instruments, pewter, china, swords, pikes, suits of armour and miscellaneous portraits. His photographs show an atmospheric house full of knick-knacks quite different from the empty rooms of today. This was the house where Agatha Christie stayed as a child, for her sister married the son of James Watts jnr. She dedicated to Abney her book *The Adventure of the Christmas Pudding* and recalled with affection the many Christmas holidays she spent there. It was a perfect setting for a 'whodunnit'.

The antiquarian taste of James Watts jnr. contrasts with his father's delight in the new. Watts jnr. was also what would now be termed a conservationist, for in 1899 he rescued the ruinous Buckley Hall of 1625, the home of his mother's ancestors at Rochdale, and rebuilt it in the grounds of Abney. His interest in conservation was not superficial for, despite his reaction against the High Victorian style, he carefully preserved the Crace rooms and their contents.

The rebuilt Buckley Hall was demolished by the local authority in 1963, the stables were taken down more recently still, and inside the walled garden is an unsightly group of temporary huts used as council offices. The handsome Gothic gatepiers to the main drive have been vandalised, and the gardens, once filled with rockeries and fountains, are a seedy public park. At the corner of a garden wall, an enormously tall Gothic finial stands sentinel, a ventilating shaft for some long outmoded heating system. But despite the unkempt grounds and the institutional character of the house, Abney still powerfully recalls the heyday of the merchant princes of Victorian Manchester.

T ii, 128; *ILN* 16 May 1857, 458; FM ii 1903, 390; *CL* cxxxiii, 846, 910; B. L. Thomson, *The Town Hall, Cheadle*, 1972; *V&A Album*, 1986, 77.

I. The Central Hall, Crewe Hall.

II.   The Great Hall, Adlington Hall.

ADLINGTON HALL, *Adlington*

904 805 *House and gardens open to the public. (Privately owned)*

'Descending this hill, and thro' a wooded country, came to Edlington; and then into the turnpike road, fronting which is an ugly staring red-brick house, of Mr. Leghs.' Lord Torrington, passing by in 1790, saw the classical south front of Adlington Hall, with its ungainly portico built by Charles Legh in 1757. But had he looked behind the portico he would have found an ancient half-timbered courtyard house with the finest medieval Great Hall in Cheshire.

Originally Adlington was moated and had timber-framed buildings on three or even four sides of the courtyard. The tall half-timbered porch on the north side formed the entrance to the Great Hall (the visitor now enters from the back) and was probably approached from a gatehouse where the classical portico now stands. The pair of heavy oak-studded doors displayed in the courtyard arcade is probably from the old gatehouse. The Great Hall is dated 1505 inside, but the porch was added in 1581, according to the legend carved on its lintel, 'Thomas Leyghe Esquyer who maryed Sibbell doughter to Sr Urian Brereton of hondforde Knighte and by her had Issue foure sonnes & fyve doughters made this buyldinge in the yeare of O^r lorde god 1581 And in the raigne of our soveraigne lady Queene Elizabeth the xxiijth'. Its big herringbone bracing resembles that on the east wing, housing service rooms, probably built at the same time, but in form the porch is like the two-storeyed jettied porch at Handforth Hall built 19 years earlier by Thomas Legh's father-in-law, the Urian Brereton mentioned in the inscription.

In the late 17th century the Great Hall, except for the porch, was encased in brick and tall mullioned windows were put in to light it. Colonel Thomas Legh the younger had inherited in 1644 but Adlington had been twice besieged and the estate sequestrated. He did not get it back until 1656, after paying heavy fines. Before his death in 1687 he remodelled the Great Hall inside and out and tacked on to it the irregular gabled north front, with its panelled rooms within.

The Great Hall, though lofty, is small in relation to its height. It has two very remarkable early features. At the upper end is the coved canopy, a rare wooden version of the cloths of estate hung over the high table in the Middle Ages to give splendour to the appearance of the Lord of the Manor. The carved wooden zig-zag imitates a decorative valance. The canopy is divided by oak ribs into 60 compartments each one painted with Cheshire family arms, and there are wooden letters, finely carved with decorative flourishes, spelling out 'Thomas Legh & Catherina Savage uxor eius A°.D^{ni}. MCCCCCV RRH VII XX' that is 1505, the 20th year of Henry VII's reign. Once the scheme was even grander, for an account of 1611 records an elaborate display of over 180 coats of arms in the Great Hall.

The spere-truss at the lower end is even earlier than the canopy. It consists of two massive octagonal posts rudely decorated with broad roll mouldings and cusped panels. Between the speres and the side walls are fragments of delicate Gothic tracery, and in the passage around the now blocked buttery and pantry doors are carved animals and foliage. The style of the carving suggests the early 15th century. Much has since been altered: the roof has been plastered and grained to imitate panelling, the angels on the hammer-beams have been replaced with later ones, the walls covered in murals and the spere-truss filled in with the organ gallery. To get an idea of how it originally looked one has to visit Rufford Old Hall, Lancashire, which has so much in common with Adlington that it is possible they are by the same craftsmen. Rufford has a coved canopy, a hammerbeam roof with angels and a spere-truss, the pattern of the latter

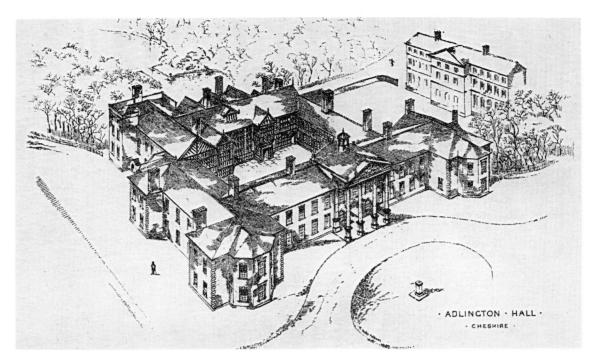

7. (*above*) Adlington Hall before demolition of the west wing: drawing by Henry Taylor, 1884.

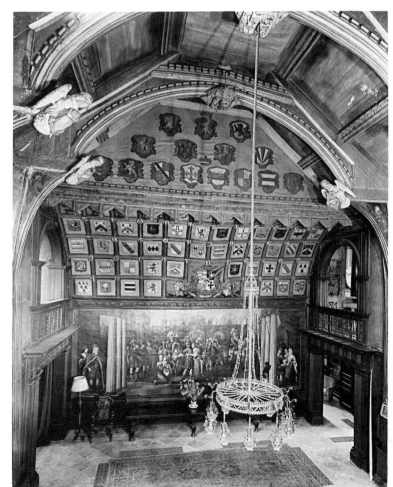

8. The Great Hall canopy, Adlington Hall.

almost identical to that at Adlington. But at Rufford all the original quatrefoil framing is still visible on walls and roof, and between the spere-truss is a unique free-standing carved wooden screen.

The organ at Adlington was installed in the late 17th century by Colonel Thomas Legh. It has two tiers of pipes arranged between carved grilles and fluted pilasters; the precision and daintiness of the gilded Baroque curves recalls the woodwork in Wren's City churches. Also of the finest quality are the carved railings in the alcoves and the organ gallery, the latter especially delicate with interlaced L's for Legh. The organ itself dates from the same period, though incorporating parts of a pre-Restoration instrument. It is one of the earliest of its date to survive virtually unaltered and is almost certainly the work of Bernard Smith, a famous organ builder, all of whose major organs, including those at Westminster Abbey and St Paul's, have been altered or destroyed. The Adlington organ includes three 17th-century reed stops, a rarity which produces a surprisingly astringent tone. Handel played the organ at Adlington in 1741 or '42 and set to music a hunting song written by Charles Legh. Handel's manuscript 'presented by him in this his own handwriting to Charles Legh Esqr. in the year 1751' is kept at the house. The organ is still used for occasional concerts.

Two slightly later embellishments are in a less urbane style. First, above the organ is a gigantic curved hood framing two overscaled gilded cherubs jauntily playing trumpets, and a pair of coats of arms with exuberant mantling surmounted by the Legh crest of a unicorn's head. This dates from 1693 and commemorates the marriage of John Legh and Lady Isabella Robartes. Second, are the wall paintings, showing the provincial taste of a country squire trying in vain to keep up with modern fashion. They were sensibly covered up at some point but revealed again in the mid-19th century. The story of Aeneas, Hector and Andromache is told in the stilted gestures and fancy costume of a comic opera, a jolly but naive imitation of the grandiloquent work of Verrio and Laguerre, fashionable late 17th-century mural painters. On the short walls by the speres, a little later in date, are Mrs. Arabella Hunt, singer and lutenist to Queen Anne, copied from an engraving of 1692 after Kneller, and St Cecilia, patron saint of music, playing the harp. The musical theme continues in the contemporary fireplace with the head of Apollo.

Charles Legh inherited in 1736 and began an extensive programme of modernisation, also somewhat provincial in style. He was responsible for the two brick ranges south and west of the courtyard, the detached stable block, and several park buildings. First came the western extension of the north wing, with a library, staircase, drawing room and dining room, the latter of 1742. The stables are dated 1749, and the south wing bears the inscription 'Charles and Hester Legh 1757'. Finally the west side of the court was closed by the long ballroom, dated 1761 on a Venetian window, now reset.

The 18th-century improvements are recorded in a series of paintings by Thomas Bardwell, all the more important as much of the work has since disappeared. Sir Hubert Worthington was called in in 1929 to reduce the house; many of the original contents had been sold in 1846 and few family papers survive. Bardwell's south view shows the front criticised by Torrington, with the Ionic columns of the portico ineptly raised upon octagonal bases and the attic storey squashed in below the pediment. This front was formerly much wider than it is now, for at either end were broad pavilions with canted bays housing the end of the ballroom at the west and the chapel at the east, both removed in 1929. Further east is the simpler and more successful front of the stable block, since shorn of its cupola. The paintings also record the garden buildings, including the surviving domed Temple of Diana, the ruinous Jupiter House and a Chinese bridge, now lacking its pagoda and railings. Not shown in the painting are the Tig House and an enchanting Shell Cottage. In each of the paintings the presiding genius is present, Charles Legh, always surrounded by a little crowd of favourite dogs.

The main 18th-century rooms which survived the demolition are the dining room and the drawing room above it, connected by a plain broad staircase. Both rooms are fully panelled in

9. The south front and stables, Adlington Hall, from a painting by Thomas Bardwell, *c.*1761.

10. The drawing room, Adlington Hall.

the classical style with pediments over doorcases and chimneypieces. The dining room is lower and lacks enrichment. It has a simple veined white marble fireplace which can be dated 1742 from a document signed by the carver Will Hall, agreeing to work it 'according to Mr. Norris' design', perhaps the same John Norris who was architect at Dunham Massey between 1732 and 1740. Like Norris' work at Dunham, the rooms at Adlington were old-fashioned for their date. It is tempting to speculate whether Norris was the architect of Adlington where, in the absence of any evidence either way, the design has been attributed to Charles Legh himself.

Much more splendid is the drawing room, taller and bolder with giant Corinthian pilasters and more generous friezes. There is vigorous wood-carving in the William Kent style over the doors, showing heads of Bacchus, Ceres, Flora and Neptune, the latter particularly good with seaweed hair, shells and ammonites. The white marble chimneypiece was carved by Daniel Sephton, a Manchester statuary; its heavy scrolls, garlands and the profile of Minerva are similar to his signed monument of 1753 in St Mary's Church, Stockport.

In the family sitting rooms of the south wing there are pretty Rococo ceilings with Gothick and Chinoiserie motifs including one with frolicking monkeys. Also preserved in this part of the house are a few fragments from the demolished rooms, overdoors of classical heads with trophies like those in the drawing room. Worthington's reductions were sensitively done; instead of simply removing the west wing and exposing the courtyard on one side, he rebuilt a screen wall housing a corridor to link the north and south wings, and replaced quoins, cornices and sashes to disguise his surgery. Thus the integrity of the house was kept; despite the demolition, Adlington's mixture of antiquity and homeliness make it one of Cheshire's friendliest houses.

O iii, 663; T ii, 100; Taylor, pl. 29; Torrington iii, 120; *CL* cxii, 1734, 1828, 1969; *Adlington Hall* guidebook, n.d.; *The Organ at Adlington Hall*, 1978; Adlington Hall, family papers.

ALDERLEY PARK, *Nether Alderley*

844 763

The Stanleys of Alderley are one of Cheshire's best known families, and their letters, edited by Nancy Mitford (a member of the family herself), provide a fascinating insight into country house life of the mid-19th century. During the Victorian period they were one of the county's biggest landowners, but a series of misfortunes has meant that not only does no great country house survive today, but the Stanley family no longer has any interest in Alderley.

The principal remnant is the Old Hall, standing close to Nether Alderley Mill at the north end of the park. This is part of an early 17th-century house built by Sir Thomas Stanley, the 2nd baronet, which was later extended and then severely damaged by fire in 1779. Besides the house he built the stone bridge over the moat, a new stable block, extensive walled gardens, and a pigeon house known now as the Apple House, all of which remain, and he was the first Stanley to plant the famous beech trees which now cover the Edge. But even before the estate was acquired by the Stanleys in 1602, the mill and its reservoir had been constructed. Nether Alderley Mill dates from the 16th century and its back wall forms the dam to the lake which provided water to power the wheel, doubling as an ornamental moat for the Old Hall. In the 18th century the house was transformed. In front of the Old Hall was placed a three-storey rectangular block with a piano nobile and a high parapet. In the centre a giant order without an entablature gave prominence to the new entrance. According to Lysons the date was 1754, but illustrations show a huge Baroque front more in the style of the very early 18th century. Though undeniably grand, like other Cheshire houses of this period it is a frankly provincial design.

The new house did not last long. In 1779 it was utterly destroyed by fire. The family was absent at the time, but most of the furniture, paintings and books were lost. All that now remains from this important period of building is a rusticated stone pier close to the road. After the fire the family moved out to the Park House, a farmhouse at the southern end of the park. At first the intention was probably to rebuild on the original site (an estate map dated 1798 shows the Hall still at the north end and the Park House as a collection of farm buildings around a garth), but in time they must have decided to remain at Park House, and a gradual programme of improvements was begun. From this period there survives extensive stabling of 1815, arranged around two courtyards connected by an archway. In the first is a handsome hexagonal dovecote with nesting boxes for over 400 birds. The new house was erected to the east of this complex, and, like the stables, was built in stages. It was in a plain classical style, low and spreading, with various rambling extensions, all faced in stucco. By the end of the century there were 40 principal bedrooms and six large reception rooms, yet still in 1904 a grand ballroom was added for the 4th baron. This was designed by Paul Phipps, a London architect, and apart from the stables is the only section of the house still remaining.

In 1931 fire struck again, and the house, already proving too large and too costly to maintain, was demolished. The ballroom now became the principal reception room and an adjoining farmhouse the family quarters. It was a short-lived arrangement, for in 1938 came the final dismantling of the estate; 4,624 acres of land, 77 farms and 170 other dwellings were sold in a four-day auction, and the 400-acre park was bought by a London developer. Though the house had already been destroyed, the park and gardens were up to this time well maintained. They included a beautiful water garden surrounded by terraces and herbaceous borders, Samuel Wyatt's delicate latticework iron gates from the Poultry House at Winnington Hall which the

11. The Old Hall, Alderley, *c.*1900.

12. (*below*) The Old Hall, Alderley, showing the 18th-century block.

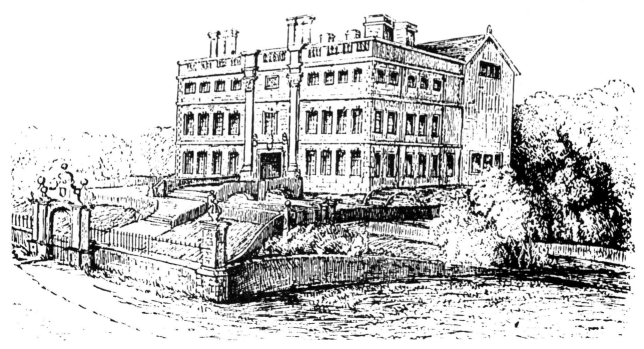

1st Lord Stanley had bought in 1809, and an obelisk of 1750 with the Stanley eagle crest. There was also a curious 18th-century deer enclosure with castellated walls designed as an eye-catcher to be seen from the Old Hall.

During the war all this fell into decay, but in 1950, after the failure of the developer to gain consent for housing in the park, the estate was acquired by I.C.I. Today park and gardens have been partially restored as the setting for a huge new complex of offices and laboratories accommodating over two thousand employees.

Lysons, 481; O iii, 578; T ii, 87; J. P. Earwaker, *East Cheshire* ii 1880, 601; *Ches Life* July 1936; Nancy Mitford, *The Ladies of Alderley, Letters 1841-50*, 1938; Nancy Mitford, *The Stanleys of Alderley, Letters 1851-65*, 1939; G. B. Mill, *The History of Alderley Park*, 1980 (typescript at Alderley Park); *Nether Alderley Mill* guidebook 1982; CRO DSA/241/1A Account Book, DSA/3177/4 Photo Album.

ARLEY HALL, *Aston-by-Budworth*

675 810 *House and gardens open to the public. (Privately owned)*

Arley Hall was designed by George Latham for Rowland Egerton-Warburton between 1832 and 1845. Though savagely truncated in recent years, it is an ambitious and single-minded creation of the early Victorian Jacobean revival. Surviving documents from the lengthy period of construction provide a fascinating picture of the relationship between the architect and his client.

The Arley estate had formed part of the extensive Warburton holdings since the end of the 12th century. In 1469 Sir Piers Warburton moved from Warburton to Arley and built himself a new house. This was at first a standard E plan timber-framed house facing south within a moat. In the 16th century the Hall was extended to enclose a large courtyard with a gatehouse. William Webb visiting it around 1623 wrote of 'the sight of that beautiful house of Arley that doth, as it well may, show itself to beholders afarre off as a place to be regarded'. By the mid-18th century it was thought less prepossessing and in 1758 Sir Peter Warburton, the 4th baronet, filled in the moat and encased the house in brick and stucco to create a more fashionable appearance. An unsigned elevation and a later watercolour show the south front which somewhat resembled the entrance front of the nearby Belmont Hall. To each side were full height canted bays and in the centre a curved bow with Gibbs surrounds to the openings and octagonal-paned sashes. More striking was the treatment of the Great Hall which was fancifully decorated later in the 18th century with Gothick pinnacles, cresting and ogee windows.

These improvements did not give satisfaction for long, for family letters complained of rats and the smell of drains. When Sir Peter Warburton, the 5th and last baronet, died in 1813 without issue, he left Arley to his great-nephew Rowland Egerton, then aged eight. In 1818 plans were drawn up by Lewis Wyatt, who was working for Rowland's uncle Sir John Grey Egerton at Oulton Park, for rebuilding the west front in a plain Neo-classical style. Then in 1826 when Rowland had reached the age of 21 George Latham was engaged and submitted four alternative schemes for a symmetrical Gothic house. Latham, an unknown local architect practising in Nantwich, was hardly older than Rowland (who with his father had now taken the name of Egerton-Warburton), and though none of these schemes was to be adopted, he was to remain the principal architect at Arley for over twenty years. It was not until after Rowland's marriage in 1831 that any real progress was made. In one of the first of a huge quantity of letters from architect to patron, Latham advised that the old house be completely demolished, and that with 'proper economical management, a superior mansion with a picturesque Elevation might be erected with from £5-6,000'. Although the final cost turned out to be nearer £30,000, Rowland was sufficiently encouraged to commence, and new plans were prepared. The style adopted was not Gothic but Jacobean, though Latham called it 'Queen Elizabethan'. He had just completed Willington Hall in this manner at a cost of £4,000, but Rowland cannot have found much to impress him about this other than value for money. Building commenced in 1832 with the service wing. The main house was planned as a large rectangular block built over the old courtyard, and continuity was maintained by rebuilding the Great Hall in exactly the same position as before. By the beginning of 1834, Rowland had become worried by the expense, and the following year, with the cost having already reached £13,000, construction stopped with the drawing room, staircase and Great Hall unfinished internally. It was not until 1840 that work recommenced.

The external appearance of the new house is derived from Crewe Hall which Latham knew well. Arley is built of diapered red brick with stone dressings, mullioned and transomed windows

13.   The entrance front, Arley Hall, *c.*1880, showing the tower, now demolished.

and small shaped gables. Throughout the long period of construction Latham's letters show the degree of interest which Rowland took in every aspect of the work, leaving little to the discretion of his architect. He was a difficult patron, demanding constant alterations to details, replanning the layout of rooms and issuing curt criticisms when the results did not please him. Latham, who lacked the self-confidence of greater architects, was easily hurt and wrote long defensive replies. Most trying must have been the abuse he suffered whenever he submitted his hard-earned fee accounts; and then in 1841 when dry rot was discovered in the new building he was held directly responsible. The reason for Rowland's intolerance was perhaps because, as the work proceeded, so his discernment grew and he recognised the limitations of his architect. But as Latham was a local man he was always on hand, whereas a metropolitan architect would probably not have been able to cope with the piecemeal programme of construction.

Rowland's doubts about Latham's abilities led him to look elsewhere for an architect to design him a chapel. Formerly the chapel had been a separate structure within the park, but Rowland, much influenced by the Oxford Movement, resolved to have a building attached to his house more suited to the ritual of Catholic worship. This meant a Gothic chapel in the style of the 13th century. This time he went to a London architect, Anthony Salvin, who, though principally a designer in the Tudor style, had erected one church along thoroughly Ecclesiologi-cal lines, Christ Church, Kilndown in Kent for Viscount Beresford, step-father of A. J. Beresford-Hope, a founder member of the Cambridge Camden Society. Latham was understandably vexed, describing Salvin's design as 'a breach of good taste', because it would destroy the unity of the east elevation. Rowland retorted by quoting Pugin's views on the dishonesty of uniformity in architecture, but Latham would not give way and made his own plans for a chapel in the 'Queen Elizabethan' style. When these failed to meet with approval, he tried a Gothic design, finally urging his patron to convert the new Great Hall to a chapel. Rowland however had decided that the Great Hall was to become the dining room, and there the matter rested. Salvin built the chapel and Latham continued as architect for the house.

Salvin too was subjected to lengthy correspondence on every detail, but knowing how to deal with his difficult client he was treated with much greater respect. On completion Rowland expressed great satisfaction with the effect of the chapel, and indeed the result is a perfect example of the Ecclesiologists' liturgical requirements. Pugin would have appreciated the composition of steep roofs, octagonal belfry and oriel window grouped round the porch which originally connected the chapel to the house. Inside the chapel are angel corbels holding shields, each one different, just like those in the chapel at Pugin's Alton Castle. More remarkable are the fittings added later by G. E. Street, to whose design the north aisle and servants' porch were built in 1856-7. Street's ironwork is exceptionally beautiful, especially the radiator cover in the form of a 13th-century tomb with lily finials. The chapel was consecrated in September 1845, but during its construction progress was being made on the house itself. By this time the shell, with the exception of the south front, was completed, and the service wing was in operation, but none of the main rooms had been decorated. In 1840 the design of the south front was agreed, and the old range was demolished. As in the layout of the former house the entrance was placed in the centre, but the appearance of this elevation has been radically altered by the removal in 1968 of the octagonal domed tower which rose above the porch. This was a curious feature, probably modelled on the entrance tower of Holland House, Kensington, but made much taller. It gave the design a strong verticality, and without it the elevation is a lack-lustre version of the entrance front of Crewe Hall. The heraldic animals perched on the gables are reminiscent of those on the staircase at Crewe and originally held pennants. They were carved by John Thomas, sculptor of the huge lions guarding the approach to the Britannia Bridge over the Menai Straits.

In 1842 work started on the interiors of the principal rooms, but Rowland, impatient to receive drawings, maintained that Latham was devoting too much of his time to John Tollemache and his plans for Peckforton Castle. Relations deteriorated over the execution of the library ceiling, and there was criticism of details, including a dubious warm air heating system which Latham had recommended. In November 1846 Latham was invited to submit his account for work done since 1837, and after three months' wrangling he was dismissed. Having been employed by Rowland for 20 years he wrote sadly 'it would certainly have been a matter of the highest gratification to me to have had the honour of completing as well as of beginning your house'. However it was not the end; in 1861 the architect was back in favour redesigning the ceiling of the new library and in 1865 the final decoration of the entrance hall and morning room.

For all the hours spent on them by both architect and patron, the interiors are frankly a disappointment. The ceiling designs were based, as Latham was keen to point out, on actual examples recorded in such books as Richardson's *Old English Mansions*, but their execution is mechanical. There is also a monotony of scale and a repetitious character about the rooms, something skilfully overcome by Salvin in his designs for Peckforton (for by this time Salvin had replaced Latham as the architect for Tollemache's new castle). The main rooms lie to either side of a large front hall. Originally the entrance opened into a screens passage with an elaborate carved screen, but complaints of draughts led to its removal in 1861. In the front hall and gallery are broadly moulded plaster ceilings executed by John Hughes of Manchester, and the drawing room has an attractive frieze of birds pecking at grapes. The most comfortable room is the library, housing Rowland's fine book collection in a set of Jacobean-style bookcases and

14. (*above*) The chapel interior, Arley Hall.

15. (*below*) The dining room, Arley Hall, now demolished.

lit by stained glass windows by Lusson of Paris. But luxury was not Rowland's way of life; he saw little merit in acquiring sumptuous furniture and expensive paintings.

Lord Halifax, the leading Anglo-Catholic, described Rowland as 'a perfect combination, a good churchman, a good landlord, a keen sportsman and a man of literary tastes'. During the 78 years he held the estate, he carried out extensive agricultural improvements, but his passion was building. At Great Budworth he repaired the church, built a school and restored the houses using Butterfield, W. E. Nesfield, John Douglas, Edmund Kirby and William White as architects to create one of the most attractive villages in Cheshire. White also designed estate cottages at Arley Green, where the beautiful setting and sensitive grouping of buildings illustrates well the picturesque qualities for which Rowland strove but sadly did not achieve in the design of his own house.

The only part of the Old Hall to survive is a large cruck barn, converted into a ride in the early 19th century. Rowland had the end bay removed in the 1850s to form an approach to the new house, and erected the Bavarian-looking clock tower to his own design. The adjacent barn, now the tea room, contains a fragment of a 16th-century overmantel depicting Mars and Venus with Cupid, presumably from the Old Hall, and two large coats of arms, one Egerton, the other Warburton, with lines of Rowland's celebrated doggerel below, from the demolished dining room of the new house.

A Jacobean-style house required formal gardens, and from W A. Nesfield Rowland commissioned an elaborate design of parterres for the east side. These no longer exist, but the gardens south-west of the house have not only been well maintained but also enlarged by his great-grand-daughter Viscountess Ashbrook. Within an appropriately architectural framework they contain a number of exceptional features, including the Furlong Walk along a raised terrace, the Ilex Avenue leading to two magnificent urns from the gatepiers of Marbury Hall, and the herbaceous border, one of the earliest and most beautiful examples of this most English of garden forms. In the walled garden created in 1960 are four of the heraldic animals from the demolished parts of the house. Also from the house are plaques painted with verses by Rowland which now line the walls of the small tea house. These refer to the neighbouring estates which were visible from the tower when it was built. The unsightly scars left by the truncation of the house in 1968 are shortly to be concealed as part of a sensitive scheme of rebuilding on the lines of the demolished wings. This will provide an endowment for the house, and ensure that the gardens, now one of the sights of Cheshire, are maintained for the future.

O i, 410, 613; T ii, 61; *CL* xvi, 942; *Ches Life* July 1935, January 1940, September/October 1955; Charles Foster, *Arley Hall* guidebook 1982; JRL and Family collection, Egerton-Warburton papers.

BAGULEY HALL, *Baguley*

816 887

The 14th-century Baguley Hall is one of the earliest timber-framed houses in Cheshire, and is of extremely unusual construction. It was originally built by the Leghs of Baguley and after many changes of ownership became part of the Wythenshawe estate when, according to Ormerod, it was well preserved by the Tattons of Wythenshawe. It came into the hands of Manchester Corporation when the estate was acquired for council housing; at that time Baguley Hall was occupied by a tenant farmer. When he left, a housing estate had grown up all round it and the hall was used as a timber store. It later deteriorated so much that in the *Buildings of England* Pevsner called the way Manchester treated Baguley 'a scandal'. Fortunately it was taken over by the Ministry of Public Building and Works and is now gradually being restored.

It is ironic that it was acquired along with Wythenshawe Hall and that it was Wythenshawe which the City turned into a museum for, as a house, Baguley is far more distinguished. Unlike Wythenshawe, it sank down the social scale and so was spared the remodellings and additions which removed so much of the character of Wythenshawe. Baguley has been truncated; it has lost the upper end bay of the Great Hall sheltering the dais, and its two cross wings have been rebuilt in brick. Some medieval timbers survive in the service wing, though the domestic wing is all of 17th-century brickwork. But the Great Hall itself, forming the central bar of an H-plan, is remarkably unchanged from the 14th century.

The Hall faces west with, on the left, an entrance porch added in the 16th century in front of the door to the screens passage. Even from the outside the unusual construction is very noticeable. The west wall is lit by tall straight-headed windows and is framed by extremely broad timbers, up to two feet seven inches wide, much bigger than is commonly met with. All the timbers share a common thickness of seven inches; it is not so much a case of post and beam as of plank construction. A further stylistic rarity is the wall panelling, which has diagonal struts in the form of a cusped St Andrew's cross, again composed of broad planks. All the timbers on this wall have been stripped of their black coating to show the gnarled, twisted grain of the oak, weathered to a pale grey. Into the beams has been inserted a jigsaw of timber patches of various shapes and sizes, all held in with wooden pegs, completing an impression of venerable antiquity; there is none of the large-scale timber replacement seen at Wythenshawe or indeed seen in the porch where the regular grid of the present framing differs considerably from the herringbone patterns shown in older photographs.

From the outside, the half timbering is almost overshadowed by the two cross wings of brick and the steep roof of stone flags, but even so the width of the timbers and the simple form of the windows gives an impression of rustic solidity which contrasts with the busier, tinier patterns of later Cheshire houses. The breadth of the constructional members is seen to even better effect within the Great Hall, particularly from the viewpoint taken by J. C. Buckler in his watercolour of 1826. Turning his back on the rebuilt upper end of the hall, he looked northwards to the spere-truss and to the wall beyond, where the three openings to the service rooms are separated by massive jambs, their arched heads cut out of a broad horizontal beam. Above is a row of cusped blank arches, and the king-post on the upper part of the wall, which is tenoned into the roof, broadens out at its foot to a width of over four feet. The distinctive cusped arches are repeated at the sides of the spere-truss which separates the hall from the screens passage.

There are other peculiarities at Baguley; firstly the roof has trussed rafters and each pair is connected by curved scissor braces, a hybrid form. Secondly, the plan of the hall, which was

16.   Baguley Hall, 1919.

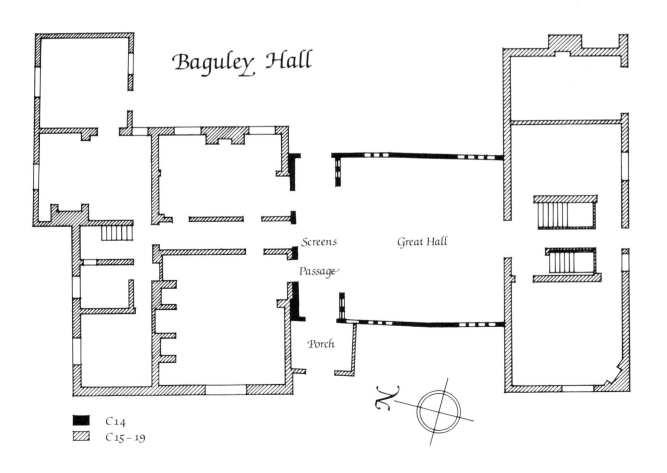

Baguley Hall

Screens   Great Hall

Passage

Porch

N

C14
C15 – 19

17. The Great Hall, Baguley Hall: watercolour by J. C. Buckler, 1826.

originally one bay longer, has sides which bow out slightly in the centre. As Baguley is in an area associated with 10th-century Viking invasions, this suggested a connection with the boat-shaped plans of Viking houses, though the Baguley plan has only a very slight bow. The plank construction is also associated with Norse and Saxon houses and the diagonal cross braces are found in the early wooden stave churches of Norway. On the other hand, the spere-truss and screens passage arrangement is English in origin.

Baguley is not quite alone in its distinguishing features. From what is known of Tabley Old Hall, now a ruin, it too had a similar plan and plank-like timbers. Farther north, in Lancashire the same characteristics seem to have been present at the demolished Radcliffe Towers and at Stand Old Hall. One related house survives, Smithills Hall near Bolton, which has plank construction and very similar service doorways, though the roof construction differs. All share a connection with ancient Scandinavian forms; Baguley is the most complete example and vividly illustrates the remarkable persistence of Scandinavian building traditions over several centuries.

O i, 553; Taylor, 136; *Antiquaries Journal* xl, 131; *JCAS* lix, 60.

III. The Saloon, Doddington Hall.

IV. The Great Chamber, Dorfold Hall.

V.   Henbury Hall.

BELMONT HALL, *Great Budworth*

654 784

The architect James Gibbs, according to the manuscript account of his work in the Soane Museum, 'contrived a very Convenient Small house of six room on the floor for the Honble John Smith Barry at Aston Park in Cheschire'. This house has been identified as Marbury Hall, near Great Budworth, greatly enlarged by Salvin in the mid-19th century and demolished in 1969. But this is incorrect. John Smith Barry's new house was Belmont Hall, still standing, adjoining the Marbury estate. The confusion is understandable for the history of the two houses was closely linked and both were owned by members of the same family. The Smith Barrys sold Belmont in 1801 and Marbury became better known as their seat whilst Belmont slipped into obscurity. It was assumed that Gibbs' 'Convenient Small house' disappeared somewhere inside Salvin's grandiose remodelling.

Marbury was the more ancient of the two. The seat of the Merbury family in the Middle Ages, it was acquired in 1684 by Earl Rivers. His daughter married the Irish peer James, 4th Earl of Barrymore, and in 1714 the Marbury estate came to his family, the Barrys. Lord Barrymore, one of the leaders of the Jacobite movement in Engand, enlarged Marbury, a vernacular brick house, adding wings and a portico. On his death in 1748 it was inherited by his second son by a later marriage, Richard Barry, the eldest son taking the title and the Irish seat at Fota Island, County Cork.

Meanwhile in 1746 Richard's younger brother John married a wealthy Essex heiress Dorothy Smith and changed his name to John Smith Barry. Whilst living at Aston Park, a small house on the Arley estate, he purchased the site of Belmont Hall in 1749; the new house was completed by 1755, the date on two insurance plaques on the entrance front. Gibbs would have been a natural choice as architect. He and Lord Barrymore had been near neighbours in London and a number of Jacobites were patrons of Gibbs.

As the Gibbs manuscript implies, Belmont is not a grand house of parade but a compact villa of the type popular in the 1750s, without a portico or a high basement, but planned in accordance with the Palladian idea of a small central block of living rooms with lower separate office pavilions at the sides, stables on the west, kitchens on the east. They are linked to the central block by low screen walls fronting courtyards entered by rusticated arches of a kind favoured by Gibbs, picking up the rusticated form of the central doorcase. The front is of seven bays with a three-bay pediment; its main feature is the pair of big semi-circular bow windows running up two storeys and glazed in octagonal patterns of a currently fashionable kind, seen for instance in the villas of Sir Robert Taylor.

But the proportions and detailing at Belmont have an awkwardness which seems to belie the involvement of anyone of the calibre of Gibbs. The curved bows, their fine glazing bars and octagonal patterns at variance with the thick sashes elsewhere in the house, seem an afterthought on such a rectilinear composition, as though trying to bring relief to a facade without projection or recession. Even the pediment does not mark a break in the flatness of the front as it should if correctly understood. The string courses are badly detailed and the back of the house is poorly proportioned even taking into account the later alterations to the windows.

The infelicities of design may be explained by the supervision of another architect, perhaps the same person who refronted Arley Hall around 1758 with octagonal glazing and a central bow, similar to Belmont. It was quite common in the 18th century for an architect to supply a design for a fee and then to leave his patron to employ an executant architect or builder. In his

18. The entrance front, Belmont Hall.

19. The drawing room, Belmont Hall, 1937.

Book of Architecture Gibbs wrote that the designs it contained 'may be executed by any Workman who understands lines, whether as here Design'd, or with some alterations, which may easily be made by a person of Judgement'. In the 1750s in any case Gibbs was unwell and it is possible that he was prevented from executing Belmont by his death in 1754.

Though the bow windows are bonded into the brickwork of the facade and so are part of the original build, they are not a Gibbs idea and must be an interpolation into his design. Without them Belmont is in its essentials not unlike some of Gibbs' plainer designs such as the unexecuted drawing for Catton Hall, Derbyshire. Within, however, Belmont's richness of decoration, its principal point of interest, is a direct reflection of Gibbs' ideas on interior treatment. The 'six rooms' mentioned in the manuscript are, clockwise from the entrance, the hall, the front drawing room, the back drawing room, the staircase hall, the dining room and the study or morning room (the extra room built out into the kitchen court was added in the 19th century). The hall is austere with a stone floor, a stone fireplace and heavy pulvinated friezes over the doors. The carving in the panelled study is of finer quality with doorcases, chimneypiece and overmantel all decorated with naturalistic flowers and fruit. More characteristic of Gibbs are the drawing rooms, adorned with delicate stucco decoration. They both have excellent Rococo ceilings similar to the work at Gibbs' Bank Hall, Warrington, 1749-50. The room facing the garden has plain walls, and photographs taken in the 1930s show it hung with tapestries. But the front room is more elaborate with *rocaille* work dancing round stucco wall panels, and over the (altered) chimneypiece is an especially splendid overmantel with Chinese birds and naturalistic flowers among swirls and scrolls. On the ceiling of the room above there is a greater accent on Chinoiserie with trellises, pagodas and more birds.

Finest of all the stucco decoration is the wall panel between the windows lighting the staircase. A portrait medallion, perhaps of Diana, is surrounded by a froth of beautifully modelled ornament and from a fluttering ribbon hangs a trophy of hunting horns, bows and arrows. This

20. Plasterwork on the staircase, Belmont Hall.

33

is similar to trophies executed in 1758 at Hagley, Worcestershire, by the Italian *stuccatore* Francesco Vassalli, who had worked for Gibbs at Ditchley. John Smith Barry was a great sportsman, hence the allusion to hunting. His famous hound Bluecap which won the 500 guineas at Newmarket in 1762 is commemorated in a public house at Sandiway near the site of his kennels.

Smith Barry was still living at Belmont in 1777 when he was in financial difficulties, for he seized profits from the estates of his son, still a minor, and by the time of his own death in 1784 he was in debt. Nevertheless his son James Hugh Smith Barry inherited Belmont and, as Richard Barry was childless, also inherited Marbury in 1787. James Hugh was a passionate collector of paintings and sculpture and was in Rome in 1780, the date Angelica Kauffman signed his portrait. He brought back to Belmont quantities of antique statuary including a fragment of the Parthenon frieze now in the British Museum and a colossal statue of Zeus now in the Getty Museum, besides many Old Master paintings. When he died in 1801 Belmont was sold to Henry Clarke who sold it to the Leighs whose descendants the Mosley Leighs own it still.

James Hugh was succeeded by his illegitimate son John, a minor. By the terms of his father's will, the paintings and sculpture were moved to Marbury where they were to be preserved as heirlooms in a special gallery to be built for them. The will also required that a mausoleum be built near the house. John succeeded in 1821 when he was able to take the name and arms of Smith Barry but he was more interested in hunting than in architecture. The house was not enlarged until 1856 when John's son James Hugh turned the irregular brick building into a vast French château, a cluster of heavy mansard roofs, dormers, turrets and a dome. The collections remained intact there until the 1940s. Marbury was demolished in 1968-9 and the grounds are now a country park, but Gibbs' 'very Convenient Small house' is now in use as a school.

Lysons, 519, 529; Hanshall, 381; O i, 607, 635, 718; T ii, 64, 69; Neale; *Ches Life* April 1937; T. Friedman, *James Gibbs*, 1984, 296; *CL* clxxxix, 1784; CRO DCN/1984/50.

BOLESWORTH CASTLE, *Tattenhall*

495 560

The Bolesworth estate includes some of the most romantic country in Cheshire. The Castle is set high on the western slope of the Broxton Hills, backed by rocky wooded escarpments. A house was first built by James Tilson who bought the estate in the mid-18th century. Altered in 1777 by Robert Mylne for John Crewe, and sold several times subsequently, the house was acquired in 1826 by George Walmesley who erected the present castle. Walmesley's architect was a pupil of Thomas Harrison of Chester, William Cole, who became County Surveyor on Harrison's death in 1829. Cole was not principally a country house architect, though he designed garden buildings at Tatton and Eaton. He produced churches in the Gothic style, but even as late as 1857, the date of the Congregational Church at Birkenhead, his Gothic was unscholarly and paper thin. Harrison, principally a Greek Revival architect, had designed two Gothic houses in Shropshire. One of these, The Citadel at Hawkstone, a triangular dower house with circular towers at each corner, is a source for Bolesworth, and Cole may well have been involved in its design. But stripped of its towers and castellated parapets, Bolesworth is in essence still classical. The five main rooms of the house are stretched out across the west side to take advantage of the spectacular view. In the centre behind a canted bay was the former library, on the right a circular billiard room, on the left an octagonal drawing room, and the flat walls between marked the dining room and morning room.

21. The garden front, Bolesworth Castle.

Perhaps another influence on the design was the nearby Cholmondeley Castle, which, together with Porden's exotic Eaton Hall, set an architectural fashion Walmesley must have felt bound to follow. His ambition to build a new Gothic house to compete with his wealthy neighbours was realised, but it ruined him, and in 1836 the estate was sold. Twenty years later it was purchased by Robert Barbour, whose family still remain at Bolesworth. Barbour was a successful Manchester businessman and banker who could afford not only to maintain the house but also to increase the holdings of the estate. He built several model farms in the Tudor style to the designs of James Harrison (another pupil of Thomas Harrison, though no relation), as well as a dower house and a lodge, both by Waterhouse. In the churchyard of All Saints, Harthill is a huge mausoleum where Barbour was buried in 1885, aged eighty-seven. For the next 35 years the estate changed little but, on inheriting it in 1919, his grandson Major Robert Barbour decided upon a thorough modernisation of the house.

22. The drawing room, Bolesworth Castle.

The popularity of the 19th-century Gothic Revival was at a low ebb in the 1920s and Bolesworth Castle was regarded by its new owner as an anachronism. The *Architects' Journal* which featured the reconstruction carried out between 1920 and 1923 remarked on the unfashionable nature of the Gothic decorations, 'gothicky glories . . . [which] departed with the cartloads of dingy lath-and-plaster rubbish into which they so pathetically dissolved at the touch of the house-breaker'. It was therefore fortunate that Major Barbour selected as his architect Clough Williams-Ellis who not only understood the spirit of the Picturesque which had spawned Bolesworth Castle, but also had the skill and sensitivity to give it a new individuality without sacrificing the architectural integrity of the original design. Williams-Ellis, a relation of the Barbours, was more experienced than any of his contemporaries in country house work; he also had a facility for dealing with crusty and eccentric landowners. In his autobiography he explained, 'I have generally done my best to keep anything that I could of earlier work, even against my clients' wishes, for the sake of history and continuity, so long as it was good of its kind, no matter what period, and provided it could be reasonably harmonised with the overall mood of the new deal'. Perhaps therefore it was at his insistence that the decoration of the octagonal drawing room was retained, for it gives a good idea of the former character of the house. The ceiling has Gothic rib vaults and the doors are decorated with tracery, but the old fireplace was removed and a fine 18th-century classical one of white marble installed on a different wall. At the other end of the enfilade, the circular billiard room was converted to a servants' hall. An extra floor was inserted above this which affects the exterior, for an additional set of windows was squeezed in and all the hood moulds removed. The library, the most sumptuously decorated room of the house, was extensively altered. Before the changes it had spiky canopies lining the walls and an enormous fireplace supporting tall figures on pedestals in a coarse Gothic, taking after Porden's Eaton Hall interiors. Books however played little part in the life of Major

23. View from the outer hall, Bolesworth Castle.

24. The saloon, Bolesworth Castle.

Barbour, and the library became a new classical dining room. The canopywork was all removed, and to decorate the room Hammonds of Sloane Street were brought in to give it a fashionable early Georgian look. Their striking colour scheme of dark green with gilded panel mouldings and frieze still survives, and the effect is well complemented by good 18th-century furniture and paintings.

The principal alterations involved the reconstruction of the centre of the house to form a spacious new hall. Previously the entrance had been on the south front, recessed behind tall pointed arches. Clough moved it to the east, forming a splendid outer hall painted to resemble fine-jointed sandstone with raised panels and a bold modillion cornice. The floor is paved with black and white marble, and in the centre hangs an early 19th-century colza lamp. It is a most accomplished neo-Baroque interior which owes much to Lutyens, whose work Clough admitted influenced him more than any other architect. The large main hall, reached through a screen of yellow veined scagliola columns, is divided into two parts, a square galleried space lit by a lantern, and a saloon formed from the original entrance hall and recessed porch. The two sections are united by common panelling and dado, but the galleried part is more formally treated. However it is a lighthearted and theatrical formality. For example, the Soane-like balustrading of the gallery with its coats of arms and flat urns is designed specifically to be seen from below, and in the saloon is an extraordinary stylised frieze of bucrania and swags, almost Art Nouveau in character. It is this free and lively approach to classicism, and an interest in the picturesque qualities of architecture which Clough developed as his hallmark. 'Except in a completely formal setpiece', he wrote, 'I think there is much to be said for allowing minor stylistic surprises to break a rhythm and coherence that might also be monotonous – something not actually to shock the spectator – but to give his perhaps flagging attention a little jolt and set him wondering just why one had done whatever it was and whether it was justified, aesthetically or practically'. This principle can also be seen in the exterior, where round-headed windows replace the pointed arches of the former entrance, or where the castellations turn into a balustraded parapet surmounted by urns. And yet great pains were taken to match the quality, texture and craftsmanship of the stonework.

Urns too are a feature of the gardens which were remodelled by Clough. Originally there was just a castellated wall at the foot of the garden which divided the house and its lawn from the park. However the lawn was given greater interest by terracing, steps and alcove seats. By the upper drive is a small rotunda sheltering a statue of Diana the huntress.

Following the completion of this work in 1923, Clough was commissioned by Major Barbour to build some cottages at Tattenhall. They are arranged in two groups around the junction with the lane leading to Bolesworth, and are named 'Rose Corner' and 'Rosemary Row'. Rose Corner dated 1927 is the more ambitious, a Palladian facade in miniature, straight out of a Rex Whistler mural. The giant portico with Clough's favourite lotus leaf capitals contains an archway leading only to the back yard of some existing cottages, though these are provided with a tall Flemish gable to fit the illusion. Like Portmeirion, Clough's sparkling seaside village in Merionethshire, it shows his unique skill at scenic effect.

These improvements ceased in 1928 when Major Barbour was tragically killed in a riding accident and joined his father and grandfather in the gaunt mausoleum at Harthill. The house however survives untouched since that time, and whilst the architectural commentators of the 1920s saw the alterations as 'replacing the wan ghosts of misunderstood mediaevalism by a robust classicism', we can enjoy in the work of both William Cole and Clough Williams-Ellis a correspondingly picturesque response to the romantic situation of Bolesworth.

O ii, 676; T i, 45; *Architects' Journal* lviii, 792; *Country Heritage*, 15; *Ches Life* November 1956; Clough Williams-Ellis, *Architect Errant*, 1971, 161.

BRAMALL HALL, *Bramhall*

890 864 *House and park open to the public. (Stockport Borough Council)*

Lord Torrington called Bramall the 'oldest of all the old striped houses; black and white, flourished into as many devices as a boy would draw upon his kite'. One of the grandest timber-framed houses in the county, its earliest parts are older than Little Moreton Hall, but it is less well preserved. In the late 18th century it was, to quote Torrington again 'trick'd up à la mode' and in the late 19th so heavily restored that Alec Clifton-Taylor called it 'in effect a Victorian reproduction, and a none too faithful one at that'. Nor has the 20th century treated it well. As a result, Bramall cannot equal the authentic patina and crooked charm of its rival.

It is now U-shaped in plan. In the centre of the U on the east side of the forecourt is the Great Hall, once full height but now divided into two storeys. Flanking it on the north is the kitchen wing and on the south an intermediate range with an ante-room leading to the southern cross wing containing the chapel, parlour and two large chambers above. Originally, as at Little Moreton Hall, there was a gatehouse wing, now demolished, making a quadrangle, and the whole was surrounded by a moat. But Bramall's development was more complex than Little Moreton's. The components were built and rebuilt at different times, the levels of the upper floors and the roofs do not match and the sides of the courtyard do not join directly to the Great Hall block.

The house was described in 1541 in William Davenport's will, which mentions the chapel and gatehouse, but the earliest surviving features date from the late 14th century. In the roof structure of the north wing are two curious X-shaped cusped scissor-braces, probably of the 14th century, similar to the roofs of Welsh houses. The intermediate range joining the Great Hall to the south cross wing also shows evidence of the earlier period, including heavy quatrefoil patterns on the exterior and particularly massive framing in the Plaster Room on the upper storey, so called from its original flooring. In the cross wing itself, the upper chamber overlooking the courtyard is lit by an oriel window supported by a chubby angel bearing the arms of the de Bromale family which owned the house until about 1375 when it came by marriage to the Davenports. The wooden mullions with cusped traceried tops are characteristic of the late 14th century, and similar tracery survives in a blocked window in the chapel on the ground floor. A view of the house in 1826 by J. C. Buckler records more of these windows in the intermediate range.

In the late 15th or early 16th century the south cross wing was substantially reconstructed. Both the rooms on the ground floor, the chapel and parlour (now called the banqueting room) have low ceilings divided by moulded beams. The chambers on the floor above, known as the Chapel Room and the Ballroom, are much taller: their elaborate open roof has cusped wind braces and big cambered beams, very like the roof at Tatton Old Hall. The roof is exposed in the Ballroom but in the Chapel Room it is hidden above the Victorian ceiling. The general arrangement of the two floors is like Sutton Hall though the woodwork at Bramall is not nearly as fine. In the late 16th century these rooms received elaborate painted decoration. On the west wall of the chapel is the figure of Christ, covered up after the Reformation with the Ten Commandments. In the Plaster Room and concealed over the Chapel Room ceiling is red and black cusped stencilling. But the most remarkable of all the painted decoration is on the walls of both upper chambers, some concealed above the Chapel Room but also magnificently exposed in the Ballroom. Now somewhat faded, the work imitates tapestry in its crowding of motifs, a mixture of up-to-date classical grotesques with figures in medieval dress, foliage, animals and

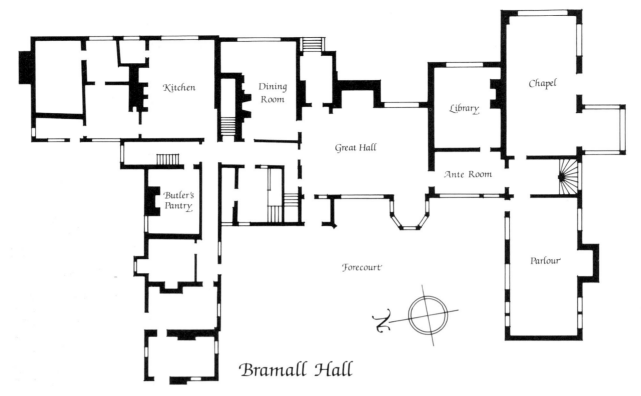

Kitchen

Dining
Room

Great Hall

Library

Chapel

Butler's
Pantry

Ante Room

Forecourt

Parlour

Bramall Hall

25. The east front of Bramall Hall in 1818, before demolition of the Long Gallery.

26. The west front, Bramall Hall: watercolour by J. C. Buckler, 1826.

27. The west front, Bramall Hall, *c*.1900, with additions for Charles Neville.

musicians. With their splendid roof and painted walls, these were very grand chambers, and they probably assumed a new importance with the decline of the Great Hall.

The original form of the Great Hall is not known, but the intermediate range may well have been part of the old Great Hall block before it was rebuilt in busily-patterned timber framing by William and Dorothy Davenport in the late 16th century. They inserted a floor, making a lower ceilinged entrance hall and over it a withdrawing room. This is dated WDD 1592 over a door, and has doorcases inlaid with geometrical patterns, a plaster ceiling with pendants and a plaster overmantel with crude caryatids and the arms of Elizabeth I. Facing the courtyard, the new porch and the polygonal bay window recall the slightly earlier examples at Little Moreton. The most prominent addition made by William and Dorothy no longer exists. It was a Long Gallery placed on the second floor, not over the gatehouse as at Little Moreton but on top of the new withdrawing room. Its oddly proportioned expanse of closely set-timbers dominates early views of the house.

Bramall was noteworthy for the excellence of its needlework. In the Plaster Room is exhibited a remarkable 16th-century heraldic table carpet formerly on the high table in the Great Hall. The adjoining bedroom is known as the Paradise Room after a bed hung with tapestries telling the story of Adam and Eve in the Garden of Eden, exquisitely worked by Dorothy Davenport who completed them in 1636. The hangings are now at Capesthorne, for the Bromley-Davenports bought them at the Bramall sale of 1877 to prevent them passing out of the family.

The 18th century saw little building activity until the advent in 1767 of the 10th William Davenport and his wife, whose activities were deplored by Torrington. By 1774 the gatehouse wing had been removed and by 1826 the Long Gallery had also disappeared. Sash windows were put in the withdrawing room, seen in Buckler's drawing, and the chapel was altered. Torrington would have had further reason to complain if he could have visited the house in 1890 instead of 1790. During the 19th century the Davenports fell on hard times, part of the estate was sold for building land and the house was let. In 1877 it was sold and the family moved to Clipsham Hall, Rutland, taking a few portraits and other items with them. Everything else went under the hammer. Bramall was threatened with demolition but in 1882 T. H. Neville of Strines Printing Works, Marple bought it for his son, Charles. Charles Neville undoubtedly saved the house. He took out the sash windows and revealed period features such as the wall paintings and the chapel windows. He must have expended large sums on structural consolidation. But his taste was for the somewhat too picturesque and he turned Bramall into a late Victorian country house in the Old English style. George Faulkner Armitage provided much attractive and fanciful metalwork including lamps, door furniture, fenders and firedogs. He also refitted several rooms in an unsympathetically glossy neo-Jacobean style, as seen in the Chapel Room, where Pugin furniture from Abney is now shown, and in the former dining room, now the shop. Less fortunate still was Neville's fondness for the sentimental paintings of the aptly named Herbert Schmalz, some of which are still in the house.

On the exterior Neville is said to have been his own architect and what he did was undeniably effective; the discriminating Edward Ould wrote that the restoration had been 'on the whole, judiciously done'. But it was also deceptive. The most picturesque part of Bramall is the courtyard front of the Great Hall. What could be more typical of Cheshire black and white work of the 16th century than this? It has large areas of small-paned glazing, patterned timbers and lively gables surmounting the porch and the polygonal bay window lighting the dais end of the hall. It comes as a shock to learn that all the gables were placed there in the 1880s in self-conscious homage to Little Moreton Hall: the roofline was formerly flat and Neville's picturesque additions were intended to break up the stark horizontal skyline left after the removal of the Long Gallery.

In contrast, the unco-ordinated ragbag of patterned gables on the garden front was made less picturesque. Pleasingly uneven roof ridges and timbers were straightened out and chimneys

28. The drawing room, Bramall Hall, *c*.1900.

rebuilt in harsh red moulded brick. On the cross wing the entire south and west walls were rebuilt in brick. Some of this work may post-date Neville. The family left in 1926 and the house changed hands again, but in 1935 it was acquired by the local authority. Soon afterwards services were resumed in the chapel and the house was opened to the public. Since then much restoration has been carried out, some even more drastic than before, such as the complete rebuilding of the north wing with applied half timbering imitating the original exterior but modernised within. As a result the house has not managed to escape a certain hardness, emphasised by the insensitive municipal landscaping of the east terracing. But few houses of its type survive at all and even in its truncated, over-restored form Bramall is still full of interest.

O iii, 829; T ii, 89; *The Cabinet Maker and Art Furnisher*, v, 1 December 1884, 101; P&O, 38; Torrington ii, 202; A. Clifton-Taylor, *The Pattern of English Building*, 1972, 325; *Bramall Hall* guidebook 1976; E. B. Dean, *Bramall Hall*, 1977.

BRERETON HALL, *Brereton Green*

782 650

'The stately house of Brereton', as Webb called it, is an Elizabethan hall built in 1585 by Sir William Brereton of Brereton, not to be confused with the Breretons of Handforth or of Malpas. It is unusual for its date in Cheshire in being of brick and not half-timbered. It has a splendid centrepiece to the main front with twin octagonal towers flanking an entrance arch. The towers were originally higher with glazed look-out rooms and ogee caps, and in front was a walled forecourt recorded in an embroidered hanging of 1744 at Aston Hall, Birmingham. By the early 19th century, the formal approach had gone; an engraving of 1819 after de Wint shows the house set in meadowland sweeping down to a lake with cattle drinking, a romantic prospect sadly now spoiled by the draining of the lake.

Brereton presents an enigma, for the towers recall the Tudor gatehouses of the early 16th century such as Hampton Court or Layer Marney, or the fronts of later courtyard houses such as Old Chatsworth or Burghley. But Brereton does not seem to have had a courtyard. Its

29. The entrance front, Brereton Hall, 1909.

44

plan is U-shaped, with two wings extending behind the house. The ends of the wings have gabled and mullioned windows which do not appear to have been altered; there is no sign of the wings having been carried round to form a quadrangle. The plan may indeed have been an E for the brickwork in the centre of the rear has been changed and there is now a Victorian glazed conservatory projecting there. The centrepiece of the front is marked by stone quoins and surface enrichments. Running across the towers and above the doorway is a continuous band of windows, and above and below are carved stone panels separated by coupled pilasters. In the centre are the Brereton and the Royal arms and the date 1585. At roof level is a scrolly parapet and a little curved pediment, and the relieving arch, probably added to stabilise the towers quite soon after they were built, has a classical frieze.

The design of this centrepiece does not link up with the rest of the house: the string courses and windows on the towers are not continuous with the sides, and indeed the whole centre seems awkwardly grafted on to a plainer, more standard type of front with simple rectangular mullioned windows, gables and projecting bays. Lysons in 1810 wrote that some of the armorial windows then in the house bore the date 1577; it is possible therefore that the towered centrepiece was an afterthought added in 1585. The row of windows on the towers recalls Barlborough Hall, Derbyshire, of 1583, otherwise dissimilar. Much closer is Rocksavage, now lost, but known through an engraving also after de Wint. Rocksavage stood on a cliff overlooking the river Weaver on a site now engulfed in the industrial development of Runcorn. The engraving of 1819 shows it already ruinous. It was built around 1565-6 by Sir John Savage. Brereton knew it well for he was Savage's ward and when he came of age he married Margaret Savage, his guardian's daughter. The twin octagonal towers with domed tops at Rocksavage formed the model for those at Brereton. But there are important differences. At Rocksavage the string courses of the towers continued along the adjacent walls, and according to an 18th-century estate plan, it was a courtyard house.

The enigma of Brereton's plan cannot be solved by reference to the internal layout of rooms, for this has been altered and the original position of the Great Hall is unknown. There are however a number of original features inside. Royal heraldry is prominent; Sir William was a loyal soldier to Elizabeth I. His father had served her in Ireland and he himself is shown wearing in his cap a miniature of the Queen on his portrait dated 1579, now in the Detroit Institute of Arts. There was formerly at Brereton a portrait of Elizabeth of the same date. The Royal arms are more conspicuous than Brereton's own on the entrance or west front and, within, the best surviving overmantel shows again Elizabeth's arms and the date 1585. This is in the room in the south wing perhaps originally a withdrawing room. Here the plasterwork frieze justifies Camden's contemporary description of the Hall as 'magnificent and sumptuous'. Over the Royal arms on the overmantel is the globe of the heavens, and running round the room is a series of crowns and arms of 43 different European states and principalities. To each is attached the name of its ruler in Latin on a scroll curling round a red and white rose. The shield for the King of Jerusalem bears a cross and his crown is a crown of thorns. In the large bay window looking south-east was formerly stained glass depicting the Nine Earls, two of Mercia and seven of Chester. The glass is now at Stoneleigh Abbey, Warwickshire.

In the corresponding room in the north-east wing, called the kitchen, large cartouches set into the walls frame moral inscriptions: for example, 'Doe nothing this day whereof thou mayest repent tomorrow'. Of several other heraldic chimneypieces in the house the most interesting is in an upstairs room over the north entrance, an elaborate but naively carved alabaster chimneypiece dated 1633 commemorating the marriage of William, 2nd Lord Brereton with Elizabeth Goring. Numerous coats of arms and two delightfully awkward winged harpies are supported by two herm busts, perhaps portraits, for arms identify the man as a Brereton and the woman as a Goring.

The Brereton line became extinct in 1722 and the estate passed to the Holtes of Aston Hall,

30. Dining room fireplace, Brereton Hall, 1909.

where some Brereton portraits still hang. In 1817 both the Aston and the Brereton estates were sold. Brereton was bought by John Howard of Hyde, who 'improved' the Hall in a drastic and insensitive manner. He removed the cupolas and built onto the towers what *Country Life* in 1909 called 'battlements of outrageous proportions and cumbersome mouldings'. He also replaced the stone flags on the roof with slate, put plate glass in the lattice windows and radically changed the interior which is now full of rather coarse work of the early 19th century, a mixture of Gothic and classical. A transverse corridor runs along the back of the main part of the house, destroying the original disposition of the rooms. Now the dormitories and desks of a girls' school have taken over, but from the outside Brereton is still almost as romantic a sight as it appeared to Peter de Wint in 1819.

Lysons, 458; O iii, 87; S. C. Hall, *The Baronial Halls and Picturesque Edifices of England*, i, 1848; T i, 141; *CL* xxvi, 388; *Ches Life* March 1937; A. L. Moir, *The Story of Brereton Hall*, 3rd ed. 1976.

CAPESTHORNE HALL, *Siddington*

841 728 *House and gardens open to the public. (Privately owned)*

Seen from afar, Capesthorne is a fantastic Victorian vision of a red brick Jacobean mansion spread out across the landscape with a romantic skyline of towers, domed turrets and shaped gables. The air of unreality is enhanced by the misty outline of the Jodrell Bank radio telescope rearing up in the distance. The house is magnificent scenery, partly the work of Edward Blore who refronted it in 1837, and partly Anthony Salvin who reconstructed it after a fire in 1861. Nothing could be more different from the four-square 18th-century house built for John Ward. The Wards settled at Capesthorne in the reign of Edward IV. The site of their earlier house is marked by a brick column in the park to the left of the drive. In 1719 John Ward engaged William Smith to build on a new site. First to be constructed were 'two wings, the one for domestic offices, the other for stables and coach houses'. Smith's plans for the ground floor survive and show the wings as detached pavilions each seven bays wide. Though now linked to the main house, these blocks still exist as the courtyard fronts of the two side wings; beneath their Jacobean trimmings are classical quoins and sash windows.

William Smith's estimate for building the chapel is dated 1720. Though his surviving plans differ from the chapel as built, the brick box with an apsidal end is recognisably his work. Finally the house itself was built, a simple seven-bay classical block, the central three bays breaking forward beneath a pediment; on the back the centre was slightly recessed. The designer was probably Francis Smith, William's younger brother (William had died in 1724). Francis's estimate dated 1731 specifies a house of brick with stone dressings. A letter of 1749 from a Sarah Clayton of Liverpool about the new Town Hall there stated that its architect, John Wood of Bath, had 'planed Mr. Wards house at Capesthorne', but this is probably erroneous. A good idea of the interior of the 18th-century house is given in a set of charming watercolours by James Johnson of Macclesfield, a joiner who worked for Blore. Though they record Blore's decorations of around 1840, a great deal of what was there before was retained. The plan was a double pile with a central entrance hall and a corridor leading off it on either side down the middle of the house. The skeleton of this plan survives in the centre of the present much larger building.

John Ward's son and heir died in 1726 and, when he himself died in 1748, Capesthorne passed to the Davenports of Woodford and Marton through the marriage of John's daughter Penelope to Davies Davenport. Their grandson Davies Davenport III improved the house; Johnson's views show two adjoining rooms with elaborate Wyatt-style ceilings perhaps of the 1790s. Shortly afterwards the house was extended on either side with low additions in a plain classical style with flat pilasters, on the south-west a single storey orangery and echoing it on the north-west a drawing room in the position of the present saloon.

Davies Davenport III was Tory M.P. for Cheshire. His son, Edward Davies Davenport, set himself in opposition to his father, becoming Whig M.P. for Shaftesbury. He was a man of radical sympathies, culture and learning. Most of the books now at Capesthorne bear his bookplate. He corresponded with intellectuals like Harriet Martineau and William Roscoe and politicians such as Richard Cobden and Lord John Russell. Davenport travelled in Italy, bringing back marbles, casts, vases and bronzes including Graeco-Egyptian and Roman busts, casts after Canova and a notable group of Attic vases. On his father's death in 1837 Davenport called in Blore who had lately remodelled Keele Hall, Staffordshire for the Sneyds, Davenport's mother's family, and had worked on a lesser scale in Cheshire at Vale Royal, Dorfold and Combermere. The grand Elizabethan style was his speciality, but he had a large practice and his work has an air of sameness about it; the fronts of Capesthorne and his contemporary house,

31. Capesthorne Hall.

Merevale in Warwickshire, are very similar. Both take their inspiration from the Jacobean prodigy houses Hatfield and Aston.

Blore joined the three parts of the old Capesthorne into one, extending the central block to meet the wings by creating new rooms at each side, widening the wings and building new stable and service courts on the north and south to form an immensely broad, totally symmetrical composition with a recessed centre and a large forecourt. To the front he applied a facade of brick and stone, full of incident compared with what was there before; mullions replaced sashes, a ground floor loggia replaced the central entrance and the skyline was enlivened by turrets with ogee caps and shaped gables. In the centre was a raised attic with a clock and bellcote. The design looks attractively picturesque in Blore's drawing, but it was all front; the sides look confused, and at the back no attempt was made to disguise the square Georgian block with its classical architraves and parapet.

The entrance, placed in the angle between the house and the north wing, led into a new entrance hall with a billiard-table in a recess. Beyond was a dining room and behind it an arcaded sculpture gallery on the line of the old central corridor. The new rooms had shallow strapwork ceilings but the old ceilings were preserved in the existing suite of rooms on the garden front, fitted out as libraries with bronzes and terracottas displayed on top of bookcases. The low orangery was replaced by a vast conservatory designed by Joseph Paxton, now demolished. Contemporary with his Great Stove at Chatsworth, it led directly into the family pew in the

49

32. (*above*) The garden front, Capesthorne Hall: a watercolour by Blore, *c*.1827, showing the 18th-century house behind Blore's facade.

33. (*below*) The entrance hall to Capesthorne Hall, from a watercolour by James Johnson, 1840.

chapel. Blore built lodges in matching style but the grand entrance arch which he proposed was not executed.

In 1861, during the time of E. D. Davenport's son Arthur Henry, a disastrous fire destroyed most of the central part of the house, contents and all. The wings survived, but of the main block only the loggia and part of the front wall remained. Blore was by now in retirement, so Anthony Salvin was engaged instead. He kept to Blore's general arrangements, recreating the wide frontage but making certain changes which altered the character of the house. He removed the central accent of the east front, making three shaped gables of equal height along the top; he rebuilt the garden front and the rooms along it in Jacobean style as Blore had failed to do; and, most radically, he altered the proportions of the storeys, making much more lofty rooms on the ground floor. The present family dining room on the south-east corner preserves the pleasant proportions of the old house, in contrast to the taller state dining room with its pompous neo-Jacobean chimneypiece replacing a much smaller one by Blore. In the drawing room, two Coadestone fireplaces of 1789 were brought up from the family's Belgravia house. On the staircase landing, amusing wrought-iron balustrades were installed, incorporating in the Davenport crest of a felon's head a portrait of Gladstone, political enemy of William Bromley-Davenport, Tory M.P. for North Warwickshire. He had succeeded Arthur Henry in 1867, whilst Salvin's work was still proceeding. Salvin followed Blore's interior detail in the entrance hall and gallery but elsewhere introduced his own thinner, fussier strapwork ceilings. His work at Capesthorne lacks both the convincingly historical texture of Peckforton and the opulence of his contemporary Thoresby, Nottinghamshire. His budget may have been restricted, for in re-erecting Blore's square towers he left their top storeys open on two sides, so that they appear solid from the front but decidedly odd from the back, a purely scenic device.

The saloon was remodelled in 1879 and the chapel in 1884; the box pews were removed and a High Church dignity was introduced with an Italianate gilded and coffered ceiling, stained glass, terracotta reliefs by the Victorian art potter George Tinworth, and a large Salviati mosaic reproducing Giotto's *Dormition of the Virgin*, then at Capesthorne. The Giotto, now in Berlin, was one of an outstandingly important picture collection formed by E. D. Davenport's brother, the Revd. Walter Davenport Bromley, and originally kept at Wootton Hall, Staffordshire and his London house. He was one of the earliest British collectors of Italian primitives, a very advanced taste for the period, and besides the Giotto his collection included pictures by Giovanni Bellini, Signorelli and Duccio. Also from Wootton is Allan Ramsay's portrait of Jean Jacques Rousseau who stayed there with Richard Davenport; from Bramall comes Dorothy Davenport's fine embroidered bed hangings of the Garden of Eden; from the demolished Calveley Hall is a fireplace in the state dressing room and from Marton Hall, also taken down, came panelling re-used in the comfortable family library.

During the Second World War, the house was used by the Red Cross and became run down, but it was revived by the present Lady Bromley-Davenport who was born in Philadelphia. Her redecorations favoured the clear, bright colours and contrasting white paint of the 1950s, when the house was first opened to the public; the red of the staircase hall was chosen to match a favourite rhododendron from the garden. A bedroom was installed with Colonial furniture, pictures and Americana from her childhood home, and paintings of the house were commissioned from John Ward, C. F. Tunnicliffe and L. S. Lowry. But the picture most true to the spirit of Capesthorne is by John Piper, who has captured the scenic qualities of the entrance front with an apt flair for the theatrical.

O iii, 722; T ii, 103; *THSLC* cxxi, 23; L. Bromley-Davenport, *History of Capesthorne*, 1974; *CL* clxii, 535, 607; J. Cornforth, *The Quest for Comfort*, 1978, pls. 75-80; L. Bromley-Davenport, *Capesthorne Hall* guidebook 1980; BM Add. Mss. 42028-9, Blore drawings; JRL Bromley Davenport papers.

CHOLMONDELEY CASTLE, *Cholmondeley*

536 514 *Gardens open to the public. (Privately owned)*

Cholmondeley is the first of the 19th-century Cheshire castles. Unlike the others, it was built for an old family which had occupied its estates since before Domesday Book. A small fragment of the early house survives on a different site and not far from it is the family chapel. Its outer walls date from the 18th century but the original licence to celebrate divine service was granted in 1285; within the present chancel is the medieval hammerbeam roof, one of its beams carved with the date 1300. The old house was described by Leland in 1538 as a 'faire building of tymbre, and motid about with the water of a poole'. It was rebuilt by Sir Hugh Cholmondeley as a jettied, timber-framed courtyard house; carved over the door was 'William Fawkoner, Master of the Carpentry and Joynery worke, 1571'. The Hall and chapel were damaged during the Civil War by the Parliamentarians, but were repaired by Robert Cholmondeley. He lavishly refurnished the chapel with a superb set of oak fittings, a magnificent set piece of Laudian High Anglicanism, though actually constructed during the Commonwealth, for the screen is dated 1655.

34. The screen, Chapel of St Nicholas, Cholmondeley.

In the late 17th century Hugh, 1st Earl Cholmondeley gave his support to William III who rewarded him with court office. The Earl created extremely large formal gardens in the French style, with canals and allées laid out by the gardener George London, gates and railings by Jean Tijou, and lead statues by Jan van Nost, some surviving. In 1701 the architect William Smith of Warwick was brought in and encased the wooden house in stone; his south and west fronts, with giant orders and heavy balustraded parapets supporting urns and statues, were engraved in *Vitruvius Britannicus*. The plan and the not quite regular elevations show the problems of trying to make a symmetrical classical house out of an old-fashioned arrangement of courtyard, Great Hall and screens passage; Leoni was to face similar difficulties some years later when remodelling Lyme. In 1712 the 1st Earl fell out with his architect, vowing 'never to employ Mr. Smith More if ye staire case is not finish'd this winter', and called in Vanbrugh. The latter's north front design, also shown in *Vitruvius Britannicus*, has characteristic arched windows, curved bows and a low wall screening the courtyard; but it was not executed and the forecourt was closed by magnificent wrought-iron railings and gates by Robert Bakewell, supplied in 1722. Smith also rebuilt the chapel in pink brick with a hipped roof, stone quoins and tall arched windows, preserving the internal woodwork; the contract is dated 1716. The matching transepts are an addition of 1829 and the gates and railings outside, made by Bakewell for the old house, were placed here after 1801.

Cholmondeley was neglected in the 18th century as the 3rd Earl frittered away his money, but eventually the family's fortunes were saved by his marriage to Sir Robert Walpole's daughter Mary. When in 1797 her brother, the antiquary Horace Walpole, died childless, he left the Walpole estates, including the palatial but ruinous Houghton in Norfolk, to his great-nephew the 4th Earl of Cholmondeley. The Earl demolished most of the old Cholmondeley and built a new house, choosing not to go to Houghton perhaps because of the long continuity of family possession in Cheshire. His choice of Gothick, deliberately underlined this and may also owe something to his great-uncle's pioneering taste for the style at Strawberry Hill.

The 4th Earl had already remodelled the formal gardens, employing William Emes in 1777; he began his new castle in 1801. Like Horace Walpole at Strawberry Hill, he acted as his own designer in collaboration with a minor architect, in this case William Turner of Whitchurch, and though some of Turner's suggestions, such as an entrance loggia and turrets, were eventually adopted, in general the Earl's directions were given with imperious curtness and Turner was left in no doubt about his role: 'Lord C. has sent the Idea of a Front, & if Mr. Turner will make a Sketch or two in pencil to accompany the Plan to be drawn by Mr. Hill, he will be glad; they must accord with his Idea'. 'The Ornaments on Door unnecessary . . . The upper storey of the Turrets I disapprove. The Battlements to be continued as marked in Ink. The Ornaments under Battlements useless'.

Like Walpole, the Earl seems to have been remarkably clear as to what he wanted: 'It is intended that the new Hall shall in every Respect have the appearance of an old Gothic castle, as much as possible consistent with neatness, & peremptorily to exclude both from without and within *everything that is new fashioned*'. 1801 was well in advance of the taste for large castles, and indeed before its later enlargements Cholmondeley was quite compact, like a Gothick villa on the scale of Nash's Luscombe, Devon of 1801. But unlike Nash's building or Payne Knight's influential and picturesque Downton Castle of 1784, Cholmondeley was symmetrical. The neatness desired by Lord Cholmondeley is apparent from the entrance front, facing west; the nucleus of the castle consists of two matching castellated blocks joined by a single-storey entrance loggia, behind which rises a third block, that of the full-height entrance hall. Beyond are the three principal staterooms looking east over the park. This is the extent of the house finished in 1805, distinguished from the later additions by its somewhat smaller blocks of pinkish grey stone, and its untutored Gothick windows each divided by a Y-shaped central bar.

The Earl's insistence on the exclusion of everything new fashioned also had a practical aspect, for a great deal of the material from the old house was re-used in the new. Bricks, glass, panelling, marble chimneypieces, stone flags and steps were all carted to the new site. The wainscoting from the old house was altered to form dadoes for almost all the rooms, sash windows were re-used in the basement, and doors, shutters and architraves, shorn of their pediments, were altered 'to accommodate the Gothic form'. On the main drive was re-erected Bakewell's wrought-iron screen, now without its gates. The re-use of old materials was included in Turner's original estimate of 1801, from which the Earl refused to deviate; he turned down Turner's suggested addition of turrets, unimpressed by his argument that they would 'realize the sentiment in Milton, "Towers and Battlements he sees, bosomed high in tufted trees" '. But later such poetic associations were acceptable, and in 1817 a series of irregular enlargements was begun, resulting in the impressively baronial-looking castle of today. In 1815 the Earl had been created 1st Marquess of Cholmondeley; through his marriage he had become Hereditary Lord Great Chamberlain, giving him a leading role in royal ceremonials including the coronation (the office is held by the present Marquess). In 1817 a new dining room was added on the north, followed in 1819 by a family wing to the south, with a tall rectangular tower to the left of the entrance front, both additions to the designs of the Marquess. Two octagonal angle turrets were

35.   The entrance front, Cholmondeley Castle.

36.   Cholmondeley Castle from the south-west.

37. The hall, Cholmondeley Castle.

added after 1819, and finally, soon after the death of the 1st Marquess in 1828, Sir Robert Smirke added a round tower on the south-east corner of the family wing, and brought forward the central tower of the east front with a canted bay, an improvement first proposed by Turner. Both Smirke's towers are castellated, with distinctive machicolations in three steps as at Lancaster Castle (a model which had also been suggested by Turner), and the round tower has deliberately small windows to emphasise its bulk. By these means Smirke gave greater strength to the diffuse composition of the 1st Marquess's castle, and made its elements group impressively from a distance; the cluster of towers of the east front raised up on the hillside can be seen from many viewpoints in the park.

The entrance loggia, with roughly tooled grotto-like walls, leads to a double-height hall lined with Gothick panelling and originally filled with banners, pikes, swords and helmets. Over the chimneypiece is an elaborate genealogical display. A letter survives from the 4th Earl instructing the painter to 'go to Crewe Hall & ask permission to look at the Antient Hall in which Mr. Crewe sits of an Evening, it is painted between white and a light lead colour . . . I think that near the Colour I wish for my rooms at the castle'. However when the present Lord and Lady Cholmondeley inherited the castle they found dark and heavy Victorian colours and have simplified and lightened them. The hall is now painted apricot and portraits and sporting pictures replace the military trophies. A screen of arches leads to the saloon or ante-room. The upper parts of its windows were formerly filled with stained glass, acquired by the 1st Marquess on his diplomatic travels in Europe. Both the ante-room and adjoining drawing room are hung with a set of 17th-century tapestries after Teniers, brought from the old house. In the drawing room is an original Gothick fireplace in pink and grey marble; the dado and the cornice is Gothick. The scheme for this room was by the Regency designer George Bullock who also supplied rich furnishings for other rooms, including fake armour of wood and ceramic for the entrance hall. The dining room is classical, with a frieze of vines and a grey marble chimneypiece. In the staircase hall there are Gothick cast-iron brackets supporting the staircase but the black marble steps and Bakewell's fine wrought-iron balusters come from the old house. The kitchens and domestic offices, placed in the basement, are lit from sunken areas on the west and north sides. To the south stretch the colourful gardens created by the present Lady Cholmondeley.

Two later buildings continue the Gothic tradition. At the north entrance to the park is the Beeston lodge, a rugged High Victorian creation of 1854 by S. S. Teulon, with stepped gables, arrowslits, steep roofs and castellations. Closer to the castle is the brick pool house of 1972 by Roderick Gradidge. Its arches echo those of the loggia, the cornice copies that in the drawing room and it incorporates 18th-century wrought-ironwork found languishing on the back stairs. Its playfulness harks back to the pretty Strawberry Hill flavour of the 1st Marquess's neat castle.

Colen Campbell, *Vitruvius Britannicus*, ii 1717, 31-4, iii 1725, 79-80; Hanshall, 355; O ii, 635; T i, 18; Leland iv, 2; *CL* cliv, 154, 226; *Apollo* ci, 22; CRO DCH/x/20, Album of letters.

CHORLEY HALL, *Alderley Edge*

837 782

Tucked away down a quiet lane not far from the Victorian villas of Alderley Edge is a medieval manor house, the oldest inhabited country house in Cheshire. It dates from the 14th century and stands in a cobbled courtyard approached by a narrow stone bridge across a moat. Next to it in startling contrast is a detached Elizabethan building with busily patterned half timbering. The stone house can be dated on stylistic grounds to around 1330 and was probably built by Robert de Chorley who was recorded here during the reign of Edward III. Another member of the de Chorley family was Keeper of the Park of Macclesfield, an important horse breeding area, and it is likely that the de Chorleys supplied horses to the Crown for the Hundred Years War.

On the entrance or north front the stone house is lit by heavy mullioned windows and a low arched Gothic doorway is set to the left. The roofline is broken by three half-timbered gables, though only the one on the left, the gable of a cross wing, is original. Chorley is a classic type of medieval house, a double height Great Hall with a two-storey wing set at right angles to it, separated by a screens passage. This is more apparent on the south side, which has been less altered. Here there is only one gable and the two elements of the medieval house are beautifully clear. On the east is the gabled cross wing with a three-light buttery window of the 14th century on the ground floor, and another window, later enlarged, lighting the solar above. On the west is the horizontal roofline of the Great Hall with the original tall two-light window, centrally placed, indicating that the hall was a single-storey apartment open to the roof. This window was altered in the 16th century when the sill was raised to accommodate a fireplace and chimneystack.

Chorley is built of rubble, but on the dressed stone of the openings can be seen the peculiar markings which give rise to the name robin's claw or crow's feet stone. This is only found on Alderley Edge (it is also used at Soss Moss Hall) and at Bidston Hill. Stone flags cover the roof; the original roof structure is preserved but, as the Great Hall has had a floor inserted, the timbers can only now be seen at close quarters from the bedrooms. There are four principal roof trusses including a big spere-truss and in the screens passage are four stone arches leading to the service rooms.

By 1523 the house belonged to the Davenports, who built the huge stone fireplace against the south wall. At the same time the Great Hall was split into two storeys, each divided into several rooms, and a stone staircase was built between the chimney stack and the screens passage, winding round one of the speres. To light the room at the west end of the upper floor a new gable was built on the entrance side, its timbers forming a chevron pattern. The Davenports also constructed a new half-timbered house on a sandstone plinth, entirely unconnected with the stone hall though adjoining its north-west corner. The two buildings may have been lived in by separate families. The patterned half timbering of the Elizabethan house is spectacular, with vertical and chevron studding on the ground floor, curved braces on the jettied first floor and in the gables a form of cusped lozenge similar to those at Handforth Hall which is dated 1562. The work at Chorley must be contemporary and the alterations to the old house must also be of this period. The principal apartments inside the new house are the withdrawing room on the ground floor and two chambers above; the staircase has been moved.

Shortly before 1604 the estate passed to the Stanleys of Alderley, and Thomas Stanley, who at the time was improving his seat at Alderley, also carried out work at Chorley. In the stone

38. The north front, Chorley Hall, *c*.1900.

39. The south front, Chorley Hall.

house he enlarged the windows, introducing stone mullions and transoms, and raised the central part of the roof on the entrance front into a third gable to provide better lighting for the upper chamber behind it. In the half-timbered house the withdrawing room was lined with oak panelling. The two-arched bridge and the timber-framed farm buildings outside the moat must also date from this time. In the 19th century the two blocks were joined together by a brick link containing a new staircase. The house, tenanted by farmers, became dilapidated and repairs were carried out carelessly, such as the replacement in brick of the east wall of the stone house. By 1897 it was hemmed it by 'pigstyes, dungheaps and slaughterhouses'.

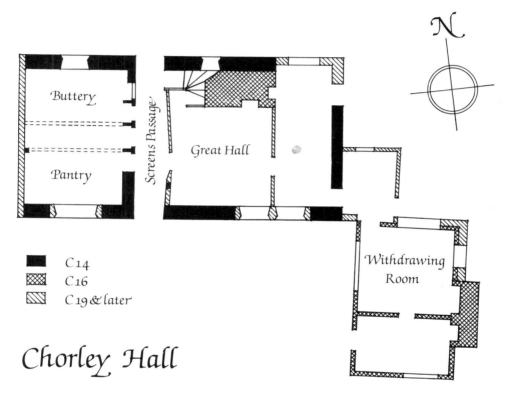

C14
C16
C19 & later

Chorley Hall

In 1915 Chorley was fully restored, as commemorated by the carved overmantel on the ground floor of the half-timbered house. More recently the east wall, repaired in brick and then rendered, has been admirably rebuilt in stone. The lower part of the Great Hall in the stone house is still divided, now into two spaces, a dining room and a kitchen, while the service rooms beneath the solar have been opened up into one large drawing room – a pity as the new kitchen would be more appropriate in this part of the house. But if the present internal spaces at Chorley Hall are confusing, this simply reflects the history of the house, which at a very early date was partitioned into rooms of odd proportions. Nevertheless Chorley is an important example of a medieval house, and its survival is surprising so close to an area where the new and smart is still preferred to the old and mellow.

O iii, 601; *TCLAS* xv, 182; *AMS* vii, 61.

COMBERMERE ABBEY, *Combermere*

587 442

Combermere Abbey is a pasteboard Gothick house of the early 19th century, idyllically positioned overlooking a lake in a distant and peaceful part of Cheshire close to the Shropshire border. The medieval abbey originally on the site belonged to the Cistercians who always preferred lonely places remote from the world. Combermere was founded in 1133 by Hugh de Malbank, son of the Norman grantee of Wich Malbank (Nantwich). The abbey was wealthy; its endowment included substantial salt revenues, but the first of many financial crises occurred during the mid-13th century. Several times the abbey had to be taken into royal custody and it developed a reputation for maladministration and indiscipline.

At the Dissolution it was granted to Sir George Cotton, an esquire of the body to Henry VIII. He demolished the church and most of the abbey buildings except for the part which he used as his dwelling. Remains surviving inside the present house (fragments of a medieval arch are hidden in a closet) suggest that it was formed from the west range of the cloister; that being so the church would have stood at right angles to the house, its west end joining up with the right-hand side of the present entrance front. Buck's engraved west view of the house in 1727 shows broken arcading, the remains of the cloister, along the front. More conclusive is the evidence of the first floor where there is the principal apartment of the house, now the library. Concealed above its plaster ceiling is an extremely fine late medieval hammerbeam roof, its timbers decorated with the abbey arms, a shield bearing a crozier. As with the contemporary hall at Vale Royal, the other Cistercian foundation in Cheshire, the original use of the room is not certain. It is traditionally said to have been the monks' refectory, but this would normally have been on the south range and placed at right angles to it instead of running along the range as here. The hammerbeam roof is exceptionally grand, too grand for a refectory, and this supports the theory that the room was the abbot's Hall, on the first floor of the west range of the cloister. During the 15th century many west ranges were lavishly rebuilt as abbot's lodgings, and it would have been only natural for Sir George Cotton to use it as his house. But over the next 250 years there are only a few shreds of evidence to explain the transformation from abbot's lodging to Gothick mansion.

Sir George's son Richard remodelled the house, for a stone tablet formerly recorded that 'Master Richard Cotton and his sons three, Both for their pleasure and commoditie, This building did edifie, In fifteen hundred and sixty three'. They probably installed a fireplace in the Great Hall and put in the plaster ceiling to cover the open timbers of the roof. It would have been logical to make a new screen at the same time, though the magnificent screen now in the library seems to be early 17th century rather than late 16th. It would also have made sense to provide a suitably impressive staircase giving access from the ground floor entrance up to the hall. But all the present staircases are later. At Vale Royal the problem was solved by an external stair, but there is no evidence of one at Combermere, and it is not shown in either of the 18th-century views of the house. The screen is a handsome and boldly-carved design with arched doors, broad fluted and banded pilasters and a crested armorial top. It originally stood at the lower or north end of the Cotton's Great Hall. This is indicated by the concealed roof structure, where a truss with moulded posts marks the dais end and a narrower north bay shows the position of the screens passage. But the screen is now at the south end, perhaps moved quite soon after it was built; it was certainly in its present position by 1690, the year William III stayed at Combermere on his way to Ireland and the Battle of the Boyne. Next to the hall at

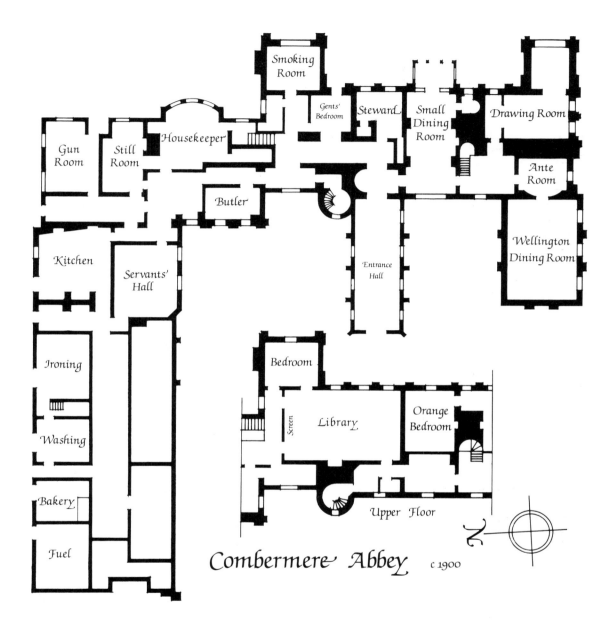

Gun Room

Still Room

Housekeeper

Smoking Room

Gents' Bedroom

Steward

Small Dining Room

Drawing Room

Butler

Ante Room

Kitchen

Servants' Hall

Entrance Hall

Wellington Dining Room

Ironing

Washing

Bedroom

Screen

Library

Orange Bedroom

Bakery

Fuel

Upper Floor

Combermere Abbey c 1900

the north end is a room known as the Orange Bedroom, where the King is said to have slept. If the screen had been in its original position it would have been impossible to enter the hall without passing through the bedroom. Odd as it is, the removal of the screen must be explained by the need to create a bedroom for royal use.

The next record of Combermere comes from two views, the Buck engraving of 1727 and a slightly later oil painting. They show a house with a hipped roof and a cupola. The ground

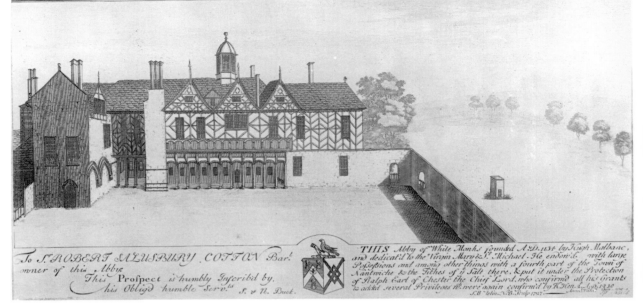

To S.ᵗ ROBERT SALUSBURY COTTON Bar.ᵗ owner of this Abby. This Prospect is humbly Inscribd by. his Oblig'd humble Serv.ᵗˢ S. & N. Buck.

THIS Abby of White Monks founded A.D. 1135 by Hugh Malbanc, and dedicat.d to the Virgin Mary & S.ᵗ Michael. He endow'd with large Possessions and amons other things with a fourth part of the Town of Nantwiche & the Tithes of ye Salt there, & put it under the Protection of Ralph Earl of Chester the Chief Lord, who confirm'd all his Grants & added several Privileges wᶜʰ were again confirm'd by K. Hen. 1. A.D. 1130. S.B. delin. N.B. Sculp 1727.

40. Combermere Abbey: an engraving by S. & N. Buck, 1727, showing the remains of the cloister on the east front.

41. West front of Combermere Abbey: detail from a painting of *c.*1730.

floor was partly of stone, the first floor half-timbered, and above, in the roof, was an attic storey with dormers. Buck shows the house from what was the cloister garth; the painting shows a bird's eye view from the other side, the west front. Spread out on the main axes are extensive formal and kitchen gardens divided by long screens of railings and gates, including the fine pair on the east side probably made by Robert Bakewell and now at Westbury Manor, Long Island. To the north is the mere. The entrance and cupola on the house, not quite central, are aligned with the screens passage. In 1774 Dr. Johnson wrote a tantalisingly vague account of a visit to Combermere with Mrs. Thrale, whose family, the Salusburys of Llewenny, Denbighshire, had married into the Cottons. The Doctor enjoyed boating on the lake and described the house as 'spacious but not magnificent, built at different times with different materials, part is of timber, part stone or brick, plaistered and painted over to look like timber. It is the best house that I ever saw of that kind'. Evidently it was still unimproved. Some changes took place in 1795 for this is when the inscribed tablet mentioned above was found during alterations made by Sir Robert Cotton. But the Gothicisation of the house must have taken place between 1814 and 1821, when it was described as 'recently coated and ornamented in the pointed Gothic style'. For in 1814 Sir Stapleton Cotton had been raised to the peerage for his military services. Rewarded by a grateful nation with a pension of £2,000 per annum, he attempted to transform Combermere into something more fitting for a hero.

Viscount Combermere, as he later became, served in India and the Peninsular Wars, notably at Salamanca. His crucial role in this decisive British victory drew from Wellington the remark, 'By God, Cotton, I never saw anything so beautiful in my life. The day is yours'. He became Baron in 1814, Viscount in 1827 and Field-Marshal in 1855, and was successively Governor-General of Barbados, Commander-in-Chief in Ireland and in India. His equestrian statue stands at Chester outside the castle. Exceedingly vain and self important, he was Thackeray's model for Sir George Tufto in *The Book of Snobs*, his 'padded breast, twinkling over with innumerable decorations . . . It is difficult to say what virtues this prosperous gentleman possesses. He never read a book in his life, and with his purple old gouty fingers, still writes a schoolboy hand. He has reached old age and grey hairs without being the least venerable. He dresses like an outrageously young man to the present moment and laces and pads his old carcass as if he were still handsome George Tufto of 1800'.

His house too exhibits a love of empty-headed show. He had it castellated and rendered in grey cement, inserting heavy-handed Gothick windows set in pointed arched recesses. He remodelled the library, added an extensive bedroom and service wing at the south, and built on a dining room at the north for Wellington's visit of 1820. Seen from a distance, Combermere appears as a romantic ivy-clad vision of battlements and pinnacles. But its detail is coarse, its massing inept and the render, applied like stage scenery to a framework of battens nailed to the half-timbered walls, left a legacy of rampant dry rot. Nothing was done to resolve the internal awkwardness caused by the moving of the screen which today still results in a cumbersome progress from the entrance to the south stair leading up to the library, still the only reception room of any size. Lord Combermere was better at winning battles than choosing architects.

He did commission two ambitious remodelling schemes, from the Morrisons of Ireland around 1829 and from Edward Blore, whose drawings for a courtyard house survive. Of these, only the Elizabethan-style lodge by the Morrisons, and a reduced version of Blore's Tudor-style stable block, dated, 1837, were built. In the beautifully landscaped park, the lake was extended so as to be seen from the west front, and beyond it is an eyecatcher in fancy brickwork with arrowslits and pinnacles, called the Brankelow Folly, a keeper's cottage with dog kennels in the side pavilions. At the far end of the park is a tall obelisk commemorating Lord Combermere, who died in 1865. Overlooking the lake is the west front of the house, an irregular E shape with a Gothick porch not quite in the centre, betraying the medieval plan. The original entrance passage was made into a pretty little narrow hall with Gothick clustered columns and delicate leaf capitals; it was later used as a small dining room. Beyond is the disused north wing formerly including the Wellington dining room, recently demolished. The present entrance was formed on the east side in 1854, originally a long entrance hall hung with military and sporting trophies and now reduced to a porch. This leads to a passage decorated with cast-iron tracery in the perpendicular style, similar to work at Porden's Eaton Hall. To the south is the service wing, reduced and lowered by one storey, neatly re-using the removed Gothick windows and replacing the battlements at the new parapet level. An attractive octagonal game larder still stands in what was the service court.

The only interior of note is the library, its old screen and ceiling dramatised in the antiquarian taste of the early 19th century. The coved ceiling fits snugly into the lines of the hammerbeam roof it was designed to hide. The plasterwork itself is difficult to date: the ornamentation on the ceiling proper may be original, but the display of heraldry on the coving is characteristic of the 19th century, looking back to the heraldic canopy at Adlington. In a photograph of 1893 the background of the coving is shown darker, giving a much richer effect that the cream colour of today, though the ceiling itself was then as now a lighter shade. 'All is dark here and gloomy rather than stately', commented the *Illustrated London News* in 1890. 'It is a room which would look best lamplit'. It was and still is a powerfully atmospheric room, formerly lined with bookcases which have now mostly been replaced with panelling brought in from elsewhere. It was not a love of books, but a desire to surround himself with the imposing evidence of ancestry which led Lord Combermere to create this room. Fictional historical portraits, including Henry VIII and Sir George Cotton, are placed over the chimneypiece, between the windows and on the reverse of the screen.

42. West front of Combermere Abbey before recent alterations.

43.   The library, Combermere Abbey.

Later the estate was sold to the Crossleys, in whose family it remains. The rambling, ill-constructed house brought problems in the mid-20th century and in 1971 Raymond Erith and Quinlan Terry drew up a scheme to rebuild it, re-using some of the Gothick elements. This was not carried out, but around 1975 another remodelling programme was begun by James Brotherhood of Chester. The south part has been successfully reduced but the north wing stands empty awaiting a decision on its fate, unless it falls down first.

O iii, 402; Hanshall, 47; Neale; T ii, 1; Mary, Viscountess Combermere and W. Knollys, *Memoirs and Correspondence of Viscount Combermere*, 1866, 109; *ILN* 8 November 1890, 590-2; Sale brochure 1893 (Copy in NMR); *Thackeray's Works*, Centenary edition 1911 ii, 46; *Ches Life* May 1936; Boswell's *Life of Johnson* (ed. Hill, rev. Powell) 1964 v, 434-5; E. Longford, *Wellington, The Years of the Sword*, 1969, 287, 355; Harris 132; VCH iii, 150-6; BM Add. Mss. 42028, Blore drawings; CRO DBC/261/Box 53, Plans by Douglas and Minshull.

CREWE HALL, *Crewe*

733 540

Crewe Hall is a difficult house to comprehend. In essence it is Jacobean, one of the finest buildings of its date in England, but it is not known as such, for, extended in the late 18th century, modernised in 1837, and then substantially remodelled after a devastating fire in 1866, it has generally been regarded as Victorian. To the present-day visitor it is not only the quantity of Jacobean work remaining which is of interest, but also the creative quality of the Victorian reconstruction.

The house was built by Sir Randulph Crewe between 1615 and 1639. The estate had been in the ownership of the de Crewe family as early as the 13th century, but it had passed out of the family until the late 16th century, when it was bought by Sir Randulph, a descendant of the earliest Crewe of Crewe. He had clearly set his sights on acquiring the estate and building a new house. Born in 1558 in Nantwich, he trained in law at Lincoln's Inn, where he made rapid progress in the legal profession, becoming Lord Chief Justice in 1625. This appointment however did not last long, for James I died in this year, and Sir Randulph incurred the new King's displeasure by declining to acknowledge the legality of a forced loan. He was dismissed from office after only two years and never regained favour, spending the remainder of his life in Cheshire.

The new house was begun in 1615. In national terms it is a conservative design: Longleat, with which it has stylistic similarity, was begun 50 years earlier. But Sir Randulph was not a young man, and by the standards of Cheshire the house was progressive. The 17th-century historian Thomas Fuller remarked, 'Sir Randal brought the model of excellent building into these remote parts; Yea, brought London into Cheshire'. A painting of about 1710 shows that the original house was a square block with sides about one hundred feet in length, punctuated by projecting bays capped with gables and surmounted by groups of octagonal chimneys. Service areas were in a series of small steeply gabled buildings on the west side. A forecourt and extensive formal gardens were enclosed by walls. How much of this can be seen today? From the outside the main part of the house would seem to be largely unaltered apart from the recent loss of its chimneys; and of the service buildings, some exist in a modified form. But in fact the house has been through many changes, and inside Sir Randulph might scarcely recognise it.

The first major change was the large service wing added to the west side at the end of the 18th century. This was designed in the style of the house, showing an unusual consideration for its date, but the proportions are more 18th than 17th century. Then in 1836 the third Baron Crewe commissioned George Latham of Nantwich to carry out extensive improvements. These included rebuilding the chimneys and remodelling the library. However, early in 1837 Latham was replaced by Edward Blore. 'I understand Mr. Blore has proposed some alterations in the interior to enlarge the Entrance Lobby', wrote Latham. 'I hope he will have respect to the original character of the house'. Although it is difficult to know precisely what degree of respect Blore did show, it is possible to trace much of what he did from a large volume of working drawings which survives in the R.I.B.A. Drawings Collection, and we know that an enormous sum of money was spent, £30,000, mostly on the interiors. Lord Palmerston, when visiting the Hall shortly after the completion of this work, was inspired to write:

44.   Crewe Hall, from a painting of *c*.1710.

Here in rude state old chieftains dwelt,
Who no refinement knew.
Small were the wants their bosoms felt,
And their enjoyments few.

But now by taste and judgment plann'd,
Throughout these scenes we find
The work of Art's improving hand,
With ancient splendour join'd.

This is something of a slur on Sir Randulph, no 'old chieftain', but the organisation of a Victorian country house was very different from that of two centuries earlier, and Blore carried out some radical changes to the plan, as well as embellishing the interiors and fitting plate glass in all the windows. This was mostly destroyed by the fire of 1866. It is said that whilst the Hall was still burning Lord Crewe wrote to his architect asking him to 'come and build it up again', but Blore, by this time in retirement, declined to undertake so large a job, and it was passed to E. M. Barry, son of Sir Charles Barry, designer of the Houses of Parliament.

E. M. Barry lacked the imagination and ability of his father; his strength was in planning, and his forte was hotels. His best known work is the Royal Opera House, Covent Garden, but Crewe Hall, where he was directed by the powerful character of the existing building, is his finest. Barry's attitude to the restoration is made clear in a lecture he later gave to the Royal Academy, in which he states that the greatest care was taken in following the original design, but 'with less roughness of execution and uncouthness of detail, particularly in respect of the human figure. Such peculiarities cannot, I think, be properly repeated in a modern reconstruction ... it is not the part of the nineteenth century restorer to reproduce matters which at best were the weaknesses of his predecessors. He is in such cases free to select, and should not seek, by a clever imitation of bygone tricks of construction or design, to deceive the spectator as to the age of his own work, and so pass off the latter as something which it is not'. As a rule Barry's work is richer, more elaborate and more regular than that which it replaced.

The exterior of the main Jacobean block exists essentially in its original state; indeed most of the masonry, including the internal walls, survived the fire, and only the stonework cresting to the gables and the lower part of the porch appear to have been replaced. The most striking addition is the tower which was required for storing water. Barry used this as a means of uniting the main house and the service block, but it is only partially successful, for he made little attempt to produce a convincingly Jacobean design. The chief internal alterations were caused by the replanning of the ground floor. At the centre of the house there had originally been an open courtyard. The main entrance opened into a screens passage and the formal route took the visitor through the Great Hall on the right to the small East Hall and then up the staircase to the staterooms on the first floor. This arrangement was not acceptable to the Victorians, and Blore had already created an entrance hall in place of the screens passage, and roofed over the courtyard to form a single storey central hall. Barry's solution was more ingenious. He made the central hall into a kind of atrium with a hammerbeam roof. A ground-floor arcade supports an open gallery at mezzanine level and above, enclosed except on the short sides, are the corridors of the first floor, lit from richly-coloured stained glass panels. It is an exciting space and Barry's brilliant planning is accompanied by a High Victorian sense of design, for every surface is embellished with carving, and the floor is paved with a glowing pattern of coloured marbles.

The central hall provides a way of reaching the staircase without having to pass through the Great Hall. It also leads to the small chapel which lies on the north side. The chapel was originally plain by comparison with the other rooms of the house, but Barry took the opportunity to make it the most lavish, commissioning stained glass and murals from Clayton and Bell, bronze medallions of biblical characters from J. Birnie Philip, and painting and stencilling from J. G. Crace. It is all uncompromisingly Victorian, and here one understands Barry's view that the detail should be of its own time. These craftsmen were amongst the best available and he had worked with them in his father's office on the decoration of the Houses of Parliament. The dining room was by contrast restored by Barry to its 17th-century appearance. This was the room least damaged by fire, and the overmantel with the figure of Plenty is original. The chimneypiece, which also survived, is however Blore's. The elaborate carved screen and the ceiling which had been recorded by C. J. Richardson are accurate reproductions of the Jacobean designs. In the Oak Parlour to the left of the entrance hall is an original overmantel, the only substantial piece of carved timber to survive the reconstruction. The main staircase, which had also been recorded, is a great piece of showmanship; there is no other Jacobean staircase of such spatial complexity, and Barry rebuilt it accurately. Like the famous stairs at Hatfield House, the carved newels were designed to display sculpture. At Crewe they support heraldic beasts which, according to Joseph Nash the antiquarian artist who visited Crewe in 1838, were formerly painted and gilded. At the first landing is the entrance to the Carved Parlour, a panelled room with an overmantel depicting the winged figure of Time chastising sloth and rewarding industry. The sharpness of the carving contrasts with the naive character of the dining room overmantel and illustrates Barry's philosophy on restoration.

The state apartments on the first floor are only loosely a recreation of the originals. These rooms had already been embellished by Blore, and Barry felt able therefore to devise his own treatment. The most impressive is the library, situated above the Carved Parlour. The bookcases which line the walls are separated by figures of bibliophiles carved by Philip, and the frieze

45. Crewe Hall, c.1900.

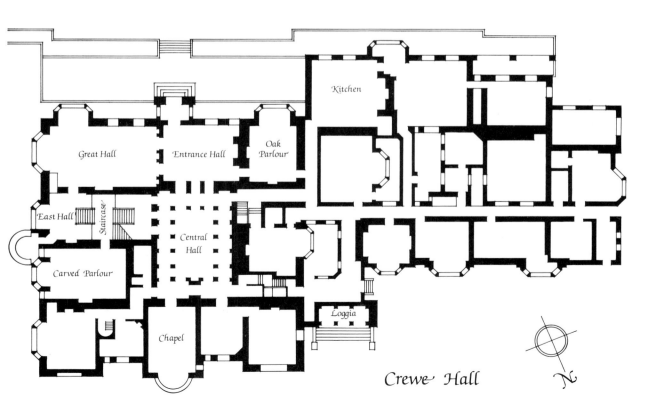

Kitchen

Great Hall

Entrance Hall

Oak Parlour

East Hall

Staircase

Carved Parlour

Central Hall

Loggia

Chapel

Crewe Hall

N

46. The staircase, Crewe Hall, 1913.

47. The Carved Parlour, Crewe Hall, 1913.

represents scenes from the poets by J. Mabey. The ceiling of the drawing room which lies opposite the library is a reproduction of the Jacobean original, recorded by the architect William Burn, a great rival of Blore's. The pattern of the ribs is identical to a ceiling formerly at the *Reindeer Inn*, Banbury, of which a replica is in the Victoria and Albert Museum. The originals of both were most likely the work of the same craftsmen. The whole north side is taken up with the Long Gallery which has at its centre the semi-circular bay forming the apse of the chapel below. Opposite this bay is a spectacular chimneypiece of coloured marbles with busts of Sir Randulph and Nathaniel Crewe, Bishop of Durham, carved by Henry Weekes. In one of the state bedrooms is an original fireplace and plaster overmantel representing the murder of Abel by Cain.

More discreet alterations by Barry dealt with the efficient organisation of the household. Additional service rooms were fitted into the ground floor, and by modifying the roof structure he provided a further 20 servants' bedrooms in an attic. Separate staircases rose from the ground floor to the menservants' and the maids' rooms, an important requirement in the planning of a Victorian house. Within the basement there existed an arrangement of tramlines with hot water encased chests on wheels to transport hot food from the kitchens to the lifts below the dining room.

By the time of the fire, the park had already undergone major changes. The formal pleasure gardens shown in the early 18th-century painting had given way to a more picturesque landscape, the work of William Emes, and in 1791 Humphry Repton produced designs for an ornamental lake and new approaches. In the mid-19th century W. A. Nesfield laid out parterres with statuary and gravelled walks. Terraces were formed on the north and south sides, and balustrading was erected, probably to Barry's design, incorporating heraldic beasts modelled on those of the grand staircase. The magnificent entrance gates made by Cubitt and Co. were exhibited at the Paris Exhibition of 1878. Of these formal gardens only the gates, the statuary and the terraces survive. The beds have been mostly grassed over, and the lake drained away in 1941 when the dam collapsed. There are however a number of interesting estate buildings. The stables date from the 17th century, though the centrepiece is by Blore. More remarkable are Stowford and Smithy Cottages, designed by Nesfield's more famous son, W. E. Nesfield, the early partner of Norman Shaw. Erected between 1860 and 1866, these owe nothing to the Jacobean style of Crewe Hall, but are loosely derived from the vernacular architecture of the south-east with tile hanging, pargetting and tall chimneys.

Hungerford Crewe, the 3rd Baron, who rebuilt after the fire, never married. On his death in 1894 the estate passed to his nephew Lord Houghton, who in 1931 offered the Hall as a gift to Cheshire County Council. The offer was declined and, to protect the interests of his tenants, the bulk of the estate was sold to the Duchy of Lancaster. Following the war, the Hall was leased as offices, and since 1966 it has formed the U.K. headquarters of the Wellcome Foundation.

O iii, 312; J. Nash, *The Mansions of England in the Olden Time* i 1839, iv 1849; C. J. Richardson, *Studies from Old English Mansions* i 1841, ii 1842, iii 1845; T ii, 5; B xvii, 485; *The Architect* ii, 58; E. M. Barry, *Lectures on Architecture*, 1881, 318; *CL* xi, 400, xxxiii, 634; *Ches Life* December 1967; Girouard 178; Harris 24, 151; Cambridge University Library mss 3945-6, Blore wages book; RIBA Blore and Barry drawings.

See also plate I, facing page 14.

DODDINGTON HALL, *Doddington*

709 465

48. The tower house, Doddington.

The early career of Samuel Wyatt was spent in the shadow of his younger brother James. The commission in 1776 by Sir Thomas Broughton of Doddington offered him his first opportunity to design a completely new house. It was an important step and Doddington established his reputation as the most fashionable architect of late 18th-century Cheshire. Sir Thomas Broughton inherited the estate from his brother in 1776. Doddington had passed to the Broughtons of Staffordshire from the Delves family in the early 18th century. John de Delves, a highly placed royal servant and Justice of the King's Bench, purchased the manor in 1352. In 1365 he was granted a licence to crenellate, and the tower house which stands in a field below the hall may have been the result. His great-nephew John Delves also obtained a licence to crenellate in 1403 and stylistically the building could be of either date. It is a pele tower, a type of fortified house with a vaulted chamber at the base, of which the only other example to survive in Cheshire is at Brimstage Hall. On the east side an elaborate staircase and loggia are attached, remnants of the 17th-century Doddington Hall, a moated courtyard house which was demolished at the time the Wyatt house was built. Also from the old Hall are the life-sized carved figures of the 'Four Esquires', Dutton of Dutton, Delves of Dodynton, Foulshurst of Crewe and Hawkestone of Wrinehill, who served under Audley with the Black Prince at Poitiers. These figures now stand at the outer sides of the loggia within which are larger ones of the Black Prince and Audley. All are depicted in the fashions of the time they were carved with bushy moustaches and Jacobean armour.

When Thomas Broughton inherited Doddington, the old Hall was ruinous and in use as a farm. The needs of his family, which grew to 14 children by 1785 when his wife died in childbirth, and the increased yield of his estates must have determined him upon moving to Doddington and rebuilding. He first went to 'Capability' Brown who produced designs in 1770 both for improvements to the grounds and for a new house. These plans were rejected in favour of those of Samuel Wyatt, though part of Brown's landscape designs, for which he made a charge of £98 10s. 0d., may have been adopted. Samuel Wyatt, whose family business was based in Staffordshire, was probably known to Sir Thomas through his work at Blithfield Hall for the 1st Lord Bagot, though the Wyatt style had gained wide publicity from the exhibition at the Royal Academy in 1772 of the designs for Heaton Hall by his brother James. Drawings for

49. (*above*) The south front, Doddington Hall.

50. (*below*) The entrance hall, Doddington Hall.

Doddington signed by Wyatt and dated 1777 survive at the Hall and, although the house was not completed for 21 years, there was no significant alteration in its execution.

The new Hall is a large rectangular block with a tall rusticated basement and one-and-a-half storeys. It is unusually broad and, unlike most Wyatt houses, has no portico but instead a double projecting staircase modelled on that at Kedleston Hall by Robert Adam, where Samuel had been engaged as Clerk of Works from 1759-68. The three main elevations are symmetrical, faced with beautifully set ashlar, and show the Wyatt style at its purest. Apart from the staircase, the north-facing entrance front is broken only by the merest projection of the pedimented centre and of the two end bays. The latter contain tripartite windows within blank arches, a Wyatt hallmark. Between the plain unmoulded windows of the piano nobile and the upper floor are panels with garlands, and within the blank arches of the projecting bays are Coadestone medallions depicting the signs of the zodiac. These same elements are used in the composition of the south front, though here a broad semi-circular bow with a shallow dome replaces the pedimented centre and staircase. On the west side is an unusual serpentine service wing.

The plan of the house is also strictly ordered. As at Kedleston the two principal rooms of the piano nobile are a rectangular entrance hall and behind this a circular saloon, both on the central axis. In the entrance hall an austere Doric order of dark grey scagliola columns supports an entablature with the metopes containing pelicans, the Delves crest. Within deep niches are marble-topped tables supported on scrolls, and over the doors are panels of frolicking putti painted in grisaille to imitate carving in stone. The saloon is the great climax of the house, a circular room 36 feet in diameter, 20 feet high and surmounted by a graceful saucer dome. It is entered directly from the hall, through double doors fitted with 'sympathetic hinges', probably the first use of Wyatt's patent device for opening both leaves simultaneously. The wall is divided by pilasters into panels, some enclosing tall pier glasses, others shallow alcoves for daybeds. At the top of each panel is a classical scene in grisaille, and above is a rich gilt frieze and a cove of octagonal coffering. The decoration of the pilaster strips incorporates medallions of maidens and trophies of musical instruments in imitation of dark blue Wedgwood Jasperware. Within one of these, on a music sheet, is the signature of the decorator McLachlan for Morant. Morant and Co. was a firm of late Victorian and Edwardian decorators, and this scheme, thought previously to be by Wyatt, dates only from the turn of the century, with the exception of the classical scenes in the manner of Biagio Rebecca. In fact Wyatt drawings at the Cheshire Record Office show that the decorations were strikingly different. Whereas at present the ceiling and cornice are largely gilded, Wyatt intended the plasterwork to be picked out in pastel colours on white, and for the pilasters he showed brightly coloured arabesques sprouting from vases. In changing the tone of the room, Morants were reflecting the more sombre taste of the late 19th century, but if the gaiety of the decoration has been lost, the richness and delicacy has not.

Around these two great rooms the remainder of the floor is symmetrically disposed. Two top-lit stone staircases with slender iron balustrades fill the narrow central spaces to either side of the hall. To the east are a small drawing room, a breakfast room, and the large dining room with shallow apsed ends and a frieze of bellflowers, later used in the music room at Heaton Hall. The original colour scheme was pale green as at Heaton. On the west side of the house are the library containing original bookcases, formerly painted and gilded, and Sir Thomas's octagonal dressing room. The circular space above the saloon is divided ingeniously to form two hexagonal bedrooms with vaulted ceilings, and in the basement below is a circular billiard room.

Samuel Wyatt also designed the stables, the north lodges, like salt and pepper pots, and the model farm built north-east of the castle in a rustic classical style. Within an octagonal enclosure stands a tall barn with lower cowsheds and fodder stores radiating from its corners. The purpose of a model farm was to increase agricultural efficiency through an ordered and practical layout, and Wyatt was a pioneer of such buildings. Wyatt's practicality was recognised by his client,

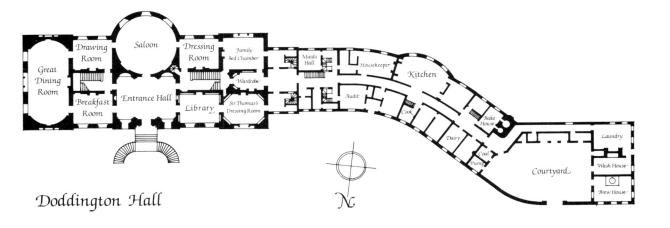

Doddington Hall

N

for Sir Thomas considered it 'one of the happiest circumstances' that he employed 'an architect who whilst he had paid every proper regard to elegance and embellishment has in no respect neglected the important considerations of solidarity, utility and convenience'; he commissioned two portraits of himself, about 20 years apart, both showing him holding the plans for the house. It was an ambitious programme of building and few families in Cheshire could match it. When Sir Thomas died in 1813 aged 68 it was recorded on his memorial in the church at Broughton that he had not encumbered the family estates by a shilling in the building of it. Perhaps if it was built only from income, this is why it took 21 years to complete. In any event, his son Sir John Delves Broughton did not feel financially constrained, for in 1815 he engaged Jeffry Wyatt (later Sir Jeffry Wyattville), Samuel's nephew, to enlarge the stables. This was not carried out, but surviving drawings show that the scheme involved re-use of the curved stonework and pilasters of the 'temple', a domed banquet house which stood on an island in the lake. Besides being a country gentleman, Sir Thomas Broughton was also a clergyman, becoming rector of St Mary's church, Cheadle in 1794. It is therefore strange that no chapel was included in the plan of the house. It was not until 1837 that a chapel was built within the park for his son. A

51. The model farm, Doddington.

dull exercise in the Gothic Revival, it was designed by Edward Lapidge, whose father was 'Capability' Brown's chief assistant and successor.

It is fortunate that all later improvements were restricted to erecting new estate buildings and cottages, for the house survives remarkably unaltered. Anonymous drawings exist for an insensitive scheme prepared around 1900 for modifying the north elevation by the addition of a balustrade and placing pediments over the tripartite windows and doorway. Mercifully it was never carried out. Apart from commissioning some new furniture and decoration, the family did not radically change their chaste Wyatt interiors, and left only at the outbreak of the Second World War. Until recently the house has been let to a girls' school; now the school has closed and the future is uncertain.

O iii, 524; T ii, 13; Sir Delves L. Broughton, *Records of an Old Cheshire Family*, 1908; *Ches Life* March 1936; *CL* cxiii, 344, 414; D. Stroud, *Capability Brown*, 1975, 213; Robinson, 256; J. M. Robinson, *Georgian Model Farms*, 1984, 71, 122; Doddington Hall, Wyatt drawings; CRO DDB/Q/1, DDB/Q/Z, DDB/G/B, drawings and estate maps; RIBA Lapidge drawings.

See also plate III, facing page 30.

DORFOLD HALL, *Nantwich*

636 526 *House and gardens open to the public. (Privately owned)*

The history of Dorfold is linked to the practice and profit of the law, for the estate was bought by a distinguished Elizabethan lawyer, Sir Roger Wilbraham and, when the Wilbrahams sold it in the 18th century, it was purchased by another lawyer, James Tomkinson. Sir Roger was a younger son of the Wilbrahams of Townsend house, Nantwich, a junior branch of the Wilbrahams of Woodhey. Solicitor-general of Ireland for Elizabeth I, Sir Roger served James I as Master of the Court of Requests and Surveyor of the Court of Wards and Liveries. He purchased the Dorfold estate but, being childless, passed it to his younger brother Ralph, Feodary of Cheshire and Flintshire. It was Ralph who built the present house, begun in 1616, the year of Sir Roger's death: the date is carved over the entrance and occurs inside on the Oak Room fireplace. The overmantel in the King James Room is dated 1621, giving a possible finishing date for the house.

A Jacobean house, Dorfold is today seen through Victorian eyes. Until then, there was no formal approach, no neat lodge and gates, no avenue of limes and no shaped forecourt, just a long irregular drive coming in at an angle and skirting a dank pool; in front of the house but detached from it were just two low brick pavilions with curly shaped gables. Now that the pavilions and their gables have been repeated in the 19th century to form a forecourt enclosed on three sides, Dorfold looks busier and prettier than it must have done originally, for the house itself is rather stark of outline. It has a rectilinear frontage with three big straight triangular gables, and large windows with stone mullions and transoms. The plan consists of a central block containing a hall with a Great Chamber above, and two cross wings. The facade, of brick with diaper patterning, steps back towards the centre, each step marked by long and short quoins. In the return angles between the outer gables and the centre are two double-storey projections with flat balustraded tops. These contain the hall bay window on the right and the porch on the left, with the entrance door on the inner side not the front. This type of entrance arrangement occurs at other late Elizabethan houses including Burton Agnes, Yorkshire and Chastleton, Oxfordshire, both of which have in common with Dorfold a large barrel-vaulted upper chamber. Similar entrances are seen on a smaller scale in Cheshire at Harden Hall, Tattenhall Hall and Lower Huxley, the latter perhaps influenced by Dorfold as it belonged to Ralph Wilbraham's nephew Thomas.

On the garden front of Dorfold, which looks south, the two outer gables correspond to those of the entrance front, but the centre is curiously flat, with a dropped string course and windows which seem to have been altered. The door, now in the centre, was originally to the right, aligning with the entrance passage and porch. The canted bay at the west end, and the eastern extension, originally a larger service wing, are both later additions.

The Jacobean interiors survive only on the first floor, reached by the original oak staircase in the west cross wing. First there are two bedrooms. The Oak Room is panelled to the ceiling and over the fireplace are painted coats of arms of Wilbraham family connections, one dated 1616. The adjacent half-panelled room with a grotesque plaster frieze is called the King James Room after its plaster overmantel displaying the arms of James I and the date 1621 with strongly modelled heraldic mantling.

Occupying the centre of the upper floor is the Great Chamber, one of the most splendid rooms in Cheshire, warm, spacious and light, with panelled walls and a spectacular plasterwork ceiling, a broad, high barrel vault richly modelled with fanciful pendants and a complex design of superimposed strapwork patterns with many little studs and cartouches, incorporating thistle,

52. The forecourt, Dorfold Hall.

53. Fireplace in the King James Room, Dorfold Hall, 1908.

rose and fleur-de-lys. Similar work, with elaborate openwork pendants and patterns of even finer quality, is seen at Blickling Hall, Norfolk, where the patron, Sir Henry Hobart, is known to have employed a London plasterer, Edward Stanyan, in 1620. Hobart was Lord Chief Justice to James I and so came from the same circle as Sir Roger Wilbraham, Ralph's brother. The common background of the patrons, and the similarities of design, suggest the work at Dorfold was carried out by London plasterers. In the lunettes at each end, in a different craftsman's hand, are birds and little winged sprites emerging from cornucopiae, motifs also found in East Anglia, at Audley End.

The Great Chamber at Dorfold also has painted coats of arms, representing famous courtiers: Sir Thomas Egerton and Sir Randulph Crewe over the doors and Lord Burghley, Sir Christopher Hatton and Lord Derby over the fireplace, but strangely enough there is no display of Wilbraham heraldry. Neo-Elizabethan embellishments were added in the 19th century, as in the case of the forecourt: the doors and the fancy aedicules surmounting them are Victorian trimmings, and in 1837 the architect Edward Blore designed a fireplace, though the inner part has since been removed to reveal the original stone arch. (A design by Blore dated 1843 survives for the fireplace in the dining room.)

In 1754 the Wilbrahams sold Dorfold to James Tomkinson, a wealthy lawyer from Bostock. The Tomkinsons had for many years been managing the affairs of the Wilbrahams and clearly knew more about the estate business than the Wilbrahams themselves. Over a period, James Tomkinson had the ground floor of Dorfold remodelled, separating the screens passage into a corridor, turning the hall into a dining room and making a library in the south-west corner. He also added a five-bay brick service wing in a plain classical style. The architect William Baker may have been responsible for these alterations. His account book records that he supervised repairs at Dorfold, which were carried out by a builder, Roger Eykin, between 1757 and 1759, though the nature of the work is not specified. The simple classical cornice of the dining room ceiling is consistent with Baker's style and with this date. The service wing could be later: it was definitely in place by 1789 as it is clearly shown on an estate map of this year. (It was demolished in 1951, except for one bay.) The library interior is certainly later than the 1750s. The ceiling is in a busy Neo-classical style, with garlands at each corner representing the four seasons, and a pair of cooing doves in the middle, probably celebrating the marriage in 1771 between James Tomkinson's youngest daughter Catherine and George Cotton. The design has been attributed to the young Samuel Wyatt. A fireplace in the Wyatt manner has since been removed.

In the early 19th century the house must have been found inconvenient, and various schemes exist to provide larger kitchens, dining room and library; there are drawings and proposals by Thomas Harrison of Chester (1816, 1822-3), Lewis Wyatt (1825) and George Latham of Nantwich (1827). None of them was executed. But in 1824 the front of the house was made to look more picturesque for James Tomkinson's grandson, the Revd. James Tomkinson. An enclosed forecourt was ingeniously created by attaching to the outer corners of the facade replicas of the two original low L-shaped pavilions, and the new ones were joined to the originals with screen walls which also repeated the shaped gables. Over the doorway in the centre of the east screen is carved the date 1824. Of the architects consulted, George Latham is the most likely candidate to have carried out this kind of work.

In 1849 the landscape gardener W. A. Nesfield came to Dorfold to advise on further improvements. His plan for a formal parterre dated 1850 survives. He suggested doing away with the untidy old pool so that a new axial carriage drive could be formed; the old approach he likened to a back entrance. Nothing was done, perhaps because of opposition from Mrs. Tomkinson senior but, as soon as she died in 1861, Nesfield was again invited to work at the house. With her death, by a quirk of history Dorfold reverted to the descendants of the Wilbrahams of Woodhey, for it was inherited by the Revd. James Tomkinson's daughter Anne, wife of Wilbraham Spencer Tollemache, the younger son of Admiral Tollemache of Tilstone Lodge. Opposition to changing the approach at Dorfold was endemic in the Tomkinson ladies for Anne wanted not only to keep the pool but to enlarge it, whilst Nesfield dismissed it as 'a receptacle for sewerage and decaying vegetable matter'.

In 1862 Anne came back from a visit to France to find trees cut down, the pool being drained and the land dug up for a drive. She is supposed not to have spoken to her husband for six months. Meanwhile, Nesfield remodelled the approach, planted the avenue, paved the forecourt and closed it with a balustrade; lodge, coach house and clock tower were also built at this time. In the centre of the court is a large bronze of a mastiff and her puppies, This and the iron gates at the end of the avenue were bought at the Paris Exhibition of 1855. From nearer home came other garden ornaments, the pair of stone lions from Townsend House, 1571, and the gateway from the Wilbraham almshouses of 1613. The formal parterre at the south was presumably the work of Nesfield. But Anne would have none of it. She added a codicil to her will that, at her funeral, her body was not to be carried down the new drive and, when she died in 1871, her coffin was borne to Acton church across the fields.

O iii, 345; T ii, 20; *JCAS* xv, 77; *CL* xxiv, 594; L. Turner, *Decorative Plasterwork in Great Britain*, 1927, 70; *Ches Life* May/June 1948, February 1954; Oswald, 127-8; Family collection and JRL, Roundell of Dorfold papers.

See also plate IV, facing page 30.

DUNHAM MASSEY HALL, *Dunham*

735 874 *House, gardens and park open to the public. (National Trust)*

On the death of the 10th Earl of Stamford in 1976 Dunham Massey Hall passed to the National Trust. The 10th Earl, who had held the estate for 66 years, lived alone, latterly in only a small part of the house, and the principal rooms were shuttered, their contents under wraps. During this time he did nothing to alter the decorations, and the arrangement of furniture remained as it had been placed for his parents at the start of the century when the house was restored. These Edwardian interiors are now amongst the most interesting features of the house.

The earliest record is of a castle held at Dunham by Hamo de Masci against Henry II in 1173. No trace of this has been found, but the mound beside the lake in the garden may be the remains of a Norman motte. In 1453 the manor passed to Sir Robert Booth of Barton, whose grandson Sir George Booth built the nucleus of the present house around 1616. Sir George's house was E-shaped, built of brick, surmounted by curved Flemish gables with a Great Hall lit by huge mullioned windows. It is clearly visible in the view engraved by Kip in 1697 behind the later entrance front. Sir George's grandson and heir, young Sir George, was imprisoned in the Civil War by the Parliamentarians, but after the Restoration he was made 1st Lord Delamer, and returned to Dunham to continue enlarging the house. Of his work Sir Peter Leycester records the conversion of two ground-floor rooms to create a chapel in about 1655 and the construction of the new entrance front enclosing a central courtyard. This new front, Leycester claimed, 'much beautified the manor-house', an opinion not shared by the 2nd Earl of Warrington who remodelled the Hall in 1732, for his manuscript note relating to the description observed acidly, 'He seems to speak ironically'. The new front was indeed a curious design; at each end were octagonal towers, and between them a facade divided by paired columns framing round-headed windows with external shutters.

In the next generation debts were run up by the politically ambitious 2nd Lord Delamer, later 1st Earl of Warrington, and he carried out no works at Dunham. By contrast his son the 2nd Earl took no interest in politics but devoted himself to the improvement of the estate and the Hall. A difficult and cantankerous man, he married Mary Oldbury, the daughter of a London merchant, who brought a dowry of £40,000 and restored the family fortunes, but they 'quarrell'd and lived in the same house as absolute strangers to each other at bed and board'. Although her money financed the Earl's building projects, there is no recognition of her in the many arms and crests which adorn the interiors, and the Earl's double portrait by Michael Dahl shows him not with his wife but with his daughter who was later to inherit the estate. The pose adopted by the Earl in this portrait gives new meaning to the description of him by an acquaintance as 'the stiffest of all stiff things'. Conservatism fashioned the style of his building and landscape work at Dunham, but it also led to his commissioning a remarkable series of paintings as a record of the estate and his achievements. The first were painted in 1696, immediately he succeeded: a study by Knyff of a pug with the old house in the background, and a view by Adrian van Diest, as well as Kip's engraving. Van Diest's view, which predates the rebuilding of the house, shows the earliest planting in the park.

Before starting on the Hall, the 2nd Earl concentrated on improving its setting, planting vast numbers of oaks, elms and beeches in a series of avenues radiating from the house with vistas terminated by statues and obelisks. Running parallel with the avenues are straight-sided ponds. The arrangement is similar to Bridgeman's work at Boughton and Wimpole, but it is probable that the design was made by the Earl himself. The completed planting is accurately depicted

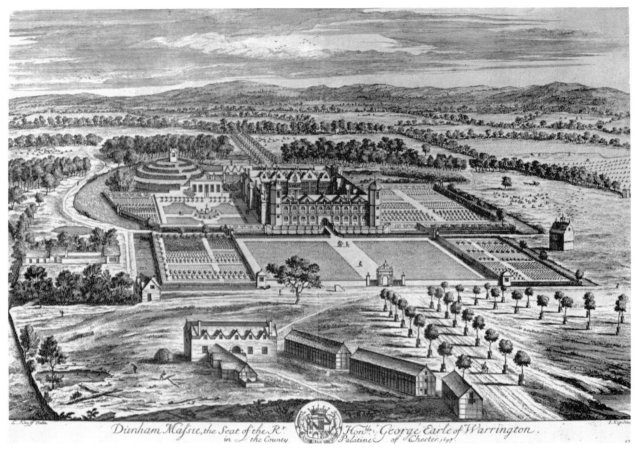

54. Dunham Massey from the south: engraving by Kip, 1697.

in the four marvellous bird's eye views by John Harris the younger, painted about 1750. These paintings also show the new house which was completed in 1740. Though the 2nd Earl had been altering the inside from early in the century, work on the exterior did not start until 1732. The architect was John Norris, an obscure figure, presumably a local man, known only as the designer of Dunham, some minor work at Atherton Hall near Leigh in Lancashire, and perhaps a fireplace at Adlington. He recased the old courtyard house in brick, retaining unaltered the arrangement of rooms in the north range, including the Great Hall, which, in a new house, was by this time an anachronism. On the courtyard side the hall is lit by tall mullioned windows which might easily be taken for part of the earlier house except that Kip had shown them in a different form. There were similar windows in the stone centrepiece of the entrance front, though these were replaced by conventional sashes in 1789 by the Liverpool architect John Hope for Harry Grey, 4th Earl of Stamford. Also visible in the Harris views are the stables stretching southwards from the house in two separate blocks.

55. Dunham Massey from the south-west from a painting by John Harris the younger, *c*.1750.

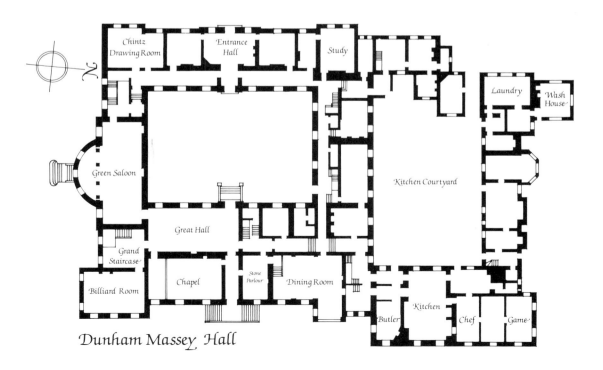

Chintz Drawing Room

Entrance Hall

Study

Laundry

Wash House

Green Saloon

Kitchen Courtyard

Great Hall

Grand Staircase

Billiard Room

Chapel

Stone Parlour

Dining Room

Butler

Kitchen

Chef

Game

N

Dunham Massey Hall

The Stamfords succeeded to the Dunham estate in 1758 through the daughter of the 2nd Earl of Warrington who married Harry Grey, 4th Earl of Stamford. In the 1820s the 6th Earl, also Harry Grey, commissioned the architect John Shaw to form a dining room from two rooms at the centre of the east range and to carry out other internal alterations. During the next 80 years there were few changes, the 7th and 8th Earls leading unconventional lives, one marrying the daughter of an Oxford College bootman and then a circus equestrienne, the other a South African negress. It was not until 1905 that the house was revived; William Grey, a nephew of the 8th Earl, inherited the title after proving his claim in the House of Lords. The house was in need of considerable repair, and, following the family tradition, the 9th Earl commissioned another unknown architect, J. Compton Hall, whose most conspicuous contribution was the clumsy remodelling of the stone centrepiece to the entrance front, based loosely on Sudbury Hall, Derbyshire. He was clearly not up to the creative side of the work and, on the insistence of Lady Stamford, her relative the furniture historian Percy Macquoid was called in to advise on decoration. Unhappy with this interference, Compton Hall wrote pathetically to Lord Stamford in 1907, 'I expect others have freely expressed their views as to what should be done, and what is good taste in decoration – and I fear I have run the risk of appearing to lack ideas – in my endeavours to ascertain rather what was desired than to push my own views – I think the house . . . would not be improved by too lavish a decoration of the sort which would possibly be recommended in West London'. The rooms remain largely as they were completed by Compton Hall and Macquoid, and it is those where the latter was involved that are the more successful.

The main entrance below the new centrepiece leads into a vestibule panelled by Compton Hall, who removed an incongruous covered passage across the courtyard installed in 1823 to link the entrance with the Great Hall. This meant forming a route through the east range, that taken by the visitor today. The central part of this range is taken up by the Green Saloon which was used in the 19th century as the dining room. The wide bow window with its screen of scagliola columns was formed by John Shaw in 1822 when the room was converted from the 2nd Earl's parlour and withdrawing room. But as it was conveniently placed far from the kitchen, the 9th Earl decided that it should once again become a drawing room. The colour scheme and furnishing is by Macquoid, the strong green of the walls and dyed carpets offset by yellow silk upholstery supplied by Morant and Co., his favoured decorators. In a letter to Lady Stamford he banned any shade of red which he cautioned 'will look poisonous in the room'. The present arrangement of the Great Hall is also Edwardian. Old photographs show that in its early 18th-century form it was exceptionally austere, the only decoration being the splendid carved stone chimneypiece. This was designed by Boujet, a Huguenot architect, by whom there are drawings for similar overmantels with the Booth crest in the R.I.B.A. Drawings Collection. Boujet, another obscure architect, must have been employed by the 2nd Earl before he engaged John Norris. The present plasterwork in a free 17th-century classical style was introduced by Macquoid, and this together with his skilful colouring and selection of furniture turned a cheerless room into something rich and stylish. The chapel which lies off the lower end of the hall was made for Lord Delamer in 1655 out of two ground floor rooms. The Booths were strict Protestants, and the simple character of the chapel reflects their religious convictions. The timberwork was installed in 1710, and the blue Spitalfields silk damask inset within the reredos provides a subtle note of richness. The Stone Parlour beyond the chapel, which is not at present included in the visitor's tour, also survives from the earlier house.

At the head of the main staircase is the Summer Parlour, formerly the principal bedchamber, once housing the 2nd Earl's state bed with its magnificent crimson velvet hangings fringed in gold and silver. The present character of the room derives from a scheme of the 1930s, with a comfortable clutter of objects from many periods dominated by a large Edwardian portrait of the Countess with her children. The Great Gallery has paintings, including the Harris views of

56. The Great Hall, Dunham Massey Hall.

57. The library, Dunham Massey Hall.

the estate, and in the tea-room are Grand Tour souvenirs. In the Stamford Gallery, a wide bedroom corridor stretching the full length of the courtyard, Macquoid assembled a series of splendid early 18th-century walnut chests. But most appealing of all is the library, unchanged from the 1730s, scholarly but cosy with its rows of faded bindings and gleaming astronomical instruments. Over the fireplace is the famous Crucifixion after Tintoretto believed to be the earliest documented carving of Grinling Gibbons. The tour of the house is concluded by a visit to the kitchens and domestic offices. Close by is the new dining room which was formed by Compton Hall from pantries and storerooms, a gloomy interior in a loosely-based Queen Anne style which Macquoid was not invited to enliven. Compton Hall had however anticipated that it might be bleak, for he suggested stained glass to 'warm up a sunless room', an idea which Lady Stamford was not keen to adopt for it would have required mullioned windows and these would have unbalanced the north elevation.

The park at Dunham, long open to the public for recreation, has always been more widely appreciated than the house. Medieval in origin, it had already been enclosed for hunting by the 16th century. The 2nd Earl's planting transformed it into one of the most ambitious formal parks in the north-west. Though by the time it was completed such formality was outmoded, the layout has never been destroyed, and with the aid of John Harris's meticulous views the National Trust has begun to ensure the future of this grand design by a huge programme of new planting.

O i, 533; T ii, 28; *TLCAS* xlii, 53; Torrington ii, 205; *CL* clxix, 1562, 1664, clxx, 18, 106; *Dunham Massey* guidebook 1981; JRL, Dunham Massey papers.

EATON HALL, *Eaton*

414 607

The first impression of the Eaton estate is one of prodigal generosity with space. The Hall is approached axially for two miles down the immensely broad and straight Belgrave Avenue, skirted by wide lawns. After a time an obelisk appears on the horizon, beyond it a glittering screen of gates and to one side rises a tall Victorian clock tower, like Manchester Town Hall set down in the midst of flat parkland. Beyond the gates, instead of the expected grand statement is a modern house, white and stark. The new Eaton Hall, built in the 1970s, is the latest in a succession of houses on the same site, each one remodelled or demolished as fashion changed. Like most of the others before it, this one too was greeted with loud accusations of vulgarity and inappropriateness.

The Grosvenor family is of Norman descent and originally held lands at Lostock in east Cheshire; in the 15th century the family acquired the estates at Eaton by marriage. The first Eaton Hall appears on an early estate map as a gabled, moated manor house a little way south of the present Hall. It was retained as a farm building throughout the 18th century. The first house on the present site was built between 1675 and 1682 by Sir Thomas Grosvenor, 3rd Baronet, who in 1677 married Mary Davies of Ebury. It was the London property which she inherited which was to make the fortune of later generations of Grosvenors. Sir Thomas' mansion was designed by William Samwell, one of the gentleman architects of the Restoration. Like Sir Roger Pratt's influential Clarendon House, Piccadilly, Eaton was a symmetrical block with a central pediment, a hipped roof and a cupola on a balustraded platform. The plan was a double pile with detached wings coming forward to make a forecourt, closed at the front with a curved line of railings. The present axial approach dates from this period, Early in the 18th century the Davies brothers supplied wrought-iron gates. East of the Hall were extensive formal gardens with parterres, water basins and allées in the French style. Around 1768 Robert Adam made proposals for altering the house but they were not executed. To the south some landscaping with sweeping lawns and clumps of trees was carried out, possibly by 'Capability' Brown, whom Lord Verulam recorded in 1769 as improving the park. But radical changes to the house and grounds took place only after 1802 when the 2nd Earl Grosvenor (later 1st Marquess) inherited. He employed William Porden as his architect and John Webb as his landscape gardener. The means to do this were provided not yet by the London estates, but from the family lead mines at Halkin in North Wales, which began to produce an income of £50-£60,000 a year, enabling the Earl to buy a London house and form a celebrated picture collection as well as to reconstruct the family seat.

Porden had been surveyor of the London estate since about 1785 but before that he had worked for James Wyatt on his Gothic houses and at Westminster Abbey. Porden's work at Eaton was carried out between 1804 and 1812. He first envisaged a Grecian recasing, but persuaded the Earl to adopt Gothic for its historical associations. Porden demolished Samwell's wings but retained the main block as the core of his house, keeping the double pile plan, with a hall and saloon on the entrance axis. But each corner was extended outwards with low wings, a loggia was added on the garden side and in the centre of the entrance front was a prominent porte cochère. The whole was clad in an array of spiky buttresses, pinnacles, battlements and turrets, mechanical and repetitive in detail. Much of the ornament was cast from models by the sculptor Charles Rossi. The windows were an uneasy combination of cast-iron Gothick tracery above slender glazing bars of bronze and copper. Within, all was expensively fitted out, with cusped

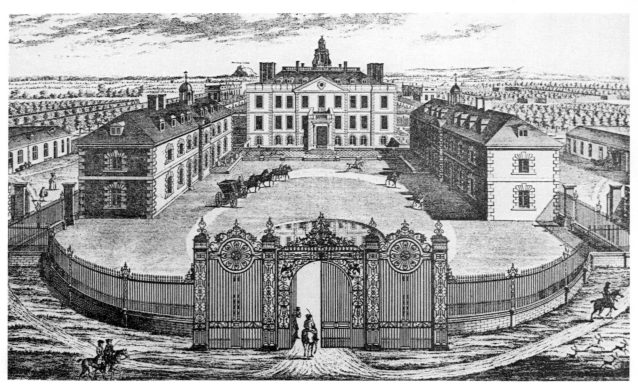

58. Eaton Hall by Samwell, entrance front: engraving by Thomas Badeslade, *c*.1740.

59. Eaton Hall by Porden, garden front: lithograph by J. & J. C. Buckler, 1826.

tracery designs applied everywhere, on carpets, chimneypieces, grates and fenders, on suites of Gillow furniture of Regency form to which gilt Gothick knobs and crockets were attached. Gothick too was the organ and the lacy plaster fan vaulting in the saloon (probably by Bernasconi) though some plasterwork from the previous house was retained. In the dining room were Gothick niches housing Westmacott's statues of medieval Grosvenors, now banished to the garden. For the saloon windows, heavily draped and fringed, the artist Henry Tresham designed stained glass, restricted to the upper and outer panes to retain the views over the park. Here Webb introduced two serpentine lakes to the east, between the house and the river Dee, and almost completely removed the formal gardens, though keeping the Belgrave approach.

Porden died in 1822; between 1823 and 1825 the house was greatly extended by Benjamin Gummow but probably to Porden's designs, as Gummow had been his clerk of works. The additions, two side pavilions attached to the central block by octagonal ante-rooms, contained a large rib-vaulted library to the south, and a chapel to the north. Porden cited medieval precedent for much of his detail; 'My cradle was rocked in York Minster', he wrote to the Earl, 'and . . . I can tell the place where every ornament you have looked at may be found'. But the result of his labours not only lacked the asymmetry of medieval architecture, as it stuck to Samwell's classical plan, it also lacked medieval dignity and patina. So it appeared to many visitors: 'a vast pile of mongrel Gothick which cost some hundreds of thousands and is a monument of wealth, ignorance and bad taste' (Charles Greville); 'the most gaudy concern I ever saw. It looks like the new bought & new built place of a rich manufacturer . . . the house decorated with a degree of gorgeousness that is quite fatiguing' (Mrs. Arbuthnot): 'in this chaos of modern gothic excrescences, I remarked ill-painted modern glass windows and shapeless tables and chairs which most incongruously affected to imitate architectural ornaments' (Prince Puckler-Muskau). The same writer complained that 'Treasures of art I saw none', for unlike Fonthill, which had set the fashion for this kind of bizarre Gothick palace, Eaton was not designed as a setting for works of art. Most of the Grosvenor pictures were kept in London.

By 1846 Porden's frilly Gothick was hopelessly out of date and the house was beset by practical problems: Lady Belgrave had reported all the pipes frozen up in 1826 when she was expecting guests, and a few years later she had written that it was 'cold and comfortless as usual'. William Burn was called in to remodel it for the 2nd Marquess who had inherited in 1845. Burn's forte was efficient planning at a time when country house technology and the organisation of large numbers of servants were becoming more complex. He modified the basement and foundations to eliminate damp, changed the heating system, introduced gas lighting and enlarged the stables and the servants' wing. He installed a bathroom, three W.C.s and a dinner stair, as it was unacceptable in the 1840s for meals to be seen being carried across the main corridor between the kitchen and dining room. Burn also did his best to make Porden's Gothick appear more solid. The corners of the house were strengthened with octagonal turrets, the skyline on the garden side was raised an extra storey and an octagonal tower placed in the centre. Thicker and more correct stone tracery was put in the windows. The interior was redecorated, but Porden's main features were kept; the saloon with its fan vaulting was improbably done up in the fashionable Alhambra style. Nesfield, the landscape gardener, was employed to bring back formal gardens with statues, terraces and walks.

Burn's alterations were completed in 1851 but the house was still recognisably Porden's. In 1869 the 3rd Marquess succeeded (he became 1st Duke of Westminster in 1874) and he promptly embarked on a yet more extensive campaign of rebuilding. He had Eaton completely transformed by Alfred Waterhouse. This too was a recasing, keeping the nucleus of Samwell's plan and even elements of Porden's house such as the porte cochère. But all frivolous Gothick was expunged; Waterhouse was a serious Gothic revivalist who had made his name with the Ruskinian Manchester Assize Courts and had just won the Manchester Town Hall competition. He had a thorough understanding of European Gothic, an inventive repertoire of detail and a feeling for

60. Eaton Hall by Waterhouse, entrance front, c.1900.

spatial values lacking in both Porden and Burn. Waterhouse's Eaton was built from 1870 to 1882 and cost over £600,000. The legacy of Mary Davies meant that by 1869 the Grosvenors were receiving £115,000 a year from their London estates, the sum increasing annually as leases fell for renewal, and this was in addition to the £37,000 a year from the Cheshire and Welsh lands. Eaton was the most expensive and lavish of all Gothic revival country houses.

Waterhouse raised the skyline with steeply pitched roofs and big conical and octagonal turrets, and throughout introduced bolder massing and more substantial detail. But he did not much extend the main part of the house, keeping to the nine-bay nucleus of Samwell's main block with its hall-saloon axis and the lateral extensions of Porden. Though he retained Porden's disposition of dining and drawing rooms on the south, he otherwise totally reorganised the plan with characteristic flair. Porden's kitchen on the north-west corner of the entrance front became the smoking and billiard rooms, and the Gummow chapel pavilion was turned into kitchens.

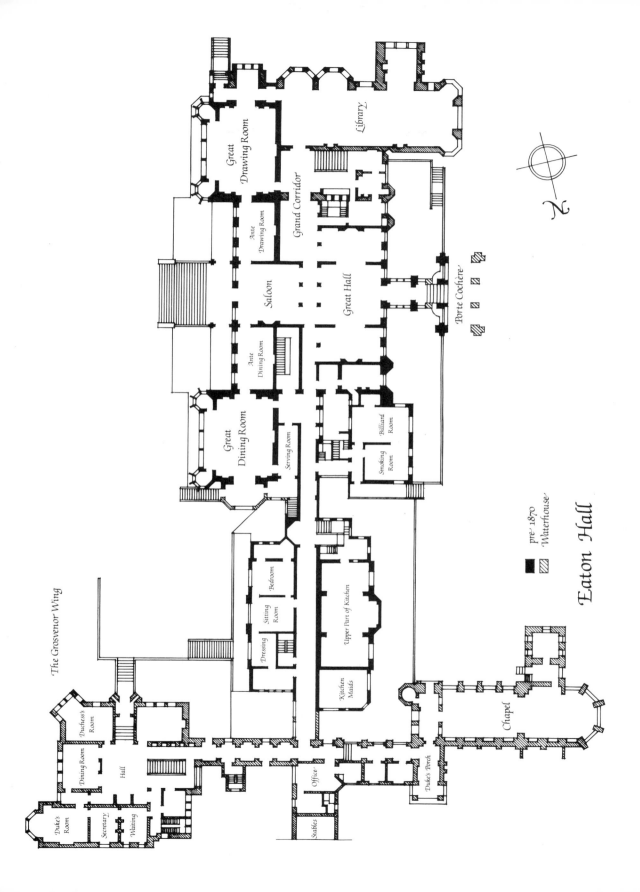

Great Drawing Room

Library

Ante Drawing Room

Grand Corridor

Great Hall

Saloon

Ante Dining Room

Porte Cochère

Great Dining Room

Serving Room

Billiard Room

Smoking Room

The Grosvenor Wing

Bedroom

Sitting Room

Dressing

Upper Part of Kitchen

Duchess's Room

Dining Room

Hall

Kitchen Maids

Duke's Room

Secretary

Waiting

Office

Chapel

Stables

Duke's Porch

pre 1870
Waterhouse

Eaton Hall

The library pavilion was demolished and a new library brought to the south-west corner, where it projected from the main body of the house beneath a big tower with a pyramid roof. The stable court was further enlarged and two new elements introduced, a chapel with a lofty clock tower and a new family wing. Though the core of the main block was still symmetrical, Waterhouse's additions brought a variety of grouping much more medieval in feeling than the previous houses.

The interior was sumptuously fitted out in a variety of materials, all coloured, carved and inlaid in the hard and bold manner favoured by Waterhouse, using a characteristic mixture of medieval and aesthetic motifs. A feature of the house was the extravagant use of coloured marbles, granites, alabaster and porphyry for dadoes, walls, chimneypieces and floors, elaborately inlaid in patterns inspired by the pavements of St Mark's and Pisa cathedrals. The entrance hall was panelled in alabaster and sea-green marble with a gallery at one end and two vast alabaster fireplaces carved with friezes of Grosvenor history. Through an arcade was the saloon with a painted frieze of the Canterbury Pilgrims by Stacy Marks and Moorish vaulting above, a remnant of the previous house. The chimneypiece from this room, carved with pairs of lovers from history and literature, is still at Eaton, now in the stable wing. The dining room walls were adorned with the Grosvenor wheatsheaf and the Westminster portcullis, and the drawing room walls hung with purple silk embroidery. The ante-drawing room had wall panels of birds by Stacy Marks, a ceiling and shutters diapered with flowers, butterflies and birds, and illustrations of Aesop's fables. Over the library entrance was a relief of Caxton with his printing press and the interior was wainscoted in walnut and mother-of-pearl.

Everywhere were works of art of the grandest kind; stupendous hunting scenes by Rubens and Snyders hung in the dining room whilst Rubens' *Adoration of the Magi* (now at King's College Chapel, Cambridge) was in the Grand Corridor. Suits of armour bought at the Strawberry Hill sale climbed the staircase and marble statuary stood in the corridors. The Duke patronised contemporary artists including G. F. Watts, whose grandiloquent lifesize equestrian statue of Hugh Lupus, Earl of Chester, the Duke's ancestor and namesake, stands outside the house. In front, the magnificent 17th-century gilded wrought-iron gates, previously banished to a lodge entrance, were extended by Skidmore of Coventry and set between little Waterhouse pavilions. In the chapel, tall, narrow and aisleless, Frederic Shields, the Manchester follower of Rossetti, designed the stained glass and mosaics to a symbolic programme based on the *Te Deum*, showing apostles, prophets and martyrs joining in praise of God. This is the only remaining Waterhouse interior at Eaton, dignified, rich and claustrophobic. From the clock tower above, the 28-bell carillon played a repertoire of 28 tunes throughout the day and night, much to the annoyance of guests. Whenever the Duke returned, it rang out 'Home Sweet Home'.

Superb though it was, Waterhouse's Eaton had a heavy quality about it, more urban than rural: it was not the sort of building to weather or soften. George Wyndham, a guest at Eaton in 1885, wrote to his mother, 'I am quite sure I do not like Gothic architecture', and even the Duke found it oppressive. In 1881 he wrote, 'Now that I have built a palace, I wish I lived in a cottage', and was afterwards heard to say that if his heir had any sense he would pull the house down and build another.

Eaton was built as a public statement of landed power, wealth and political position and it was meant for formal entertaining. But the Duke's personal tastes were unostentatious: for the family there was a separate wing, more domestic in style, providing rooms for the Duke, the Duchess and the secretary, a small dining room and bedrooms. 'Very snug' was how Lady Frederick Cavendish described the 'little semi-detached "living house" at Eaton'. The stables were also simpler, built in a vernacular mixture of stone, brick and half timber with steep roofs and timber flèches. But the Duke did not stop at remodelling the house. Philanthropic, devout and energetic, he was, like Lord Tollemache, a model improving landlord, unfailing in his sense of public duty. Throughout his estates he initiated extensive building programmes, and the variety and quality of the lodges, farms, cottages, churches and village buildings testify to

61. The library, Eaton Hall, *c*.1900.

62. The staircase, Eaton Hall, *c*.1920.

his keen interest in the welfare of his tenantry as well as a love of architecture. Much of his work, like his patronage of Waterhouse, was directed at the elimination of early 19th-century Gothic, but he retained one of the chief examples, the Iron Bridge of 1824; it carries the drive over the river Dee at Aldford with a graceful sweeping curve decorated with pretty tracery designs. Most noteworthy among the Victorian estate buildings are G. F. Bodley's inspiring church at Eccleston with its noble monument to the 1st Duke, and the numerous works by John Douglas of Chester. Douglas had worked for Burn at Eaton, but his independent work on the estate includes sensitive domestic revival buildings in his characteristic interpretation of the Cheshire vernacular. His feeling for the picturesque massing and steep roofs of French late Gothic is displayed in The Paddocks, for the Duke's agent and Eccleston Hill, for his secretary. The Duke's gardens too are outstanding, based on Nesfield's formal gardens for Burn's house. There are temples and summerhouses by Douglas and Waterhouse, and later additions to the layout by Lutyens, Mallows and Detmar Blow, the latter for the 2nd Duke.

63.   Eaton Hall by John Dennys, entrance front, 1975.

In the 1950s, wrecked by army occupation, Waterhouse's palace must have seemed like a colossal white elephant; everything but the chapel and stables was demolished in 1963. It was a bold step to commission a new house on the site. The new Eaton Hall was built from 1971-3, to the designs of John Dennys, the Duke's brother-in-law, who had previously remodelled

Saighton Grange on the estate. Faced somewhat inappropriately in gleaming white Travertine marble, it bravely follows the previous house not only in its position at the end of the avenue, but also in its central porte cochère. Despite an asymmetrical plan the general appearance is regular. The main rooms are arranged round a two-storey hall with a swimming pool in the basement and reception rooms on the top floor. The interiors are expensively fitted out with woodblock floors, silk wall-coverings and space for the family pictures and objets d'art. But it all has the bland and impersonal luxury of a bank or boardroom in the City. The stark white horizontality of the house is at odds with Waterhouse's tower and, though the decision to demolish the Victorian house was understandable, the new building represents a lost opportunity. History is repeating itself, for the present Duke has approved plans to install a pitched roof and more comfortable-looking detailing. Nevertheless the most apt comment was made by the Duke of Bedford; on seeing the plans for the new Eaton he wrote, 'It seems to me that one of the virtues of the Grosvenor family is that they frequently demolish their stately home – I trust future generations will continue this tradition'.

O ii, 838; T i, 1; J. Hicklin, *Guide to Eaton Hall*, 1855; *B* xxxv, 687, xxxvii, 886, xxxix, 693; *Journal of Decorative Art*, v, 667 et seq.; R. H. Morris, *The Guide to Eaton Hall*, 1888; M. Macartney, *English Houses and Gardens*, 1908, pl. 29; *Life and Letters of George Wyndham*, 1925, 141; Fulke Greville, *The Greville Memoirs*, iv 1950, 388; *Journal of Mrs. Arbuthnot*, ii 1950, 46; G. Huxley, *Victorian Duke*, 1967; *CL* cxlix, 304, 360; Girouard 1; *AR* clvii, 293; Franklin, 83, 93, 240, 222; *Journal of the Garden History Society*, 1984, 39; J. M. Robinson, *The Latest Country Houses*, 1984, 136.

64.   The entrance front, Edge Hall.

65.   The entrance front, Edge Hall, from an estate map of 1687.

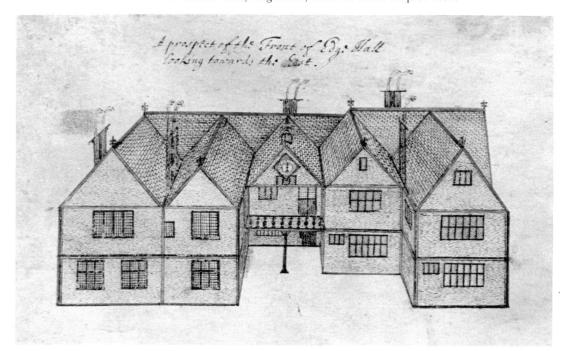

EDGE HALL, *Tilston*

481 503

Like many Cheshire houses which have been gradually improved, the history of Edge Hall is not easy to reconstruct. George Ormerod writing in 1817 commented, 'the present mansion is of considerable antiquity, but has been so repeatedly altered in various styles that no date can be inferred from its architecture'. A cursory inspection would suggest that it is a Jacobean house with a smart centrepiece inserted in the 18th century; but, as Ormerod observed, this is not the whole story. The manor has been held by the Dod family from the time of Henry II when Hova Dot married the heir to 'Egge'. The Hall remains on its original moated site, and the layout and two 15th-century arch-braced roof trusses show that the core of the house is certainly much earlier than it appears from the outside. The earliest view is a drawing of the front on an estate map dated 1687. This shows the layout not substantially different from the present house, but with five irregularly projecting brick gables, the central one deeply recessed. The refacing and enlargement of the medieval house was probably carried out for Sir Edward Dod, Baron of the Exchequer at Chester, who died in 1649. It was a sizeable house for the time: the Hearth Tax of 1663 shows it to have had 12 hearths, but it was not a building of any architectural pretension.

The first attempt to make the house look more imposing was made in 1721 for William Dod. This involved squaring off the entrance by bringing the four outer gables level, and inserting the ambitious classical centrepiece (the outer gable on the right which now unbalances the composition was not added until around 1800). It is probable that the windows in the gables were also sashed at this time. Against these plain brick gables the centrepiece makes a striking impression. It is just three bays wide, squeezed in so that the stone architraves of the windows almost touch. At the centre is a Corinthian doorcase with an open pediment containing the arms of the Dods and the crest of a serpent piercing a garb. Resting on the keystones of the first floor windows is a heavy cornice and balustrade, and then just behind is an openwork cupola dated 1721. It is a vigorous design and, if the compressed proportions give it an engagingly provincial character, this is because of its place within a vernacular scaled building. An architect of talent was responsible, perhaps Richard Trubshaw who designed several buildings in a similar spirit just over the border in Shropshire and Flintshire.

The octagonal glazing of the ground floor windows was inserted before 1768, the date inscribed on one of the panes. This type of glazing, popularised by Sir Robert Taylor, occurs in Cheshire also at Belmont and Arley in the 1750s. These windows were probably part of the extensive works carried out during the ownership of the flamboyant Thomas Crewe Dod who succeeded to the estate in 1759 aged five. Having spent his early life as a soldier he returned to Edge, raised large sums of money on mortgage and began a series of improvements. These included draining the moat to make way for a large service wing, and demolishing the south-west corner for a new saloon, though plans for a grand dining room were never executed.

Inside, the layout follows the basic form of the timber-framed house which existed before the Jacobean gables were built: the present entrance, although at the centre of the main front, leads into one end of the hall where the screens passage would have been. At the former dais end, doorways lead into the dining room and the saloon. The dining room is lined with late 16th-century panelling, though the fireplace, doorcase and Gothick niche in the end wall are alterations made by Thomas Crewe Dod whose portrait hangs in the room. It was probably also in his time that the oak panelling, the plasterwork frieze and ceiling were first painted white and gilded. The saloon is quite different, a large spacious interior intended for parade, its taller proportions providing ample space for the display of full-length portraits. One room above has panelling of similar date to the dining room and a most handsome Carolean chimneypiece with a curly open pediment, the latter probably part of William Dod's remodelling of 1721. In 1867 the estate passed through the female line to Frances, wife of the Revd. Charles Wolley, who assumed the family name Dod. He was a notable horticulturalist and embarked upon a great expansion of the gardens. A late Victorian photograph album at the house records acres of rockeries and borders, famous in their time, but long since abandoned. Trees and shrubs however remain to give the house a secluded setting in this most unspoiled corner of the county.

O ii, 678; T i, 33; *Ches Life* September 1936, January/February 1948; *CL* clxxviii, 1612.

GAWSWORTH HALL, *Gawsworth*

892 697 House and gardens open to the public. (Privately owned)

It is best to come upon Gawsworth Hall from the west, and on foot. Walking up the lime avenue the visitor passes the church, two rectories and a string of great fish ponds before reaching the Hall; there is no place in Cheshire to equal the beauty of this setting. The earliest reference to the Hall is in 1365 when a licence was granted for the administration of a chapel within the house. The manor had passed by marriage to Thomas Fitton in 1316, in whose family it remained until 1611. The present Hall was built in stages from the 15th century until about 1600. As a large part has since been demolished and the remainder greatly altered, it is difficult to determine the original functions of the rooms, but it is possible to show how the sequence of building developed.

Like many of the other great houses on the eastern boundary of Cheshire, Gawsworth is timber-framed. It was probably moated, and like the others was almost certainly a courtyard house. It is now U-shaped with the open side facing west towards the church, but we know that extensive demolition took place around 1700, and this may have included the removal of the west range. If it is assumed that the missing west side contained the gatehouse, it can be seen that the layout is very similar to Little Moreton Hall. But to explain this it is necessary to examine the structure more closely.

The earliest part of the present building is the north range which contains what is now the main entrance. From the outside this is not apparent, for the timber frame has been replaced with brickwork and applied timbering, but the great arch-braced trusses of the roof date from the late 15th century. This range was built in two sections; first the three western bays to the right of the entrance, then the two eastern bays, probably a bit later, though the construction is similar. Both sections offered fine upper floor apartments and were never part of a Great Hall. It is likely that they formed additions to an existing house, and when later phases were built they were relegated to service quarters, the two large chimneystacks being added in the 16th century. The next phase was the adjoining east block, now the Long Hall and dining room, which appears to have formed the main domestic quarters. At the northern end was a Great Hall formerly open to the roof, with a solar beyond on the first floor. The bay nearest the entrance range would have been the screens passage leading from a porch on the west or courtyard side, then two open bays forming the hall itself. The central arch-braced truss has a carved boss now concealed above the ceiling. The adjoining room on the first floor, perhaps the solar, was built with a ceiling, for the central beam and cambered joists which supported it survive above the present flat ceiling over the staircase. The east range continues south beyond this room to meet another block canted ten degrees to the east, now the Green Room. The re-alignment is puzzling and suggests that the south-east wing is part of an earlier building which was incorporated into the house when the east range was built. This block was originally open to the roof, but it was not a Great Hall as has been thought, for the timbering is far too crude. Most probably this was a barn which, until the east range was built, was a separate structure, though its length has later been much reduced. The south block, of which only a part survives, was built in the late 16th century as grand domestic apartments. It extended approximately to the present garden terrace where it probably joined on to an earlier west range to enclose the courtyard. At Little Moreton the gatehouse stands opposite the range containing the hall. The porch is in the far left corner of the courtyard and in the right corner is the famous double bay window. The same pattern can be seen at Gawsworth, and though the hall did not stretch the

66. The courtyard, Gawsworth Hall, *c*.1960.

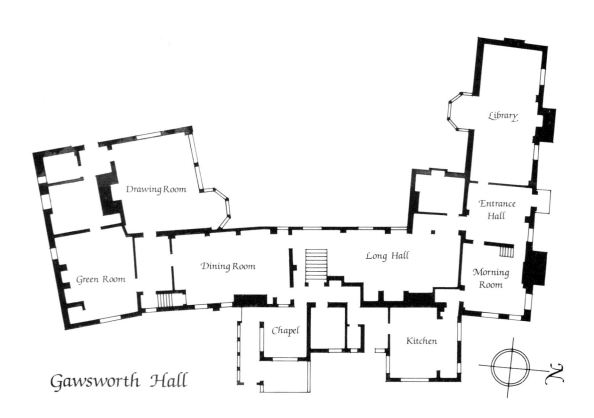

Library

Drawing Room

Entrance Hall

Green Room

Dining Room

Long Hall

Morning Room

Chapel

Kitchen

Gawsworth Hall

full width of the courtyard, the strikingly tall bay window of the south wing is squeezed into the corner in a similar fashion.

The only dated element of the building is the splendid Fitton coat of arms on the north front signed by the sculptor Richard Rany and carved in Galway in 1570. This was made for Sir Edward Fitton II, Lord President of Connaught and Thomond, and Treasurer of Ireland, and is a rare surviving example of the flourishing school of stone carving which existed in Galway at that time. As Sir Edward resided in Ireland from 1569 until his death in 1579 and saw little of Gawsworth, it is probable that it was carved for his house in Ireland. The ambitious south range of the Hall must have been built for his son Sir Edward III, Lord President of Munster, the father of Mary Fitton, supposed 'Dark Lady' of Shakespeare's sonnets. In 1643 the estate passed from the Fittons to Sir Charles Gerard of Halsall, Lancashire, and so began 60 years of legal wrangling over rightful ownership between the Fitton kinsmen and their cousins the Gerards, which ended only with the death of rival claimants, the Duke of Hamilton and Lord Mohun, in a duel in Hyde Park in 1712. The estate remained with the Mohun (or Gerard) side, but in 1725 it was sold to William Stanhope, later Earl of Harrington, whose family retained the Hall until 1935. From 1961 until his death in 1978 it was the home of the Cheshire antiquary Raymond Richards, author of *Old Cheshire Churches*, and it is he and his wife Monica who created the interiors now seen by the visitor to Gawsworth.

There have been so many changes over the years that the original features of the interior have been lost, but the rooms gain interest from items acquired by Richards from historic buildings altered or demolished in the 1960s. Richards had already used his theatrical skill in dressing up the interiors of other houses he had owned such as Stanhope House, Bromborough, and at Gawsworth, the Old Rectory, the former village school and the Gatehouse. At the Hall he added the doorcase through which the house is entered, the fine inlaid chimneypiece in the library and the two sets of Pugin bookcases from Scarisbrick Hall, Lancashire. Entirely Richards' creation is the chapel and its ambulatory, the former fitted up with panelling from Marple church, and the latter crammed with Victorian church furnishings and lit by Morris and Co. windows from All Saints, Birkenhead. Off the ambulatory is a tiny conservatory housing marble sculptures by John Warrington Wood, carelessly jammed together as if in a studio. Richards' collection of neglected sculpture is an example of his interest in the history of Che-

67. The chapel ambulatory, Gawsworth Hall.

shire, seen also in his library of local subjects. Gawsworth is essentially a comfortable family home. There are few great objects or portraits associated with the original family. Fitted carpets abound, and the chintzy furnishings and velvet drapes in shades of pink and gold suggest the 1960s rather than the 1560s. Of original plaster decoration only the modest carved frieze in the

Mary Fitton bedroom survives, and the complex timbering of the gallery is the result of *ad hoc* construction rather than any decorative intent.

If the interior of the Hall has undergone much change, the exterior is yet more altered. Only the courtyard sides of the east and south blocks give an idea of its original appearance. The north block was encased in brick and fitted with sash windows early in the 18th century, and the applied timbering is modern. The library bay dates only from 1920. The south front, which was clumsily faced in brick when the house was truncated around 1700, looks out onto parkland enclosed by a crumbly 16th-century wall of immense height, within which are a series of raised terraces and mounds. Though traditionally thought to have been for tournaments, the layout of terraces and walks is almost definitely the remains of grand Elizabethan formal gardens. These rank in size with the most important pleasure gardens of their time, and suggest that the aim of Sir Edward III in creating them was to attract the Queen to Gawsworth on her Royal Progress. Today the grounds are the repository for more of the Richards's collection of unconsidered trifles: church fonts, large statues of Manchester worthies rescued from destruction in Salford, Victorian omnibuses and even a lych gate from Southport leading to the tradesmen's entrance. In the fine church nearby are the alabaster effigies of the Fittons, amongst the best memorials in Chesire, and the tradition has been continued in the beautifully-lettered stone tablet commemorating the death of Raymond Richards in 1978.

O iii, 553; *THSLC* ii, 200; *AMS* 1957, 181, 1963, 53; *Gawsworth Hall* guidebook n.d.; G. Holland, *Gawsworth Hall*, unpublished report, 1982; *CL* clxxix, 1262; R. C. Turner, *The Gardens at Gawsworth Hall*, unpublished report, 1986.

GREAT MORETON HALL, *Moreton*

840 596

The Moreton Magna estate was always separate from the well-known Little Moreton Hall. It had been the seat of the Bellots from the mid-15th century and its Hall was a large timber-framed building erected in 1602. In 1841 this was torn down and a new house built. Its owner George Holland Ackers was a businessman from Manchester, and his extravagant new house massively upstaged its old-fashioned neighbour. The estate had been bought in 1793 by the brothers James and Holland Ackers for £57,107. The sons of a fustian manufacturer from Bolton, they made immense sums of money through land speculation in Manchester. James Ackers, the more colourful of the brothers, was a colonel of the Manchester and Salford Volunteers and Chairman of the 'Society to put down Levellers'. Clearly he was not sympathetic to the pressures for social change which had emanated from revolutionary France, and his purchase of a country estate may have been intended to enhance his respectability and position. But he never lived at Great Moreton, for in 1795 he built Lark Hill House in Salford, now the Peel Park Museum.

68. Great Moreton Hall from the west.

The Ackers brothers had begun by repairing and modernising Bellot's old Hall, but there was little change until 1836 when George Holland Ackers, aged 24, inherited the estate together with a considerable fortune and decided to rebuild. To design the new house he chose Edward Blore, the most successful country house architect of the time. Blore's early career as an

103

antiquarian draughtsman gave him a working knowledge of 15th- and 16th-century architecture; his control of the costs at Buckingham Palace after the scandal of John Nash's extravagance proved his reliability. Such qualities would have appealed to the business mind of Ackers. By 1840, the year he was commissioned to design Great Moreton, Blore had been responsible for works at 48 country houses including Vale Royal, Capesthorne, Crewe and Worsley Hall near Manchester, a major new house for Lord Francis Egerton. Clearly Ackers was in good company.

The castles of the early 19th century, represented in Cheshire by Cholmondeley and Bolesworth, belonged firmly to the picturesque tradition, comfortable and conveniently planned country houses dressed up in medieval fashion. By the 1840s medievalism was associated with the aristocratic and authoritarian interests of Disraeli and Young England, and this coincided with the attack on sham castles launched by Pugin who despised the paste-board character of the early Gothic Revival. In his architecture Blore reflected these changing trends. Thus Great Moreton marks a transition. Like Alton Towers, which Pugin was remodelling nearby in Staffordshire for the Earl of Shrewsbury, and Bayons Manor, the antiquarian dream of Charles d'Eyncourt Tennyson in Lincolnshire, Great Moreton was one of the first houses to revive the Great Hall. But what Blore did not accept was Pugin's radical approach to planning and composition. In this respect Great Moreton is conservative. The plan is essentially that of a Palladian villa, ordered and symmetrical, with the Great Hall, not as it should be at the centre of the house, but to one side of the garden front, simply one of a series of lavish rooms arranged around a large central space. For all its crenellations, buttresses and turrets, the underlying form is conventional.

The approach to the house from Ackers Crossing, the family's halt on the London Midland Railway, enters the park by a rustic lodge of 1858. Here gates were opened from inside the cottage by an ingenious underground mechanism. First into view come the aggressively fortified walls of the stable court; the driveway presses close against these rock-faced walls of Mow Cop stone pierced by a massively carved and chamfered archway. The warlike illusion dissolves when the service wing appears. Eight regular pairs of plate-glass windows must be passed before the main house is reached and the visitor arrives within the safe and convenient custody of a vaulted porte cochère. How much more convincing is Salvin's castle built just three years later at Peckforton.

From the porte cochère a broad flight of steps leads up to the entrance lobby and the large central hall, top lit by a glass lantern and decorated with a heraldic frieze. At one end is a triple arcade leading to the staircase, at the other a hooded fireplace carved with the Ackers arms. In all these lofty apartments ceilings are decorated with ribs and studded with bosses, chimneypieces are carved and fitted with figure sculpture, and oak doors and shutters are traceried. The effect when crammed with Victorian furniture was no doubt impressive, yet it is all sadly lifeless for, though Blore's antiquarian expertise provided him with the vocabulary to produce accurate detail, he used it repetitively. The working drawings at the Victoria and Albert Museum show that Blore left little to the freedom of the craftsman. The aim was a regular precision and a smoothness of finish as opposed to the individual flavour of genuine medieval work. These drawings do not cover the decorative schemes, though scraps of wallpaper revealed during recent redecoration show bold stencil patterns in a range of deep colours, and the drawing room is known to have been hung with tapestries.

The culmination of the tour is the Great Hall. Whilst this was fitted within the Palladian plan, its treatment both inside and out is truly medieval. Its steep slated roof rises high above the battlements and its richly traceried and leaded windows contrast with the plate glass of the adjoining saloon. Within are all the characteristic features: tall open roof, bay window and dais, screen and minstrel's gallery, armorial glass and a great fireplace and, if the details are again hard, their use is not just decorative but essential to the form and structure of the room. Blore's source was probably the Great Hall at Bayons Manor with which there are striking similarities,

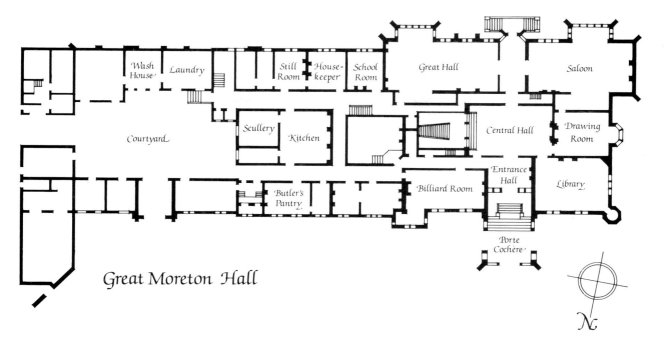

Wash House · Laundry · Still Room · House-keeper · School Room · Great Hall · Saloon

Courtyard · Scullery · Kitchen · Central Hall · Drawing Room

Butler's Pantry · Billiard Room · Entrance Hall · Library

Porte Cochère

Great Moreton Hall

N

69. The Great Hall, Great Moreton Hall:
drawing by Blore, c.1840.

but the hammerbeam roof is also like the 16th-century one at Wiston Park, Sussex which he was rebuilding at the same time. In contrast the servants' quarters are grim. Dark narrow internal corridors enable all parts of the house to be reached without passing through the central hall, whilst the servants' hall was banished to the cellars.

Little remains of the gardens, and much of the park is now farmed, for the Hall remained a residence only until 1931. Since then it has served as a school and now it is a hotel and conference centre. George Holland Ackers died in 1872 and was buried at Astbury Church. His house survives as a potent symbol of the wealth of Manchester commerce, and his life exemplifies that rapid transition from businessman to country landowner which was such a characteristic feature of 19th-century Cheshire.

O iii, 46; T i, 137; *Manchester Notes and Queries* 28 March 1885, 31 August 1894; Franklin, 132; H. Meller, *Blore's Country Houses*, Courtauld Institute thesis 1975; V&A 8710, Blore drawings; BM Add. Mss. 42027, Blore drawings.

HANDFORTH HALL, *Handforth*

863 833 House and gardens open to the public by appointment. (Privately owned)

Handforth is now an anonymous commuter suburb south of Manchester, marked by a cluster of shops on the main road. The half-timbered Hall is an unexpected sight marooned between a modern school and a housing estate down a side road, but it serves as a reminder that Handforth has a history. The extensive Handforth estates were inherited by Margaret Hondford on the death of her father at Flodden in 1513. After her first husband died she married Urian Brereton, a younger son of a different branch from the Brereton Hall family. Urian built the present Hall, setting up the inscription over the porch with his arms and the Brereton rebus of a bear and a ton, 'This haulle was buylded in the yeare of our Lord God mcccclxii by Uryan Breretooun, knight. Whom maryd Margaret daughter and heyre of Wyllyam handforth of Handforthe Esquyer and had Issue vi sonnes and ii daughters'. Urian was appointed groom to the Privy Chamber, Escheator of Cheshire and Ranger of Delamere Forest in 1526 and was knighted in 1544. At Cheadle parish church in the Brereton Chapel is a fine wooden screen bearing his rebus and initials. He died at the Hall in 1577 and was buried at Cheadle.

The date of 1562 over the Hall porch is just three years after the dated bay window at Little Moreton Hall. Both houses enjoy a similar repertoire of motifs, coved jettying on the first floor, and in the gables crossed clubs and concave-sided lozenges. Handforth is simpler and smaller. The front has two projecting gables, one at the right hand end and one in the centre over the porch. The left hand part of the front was rebuilt in brick in the late 18th century, perhaps to replace a gable matching that on the right. If so, Handforth would originally have had a symmetrical E-shaped front of three gables with a central porch, for the right hand end is certainly the original end wall, the low outbuildings being additions. On the other hand, Ormerod states that Handforth Hall is one side of a quadrangle. Whilst there is no clear physical evidence of this, an inventory of 1610 refers to a gatehouse as well as outhouses and barns of which no trace survives. These may have been grouped around a courtyard and one of them may have been joined on at the left of the Hall where it has been rebuilt in brick.

The principal room is the Great Hall on the right of the porch and screens passage; it has a bay window at the upper end but its rear portion has been partitioned off and the original fireplace has gone. On the left of the passage are three timber arches formerly leading to the kitchens, but only the arch at the back of the house has its original four-centred head. The two others have elliptical tops dating from the 17th century, probably contemporary with the insertion of the oak staircase. On an impressively large scale, it was an attempt to bring grandeur to what had become an old-fashioned house. It has a two-tier balustrade of openwork carving in an unrefined but attractive Jacobean style, recalling northern vernacular oak furniture of the period. The staircase is reached through the central arch of the screens passage. At the top it leads to a grand pair of Jacobean panelled doors opening into the upper rooms, some partitioned with original chevron framing. The staircase is not mentioned in the inventory of 1610 taken on the death of Urian's grandson William. He was succeeded by his son, a minor, also named William, who became a baronet in 1627. Sir William inserted the staircase probably in the 1620s; that he was interested in domestic improvements is evident from the fascinating diary he wrote recording his travels in Holland, Scotland, Ireland and the west of England in 1634-5. In Amsterdam he bought black and white 'stones for floors' and a great many 'painted stones for hearths' decorated with flowers, birds and soldiers, probably blue and white Delft tiles. Of these there is no trace at Handforth, nor of the pictures he bought. During the Civil War he was

70. The entrance front, Handforth Hall.

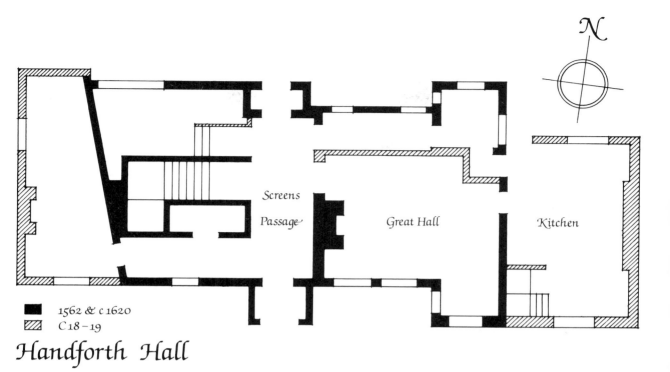

Screens

Passage

Great Hall

Kitchen

N

■ 1562 & c 1620
▨ C 18–19

Handforth Hall

71. The staircase, Handforth Hall, *c.*1900.

an important parliamentary commander, defeating the Royalist troops at the battle of Nantwich in 1643.

Part of the exterior was once stuccoed, most of the windows have been changed and many of the external timbers have been replaced or covered over. But on the broad uprights of the porch can be seen carved classical grotesques and around the Tudor arch is floral ornament in the Gothic tradition. There was more such decoration elsewhere on the house; carved designs with a letter B are visible high up at the back of the house and some of the gables have brackets carved into monstrous heads. Inside, one of the posts of the passage has original painted decoration.

With the end of the direct line of Brereton in the late 17th century, the estate was bought by the Leghs of Adlington. It later changed hands several times and when Fletcher Moss visited the Hall in 1906 it was in a state of sad decline. In the more recent past unsympathetic interior features were added, but the present owner is restoring the house as a setting for a highly appropriate collection of early oak furniture and in the grounds an ambitious geometrical garden is being planted with formal parterres, arbours and a labyrinth.

O iii, 645; *Diary of Sir William Brereton, Chetham Society* i 1884; P & O, pl. lxxviii; FM iii 1906, 325; CRO, Probate Inventory of William Brereton 1610.

HENBURY HALL, *Henbury*

869 732

The building of a Palladian villa in Cheshire in the 1980s might seem unexpected but it is in a tradition which has quietly been establishing itself in other parts of the country since the war with the building or rebuilding of country houses in the neo-Georgian or classical style. The patrons of these houses have rejected the Modern architectural vocabulary familiar from new urban buildings. It may well be that to our successors Henbury Hall, built in 1984-6, will not appear as exceptional as it does today.

Henbury Hall is based on Palladio's famous Villa Capra or Villa Rotonda of 1552, near Vicenza in northern Italy and familiar to English eyes through the variants it inspired in the 18th century at Mereworth, the Temple of the Four Winds at Castle Howard, Chiswick Villa, Nuthall Temple and Foot's Cray Place. The new rotunda is built on the site of the old Henbury Hall, erected for the Merediths in 1742. This was a classical block with a giant order of pilasters set up on high bases. Inside there was some good 18th-century plasterwork but the Hall had been remodelled in a severe Neo-classical style in the early 19th century, stuccoed and then drastically reduced in size in the 1850s. By 1957, when bought by Sir Vincent de Ferranti, it looked gaunt and awkwardly proportioned. He demolished the Hall and had the stable block converted into a house by the Manchester architect Harry Fairhurst. Sir Vincent contemplated rebuilding but it was his son Sebastian who carried the idea to fruition.

In the 1960s he considered building a modern house, seeking designs from the American-Japanese architect Yamasaki, but finally decided that a modern building would not sit well in an English park. A key figure was the painter Felix Kelly, who has for many years specialised in romantically atmospheric views of country houses and evocative architectural *capricci*. Kelly had collaborated with builders and patrons on the design of garden pavilions and had been employed by Ferranti to renovate a gamekeeper's cottage on the Henbury estate, a plain brick box to which he added side pavilions, a trellised verandah and Gothick glazing. The result, 'The Cave', is a romantic eye-catcher in the tradition of 18th-century garden follies. It is a manner of treating buildings which appeals to de Ferranti, and in the same spirit he has restored estate cottages, built a graceful Chinese bridge, and a glazed fernery housing a pool and a cascade. The new house clearly demanded something in a grander style, for the site is a prominent one on a slight eminence with gloriously uninterrupted views in all directions. In discussion with Kelly, de Ferranti conceived the idea of creating a Palladian temple in which one could live. After sketching various possibilities Kelly painted a picture of how it might look; the idea of starting with a painting and then finding an architect to realise it has a suitably 18th-century ring about it. Kelly's oil painting demonstrated his responsiveness both to the scenic qualities of architecture and to the mood of the landscape; a domed Palladian rotunda of warm golden stone and sharply cut classical detail is caught in a theatrical gleam of light against a windswept sky, a storm about to break and two figures running across the greensward to the house. It is an enchanting vision.

The natural choice of architect was Quinlan Terry, who planned a stucco house rising from the landscape with three projecting staircases spreading gently outwards at its base. It was a softer and more rustic villa than Kelly's and was not to de Ferranti's taste; in 1983 Julian Bicknell was called in. He was engaged in reinstating interiors destroyed during the wartime fire at Castle Howard, where Kelly had painted murals. A surprising choice, Bicknell was a young architect not trained in classical design but with experience of both classical and Gothic,

111

72. Henbury Old Hall prior to demolition.

73. Henbury Hall from a painting by Felix Kelly, 1981.

the kind of stylistic pluralism common in earlier periods. He learned classical proportion through studying Hawksmoor and Vanbrugh at Castle Howard, and classical detail from the inventive carving of their craftsmen. This was supplemented by the study of Batty Langley and other 18th-century pattern books. Where Terry's approach to classical architecture is grounded in moral conviction, Bicknell's is more pragmatic. His house is closer to the painting than Terry's but is not a literal copy. He followed Kelly in giving the porticos four columns (as on the Castle Howard temple) rather than the six of the original Rotonda; this gives Henbury an attractive miniaturistic scale. Palladio's square plan was changed so that the central part projected on each side to provide more room within. Endless trouble was taken over the proportions, necessitating the construction of a beautifully detailed wooden model; even so, during the building work the silhouette of the dome was raised to create a more substantial impression from ground level. Throughout all these changes de Ferranti played a decisive role. Whilst based on a study of the precedents, Henbury is the result of a collaboration of enthusiasts – artist, architect and patron.

74. Section of Henbury Hall looking west: drawing by Julian Bicknell, 1985.

The Hall is faced in French limestone of a creamy colour, superior in texture as well as more reliable in supply than English. On the pediments stand full-size stone statues carved by Simon Verity. The roof is of local stone flags and above is the tall outline of the dome and its scrolled cupola, the lobed pattern of the leadwork taken from Colen Campbell's design for Mereworth. Standing on a rusticated basement are four Ionic porticos, each one fronting a giant Venetian window. But there is only a single flight of steps marking out the principal front on the south; unlike Palladio's Rotonda, identical on all four sides, Henbury is axial, the axis extending inside. Where Palladio and his English followers have an enclosed and symmetrical central space under the dome, Bicknell has opened up the central hall linking it up with the north and south porticos. He thus creates a magnificent long saloon soaring up the full height of the house to the dome in the centre and looking out north and south through the porticos to the views beyond. The rooms to east and west behind the side porticos are the dining and drawing rooms, separated from the central space by immensely tall arched doors. In the small but high spaces left in each corner are the library, the morning room, a pantry with lift and a cantilevered staircase rising on an oval plan. The basement consists of a large central sub-hall surrounded by kitchens and staff accommodation. On the first floor bedrooms and dressing rooms are arranged round a gallery looking down on the shining inlaid marble floor of the saloon. The interior decoration of the principal rooms is by David Mlinaric, with doorcases sensitively carved by Dick Reid of York.

Henbury Hall is a small house, smaller than its Palladian ancestors and smaller than most country houses. Everything has been neatly fitted into a plan 56 feet square. Nevertheless it is not, like Chiswick, an occasional retreat, nor a rustic villa in the original Palladian sense of something close to a farm. It is an ambitious and cultivated country house. The principal room is a room of parade, a grand hard space utterly unlike the cosily furnished living halls of the John Fowler era. Comfortable rooms with sofas and cushions are provided but these are subordinate to the architectural statement. Faced in stone, with statuary, giant order, dome and saloon, Henbury marks the coming of age of the new Palladian revival.

O iii, 706; T ii, 125; J. M. Robinson, *The Latest Country Houses*, 1984, 192.

See also plate V, facing page 31.

HILL BARK, *Frankby*

244 858 *Park open to the public. (Wirral District Council)*

75. The entrance courtyard of Hill Bark (Bidston Court) in 1894, before resiting.

The history of Hill Bark is brief but eventful. It was built in 1891 as Bidston Court on the slopes of Noctorum for Robert Hudson the soap manufacturer. In 1929, after only 38 years, it was totally dismantled, moved and re-erected five miles away on its present site at Frankby. Hudson lived in the house only briefly, for, having transferred his enthusiasm for building to Buckinghamshire, between 1895 and 1901 he rebuilt Medmenham Abbey and erected for himself Danesfield, a pompous neo-Elizabethan mansion of stone to the design of R. H. Romaine Walker. Bidston Court was a very different affair, for, although built on a lavish scale (it cost £150,000), it is a house in the Cheshire vernacular style. The architect was Edward Ould, a pupil of John Douglas, from whom he gained a respect for the traditional methods of timber-frame building. In his book *Old Cottages, Farmhouses and Other Half Timber Buildings in Shropshire, Herefordshire and Cheshire*, he must have had Hudson in mind when he concluded, 'The question naturally arises, whether timber nogging is a suitable style for a modern house, and as one who has had some experience of such building, I would say that, given a suitable client, one who is worthy of the privilege of living in a timber house, who will appreciate the advantages and put up with the drawbacks – it is an eminently suitable style for a house of moderate dimensions'.

115

The site chosen for the house had fine views, but it lay on a steep west-facing slope and much excavation was necessary to form a flat base on which to build. Ould exploited this brilliantly by creating an irregular entrance courtyard enclosed on three sides by the wings of the house and on the fourth by the natural rock face. But there were disadvantages. The restrictions of the site and the closeness of a public road made the courtyard side cramped. Furthermore, by the 1920s development was spreading rapidly across the land below Bidston Hill and affecting the outlook. These factors led its new owner Sir Ernest Royden to dismantle the house and rebuild it at Frankby. Only the lodge with its tall twisted chimneys now remains at Bidston, though the grounds of the house are retained as public gardens.

The site at Frankby is one of the best on the Wirral. When inherited by Royden there stood upon it a stone house of 1868 designed, ironically, by Ould's partner G. E. Grayson. This Royden demolished, and in its place erected the timbered house from Bidston under the direction of the architects Rees and Holt. Though the views were much finer and the grounds more spacious, the house suffered architecturally from the move, for the geometry of its layout and the irregularity of its elevations had been designed to suit the restrictions of the original site. As at Bidston the house is set against a rocky bank and the drive takes a similar route, unfolding a marvellous vista of complex half timbering and gabled stone roofs as the extent and outline of the courtyard is gradually revealed. This courtyard elevation is one of the most convincing

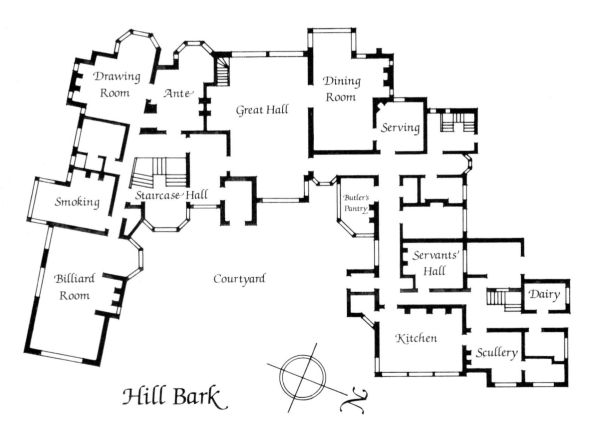

Hill Bark

116

76. The drawing room at Hill Bark (Bidston Court) in 1894, before alterations.

77. The Great Hall at Hill Bark (Bidston Court) in 1894, before alterations.

compositions in the Victorian revival of timber-framed building. Its most striking feature is the pair of gabled bays and the porch which are built in homage to Little Moreton Hall. Except that they are in reverse order, these exactly reproduce the south side of the Little Moreton courtyard, and the inscription over the bays reads, 'This House was builded by Robert Hudson and Gerda his wife Anno Dom MDCCCXCI. These bay windows being copied from those at Old Moreton Hall in the hope that when they have perished these may remain'.

The archaeological approach of the courtyard elevation, suggesting a history of additions and modifications, did not extend to the interior which aimed to satisfy all the requirements of Victorian comfort. At the centre is a Great Hall, entered through an outer hall, and to either side are drawing room and dining room. These principal rooms all have large windows facing the view to the west (the orientation was the same on both sites). In the south wing were the smoking room and billiard room, and to the north was the service wing. The staircase hall is fitted into the angle between the main block and the south wing, lit by one of the large bay windows. As with Ould's other great house of this period, Wightwick Manor near Wolverhampton, Bidston Court was originally furnished and decorated in the Arts and Crafts manner. Royden's taste in the 1930s however was somewhat different, for although he clearly liked the architecture, he was less wholehearted in his endorsement of Arts and Crafts ideals. As a shipowner, his taste in pictures was for seascapes, and his furniture was largely early Georgian. Amongst the alterations he made to the interior was to create a large neo-Georgian drawing room from two smaller spaces. In the Great Hall he removed a broad inglenook fireplace with a secret staircase which had led to Hudson's bedroom, replacing it with a spectacular Jacobean carved chimneypiece dated 1627 (the date has been re-touched to read 1527), said to have come from South Mimms in Hertfordshire. Opposite he installed a beautiful 15th-century Gothic screen. The hall has since been partitioned as Hill Bark is now an elderly persons' home, but with its open hammerbeam roof and decorative timberwork it remains an imposing yet very welcoming space, still the hub of the house. At the east end is an organ gallery with the jolly inscription 'A Hall! A Hall! Give room and foot it girls. More light ye knaves and turn the tables up'. At the other end is a clerestory with eight stained glass panels of poets by Morris and Co.

Both Great Hall and dining room are lined with Jacobean panelling said to have come from Sir Walter Raleigh's house at Sherborne. There is also 17th-century Flemish timberwork in what was the billiard room. As at Portal, old materials were used to give a period character to many of the interiors but, unlike the architects of Portal or Tirley Garth, Ould never belonged to the progressive wing of the Arts and Crafts movement. His principal attraction to half-timbered architecture was an emotional one. 'No style of building', he wrote, 'will harmonize so quickly and so completely with its surroundings . . . In its cap of virgin snow, in its gorgeous garb of virginia creeper or its purple veil of wisteria it is equally bewitching. At noonday it throws the broadest shadows, and at eve (as no building can) it gathers on its snowy breast the rose of sunset, and responds to the silver magic of the moon'.

There is no doubt that the house now harmonises with its surroundings less happily than when built by Ould on the slopes of Bidston Hill amongst formal gardens with parterres, cobbled paths and terraces. But, if it has lost its sympathetic setting, it has gained by the process of ageing. Even in 1894 *The British Architect* remarked, 'What must strike everyone who sees Bidston Court is the extraordinary appearance of age it has managed to put on in its short life of two years'. Ninety years later it looks very convincingly old.

BA xli, 308; *The Architect* liv, 332, lv, 236; *Builders' Journal* viii, 358; P & O, 39; Pike 1904, 97; *Country Heritage*, 45; *Ches Life* January/February 1954; Franklin, 195.

LITTLE MORETON HALL, *Moreton*

833 589 House and gardens open to the public. (National Trust)

Familiar from a thousand calendars and picture postcards, the busily patterned black and white Little Moreton Hall is the most complete example in Cheshire of a moated half-timbered courtyard house. It was built in stages in the 15th and 16th centuries by three generations of Moretons, a family of prosperous gentry, who enlarged their house as their lands and wealth increased. The earliest part is the Great Hall. Construction progressed clockwise round the courtyard on three sides, leaving the fourth side open. The last part to be built was the Long Gallery, over the gatehouse range. The additions were made in a somewhat unco-ordinated manner, leading to the higgledy-piggledy appearance which gives the building such charm.

The Great Hall has its service wing and screens passage to the left, the entrance marked by the elaborately carved porch with twisted shafts and colonettes. Originally it seems to have been the other way round with the service wing where the parlour is now; a blocked doorway between the two bay windows may mark the original screens passage. The present orientation dates from around 1480 when William Moreton built the present porch and service wing. In the mid-16th century his son and namesake inserted a floor into the Great Hall (since removed), built a staircase and continued round the corner with the east wing, containing reception rooms and a chapel. He built the two bay windows, dated 1559 and carved with the inscription, 'God is Al in Al Thing: This windous Whire mad by William Moreton in the yeare of our Lorde M.D.LIX. Richard Dale Carpeder made thies windous by the grac of God'. Thrown out into the courtyard to light the Great Hall and the withdrawing room and their new upper floors, the generously sized bays are built so close up against each other that their overhanging tops collide and create a useless space in the angle between them. Nevertheless they give the courtyard an appealing variety of shapes and angles and a picturesque skyline. Of the proud craftsman nothing is known, though his son and namesake worked at Congleton church and at the Grammar School at Nantwich, where he is recorded as a Free Mason and Master Carpenter. William Moreton died in 1563 and his will instructed his executors to 'make an ende and finishe in all poyntes such a frame as I have in hand'. Accordingly his son John, who died in 1598, continued with the south wing, including the gatehouse, the spiral stair, guestrooms and the garderobe projecting over the moat. Finally came the Long Gallery.

Little Moreton Hall

78.   The courtyard, Little Moreton Hall.

The changing history of timber framing can be followed in the growth of the house. The 15th-century work on the Great Hall block uses heavy quatrefoil panels particularly on the side facing the garden; the timbers on the gatehouse wing are lighter and busier, with a delightful variety of motifs including star shapes and concave-sided lozenges. A similar richness of texture can be seen in the large areas of window. The glazing, dating from the later 16th century, uses countless tiny leaded panes with different patterns in each room, and much old glass with attractively variegated colouring survives. There is also a small amount of heraldic stained glass. The 16th century saw greater luxury in the interiors. The walls of the parlour are painted with illusionistic panelling decorated with imitation coloured marbling and inlay; above are brightly-coloured, crudely-painted scenes telling the story of Susannah and the Elders. The Moreton wolf's head crest and the initials J.M. date the decoration to before the death of John Moreton in 1598. This type of painted decoration is found elsewhere in the county in the late 16th or early 17th century; it must have been preferred to real panelling or tapestry on grounds of expense, but when fashion changed it was boxed in. Painted Biblical texts and borders are also found in the chapel but were never covered up in this way.

120

79. The Withdrawing Room, Little Moreton Hall.

80. West end of the Long Gallery, Little Moreton Hall.

Real wooden panelling of the 16th century lines the walls of the adjoining withdrawing room, where it is more deeply cut than the 17th-century wainscoting fitted in the other rooms. Even more solid is the very heavily moulded coffering of the handsome wooden ceiling which gives this room such a rich character. The beams are similar to the sawn-off remnant of the Great Hall ceiling, suggesting that both are of 1559. The plaster chimneypiece, with the arms of Elizabeth I and crude female caryatids, shows traces of original colouring and gilding. Perhaps the most obvious example of domestic improvement is the Long Gallery, a fashionable type of room for the latter part of Elizabeth's reign, though at Little Moreton Hall almost certainly an afterthought, superimposed without concern for the symmetry or the new classical ideas influencing up-to-date architects. Long Galleries were commonly placed on upper floors to take advantage of the prospect and at Little Moreton windows run almost continuously round the room. Though marred by ugly modifications to the roof structure, it is a gloriously long and crooked space, the wide floorboards rising up and down like waves and the walls leaning outwards at different angles. In the gables at each end are emblematic plaster reliefs copied from a book of 1556, *The Castle of Knowledge*. They show the figure of Destiny with compasses and a sphere representing knowledge, and Fortune, blindfolded, holding a wheel and standing on an unstable globe. In the adjoining upper porch room is a fireplace with overmantel figures of Justice and Mercy similar to those at Gawthorpe, Lancashire of around 1603. In the wing below are a variety of props and console supports which suggest that the Long Gallery unsettled the structure of the house quite soon after it was added.

An inventory of 1654 shows the Moretons still prospering as the house had plentiful hangings, curtains, feather beds and upholstered furniture. But the family was Royalist and during the Civil War its estates were sequestrated. By the early 18th century the Hall was let to tenant farmers. Eventually antiquarian taste came to appreciate the house for its picturesque qualities; in 1807 John Sell Cotman came to draw it for Britton's *Architectural Antiquities*. His sketch of the Great Hall interior shows it restored to its original height, a neglected but magnificent apartment with massive timbers of pleasingly irregular lines, and chickens scratching for food in the passage. Another artist James West visited it in 1847 and enjoyed its dusty atmosphere, though noting that the chapel was used as a coal store. When the Moreton line died out in 1913 the Hall was left to a cousin, Charles Abraham, later Bishop of Derby, who appreciated its importance, maintained it and secured its future by presenting it to the National Trust in 1937. Since then comprehensive repairs have been carried out involving complete re-roofing, the replacement of defective timbers and the careful restoration of the appearance of the exterior. Much of the coving on the jetties was originally blank and this can be seen in early photographs, but painted quatrefoils resembling authentic timber patterns elsewhere on the house had been liberally added by late 19th- and early 20th-century restorers. These have now been removed. More controversial has been the recolouring in mellow brown and cream instead of stark black and white. Other half-timbered houses have been classicised, Victorianised or over-restored; used as farms or simply left to fall down. But Little Moreton Hall remained, resolutely unfashionable, until time caught up with it. Now, charmingly crooked and top heavy, it is appreciated as the most picturesque of all Cheshire houses.

O iii, 49; *Little Moreton Hall* guidebook 1979.

See also plate VI, facing page 142.

LYME PARK, *Disley*

965 824 *House, gardens and park open to the public. (National Trust/Stockport Borough Council)*

The Leghs came to Lyme, high up on the edge of the Peak District, in 1388. Sir Piers Legh, younger son of the Leghs of Adlington, married the daughter of Sir Thomas Danyers, who had been granted the Lyme estate by Edward III for services in battle. The Leghs also gave the crown distinguished military service. They hunted deer and bred the famous Lyme mastiffs; one of these dogs accompanied Piers II at Agincourt, and another, a gift from King James I to Philip of Spain, is seen in Velazquez's famous painting *Las Meninas*. Lyme is now built round four sides of a courtyard, but the older work is in the north and east ranges, suggesting that the house was originally L-shaped. In the north wing is the gatehouse arch and in the east range is the entrance hall. This hall and the withdrawing room upstairs were probably the principal rooms referred to in the earliest description of Lyme in 1466 as 'one fair hall with a high chamber, kitchen, bakehouse and brewhouse with a granary, stable, and a bailiffs house, and a fair park, surrounded with a paling'.

The oldest surviving work is Elizabethan; there are several fine plaster overmantels, though not necessarily in their original positions. An especially rich one with Elizabeth I's arms is in the Long Gallery. On the exterior the most prominent Elizabethan feature, of about 1570, is the centrepiece of the north front over the entrance arch. This apes London fashion; the paired windows under a pediment are derived from the recently-built Somerset House in the Strand, though a column is incorrectly placed on the apex of the pediment. There is a puzzling lack of continuity between the centrepiece and the ranges on either side; the number of storeys and the style of stonework do not match. Also Elizabethan are the blocked mullioned windows on the courtyard side of the front. It is known from a painting that the entrance side was formerly asymmetrical and had windows of this type, now altered.

The painting shows certain features of the late 17th-century such as the cupola over the centrepiece (no longer there: it is now a belvedere in the park and a statue replaces it). The delicately executed lead hopperheads on this front bear the date 1676 and the initials of Richard and Elizabeth Legh, who improved the house; the marble chimneypieces in the north wing were installed for a visit from the future James II, then Duke of York, who came to hunt the stag in 1676. Richard's most important

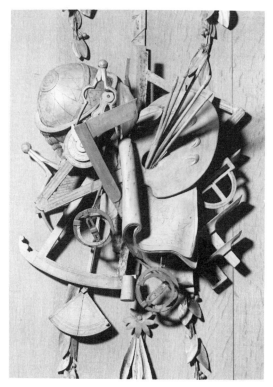

81. Woodcarving by Grinling Gibbons in the saloon, Lyme Park.

123

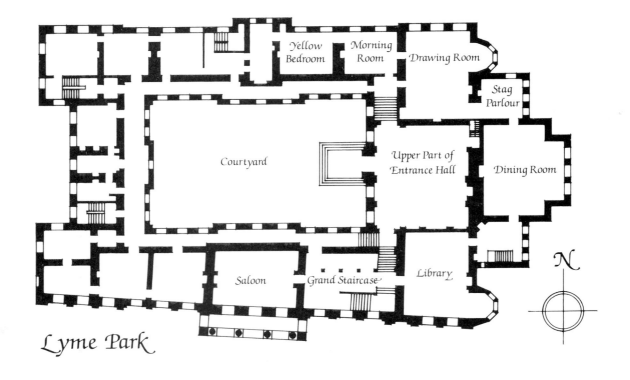

Lyme Park

82. Centrepiece of the north front, Lyme Park, 1904.

addition came after this visit; a contract to build a new parlour was signed in 1680 by John Platt, the first mention of the dynasty of masons who were to work at Lyme for several generations. The parlour was built out behind the hall, its most notable feature being the woodcarvings, probably by Grinling Gibbons. These have since been repositioned in the saloon and represent with crisp fidelity flowers, fruit, scientific and musical instruments, a palette, brushes and daintily curled up paper. Richard also planted formal gardens including an avenue of limes to the south, but his gardener complained 'what a strange, cold place it is', and that he could not 'have things soe early as his neighbours'.

In 1687 Richard died and was succeeded by Peter X, one of the Cheshire gentlemen whose portraits are now at Tatton. By degrees he brought scale, grandeur and symmetry to Lyme, adding two new wings to make it a courtyard house. First, he tackled the lopsided north front, adding an extra bay at the west to make it symmetrical, and he began to classicise it by refacing the ends with a giant order of pilasters. The unfinished edges of this work show it was intended to extend further; in an unexecuted design, the front is seen entirely refaced with a giant order, obliterating the Elizabethan centrepiece. The alterations to the north front were designed and carried out by the Platts, but in 1725 Legh brought in Giacomo Leoni, an architect of a different calibre, in touch with European classicism. Born in Venice, he had worked in Germany, published an English edition of Palladio and designed two London town houses. At Lyme he was responsible for the new south wing, the courtyard and the hall. Many of his drawings and letters survive and these show that the west front, also built in the classical style at this time, is not his. Writing to Peter Legh in May 1725 he criticised a design for it, presumably by the Platts, but his own alternative proposal was not adopted, perhaps as the work on the west front was already too far advanced to be changed. The result is that the west lacks polish compared to Leoni's south front. This has on the piano nobile a giant order of Ionic pilasters extending the full width of the front and in the centre an amply proportioned portico with square columns at each end. The effect looks rich and heavy to English eyes, accustomed to the chaste, staccato qualities of Lord Burlington's Palladianism; Leoni's interpretation of Palladio brought to Cheshire the monumental scale and texture of a European palace.

The south front was intended to be even grander than executed, for Leoni planned a cupola over the portico. The cupola was not built 'because Madam Legh did not approve of it . . . Also shee objected at the three Arches, thinking they should draw so much wind into the Court and make the House so Could'. Despite her objection, the basement of the south front is pierced by an open arcade leading through to the courtyard. Round the inside of the court Leoni provided a rusticated loggia and masked the old work on the north side by a new upper corridor giving separate access to the old enfilade of rooms. He brought forward the front of the old hall, raised it up on steps and gave it a grandiose classical portal, intended, according to his drawing, to have Michaelangelesque sculpted figures reclining on the pediment. Even without them the courtyard has a Mannerist flavour. The masonry work here and on the south wing was carried out for Leoni by the Platts. They were also responsible for remodelling Lyme Cage, the Elizabethan hunting tower and banqueting room in the park; it was rebuilt with quoins and corner turrets as a Keeper's house and poacher's lock-up.

The principal interior of this period was the entrance hall, its assymetry cleverly disguised by a screen of columns. Its most notable feature, sadly removed early this century, was a chimneypiece with plumed helms at either side and a portrait frame over it with military trophies in a Baroque style more like Vanbrugh than Palladio. Leoni may have been responsible for the design but the execution here and in the other rooms must have taken place after his supervision had ceased; much of the interior work is old-fashioned for its date. The rococo plaster ceiling in the staircase hall is of 1733, by Francesco Conseiglio and Joseph Palfreyman, and the great staircase itself was carved by the joiner John Moore in 1734-5.

No further alterations on a large scale took place until 1814 when Lewis Wyatt began to

83. Lyme Park from the south-west, 1904.

84. The drawing room, Lyme Park.

reorganise the confusion of irregular extensions and changes of level on the east wing. His survey drawings incidentally reveal much about the earlier house. His patron was Thomas Legh, traveller and archaeologist in Egypt and the middle east, who excavated the three Greek funerary monuments shown in the library. Wyatt replaced the new parlour of 1680, built at ground level, with a grand dining room at the same level as the drawing room. The new room is an early example of the revival of the Wren style but the reliefs, carried out in plaster and grained to look like oak, do not quite convince; the magnificence is a little forced. This room is entirely a Wyatt creation though he took its period from what was there before. But in several other rooms he mixed his own historicist work with authentic elements from the old house. An example is the Stag Parlour, named after the series of plaster reliefs in the frieze showing the hunting of the stag and including a view supposedly of the old house but oddly unlike it. The clumsy overmantel includes the arms of James I and the general style is Jacobean. Wyatt raised the room to a higher level and reset the reliefs, but drawings for some of the Jacobean ornament survive in his hand and these raise questions as to just how closely the Parlour is related to the room it replaced.

The drawing room is a more successful mixture; genuine survivals such as the fine chimneypiece and wainscoting are complemented by 19th-century features such as the bay window arch and the glowing stained glass brought by Thomas Legh from Disley parish church. The strapwork ceiling must be by Wyatt as it is a concentric design made for a central chandelier. All is combined to evoke a luxurious atmosphere, more Elizabethan than the Elizabethans. Some of Wyatt's alterations were more practical. He altered the Elizabethan Long Gallery to fit in a corridor to the bedrooms inserted by Leoni. Underground, he built a passage linking the new dining room with the kitchens. He also began work on the garden terraces and conservatory, and planned new stables (completed by Alfred Darbyshire in the 1860s). To provide more servants' bedrooms Wyatt boldly placed over the portico a heavy attic where Leoni had wanted a cupola. This considerably altered the balance of Leoni's design. It is fortunate that Wyatt was prevented from also spoiling Leoni's courtyard for some of Wyatt's drawings show a curved corridor crossing it from the entrance arch to the hall.

The Leghs profited from the industrial expansion of Wigan and were politically active; in 1892 W. J. Legh was created 1st Lord Newton for political services. His son the 2nd Lord Newton, who succeeded in 1898, reacted against High Victorian taste preferring the ancient look of the Elizabethan style to the showy magnificence of the more recent apartments. He employed Joubert, a fashionable though uninspired decorator, to alter the entrance hall with tapestries and a bland neo-Palladian overmantel, and even had gilt furniture wood-grained. Disdaining what he saw as vulgar modern luxury, he dressed his children shabbily and ate simple food in preference to the concoctions of French chefs. Lyme was maintained in the old style until the First World War, but its upkeep was crippling and in 1946 the 3rd Lord Newton announced his intention to sell. In the event, he gave Lyme to the National Trust, though this was still a bitter blow to the proud family. Lord Newton's sister, revisiting Lyme and recalling her life there with her parents, wrote, 'now it was dead, just as they were dead; It had died when it ceased to be a home'. But lately she has written more kindly of the efforts at restoration, which in recent years have been extensive and costly.

Lysons, 729; O iii, 678; T ii, 92; *CL* xvi, 906, xcvi, 684, c, 210, clvi, 1724, 1858, 1930, 1998; P. Sandeman, *Treasure on Earth*, 1952; *National Trust Studies*, 1981; *Lyme Park* guidebook 1984; Stockport Library, Account Books; JRL Legh of Lyme papers; Lyme Park, Lewis Wyatt drawings; Merseyside County Archive, Lewis Wyatt letter and drawings.

MOTTRAM HALL, *Mottram St Andrew*

885 794

Tantalisingly little is known of the history of Mottram Hall. No family papers survive and no contemporary descriptions explain its development. Yet it is an ambitious house and its builder William Wright was a major 18th-century landowner. Wright came from Offerton Hall near Stockport and he bought the Mottram estate in 1738. The new house dates from shortly before 1753 as it was intended for his son Randal who died aged 21 in that year. The death of his son, which followed those of his six other children all before they reached the age of 20, was a bitter blow, and he displayed his grief in a huge and magnificent monument in St Mary's church, Stockport, erected to their memory in 1756. His own memorial in St Peter's, Stockport, records 'a Life of Seventy-three years, embittered with Pain and Trouble'.

The Old Hall which Wright acquired was erected by the Calveleys in the late Middle Ages as a semi-fortified manor house. The lower section of ashlar to one side is part of this original building containing an undercroft. The L-shaped portion on the other side is the remains of an early 17th-century timber-framed extension. Wright converted the Old Hall as his agent's house, thus ensuring its survival after the new house was built.

The new Hall, erected a quarter of a mile to the east, is a large brick mansion with a monumental central block and low wings of 11 bays projecting out and then forward to create a broad open forecourt of the kind common in early 18th-century country houses. In

85. The entrance front, Mottram Hall.

128

recent years the expansion of the building as a hotel has involved the extension of the wings sideways, and this has changed the balance of the composition, but even within the original part there are ambiguities, for the details of the central block and the wings do not entirely match. The main block is surmounted by a wide pediment stretched across the entire front and resting on a giant order of six stone Doric pilasters. Within the pediment is a fine Rococo cartouche with scrolls containing the legend *Nisi Dominus edifice domum frustra laboratur* (Unless the Lord build the house he labours in vain that builds it) taken from Psalm 117. The order stands on a rusticated plinth which is broken in the centre by a doorcase, originally the main entrance. The much lower wings are set back from the centrepiece and are punctuated by pediments at the centres of each part, two facing forward and two facing each other across the forecourt. Below each is a doorway and a window with Gibbs surrounds. In contrast to the centre block, the plinth is low and plain, and the cornice and pediments are of timber. The logical explanation of these differences would be that the wings were built later than the central block, for perhaps work would have stopped after the death of Wright's son. But in style the wings appear slightly earlier with heavy architraves and some sashes with thick glazing bars. The awkward junction between the pedimented front and the curious swept gable ends on the sides of the central block suggests another explanation: that the centrepiece was refronted some time after the house and wings were completed. On the garden elevation the awkwardness is yet more pronounced because the centre projects far forward of the wings. In the simpler pediment of this front is

mis-spelt the inscription *Rura miih placeant*, taken from a verse of Virgil's *Georgics* praising the delights of the countryside.

The main block contains four principal rooms with a wide central corridor and staircase. In the left wing were service quarters and on the right the chapel and other family accommodation. The central entrance led into a hall, but the function of the four subsidiary doorways in the wings is not clear. The two facing each other across the forecourt may be later, for the Gibbs surrounds are coarser and have chamfered rustication. Inside the decoration is of many periods, but nothing appears to survive from the 1750s. The best is in the former entrance hall and the central corridor. These are decorated with good Wyatt-style plasterwork of the late 18th century, including a ceiling in the hall with vines and hunting trophies. The delicate vaulted ceiling of the corridor is very similar to that of the gallery at Winnington Hall and was perhaps carried out by Wyatt-trained craftsmen. Unfortunately the present hotel decorations detract from the quality of these rooms, and the corridor, shown in earlier photographs with a floor of black and white marble, is now carpeted.

86. The central corridor, Mottram Hall, 1923.

The chapel, now converted to a banqueting suite, is lined with panelling from Offerton Hall. Wright was a pious man; his use of a religious inscription over the entrance was unusual for a domestic building of this time, and he used his estate to endow St Peter's church, Stockport, which he built in 1768. Though large, this church is architecturally undistinguished and has little in common with the house. The memorial to his children in St Mary's however is an ostentatious work, the *magnum opus* of the Manchester sculptor Daniel Sephton. Sephton almost certainly carved the cartouche in the pediment at Mottram too, for it is very similar in style to the monument. Daniel Sephton's father Henry was the leading Liverpool architect of the second quarter of the 18th century and his major country house, Ince Blundell Hall, Lancashire was closely based on the influential Buckingham House which had side wings flanking a forecourt. Few buildings by him are recorded, and it is possible that Henry Sephton was the architect of Mottram Hall.

O iii, 695; T ii, 119; Heginbotham ii, 203; S. C. Ramsey & J. D. M. Harvey, *Small Georgian Houses and their Details 1750-1820*, 1972 edn., II pl I.

PECKFORTON CASTLE, *Peckforton*
534 580

87.   Peckforton Castle from the air.

In the centre of the Cheshire plain is a group of impressive hills which can be seen on a clear day from the far corners of the county. Closer views reveal that on the crests of two of these hills stand fortifications. On the greater are the ruins of Beeston Castle, built by Randle Blundeville, Earl of Chester in 1220. Nestling amongst the tall trees of the lower hill is the sinister outline of Peckforton Castle. The unlikely proximity of two great castles facing one another across a narrow valley has an explanation: Peckforton is Victorian, a building erected between 1841 and 1850 by John (later 1st Baron) Tollemache as his country residence. That he should erect a modern castle so close to a true medieval one is evidence of the ambition and self-confidence of this remarkable man.

88. The walls of Peckforton Castle from the south-west.

Gladstone called Tollemache, a Member of Parliament for over thirty years, a man of 'great practical ability'. As a young man he was a considerable athlete; in marriage he produced 24 children; and in his eighties he still drove a four-in-hand. His death was caused at the age of 85 through a cold caught driving on a wintry day to give help to one of his tenants. It was this concern for his tenantry which brought him renown as a reforming landlord. 'The only real and lasting pleasure to be derived from the possession of a landed estate', wrote Tollemache, 'is to witness the improvement in the social conditions of those residing in it', and in Cheshire he proved his word by dividing his estate of 26,000 acres into units of 200 acres and building over fifty new farmsteads. Each labourer was provided with a cottage and three acres of land which he could farm as a means of supplementing his wages. All this cost £280,000 compared with £68,000 spent on the castle. It was a feudal concept, and the siting of the house high on a rocky outcrop emphasised the dominance of the landlord over his tenantry. Tilstone Lodge, the nearby house built by his father Admiral Tollemache only 23 years earlier, was not for him an appropriate symbol. It is a feature of John Tollemache's conservatism that he chose to build a castle, for by the 1840s this was no longer a fashionable concept for a country house. The romantic spirit of the late 18th century had produced scores of sham castles, such as, in Cheshire, Bolesworth and Cholmondeley, but in an influential book *Contrasts*, published in 1836, A. W. N. Pugin had launched a fervent attack on such architecture which he saw as deceitful: 'on the one side of the house machicolated parapets, embrasures, bastions, and all the show of strong defence, and round the corner of the building a conservatory leading to the principal rooms, through which a whole company of horsemen might penetrate at one smash!' Tollemache chose as his architect Anthony Salvin who, like Pugin, was not interested in building a sham, but set about recreating a genuine castle of the time of Edward I.

Salvin was not the first choice, for building had started in 1841 under the direction of George Latham of Nantwich. Latham had designed the chapel at Tilstone Fearnall for Tollemache's father and had advised on repairs at Helmingham, the family seat in Suffolk. His work at Arley for Rowland Egerton-Warburton had not always given satisfaction and led to the latter employing Salvin for his chapel. After Tollemache visited Arley in 1845 he dismissed Latham, generously paying him £2,000 in compensation, and engaged Salvin instead. Salvin had by then already a reputation for restoring and extending genuine medieval buildings. 'Mr. Salvin is, of course', later wrote the architect Alfred Waterhouse, 'celebrated for the way in which he can combine the exterior and plan of an Edwardian Castle with nineteenth century elegance and comfort'.

It is the exterior and plan which make Peckforton so convincing. The outline is long and businesslike, looking as if it would actually withstand attack. The accommodation is arranged around a large courtyard enclosed, in true medieval fashion, by a defensive wall incorporating

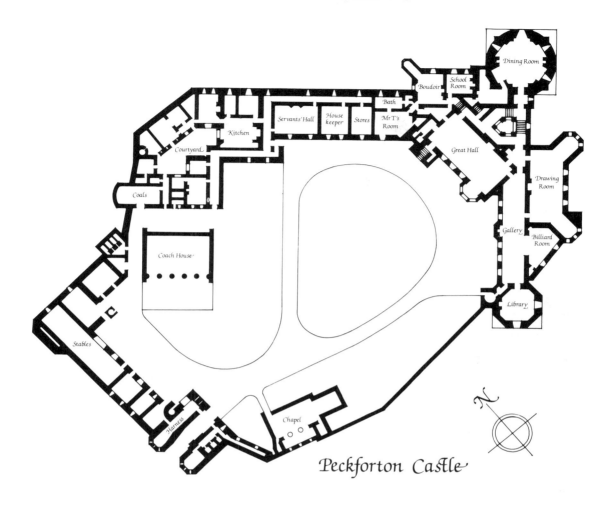

Peckforton Castle

89. The Great Hall, Peckforton Castle.

90. The staircase, Peckforton Castle.

battlements and towers. The visitor is led into this courtyard through a gateway on the west side. The reception rooms lie opposite, the domestic quarters, coach house and stables are strung out along the north wall, and to the south is the chapel. What is remarkable about this plan is its geometry. Medieval castles took their complex layout from the needs of military defence. Whilst this was not a necessary consideration for Salvin, in order to achieve an authentic outline he departed from the strict rectangular plan which made so many 18th-century castles look bogus, adopting two separate axes set at 45 degrees. The complex interaction of these axes leads to the distinctive shapes of the dining room, library, drawing room and staircase, and is even used in the arrangement of rooms around the kitchen court.

The most striking feature of the interior is the absence of ornamentation: ceilings are vaulted with plain ribs, walls are faced with smooth cut ashlar, mouldings are broad and simple, and little is plastered. From the courtyard the main entrance leads directly into the Great Hall which is lit from one side by tall traceried windows and a polygonal bay. This room sets the tone for the interiors: there are no concessions to elegance or finery. The great hooded fireplace is impressive by its severity and size, whilst the bands of Minton floor tiles and the precisely carved timber screen give the room a hard mechanical character. The dining room is octagonal and sits within the thick walls of the big circular tower. Below is an impressive circular wine cellar with a flat vaulted ceiling supported on a massive central pier, but the kitchens are situated 180 feet away at the end of a long underground passage. The drawing room is a most unusual shape, with two deep canted bays running off at 45 degrees from the outer corners. Externally these bays are expressed as bastions which rise above the line of the battlements. But the most spectacular interior space is the main staircase. This forms a pentagon in plan, with broad flights of stone steps rising dramatically around a deep top-lit well. The geometry affords striking vistas of dimly-lit vaults and gloomy corridors. The chapel, a separate building to the south of the gateway, is a simple structure in the Decorated style, and its layout, like the one at Arley which had impressed Tollemache, followed Ecclesiological principles. Yet Tollemache was an evangelical Calvinist of strict persuasion. The services held in the chapel during his lifetime were non-conformist, and though Tollemache had it licensed by the Bishop of Chester, it was never consecrated or endowed.

Some rooms of the house such as bedrooms and other family quarters have a more domestic character, with plastered walls and ceilings, but it is hard to understand how contemporary opinion could have held that 'it would be difficult to mention a house in England more entirely suited to modern wants'. The only photographs showing furnished interiors date from the 1930s, by which time the family had largely forsaken the state apartments for the more homely rooms of the west wing. In the Great Hall were portraits, armour and bulky Victorian furniture arranged formally around the walls. The dining room had a pair of canopied oak buffets elaborately carved with heraldry, and a massive circular table over fifteen feet in diameter. In the drawing room a vain attempt had been made to soften the gloom by filling it with comfortable sofas, Rococo style mirrors and ormolu electroliers. Of the original furniture supplied by Dowbiggin of London, much had already gone by the 1930s, and what had not was disposed of at an auction in 1953. The house was lived in to some degree by the Tollemache family until the Second World War, but since that time it has remained largely empty, the uncompromising nature of the interior, even if suited to life in the 1850s, defeating any attempts at modern day occupation.

O ii, 304; T i, 110; *ILN* 26 April 1851; L. Tollemache, *Old and Odd Memories*, 1908; *Ches Life* February 1936; Sale Catalogue, Browns of Chester 1953 (Copy at Chester Public Library); *CL* cxxxviii, 284, 336; Girouard, 73; R.I.B.A. Salvin drawings; Arley Hall, Latham letters.

PEEL HALL, *Ashton*

498 697

What remains at Peel Hall is sufficient to show that it was a Jacobean house of importance and distinction. From the front it appears to be a solid stone block of a house, symmetrical and ordered, but at the back, like a building in course of demolition, hang a blocked fireplace and doorways within the upper walls. Above one of the doorways is a splendid carved cartouche with the date 1637 recording the year when the Hall was erected. Its builder was most likely Henry Hardware IV who inherited the estate on the death of his father in 1613. The Hardwares, whose principal seat was at Bromborough, rose to prominence through successful trade in Chester.

The name Peel Hall derives from the pele tower which was built here as part of the defence of the Welsh border, but no evidence of it is left. The new Hall of 1637 was, for Cheshire, remarkably advanced. The present L-shaped house is little more than one-third of the original rectangular building of two storeys above a basement. What is now the main front, facing south, gives the best impression of how it looked. This is a regular facade with mullioned and transomed windows, a bold string course, and a tall parapet concealing the roof. Two flat projecting chimneystacks, formerly taller, punctuate the skyline, and at the centre is a classical doorcase. It looks out over a walled garden, originally terminated by a moat and a summerhouse on a mound. A sketch made about 1830 by the antiquary Joseph Mayer shows the house in a semi-ruinous state. It had been neglected for some time and in 1816 a wing was demolished by the then owner Booth Grey of nearby Ashton Hayes. It must have been this action which caused the doorways and fireplaces to be so oddly exposed on the outside walls.

Examination of these features and of the surface of the surrounding stonework reveals where walls were taken down, but it is difficult to understand the form of the original house until it is realised that the present main front is actually the side elevation of one of a pair of identical cross wings, and that between these was an impressive Great Hall. The entrance to the hall was on the east side and the carriage approach can be traced from the pairs of gatepiers within the high garden walls to the north-east. The hall, which was set over a tall basement, was most probably reached by a flight of external steps dividing into two, and leading up to a porch and a cross passage at each end of the hall. A parallel for this can be seen at Raynham Hall, Norfolk, a contemporary and well-known house built for Sir Roger Townsend, a country landowner with an interest in architecture. The basic plan was derived from Palladio and had been used in such houses as Somerhill, Kent, Charlton House, Greenwich, and Plas Teg, Flintshire. At Raynham and Peel however there is more of a compromise with tradition, for a truly Palladian plan would have required that the entrance be in the centre.

The evidence for believing that Peel had a similar layout to Raynham is the pattern of the suspended doorways and other carved elements which are now exposed. It can be seen from the stonework at parapet level that the present narrow rear wing was once the same height as the main block. On its east wall are a large fireplace and three blank doorways, one now concealed externally by a modern brick extension. This was the back wall of the Great Hall with its central fireplace. The two doorways on the right, one above another, indicate a screens passage with a gallery over. On the north wall of the main block is the dated cartouche and a big round headed doorway which probably led into a Great Chamber. On the left of this is a capital and a voussoir of a doorway which must have divided the porch from the cross passage, and which

91. The present main front of Peel Hall, from the south-east.

92. View of Peel Hall from the north-east.

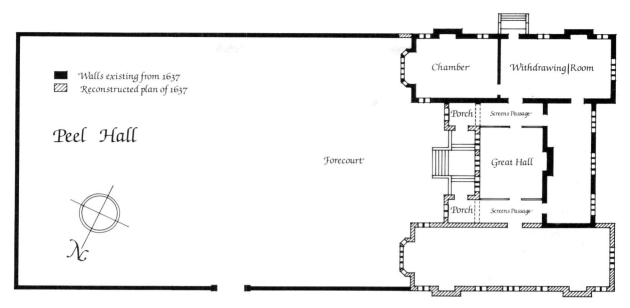

Walls existing from 1637
Reconstructed plan of 1637

Peel Hall

Chamber

Withdrawing|Room

Porch
Screens Passage

Forecourt

Great Hall

Porch
Screens Passage

N

matches the detail of the complete doorway concealed behind the modern extension. The oak staircase with carved flat balusters is contemporary with the house but has probably been moved.

While the plan of Peel Hall was advanced, its decoration was on the whole conventional and it cannot be connected with any metropolitan architect. It is however the grandest of a group of Jacobean and Artisan Mannerist houses erected by Cheshire merchants and lawyers following the fashion set by Crewe Hall. These include Dorfold, Tattenhall, Lower Huxley and Wettenhall, as well as Swakeleys, the large house built by Sir Edmund Wright of Nantwich in Middlesex in 1629-38. It is possible that Peel was never completed, for in 1639 both Henry Hardware and his only child died. Shortly afterwards it was sold to Roger Wilbraham of Dorfold. Later in the century it was acquired by Colonel Roger Whitley, a zealous royalist who had followed Charles II into exile and acted as his emissary on the rising of the Cheshire forces under George Booth. But the house was regarded with some importance for on 2 June 1690 a visit was paid to Peel Hall by King William III on his way to suppress the Jacobite rebellion in Ireland.

O ii, 332; THSLC iv, 10; *Ches Life* January 1962; R. Glasgow, *The Hardwares of Cheshire*, 1948, 31; *Cheshire Archaeological Bulletin* ix, 34; R. C. Turner, *Peel Hall, An Artisan Mannerist puzzle in Cheshire*, THSLC cxxxvi, 27.

PEOVER HALL, *Peover Superior*

773 734 *House and gardens open to the public. (Privately owned)*

93. Peover Hall from the west.

At Peover there is a 16th-century Hall, remarkable Stuart stables, fine formal gardens, and a classical chapel containing the tombs of the Mainwarings who held the estate from the early 12th century for 800 years. Their original Hall was probably on the moated site south of the stables. The new Hall was begun by Sir Randle Mainwaring in 1585; the date is carved on a panel over the doorway tucked into a corner of the north front. The mellow brick building which stands today is substantially the house of Sir Randle, for though it was later much enlarged, recent demolitions have reduced it once again to its original size. But the Hall was intended to be much larger; what was built was only a part of a grander scheme, curtailed perhaps for financial reasons, and so adapted for the family's use.

To understand the intended form of the house it is necessary to examine a plan of the ground floor. The plan is T-shaped, with the main entrance in the foot of the T facing south. If it is appreciated that the top bar of the T is one wing of a symmetrical H plan balanced about a central block, the layout falls more readily into the pattern of conventional Elizabethan houses. In such a layout the top bar of the T would have been intended to contain the domestic quarters that normally occupied half the ground floor of a house of this period. Indeed within this cross wing the large room to the west side of the central passage was certainly built as a kitchen, and those on the opposite side would have been intended to be other domestic offices. The smaller rooms to each side of the passage would have been the buttery and pantry, each with its own cellar below. But for the size of house which was actually built, the kitchen is excessively large. There is also no room which could have formed a Great Hall, for this would have been part of the central block which was not completed. In adapting the cross wing, the larger area to the east of the passage became a living hall and the adjacent room was perhaps a parlour. The plan of the first floor followed the pattern of the rooms below, with a suite of apartments west of the cross passage and the Great Chamber occupying the same area as the living hall. At the top level the building was less satisfactory, for the garret storey did not provide sufficient bedrooms, and so in 1650 the roofline was altered to give more space. Before this the south elevation would have been symmetrical. Had the house been completed to the H plan, it would have been a formidable and ambitious structure, as large as the exactly contemporary Condover Hall, Shropshire, or Montacute House, Somerset. Yet the architecture with its many gabled roofs and irregularly placed mullioned windows is strikingly unsophisticated; there is none of the showiness for example of Brereton built the same year.

If Sir Randle's taste was old-fashioned, the same cannot be said of his younger brother Sir Philip Mainwaring who became Secretary of State to Thomas Wentworth, 1st Earl of Strafford. The two are depicted in a penetrating double portrait by Van Dyck. At the time this painting was commissioned, Wentworth had just returned from his post as Lord Deputy of Ireland to become principal adviser to Charles I, and Sir Philip's exposure to court life would undoubtedly have introduced him to advanced taste. His nephew, also called Philip, inherited Peover in 1632 and died in 1647. The following year a strikingly modern chapel was erected by Philip's widow Ellen to house their monument. Built of ashlar with lunette windows set high and a pediment, the chapel is an extraordinarily accomplished piece of early classical architecture. There was not another building of such purity in Cheshire for at least fifty years. Its sophisticated form must be due to Sir Philip's connections, and it may even have been designed by John Webb or one of his circle.

Six years later Ellen Mainwaring put up another important building: the stables erected in 1654 as a gift to her son Thomas. From the outside this looks nothing exceptional, but inside is decorative work of great elaboration. The stalls are divided off by an arcade of Tuscan columns supporting a strapwork entablature, and the ceiling is decorated with relief floral patterns and strapwork fleurs-de-lis. The form of the arcaded screen is similar in style to the chapel at Cholmondeley Castle built in 1655, and represents the first use of classical columns in a secular building in Cheshire. Though the decorative work otherwise is conservative for the date, what is remarkable is the richness, and the idea of using the interior of a mere stable block for architectural display. Fortunate were the horses which inhabited this palace.

The next major development did not occur until 100 years later when in 1764 a large, three-storey extension was added to the north end of the house. In effect this fulfilled the original intentions of the Elizabethan designer, though it was built in a very different style. No concessions were made to the design of the old Hall, but the new block was not a balanced composition in its own right. It formed two-thirds of a nine-bay front around a pedimented centrepiece with the existing house occupying the place of the remaining three bays: the relationship was most awkward. The old house now became largely service quarters as had originally been intended, and the ground floor living hall was divided into three separate rooms. The Great Chamber, by this time used as the dining room, was given greater height by lowering the floor. Within the

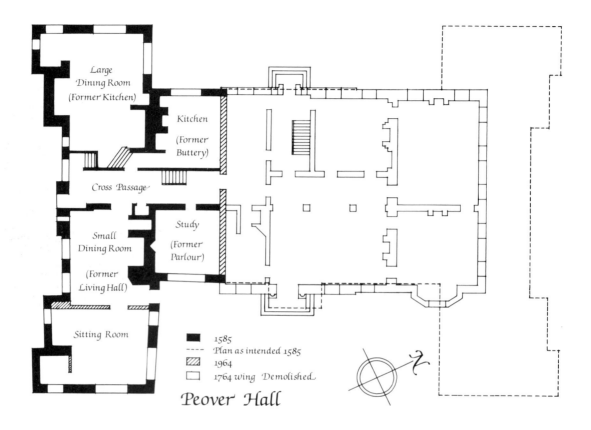

Large
Dining Room
(Former Kitchen)

Kitchen
(Former Buttery)

Cross Passage

Small
Dining Room
(Former
Living Hall)

Study
(Former Parlour)

Sitting Room

■ 1585
----- Plan as intended 1585
▨ 1964
□ 1764 wing Demolished

Peover Hall

new block were a spacious entrance hall, a drawing room, staircase, morning room and library, though none was architecturally distinguished. More handsome is the contemporary stable block with its clock and cupola built adjoining the earlier stables. These improvements were carried out for Sir Henry Mainwaring who inherited the estate at birth in 1726. There was little further change until 1919 when the estate was sold and the long association with the Mainwarings ceased. During the Second World War it served as headquarters for General Patton and the American Third Army, and when this was over it was left to decay. All but given up for lost, the Hall was fortunately acquired in the early 1960s by Randle Brooks. Since then the estate has undergone a renaissance and Mr. and Mrs. Brooks have continued the process of decoration and furnishing with considerable flair.

The plan of the house has been partially restored to its original form, and partly adapted for present-day convenience. The Georgian wing was demolished in 1964, and a new entrance was formed in the north front. This leads into the former cross passage. On the left is the original parlour, now a study, and on the opposite side is the kitchen, now the large dining room. This room has an extraordinary ceiling made up of massive timber beams set in decorative patterns, some in the form of quatrefoils. It represents, in a crude manner, the use of decorative wall framing, highly developed in such houses as Chorley Old Hall, for ceiling ornamentation, and it appears to be unique. It is likely that the ceilings in the passage and what was the living hall opposite were similarly treated, but they were removed when the first floor was lowered in the 18th century. The living hall is now separated into a small dining hall and a morning room,

94. The stables of 1654, Peover Hall.

95. Peover Hall before demolition of the 18th-century wing.

the latter panelled with an inspired mixture of woodwork from varied sources including the Mainwaring house Oteley near Ellesmere in Shropshire, and 17th-century carvings from Antwerp. The Elizabethan staircase with heavily-moulded newels and balusters has been moved more than once, and the flight connecting first and second floors is a modern copy. In the two bedrooms on the west side of the landing are fireplaces re-used from the Georgian wing, and the second of these rooms leads to the state bedroom which is dominated by a gigantic bed dated 1559, originally from Tamworth Castle, Staffordshire, but acquired from Abney Hall. Across the landing is the former Great Chamber which, like the room below, has been divided. The major part, now the drawing room, has 17th-century panelling, re-used when the floor was lowered. On the floor above this is one remaining garret, of interest chiefly for its roof which consists of a series of closely-spaced scissor trusses. At the end is a small room now known as the Priest's Room, and described in an inventory of 1713 as the Parson's Chamber. This inventory offers further evidence that the Elizabethan Hall was built no larger than its present size, for the rooms listed can all be made to fit within the existing structure.

Whilst the interiors have received careful treatment since the rescue of the house in the 1960s, the gardens too have been creatively reconstructed. Flat parkland, reputedly designed by William Emes in the mid-18th century, sweeps around two sides. On the other sides are a series of separate formal gardens, mostly laid out for Sir Philip Tatton Mainwaring between 1890 and 1905, separated by walls and high yew hedges. Remodelled by Hubert Worthington in the 1920s, these include a rose garden, a herb garden, a lily pool garden and parterres. But in recent years the compartments have been replanted and extended by Mr. and Mrs. Brooks. Small openings in the hedges lead from one 'outdoor room' to another, and in each is a surprise – fantastic topiary, arbours and classical summerhouses, statuary, colourful plants and sweet smells. These gardens with their clear architectural framework skilfully unite the rewarding group of buildings that form the heart of the Peover domain.

O i, 483; T ii, 50; *Ches Life* November 1936, October 1958; *TLCAS* lxxii, 151; *CL* clxxviii, 904.

VI. (*opposite*) Little Moreton Hall.

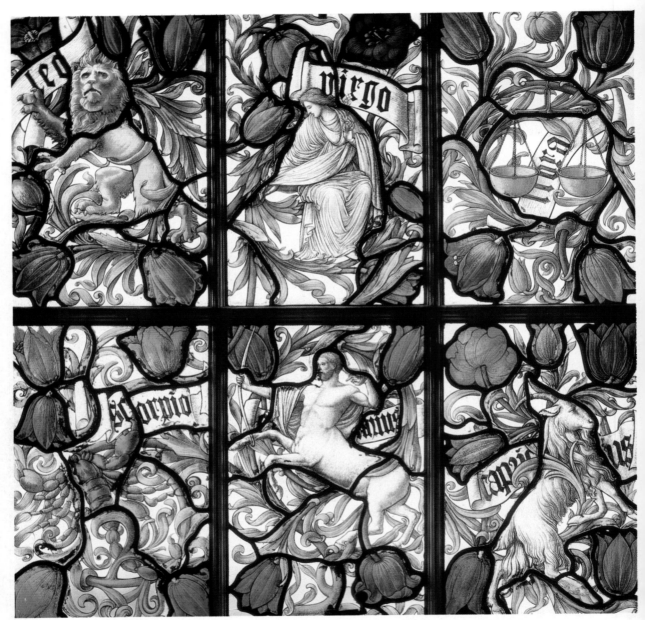

VII. Signs of the zodiac by Shrigley and Hunt in the hall windows, Pownall Hall.

PORTAL, *Tarporley*

559 634

To the north-east of Tarporley are two estates which join to form an extensive belt of parkland stretching out towards the Peckforton hills. The older is the Arderne estate, now the setting for a striking circular modern house; the other belongs to Portal, another 20th-century house, but one built in the vernacular of the Cheshire countryside. In 1900 Portal, then known as Portal Lodge, was left with its estate to the Hon. Marshall Brooks by his brother James. The Brooks family owned a successful calico printing works as well as quarries and coal mines at Crawshawbooth in Rossendale, Lancashire. Marshall Brooks was a furniture collector and

96.   The garden front, Portal.

during the 1890s he transformed the interior of Sunnyside, his house at Crawshawbooth (now the Manchester Diocesan Conference House) by introducing old panelling, stained glass, 17th-century chimneypieces and Dutch tiles. This desire to create an antiquarian interior doubtless influenced the style of the new house at Portal, as well as his choice of architect. The architect was Walter E. Tower, little known as a designer of buildings, but whose uncle, C. E. Kempe, ran a successful stained glass studio in London. Tower became a partner in this firm in the 1890s and took control in 1907. His other substantial architectural commission was Garrowby Hall, Yorkshire, a romantic courtyard house built in 1892 for the 2nd Viscount Halifax. Lord Halifax was a leading Anglo-Catholic and could well have been known to the Brooks family who erected a substantial church in Rawtenstall in 1890.

Demolition of Portal Lodge, an early 19th-century house with Gothick windows, commenced in 1900. The style of the new house which dates from 1906 was very different, for the aim was to re-create a large timber-framed courtyard house of the 16th century. Courtyard houses were a common form in medieval and Tudor mansions, but in spite of the desire of 19th-century architects to produce houses which were archaeologically accurate, the quadrangular plan was rarely used. The reason for this was convenience, for it required generous circulation space if rooms were not to be used as corridors. The courtyard plan did however become popular with Arts and Crafts architects at the turn of the century and Portal is one of the earliest examples. The house has two principal fronts. The symmetrical garden facade is punctuated by three large two-storey polygonal bays, between which are prettily decorated pairs of gabled dormers. The entrance elevation is more straightforward, having a central projecting porch and two square bays. All the usual decorative motifs of black and white Cheshire houses are used, and one of Tower's notebooks records that he visited and photographed Little Moreton, Handforth and Speke Halls. But some ideas such as the row of windows overlooking a formal garden, he took from Kempe's house, Old Place, Lindfield in Sussex.

The entrance at Portal leads into a screens passage from which a door opposite opens out into the courtyard. The courtyard here however is not part of the circulation route as in medieval houses, but merely a pleasant area to look out on with its formal cobbled paths, stone well and yews in boxes. On the right of the screens passage is the Great Hall with all its traditional elements; a hammerbeam roof, minstrels' gallery, and a massive chimneypiece carved with Marshall Brooks' coat of arms. From the upper end a doorway leads to the Great Parlour. Like all the rooms of the house with the exception of the hall this has a surprisingly low ceiling, a characteristic which is accentuated by the spectacular Jacobean-style plasterwork. This room contains one of the great south-facing bay windows, and, unlike a genuine Tudor house, or even an early Victorian recreation of the 'olden time', the interior is brilliantly lit, an effect exaggerated by the unfortunate recent stripping of all the oak panelling and carving. The middle bay belongs to the Little Parlour, and within this window are many small roundels and pieces of 16th- and 17th-century Swiss stained glass, mostly bought by Marshall Brooks at the sale in Munich in 1911 of Lord Sudeley's celebrated glass from Toddington Manor in Gloucestershire. There are scenes of Jacob's ladder, the conversion of St Paul, St Martin dividing his cloak with a beggar, and the stigmatisation of St Francis. The walls and ceiling of this room are framed in massive 15th-century timbers, and the chimneypiece with caryatids is made up of 17th-century fragments.

Beyond the hall a wide corridor passes the main staircase and runs along the south side of the courtyard to the former dining room which contains the third polygonal bay. The staircase was moved to its present position in the 1950s when a large wing beyond the dining room was demolished. This wing, which was probably part of the old Portal Lodge, contained the billiard room and schoolroom, as well as the staircase hall. At the foot of the present staircase is an archway formed of rough carved medieval timbers and some cupboards made from Flemish window shutters with decorative strap hinges. The staircase rises to a broad landing where there are panels of stained glass dated 1575 illustrating siege guns.

The bay windows look out over terraced gardens divided by lines of clipped box and yew. Beyond is a deep quarry garden with reedy pond and colonnaded walk, and then, across a clearing, a secret garden with sunken pools and rose beds. Running parallel with the drive is a long grassed avenue of topiary cut in the form of giant cones, leading to a statue of Hercules and a belvedere. Within the clear framework of this beautiful garden the intention of Marshall Brooks and his architect to create an idealised version of a half-timbered Cheshire mansion is marvellously realised.

J. Slater, *Sunnyside House* guidebook 1972; F. Latham, *Tarporley*, 1973, 68; V&A, Kempe papers.

POWNALL HALL, *Wilmslow*

837 819

97. The drawing room, Pownall Hall.

Pownall Hall, a red sandstone Georgian house dressed up in the Tudor style in 1830, does not at first look greatly distinguished. A glance at the front door hints at something remarkable. In contrast to the mechanical Gothic porch, the door has elaborately wrought metal hinges which seem to grow across it, tendril-like, branching out into leaves and flowers. There is also a knocker in the shape of a dragon, an undulating finger-plate and a sinuous Art Nouveau grille. Open the door and everywhere are curious details and mottoes, 'Salutation and greeting' on the lintel, a carved handshake, a bell pull in the shape of a trumpet flower and a legend relating that HB entered the house on Jubilee Day 20 June 1887.

HB was Henry Boddington of the Manchester brewing family. When his father died in 1886 he moved out of his home at the Strangeways brewery in Manchester and bought a house in then rural Wilmslow. He was only 30, but his tastes were advanced, and he made his house into a showcase for the most up-to-date work of the Arts and Crafts movement. His architects, Ball and Elce of Manchester, are known only in connection with the Boddingtons; they designed the Conservative Club at Strangeways and a church at Silverdale, Lancashire for Boddington snr. At Pownall they did little to the exterior but inside they quite transformed it. The rigid plan became a series of irregular-shaped rooms broken up by inglenooks, alcoves and changes of level, all flowing out of a comfortable living hall. The rooms are full of quaintly carved oak and patterned leaded windows, with carving by Milsom of Manchester, decorative painting by the Manchester artist John Dawson Watson and stained glass by the Gateshead Glass Company and Shrigley and Hunt of Lancaster.

All this was very up to the minute, contemporary with similar work at Wightwick Manor, Staffordshire, for example. But the employment of the Century Guild was *avant-garde*. Founded by A. H. Mackmurdo in 1882 to promote the equality of artist and craftsman, its members included Selwyn Image, Herbert Horne and Benjamin Creswick. The Guild provided the metalwork throughout the house and designed the dining and drawing rooms in their entirety in a style very different from the rest of the house. Much of the furniture and textiles Boddington acquired from the Liverpool International Exhibition of 1886 and the Manchester Jubilee

146

Exhibition of 1887, where the Guild exhibited. As a group the Century Guild only lasted until 1888 and the work at Pownall was its major commission.

Now a school, Pownall Hall is denuded of movable furniture, but enough remains to give a good idea of Boddington's artistic home. At the heart of the house is the entrance hall, a typical Arts and Crafts living hall with polished wainscoting, a low oak-beamed ceiling and applied half timbering in a self-consciously Cheshire style. The centrepiece is a stone fireplace, its frieze carved with the seven days of the week, and on either side a hammered brass sconce decorated with birds. In the leaded windows are vivid red poppies, tulips, and yellow foliage entwining the signs of the zodiac. Characteristic of the Arts and Crafts movement is the use of old materials recorded in the inscription 'This hall is panelled with old oak taken from the church of St Hilary, Denbigh, North Wales at the Restoration, Ano do 1881 Griffith Griffiths joyner' (the date puzzlingly suggests that work may have begun before Boddington came on the scene). Towards the back of the house are the library and morning room. The latter, devoid of most of its original fittings, still has pretty coloured glass of mythological figures but the library is much more complete. A cosy room full of built-in seats, it is divided into two parts, a low alcove lined with fitted bookcases and a taller area lit by a large window. Over the fireplace are the Seven Ages of Man painted in a flat storybook style by Watson. One of the highlights of the house was the staircase, lit by four tall lancets filled with stained glass in flowing designs by Shrigley and Hunt, a virtuoso creation in brilliantly marbled and variegated colours. The four winds are depicted each flying over a seasonal landscape of spring or summer flowers, cloudy or starry skies, icicles, rainbows or shafts of sunlight. Unfortunately an insensitively-placed fire stair prevents them from being seen.

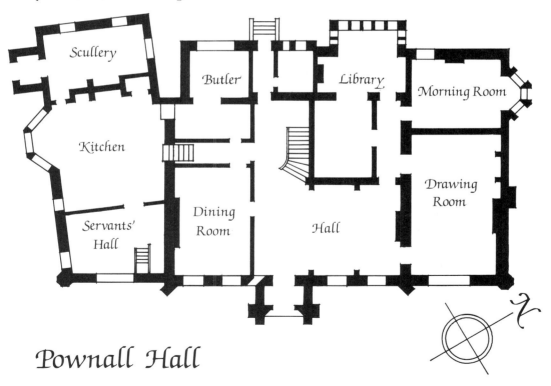

Pownall Hall

98. Fireplace in the dining room at Pownall Hall, with a painting by Selwyn Image.

99. The Fytton bedroom, Pownall Hall: drawing by T. Raffles Davison, 1891.

The two Century Guild rooms are on the ground floor on either side of the entrance hall. Unlike the rest of the house, these retain their Georgian squareness and use not oak but satinwood and mahogany. Sadly their wallcoverings have been lost. Nevertheless, in the drawing room, the woodwork on the fireplace, door, plate rail and window seat still hint at the essential character of the decorative scheme, firstly rectilinear from the slender square posts and strips (quite unlike the Art Nouveau curves in the other rooms) and secondly light and airy, from the yellow and cream colour scheme. Satinwood was combined with cream paint and with the citron-coloured fabric 'Angel and Trumpet' designed by Horne. This was gathered and hung above the plate rail as a background for fans, photographs and china. It was also used on upholstered furniture, and hung as curtains on the windows and on the canopied settle now in the Victoria and Albert Museum, probably made for the room. A pictorial frieze painted in soft colours by Image showed figures of the arts reclining beneath trees, and the same colours were picked up in Horne's ceiling decorations. The dining room was quite different, originally heavier and darker, with mahogany furniture against a dark-toned leather paper. The frieze, modelled with dogs in low relief , still remains, also the striking overmantel with another painting by Image and a projecting shelf supported by gilded atlantes modelled by Creswick in the manner of the muscular figures of Michaelangelo. The furniture in this room, including the massive buffet now owned by the Manchester City Art Galleries, was in a highly idiosyncratic interpretation of the Renaissance style.

The bedrooms are named after local families. 'Pownall' was originally fitted with Moorish screens and furniture by Liberty's, and 'Bolyn' had over the bed alcove a carved owl and the quotation from Macbeth 'Sleepe that knits up the ravelled sleeve of care . . .' Half-timbered 'Fytton' over the library, is divided into three parts for sleeping, dressing and sitting, all with fitted furniture carved with animals and birds. On going to bed in 'Dovecote', the night nursery, the Boddington children could admire the stained glass window showing an owl with poppies and bats; on waking they would see another window of the owl with birds and sunflowers. The day nursery, a double-height room with an open timber roof, is like a picture book come to life. Over the fireplace, with pretty tiles, is a large mural by Watson in the Walter Crane style, showing a medieval procession. An alcove at one end is divided into two levels, a low-ceilinged schoolroom and above it, with access from a miniature child-scaled staircase, a gallery meant for piano practice. Everywhere there is detail to delight a child: bench ends carved with pelicans, little built-in cupboards, window seats and stained glass including favourite nursery rhyme characters and pretty landscapes with fleecy clouds and flying swallows.

Once partitioned into dormitories for the school, the day nursery has recently been restored as the library. In the basement, the big oaken kitchen with 'Waste not Want not' carved on a beam, has become changing rooms and outside, the half-timbered Gallery at the back is now the school theatre. Used by Boddington for family theatricals, it also housed his important collection of early keyboard instruments and his pictures, with 200 by Watson and 33 by Ford Madox Brown. The stables have been demolished, likewise, St Olaf's chapel, a curious Romanesque-style building largely constructed of stone taken from Wilmslow parish church when it was being restored.

Near the remains of the chapel is an oak tree and here Boddington's ashes were scattered after his death in 1925. He had grown the tree from an acorn planted in the ceremonial sod cut by Lord Egerton from the Manchester Ship Canal at its inauguration. Boddington had been a director of the Canal, and had many business interests and public offices. But he was forced to resign them all in 1891 when his finances collapsed after he had unwisely lent money to friends and invested in a newspaper which failed. He spent much of his life abroad, having lived for only a few years at Pownall Hall.

It was common for Manchester or Liverpool businessmen to buy landed estates in the late 19th century and to set themselves up as country gentlemen. Like Boddington, many of them built in deliberately olde-worlde styles. But Pownall Hall is an exception because the taste which created it was sophisticated and urbane; by the standards of the average landed family in Cheshire or elsewhere the Hall would have appeared dangerously eccentric.

Art Journal 1891, 329, 354; *BA* xxxvi, 454; L. Lambourne, *Utopian Craftsmen*, 43, 46; S. Evans in *Art and Architecture in Victorian Manchester*, ed. J. Archer, 1985; Boddington papers, family collection.

See also frontispiece, and plate VII, facing page 143.

RADBROKE HALL, *Peover Superior*

768 750

The ideal of country house life had great appeal to wealthy industrialists of the Edwardian age. Backed by money from the yet booming cities of Liverpool and Manchester, this was to be the last phase of country house building in Cheshire. Its swansong was Radbroke Hall, erected with optimism for Claude and Olga Hardy during the dark years of the First World War. Hardy, a Belfast textile manufacturer, had established a prosperous smallware business in Manchester making tapes, ribbons and trimmings. His business success provided the means for a new country house; it was his wife's determination which saw it through.

Land was bought from Lord Egerton of Tatton in 1910. It was Hardy's ambition to acquire the Peover estate, but Olga favoured a smart new house rather than the decrepit and ivy-clad Peover Hall. In 1912 they appointed Percy Scott Worthington as architect. Worthington, who was at the time skillfully neo-Georgianising a nearby villa, Kerfield House, had taken over the successful Manchester practice of his father Thomas Worthington. His early houses were roughcast, with horizontal windows and sweeping roofs in the Voysey manner. But in 1912 his younger brother Hubert had joined the office after a year as a pupil of Edwin Lutyens, and it was perhaps his influence which caused the romanticism of the Arts and Crafts movement to be replaced at Radbroke by a grander classicism. The Hardys set their sights high, and for Worthington it was his most important domestic commission.

100.   Radbroke Hall: perspective by William Walcot exhibited at the Royal Academy in 1914.

First plans were prepared in January 1913. Worthington chose the type of Restoration house with a large two-storey central block and lower projecting wings flanking a forecourt. In the

101. View of Radbroke Hall from the west.

102. Curved doorcase in the dining room of
Radbroke Hall.

tall hipped roof of Cotswold stone are small-paned dormer windows, and at the centre is a giant portico approached by a curved double staircase. (The staircase was omitted in the final plans which were exhibited at the Royal Academy in 1914, the year construction commenced.) This late 17th-century style had been used by other Arts and Crafts architects, for example Lutyens. His The Salutation, Sandwich, under construction during the time Hubert Worthington was in Lutyens' office, was perhaps a model for Radbroke. There are similarities in the plan, but Radbroke differs in its use of a giant portico and smooth Portland stone instead of brick. Curiously it is a later Lutyens house, Gledstone Hall, Yorkshire, which is in appearance much closer. Indeed at Radbroke, with its touches of French classicism, Worthington anticipated Lutyens by some ten years. It is not inconceivable that in his design for Gledstone the master had learned something from the pupil. Probably because it was built during the war, Radbroke escaped attention. On completion it was not illustrated, and it has gone unnoticed ever since; even Pevsner's *Cheshire* omits all mention of it.

By April 1915 the portico was complete and work had commenced on the interior; but the following year the project was put in jeopardy by the sudden death of Claude Hardy. In spite of this blow, his widow determined to continue, and on its completion in 1917 both she and the architect were well pleased with the result. When in 1930 Worthington was awarded the Royal Gold Medal for Architecture, Mrs. Hardy wrote enthusiastic congratulations. But to him such recognition was a mixed blessing. 'This sort of publicity is dreadful to me', he replied, 'and to have to get on my legs to say thank you is purgatory.' For despite his success (he was the first exclusively provincial practitioner to be honoured with the Gold Medal), Worthington was a modest man.

There is nothing modest however about the design of Radbroke. The layout is bold and formal but, as with Lutyens' houses, it contains spatial drama and surprise. Behind the portico is a low barrel-vaulted vestibule leading on the right to a large panelled entrance hall. The core of the main block is occupied by a series of linked circulation spaces forming an enfilade through the centre. At the heart is a rotunda pierced by a circular lightwell, reminiscent of Lewis Wyatt's arrangement at nearby Tatton Hall. From this rises a white marble staircase, its broad curved steps leading to a lofty half-landing, then dividing to return to a domed circular gallery. Nor is the formality abandoned on the first floor, for a series of doorways and vaulted lobbies radiate from the centre like the spokes of a wheel. Above each bedroom door is a plaster frieze, each one different, one with a peacock, another a cockerel, the contribution of Worthington's Arts and Crafts background. The octagonal lobbies to each side of the rotunda give access to the main reception rooms. To the west is the drawing room, its end walls gently bowed, balanced on the other side by the morning room, with the oak panelled library between. Overlooking the formal garden on the east side is the oval dining room with a curved door surmounted by a frieze of acanthus leaves. In all these rooms materials and craftsmanship are of the highest quality: engraved brass locks supplied by Comyn Ching, fire grates from Lenygon and Morant, white and green marble chimneypieces, and stylish wrought-iron staircase balustrading incorporating the Hardy monogram. The contractor was the Wilmslow firm of L. Brown and Sons.

The finest interior, the music room, lies within one of the wings which flank the forecourt. Below a vaulted ceiling are walls panelled in walnut, and at each end is a screen of fluted Ionic columns. Over the big stone fireplace is a panel framed with high relief carving of fruit and flowers in the Grinling Gibbons style. This carving is an untypical insertion of earlier work in what is otherwise entirely a creation of 20th-century craftsmanship. But Hardy was a discerning collector, and these carefully designed rooms made a splendid setting for his 18th-century furniture and porcelain.

Like most Arts and Crafts architects, Worthington was much concerned with the relationship between a house and its garden. At Radbroke he laid out terraces, a sunken garden, a summerhouse linked to the Hall by high stone walls, and a bicycle shed disguised as a dovecote. But

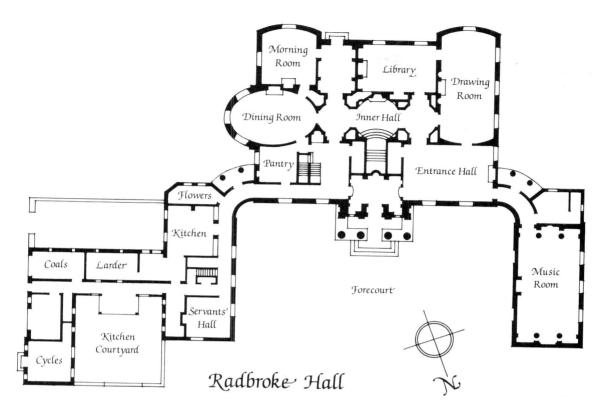

Morning Room

Library

Drawing Room

Dining Room

Inner Hall

Pantry

Entrance Hall

Flowers

Kitchen

Coals

Larder

Music Room

Forecourt

Servants' Hall

Cycles

Kitchen Courtyard

N

Radbroke Hall

the grounds were never planted as intended, for during the 1920s and '30s the house was seldom occupied, Mrs. Hardy spending much time in London. After the Second World War the family returned, but only lived in the house until 1955 when it was sold for offices. Now dominated by office blocks and car parks, the ideal is tarnished but, even before Radbroke was complete, the age of the country house had slipped away.

BN cvii, 16 October 1914; Family collection, Hardy papers.

103. The entrance front of Rode Hall in 1929, showing the earlier block on the right.

104. The garden front, Rode Hall.

RODE HALL, *Scholar Green*

819 573 *House and gardens open to the public. (Privately owned)*

Approaching Rode Hall, the first impression is of two brick houses erected side by side, a low comfortable-looking building of about 1700 with a stables, and a tall dignified block of later date. Both were built by the Wilbraham family which has held the estate for over three hundred years. In 1669 Roger Wilbraham of Townsend House, Nantwich purchased the manor from Randle Rode. There was already a house there, but the Wilbrahams probably did not move to Rode until Roger's son Randle built a new Hall which he recorded in 1708 as recently completed. This, the lower block, has a slate roof and old-fashioned cross windows with leaded panes; but some years later an attempt was made to give it a smarter look by introducing Venetian and circular windows in the wings, a new doorcase and a cupola. At the same time, the stables must have been erected, for they incorporate the same features.

It was Randle Wilbraham II, a noted barrister, who built the second new house in 1752; a portrait by Thomas Hudson shows him with a drawing of the front elevation. As built it was a rectangular structure of two-and-a-half storeys separated from the old house (which became the service wing) by an arcaded courtyard. The entrance was not in its present position, but at the centre of what is now the garden front. On the drawing included in Randle Wilbraham's portrait, the entrance is shown as a Venetian doorway, but it seems that another design was adopted, for an 18th-century estate map shows a vignette of the house with a pedimented porch. (The present portico, a severe Grecian design, was probably added in about 1820.) Also seen in the portrait drawing are stone architraves around the windows, a feature which certainly must have existed from the start, for the string course now stops short of the sides of the first floor openings. On the stylistic evidence of a floor plan surviving at Rode, it has been suggested that the architect was one of the Hiorne brothers of Warwick.

On the death of Randle Wilbraham in 1770, the Hall passed to his son Richard Wilbraham Bootle, who had taken the extra name in accordance with the will of his wife's uncle Sir Thomas Bootle. She was the heiress both to her uncle and to her father, whose estate included Lathom House near Ormskirk, a splendid Palladian mansion by Giacomo Leoni (now demolished). They continued to use Rode and were buried at Astbury Church but, in spite of his greatly increased wealth, Wilbraham Bootle carried out only limited improvements to the house, his major initiative being to commission Humphry Repton to landscape the park. 'The landscape in its present state is not unpleasing considered merely as landscape', wrote Repton in the 'Red Book' he supplied in 1790, 'but it is much more consistent with the view from a cottage or Farm house than from the Portico of a Gentleman's Seat'. But the proposals did not appear to meet with favour, and it was not until about 1805 for Wilbraham Bootle's son Randle Wilbraham III that they were carried out, and then only in a modified form. Randle inherited during the course of a five-year tour of Europe, Russia and the Middle East. On his return he married and began a series of radical changes which were to transform the interior of the house. These changes can be traced from an account book recording payments from 1799 to 1813; included in the first two years are substantial fees paid to the Liverpool architect John Hope. On the outside Hope gave the house a more fashionable Regency look by removing the architraves, increasing the height of the windows, applying stucco, and adding full height semi-circular bows at each end of the original main front. The major change was to re-site the main entrance alongside the old house. In order to produce a symmetrical elevation this required another bow which he added

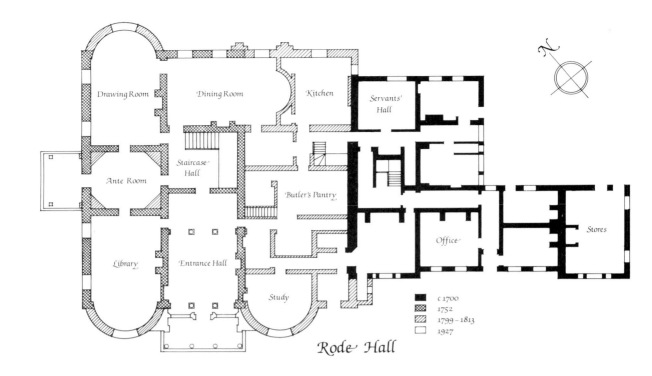

Drawing Room

Dining Room

Kitchen

Servants' Hall

Ante Room

Staircase Hall

Butler's Pantry

Office

Stores

Library

Entrance Hall

Study

Rode Hall

c 1700
1752
1799 – 1813
1927

105. The staircase, Rode Hall.

by extending across the arcaded courtyard between the old and new houses. As the building was considerably enlarged, it allowed the interior to be completely remodelled.

Before looking inside it is necessary to describe some later changes which are responsible for the present appearance of the house. Two of the curved bays had originally three windows per floor, but in the mid-19th century the pairs of outer windows were blocked, perhaps in an attempt to make the house warmer. Late Victorian photographs show the facade still covered with stucco, but refronted by a porte cochère, converted from an earlier conservatory, and called irreverently by the family the 'St Pancras'. This was removed as part of a further series of improvements made in 1927 under the direction of Darcy Braddell, who had been responsible for the restoration of the Wyatt wing at Winnington Hall. He removed all Hope's stucco, exposing the mellow, if somewhat damaged brickwork, and in place of the porte cochère constructed a wide Ionic portico. Since 1980 substantial restoration to both the exterior and interior of the house, currently under the supervision of Graham Holland, has maintained the spirit of Braddell's work, though inside some bold colour schemes have successfully replaced the muted '20s effects.

Braddell's portico leads to a generous entrance hall which had been formed by Hope from the original back stairs and breakfast parlour. In the staircase hall, the only interior remaining from the 1750s, are ceilings enriched with Rococo plasterwork and a fine oak and mahogany staircase. The octagonal anteroom, formerly Randle Wilbraham II's entrance hall, connects the library and drawing room. The library is a comfortable room with light wood bookcases by Gillow following the curves of the bow. A full-length portrait by Alphonse Legros shows Randle IV with a plan of All Saints, Rode, the church which he built in 1864 to the design of George Gilbert Scott. The best portraits, amongst which are works by Reynolds, Opie, Hoppner and Beechey, hang in the drawing room, seen against walls painted a deep pink, with picking out and marbling on cornice and dado. They are mostly of the Bakers who married into the family in the 1870s, and include Sir George Baker, 1st Baronet and doctor to George III.

The dining room by Lewis Wyatt is the most exciting of the early 19th-century interiors. It occupies the major part of the east front and was created out of the former library, enlarged to

106. Mow Cop.

incorporate part of the service court. Wyatt was a replacement for John Hope who died in 1808; the account book records a payment of £26 5s. 0d. made to him in 1810. He was working at Heaton Hall and Tatton where Randle Wilbraham must have been impressed by the forceful design for the entrance hall produced for his nephew Wilbraham Egerton; it is a version of this which was used at Rode. As at Tatton the room is subdivided by screens of Ionic columns with the ceiling forming a shallow vault. At the serving end is an apsidal alcove with a fitted sideboard made for the room by Gillows and supplied in 1813. What is particularly remarkable is the decorative scheme which survives largely in its original colours. These are predominantly black and green. The chimneypiece is of black marble and black too are the skirtings, doors and window shutters. The walls are pale green with the heavy cornice mouldings in grey and ivory, and the bold gilded capitals and bases gleam brilliantly against the dark green shafts of the scagliola columns. It is a cold and sombre effect which is echoed externally by the stark form of the primitive classical doorcase framing the garden door. In this room it is possible to appreciate how splendid the much grander space of the Tatton entrance hall must have looked in its original colouring.

During the 12 years taken to complete these improvements, work was also progressing on remodelling the grounds. Repton's plan may have formed the basis for this scheme, but the execution was entrusted to John Webb. First payments to Webb were made in 1803, but it was not until 1812 that the construction of the large lake was concluded. Family tradition holds that there was later a waterfall painted on canvas so positioned that it appeared from the house as if there was a cascade between the two lakes, and when the family was away it was taken up and stored in the stables. Further improvements to the grounds were made in 1861 by W. A. Nesfield who laid out the terraces and the rose garden, and formed the present drive leading to the west front. A contemporary scheme to dress the house up with heavy Italianate trimmings was fortunately not carried out.

Of the estate buildings, one deserves particular mention. This is a ruined castle built as an eyecatcher for Randle Wilbraham two miles away on the summit of Mow Cop. It is one of the earliest sham ruins in the country, dating from about 1754, and is conceivably the work of the Hiornes who later designed Gothick garden buildings at Gopsall Park, Leicestersire. Used by the Wilbraham family for picnics, its principal renown was as a rallying ground for religious non-conformism, and as the birthplace in 1812 of Primitive Methodism. For Randle Wilbraham IV who built the strictly Ecclesiological church of All Saints at Rode, the thought of this must have somewhat spoiled the view.

O iii, 53; T i, 129; *AR* lxvi, 61; *Ches Life* October 1937, January/February 1949; Robinson, 248; *CL* clxxvii, 1186; CRO DBW/L/1-4 and Rode Hall, Baker Wilbraham papers.

VIII.   The dining room, Rode Hall.

IX.   The Gallery, Tabley House.

X. The terrace, Tirley Garth.

SAIGHTON GRANGE, *Saighton*

443 618

Saighton Grange was the principal country house of the Abbots of Chester. Before the Conquest the manor of Saighton was held by the secular canons of St Werburgh, Chester, but in 1092 Hugh Lupus, Earl of Chester, transformed their church into the Benedictine Abbey of St Werburgh, and Saighton became part of the abbey holdings. Licences to crenellate were granted in 1272 and 1399, but the only part of the medieval building which remains today was built later. This is the gatehouse erected by Abbot Simon Ripley about 1490. Ripley was an energetic builder who brought new impetus to the works at the abbey church, completing the reconstruction of the south transept and the central tower. At Saighton his badge, a wolf's head, is carved at the base of the oriel window.

Upon the Dissolution the abbey became Chester Cathedral and the abbey lands were divided. The manor of Saighton passed through many hands before it was purchased in the 1840s by the Grosvenors, owners of the huge neighbouring Eaton estate. The 2nd Marquess of Westminster was at this time modernising Eaton Hall, employing William Burn to overcome some of its considerable practical problems. To improve Saighton, which was to be used by the Earl Grosvenor, heir to Eaton, the Marquess chose Edward Hodkinson, a local architect who had designed some cottages on the estate. Apart from the medieval gatehouse, all was rebuilt. Two 17th-century flanking wings recorded in an engraving in Ormerod, one with the remains of a garderobe, were demolished, and the gatehouse became the porch to an entirely Victorian house. The west wing was begun in 1861, the service wing in 1867 and the east wing in 1876. In the meantime the 3rd Marquess had commissioned Alfred Waterhouse, one of the most progressive architects of his day, to remodel his seat; the mechanical and unscholarly Tudor of Saighton must have looked completely outmoded in comparison.

107. The gatehouse at Saighton Grange.

The great feature of Saighton Grange is the gatehouse, a rare example in Cheshire of medieval secular stone architecture. By the end of the 15th century a heavy crenellated tower was no longer a defensive necessity, and the outline of the gatehouse is as much a picturesque as a practical device. High in a merlon of the battlements is a canopied figure of the Virgin, and below is a small decorative oriel window.

An appearance of strength comes from the way the walls are jettied out over massive angle corbels resting on flanking buttresses. The tall arched gateway now leads to the front door of the Victorian house. What this door reveals comes as something of a shock. Instead of a Tudor-style hall with heavy oak panelling and stone fireplace, the visitor enters an airy galleried room in the Regency style. To the left are two big Ionic doorcases with fluted half-columns, and directly ahead is an elegant semi-circular staircase illuminated by a shallow domed lantern. Closer examination of the staircase reveals that it is constructed of reinforced concrete, and indeed this whole classical interior dates only from 1957. The doorcase and the mahogany doors to the library, brought from Dauntsey Park near Chippenham, are the only genuine Neo-classical features. This transformation was carried out for the 4th Duke of Westminster who used Saighton Grange as his seat after Eaton Hall was abandoned. The architect was John Dennys, the 5th Duke's brother-in-law, who was later to design the present Eaton Hall. Though the creation of a grand entrance hall was an ambitious concept, the shallowness of its classical detail does not bear close scrutiny. This weakness was less apparent when the house was richly furnished with the Grosvenor treasures, but in its present sparse condition the eye focuses too much on the architecture. The most appealing rooms are those within the medieval gatehouse. The first contains the little oriel window, and above is a tower room with a painted beam bearing the motto *Tu ne cede malis sed contra audentior ito*. This Victorian sentiment, 'Do not give way to difficulties but rather strive on boldly', forms the motto of the school which now uses the house.

Saighton has an exceptionally fine garden, laid out at the end of the 19th century. This is planned as a series of formal spaces enclosed by hedging and walls with many contrasting styles of planting. On the south side is a symmetrical pattern of high yew hedges forming terraces, with a view dramatically framed by two tall Lombardy poplars. The west garden, much modified in the 1950s by Sally, widow of the 4th Duke, is more picturesque and incorporates curving paths, a lily pond and varied shrub borders. These gardens, beautifully maintained by the present tenant, Abbey Gate College, and still in the hands of the Duchess's gardener, are often open to view.

O ii, 770; *CL* xxiii, 738; *Ches Life* May/June 1958; C. Platt, *The Monastic Grange in Medieval Times* 1969, 228.

TABLEY HOUSE, *Tabley Inferior*

726 778

Tabley House, a handsome Palladian mansion, was designed in 1761 for Sir Peter Leicester by John Carr of York. The family moved there from the Old Hall, built around 1380 on an island in Nether Tabley Mere; next to it was a chapel, a gatehouse and a bridge. The chapel remained in use for family worship and the Hall was kept furnished long after the building of the new house higher up. Suddenly, one day in 1927, parts of the old building collapsed from subsidence caused by nearby brine pumping. The chapel was taken down and rebuilt close to the new house but the Old Hall was abandoned and is now a ruin. Before its collapse, it was recorded in photographs which show a Great Hall with an immense central arch formed of two massive cruck beams, each carved in crude imitation of Gothic shafted stonework. This was built by John de Leycester. In the 16th century Adam de Leycester made alterations and built the half-timbered gatehouse to the bridge across the mere, and in 1619 Peter Leycester installed a chimneypiece in the Great Hall. Crudely and stiffly carved in wood, it has painted and gilded figures of Cleopatra and Lucretia, and an emblematic female nude lying on a skull and holding a winged hourglass. The chimneypiece was rescued and is now in the Old Hall Room which links the new house with the rebuilt chapel.

Leycester's son, the scholarly Sir Peter Leycester, was the author of two celebrated volumes of *Historical Antiquities*, the first on Great Britain and Ireland, and the second on Cheshire and the Bucklow Hundred. Published in 1673 it is the earliest serious history of the area based on original documents. Sir Peter, a Royalist, had to leave Tabley in 1642, was fined and later arrested. Allowed to return, he devoted himself to his studies and in 1660 was rewarded for his loyalty with a baronetcy. In 1671 he enlarged the Hall, introducing a staircase and an upper floor. The outside was encased in brick in an old-fashioned Jacobean style with an imposing porch with lion statues. The combination of mullioned and circular windows resembles the slightly earlier Astley Hall, in north Lancashire. The chapel was rebuilt on the island in an odd mixture of Gothic and Jacobean. Sir Peter recorded that it was begun in 1674 by the master mason John Birchenough of Over Alderley and that the joiner, Ephraim Brodhurst of Knutsford, 'took his pattern from Brasen-Nose-College-Chapel in Oxford', Sir Peter's old college. As in any Oxford college chapel, the seats face inward, but the resemblance to Brasenose, completed as recently as 1666, is not otherwise marked. The tall octagonal pulpit of 1677 was made by John Brodrick as Brodhurst died before the chapel was ready. The tower was added in 1724.

Sir Peter Byrne inherited Tabley in 1742 through his mother and took the name Leicester by Act of Parliament in 1744. One of the conditions of his inheritance was a requirement to keep the Old Hall in good repair, which accounts for its long survival. But Sir Peter Byrne Leicester found it 'old and not commodious', and so employed John Carr of York to build a new house, begun in 1761 and completed by about 1769. The result is the only example in Cheshire of an 18th-century Palladian country house, and was published in *Vitruvius Britannicus* under the name Oaklands. By the 1760s Palladianism was on the wane in England, but Carr was a conservative architect working in the north. Tabley shows no signs of the Adam style which Carr was to adopt in his later works. For Sir Peter, he employed a characteristic Palladian form, a rectangular block consisting of a rusticated basement, piano nobile and attic with a projecting portico, pediment and staircase on the south front, and at the sides low pavilions attached by curved brick corridors. The canted bay on the side elevations is a motif from Kirby, Yorkshire where the young Carr had been clerk of works to Lord Burlington and Roger Morris.

108. The Great Hall, Tabley Old Hall, 1923.

109. The 17th-century front of Tabley Old Hall c.1860, with Lord de Tabley and his sisters.

110. The south front of Tabley House, 1923.

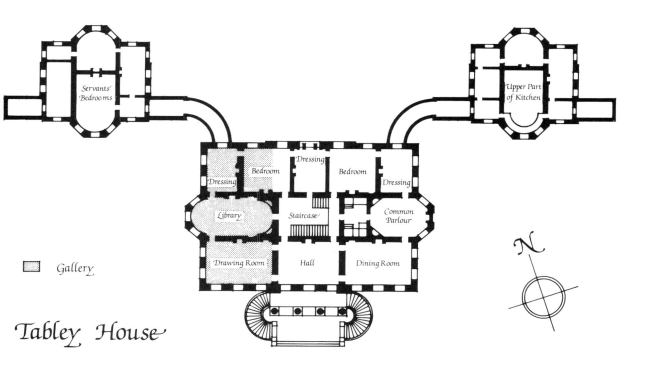

Servants' Bedrooms

Upper Part of Kitchen

Dressing

Bedroom

Dressing

Bedroom

Dressing

Library

Staircase

Common Parlour

Drawing Room

Hall

Dining Room

Gallery

N

Tabley House

Tabley is only nine bays wide, three rooms across and three rooms deep with a central staircase hall. Unlike the strung out compositions of some Palladian houses, it forms a tall compact block which looks detached from its side pavilions. This aligns it with the smaller Palladian villas pioneered at Stourhead and Chiswick in the 1720s and taken up again the 1750s by architects such as Robert Taylor and Isaac Ware. Two further features emphasise its starkness: the startlingly pink brick of its main floors which make it stand out against the landscape, and the unusual gravity of its portico which employs not the Ionic or Corinthian order, common in country houses, but the Tuscan.

111. The staircase at Tabley House, 1923.

Throughout Carr's interiors, the craftsmanship is of extremely high quality. The plasterwork by Thomas Oliver of Warrington includes the entrance hall, with delicate oval classical reliefs over the doors and fireplace; the octagonal common parlour where the ceiling is charmingly adorned with a hayrake, a pitchfork and a shepherd's crook; and the luxuriantly realistic roses and peonies on the dining room ceiling. The beautiful woodcarving of the doorcases and stair was by Mathew Bertram assisted by Daniel Shillito, a favourite carver of Carr's. The cantilevered steps with slender mahogany balusters ascend to a landing with a double screen of columns. Above is a vaulted attic lit by lunette windows; the effect is exceptionally graceful. It is a pity that the stair has recently had to be held up by ugly props as it was intended to be without visible means of support. Sir Peter was also responsible for commissioning full-length portraits of himself and his wife from Francis Cotes, a set of views recording the old and new Halls, and a limpid prospect by Richard Wilson in which the house is seen in the distance from the lake, where a couple are idly fishing.

Sir Peter's pictures were exactly what might be expected in such a country house. But his successor, Sir John Fleming Leicester, later 1st Lord de Tabley, formed a much more deliberate and original collection and carried out alterations at Tabley to accommodate it. He succeeded in 1770. In 1785-6 he went on the Grand Tour to Italy but, unusually, brought back no pictures nor marbles; he decided instead to collect modern British art. In 1806 he bought a house at Hill Street, Berkeley Square in London and formed a gallery there which became a mecca for artists and connoisseurs and was later opened to the public. Here hung pictures by Lawrence, including one of the beautiful Lady Leicester as 'Hope', and works by Fuseli, Martin, Romney and West. Turner was one of the many artists who visited Tabley; among the group of Turners owned by Leicester were a pair showing Tabley lake and tower on calm and stormy days (one at Petworth, the other still at Tabley). James Ward also painted the same scene (in the Tate). In 1823 Leicester offered the collection to Lord Liverpool as the nucleus of a National Gallery, but the offer was declined. Immediately after Leicester's death in 1827, Christie's held an auction in Hill Street and many of the best pictures were sold. The remaining works were removed to Tabley and most of them are still there.

They hang in the gallery which Leicester formed out of the rooms on the west side of the main floor; it is now one of the great rooms of Cheshire. Thomas Harrison was recorded as working at Tabley around 1810, perhaps in connection with this gallery but the extent of his work is not clear. The gallery is one long tripartite space with the canted bay window in the centre. The decoration is in the fashionable Thomas Hope taste, the doors stylishly embellished with stars and Grecian geometrical divisions, and the ceilings painted with a view of the sky seen through diagonal bars as if part of an open atrium. The chains from which the pictures hang issue from gilded lion masks placed beneath the frieze, the same method of picture-hanging used at Hill Street. There is some evidence of changes. After a fire in the east pavilion in 1819 George Moneypenny, who had just completed the Sessions House at Knutsford, carried out restoration work probably from designs by Lord de Tabley himself; Moneypenny may also have altered the Gallery, for the low bookcases with Medusa heads do not appear in Buckler's earlier watercolour of the room, and the plaster friezes over the arches were originally simpler. When Leicester became Baron de Tabley in 1826 they were altered to include peer's coronets, but he died before the work was finished and the plaster was left ungilded. The richly-coloured pictures, their wide neo-Rococo gilt frames and the deep crimson flock wallpaper give this interior a heavy sumptuousness redolent of Regency taste. It is more luxurious and architecturally more satisfying than the better known but spartan-looking gallery formed by Lord Egremont at Petworth to house a comparable collection of British art.

After Lord de Tabley's death further reorganisation took place. In 1828 the entrance arrangements were reversed by Robert Curzon, a young amateur architect and family friend, later author of *Visits to Monasteries in the Levant*. He made a new entrance on the north front, thus transforming the whole sense of the plan. The portico became redundant except as a garden entrance and the visitor, instead of approaching the house as a splendidly isolated high block, arrives through stucco entrance arches into a broad enclosed court. On the north face of the house, clumsy stucco rustication was added around the central Venetian window, spoiling the staccato quality of Carr's design. The new entrance, now through a small porch added in 1915, passes via a basement lobby up an internal staircase to a new entrance hall on the first floor, faced with marbled white stucco and adorned with classical casts. A new dining room was made in the north-east corner. These alterations were for the 2nd Lord de Tabley but it was the 3rd Baron who continued the literary interests of his 17th-century ancestor. 'He is Faunus, he is a woodland creature', wrote his friend Tennyson. He published poetry, works on Greek coinage, bookplates and the *Flora of Cheshire*. Tabley remained in private hands until 1975 when on the death of Lt.-Col. John Leicester-Warren it passed to the University of Manchester. Its future use is uncertain.

J. Woolfe and J. Gandon, *Vitruvius Britannicus*, v 1771, 16-19; Lysons, 532; O i, 623; Ackermann's *Repository*, 3rd ser. ii 1823, 2; W. Carey, *Some Memoirs of the Patronage and Progress of the Fine Arts . . .*, 1826, 22; T ii, 40; Douglas ii, 25; *CL* liv, 50, 84, 114, lxii, 997; C. Hussey, *English Country Houses, Mid Georgian*, 1956, 55; Mercer no. 32.

See also plate IX, facing page 158.

TATTON PARK, Knutsford

735 816 *House, Gardens and park open to the public. (National Trust/Cheshire County Council)*

112.   Roof structure of the Great Hall, Tatton Old Hall.

Tatton Park, the product of an association between three generations of Egertons and two of Wyatts, exemplifies the continuity of the Wyatt style between different members of the dynasty. But it was an important seat long before the Wyatts came on the scene. The Old Hall, which survived the 18th-century landscaping of the park, dates from the late 15th century. It is one of the buildings associated with Sir William Stanley, described as 'the richest commoner in England'. He rebuilt Holt Castle, on the Welsh border, and Ridley Hall: his wealth also financed a house for his son-in-law at Sutton Weaver, and Tatton Old Hall for his son William. Both houses have timber roofs, at Tatton less elaborate than at Sutton, though still impressive.

166

It has quatrefoil windbracing, two big cambered tie beams and decorated wall plates. The walls were rebuilt in brick in the 17th century. At the lower end of the hall is a modern gallery connecting with the two-storey cross wing of the late 16th century. This has been furnished partly in 17th-century style and partly as an Edwardian keeper's cottage, so that visitors can understand its changing uses.

It is not clear when the family forsook the Old Hall to live in a new house. There may have been an Elizabethan Hall on the site of the present mansion, but when Tatton was inherited by Sir Thomas Egerton, Privy Counsellor to Elizabeth I and Lord Chancellor for James I, he did not live there, nor did his descendants, the Earls and Dukes of Bridgewater. The Egertons of Tatton were a junior branch of this family. Their first recorded house was built for John Egerton, great-great-grandson of the Chancellor. Complete by 1716, it was a typical conservative Restoration-style house with quoins, a hipped roof and a one-bay pedimented frontispiece. The long straight avenue of trees leading from Knutsford which, like the Old Hall, survived the improvers, may be of this date. The contractor for 'stone-work, Lead-work and Ironwork' on John Egerton's house was John Barker, who probably acted as both builder and architect. He had already worked in this capacity for Richard Hill at Hawkstone, where John Egerton's brother-in-law Samuel Hill had supervised the work.

Samuel Hill was of great importance in the history of Tatton. He had no children so that on his death in 1758 his considerable fortune came through his sister to her son Samuel Egerton. At first Egerton planned to build flanking wings, but only that on the west was built, about 1760, containing a dining room lit by a canted bay window. This room has survived; designed by Thomas Farnolls Pritchard of Shrewsbury, its richly scrolled and garlanded plasterwork and vine frieze make the room stand out from the more chaste Wyatt interiors. A Pritchard sketchbook in Washington contains chimneypiece designs for Samuel Egerton, but the dining room now has a Westmacott fireplace of 1840. Not long after the addition of a dining room another improvement was contemplated, a scheme of 1768 by William Emes for landscaping the park, remodelling the lake and erecting various garden buildings including a banqueting room and covered seat at Old Tatton. The main house is shown on this plan as a large building on three sides of a courtyard.

Nothing further was done until 1774 when Samuel Wyatt drew up a plan to enlarge the house with a giant colonnade on the south front and a huge oval library on the south-east. Though not executed, this commission marked the start of the long connection between the Egertons and the Wyatts. In 1774 Samuel Wyatt was still overshadowed by his younger and more famous brother James, and Samuel had yet to design a major house (he had supervised the building of Heaton House, Lancashire, designed in 1772 by James for Sir Thomas Egerton, a distant kinsman of the Egertons of Tatton). It is not known why Samuel's 1774 scheme was not carried out; but in 1781, one year after inheriting the estate, Samuel Egerton's nephew William went back to the same architect, now with a great many houses to his name in Cheshire and elsewhere. Work did not start until 1789. The design finally chosen had a Corinthian portico facing the garden, just as was finally executed. The portico was intended to be in the centre of an ambitious front no less than 11 bays wide with a family wing to one side. On the central axis there was to be a hall and a saloon, with twin staircases on each side, as at Doddington. Only the western part was built; Wyatt removed the canted bay from Pritchard's dining room and replaced it with a tripartite window. Behind he built the present card room on the entrance side (originally William Egerton's study) and farther west added the low family wing. Eastwards he built three more bays including one of the staircases, its ceiling very similar to that at Heaton. But progress stopped short of the intended central hall and saloon. The extent of the work was recorded by Repton in the 'Red Book' commissioned by William Egerton in 1791. Samuel Wyatt's full design is envisaged in Repton's 'after' proposal but the 'before' view shows a house half Wyatt and half Barker.

113. The south front, Tatton Park.

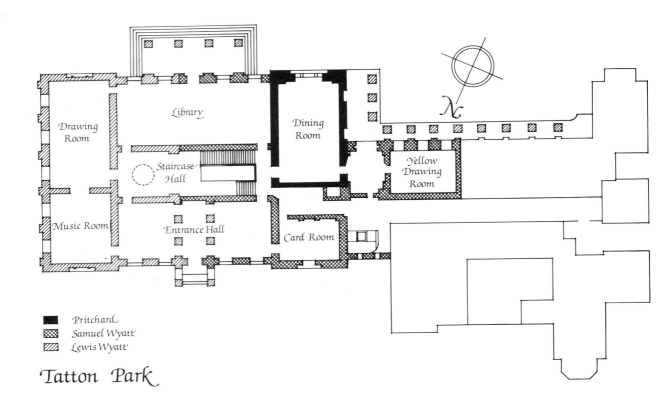

Drawing Room

Library

Dining Room

Staircase Hall

Yellow Drawing Room

Music Room

Entrance Hall

Card Room

N

Pritchard
Samuel Wyatt
Lewis Wyatt

Tatton Park

So it remained until 1806 when Samuel Wyatt supplied a revised plan to complete the house on a reduced scale. But William Egerton died in April 1806 and 10 months later came the death of Samuel Wyatt. However, William's successor Wilbraham Egerton began the last phase of the work by seeking designs from Samuel's nephews the architects Jeffry (later Wyattville) and Lewis, eventually adopting Lewis Wyatt's condensed version of his uncle's scheme. Samuel's three-bay portico was retained, now placed in front of a seven-bay instead of an eleven-bay front of smooth ashlar, with a tripartite window at the east end repeating the existing one at the west. As the western part had already been started, there was no room for the central hall and saloon or the second staircase. Samuel's existing staircase hall, cleverly extended by means of a domed ante-room, became the centre of the house and instead of a north-south progression of hall and saloon, the staterooms formed a circuit around the staircase and its extension. These two rooms, at the heart of the house, became a dynamic and theatrical space. The ante-room is lit by a shallow open saucer dome with a skylight above, an effect reminiscent of Soane. From the first floor around the well of the dome a perspective of receding arches opens up views of Samuel's earlier staircase landing, whilst a dramatic light is cast from above. The landing is now used to display the set of portraits of the Cheshire gentlemen formerly at Ashley Hall.

Though on the exterior Lewis followed the bland, understated style of his uncle, the interiors were his own. The collection of working drawings kept at the house shows his care over the tiniest details of fireplaces, cornices, carpets and furnishings, and his sophistication as a designer, breathing new life into the Grecian style. The entrance hall, antique in character, has a shallow coffered barrel vault bisected by twin screens of porphyry scagliola columns. On the trabeations above the columns and fitting neatly under the vault sit pairs of gryphons facing urns. The black marble fireplaces with panther's heads are particularly stylish, but unfortunately the present ice-cream colour scheme works against the intended gravity of marble, porphyry and stone. The music room and the drawing room en suite along the west front form a luxurious contrast with the entrance hall. The sumptuous red of the silk wall hangings, the carpet and the upholstery unite the two rooms, though their personalities are differentiated by their contents, the music room with rosewood and Boulle-work furniture by Gillow, the drawing room more full blown with bulgy gilded neo-Rococo sofas and chairs. In the drawing room hangs Nazzari's portrait of Samuel Egerton at Venice, as well as two Venetian views by Canaletto purchased there by Samuel Hill.

In all the rebuilding projects the library was a large room, for it had to house the notable book collection of Chancellor Egerton, much expanded in the 18th century in line with the cultured tastes of the family. Lewis Wyatt stretched the library out along the garden front like a Long Gallery, filling it with informally-grouped Gillow chairs and tables and lining the walls with bookcases, fronted by attractive brass grilles of intersecting curved design. But the comfortable simplicity of the scheme has been spoiled by the later introduction of a heavy neo-Palladian ceiling, matching overmantel mirrors and a highly-coloured carpet.

The park and gardens at Tatton are unusually full of interesting features. Lodges were provided by Lewis Wyatt and James Hakewill, and Wyatt also designed the flower garden and the orangery (1818). Though Repton's plans for the park were not carried out, John Webb made improvements around 1816-18. In the gardens the architect William Cole put up the temple inspired by the ancient Greek Choragic Monument of Lysicrates (1820). A more formal terraced layout of the gardens south of the house was introduced by Joseph Paxton for William Egerton, who succeeded in 1856 and three years later became 1st Baron Egerton. Paxton also built the fernery, and his son-in-law G. H. Stokes added a second storey to the family wing in 1860, somewhat unbalancing its relationship with the main house. The gardens have been considerably enlarged in this century. The delightful Japanese garden was created by Japanese workmen in 1909 for the 3rd Lord Egerton, and the 4th Lord Egerton also initiated much planting including rhododendrons, hydrangeas and azaleas.

114. The arched gallery above the ante-room to the staircase hall, Tatton Park.

115. The entrance hall, Tatton Park.

116. The drawing room, Tatton Park.

West of the entrance front, sober yellow brick Renaissance-style additions were designed in 1884 by the 2nd Baron (later 1st Earl). They include a smoking room, a chapel, later used as a cinema, a family entrance and the oak staircase removed from Hough End Hall, a half-timbered house near Manchester. B. W. Leader's oil painting of the Manchester Ship Canal commemorates Lord Egerton's role as chairman of the Ship Canal Company. A final addition was the cavernous Tenants' Hall of 1935 erected for the 4th Lord Egerton because the previous hall was too small for his immense private museum of game heads, vehicles and curios. Tatton survived in private ownership until 1958 and is now maintained jointly by the National Trust and Cheshire County Council. Its exceptional combination of old and new Halls, original pictures and furnishings, estate buildings, gardens and park make it the most complete surviving example of a great country estate in Cheshire.

O i, 444; T ii, 32; Torrington ii, 177; J. D. Mackie, *The Early Tudors*, 1962, 122; *CL* cxxxv, 16, 23, 30, clix, 884; Mercer no. 34; *Tatton Park* guidebook 1978.

THORNTON MANOR, *Thornton Hough*

300 818

There could be no-one more representative of the Victorian middle-class ideals of self-help, entrepreneurship and civic consciousness than William Hesketh Lever, 1st Viscount Leverhulme. Born in 1851, the son of a grocer, he devoted his life to the creation of wealth, and through that wealth to the education and welfare of ordinary people. The results of his benevolent despotism are seen most clearly in his works village, Port Sunlight, but three miles away at Thornton Hough is his own house, and here also is evidence of the singular character of this extraordinary man.

117. The entrance front, Thornton Manor: centre by Douglas & Fordham 1896, music room on the right by Talbot 1902, and wing on the left by Lomax Simpson 1912-14.

Lever had a passion for building. In an address to the Architectural Association in 1902 he stated that he had always wished he had been an architect. After his marriage in 1874, he lived in a succession of 13 different houses, and his son recalls that they 'seldom experienced the sensation of living for very long in a house free from the presence of workmen'. Thornton Manor, an unremarkable Victorian Gothic villa which he acquired in 1888 was the subject of a building campaign which lasted for 25 years. The work started in earnest in 1896 with the demolition of the old house and the erection in its place of a fairly modest Jacobean-style villa with three Flemish gables and large stone mullioned bay windows. It was designed by Douglas and Fordham who were already engaged at Port Sunlight. Little of this now survives other than a section of the present entrance front, for it was not long before Lever was wanting substantial improvements. First, in 1899 came the addition of stables. These were designed by J. J. Talbot, like Lever a native of Bolton, but their location (Lever's decision) too close to the kitchens was probably the reason for their later conversion to an outdoor dining room. Three years later Talbot added the music room, set at an angle on the road side of the house. This room, the great feature of Thornton Manor, is Talbot's major work, for he died aged 31 in 1902 before its completion. In 1904 followed the service quarters and 'temporary' ballroom, for which the architects were Grayson and Ould, the first of a series of ballrooms built by Lever at all his main houses. Then in 1906 a radical restructuring of the earlier parts began. Photographs of the Douglas and Fordham house show that it was entered from what is now the garden front, and the drive came all the way round. By taking a new approach directly from the road it was possible to form a garden front from the old entrance side and eliminate a length of drive. So a new porch was formed, perhaps by moving the original one, for it is dated both 1896 and 1906. However this brought the entrance extremely close to the road and, to provide privacy, in 1910 a gatehouse was built. By this time James Lomax-Simpson, son of Lever's old school friend Jonathan Simpson, had become the Lever Brothers company architect, and all subsequent work at Thornton Manor was entrusted to him. For the design of the gatehouse Lomax-Simpson departed from all that had been done before and, perhaps influenced by his former master Edward Ould, produced a striking half-timbered building. This was based on the gatehouse at Stokesay Castle which had been illustrated by Hermann Muthesius in *Das Englische Haus* published in 1904. Since Port Sunlight was also featured in this book, it is likely that Lever would have seen a copy. As built, the gatehouse is stylistically unrelated to the main house, but this would not have been the case if a scheme dated 1913 for two large timber-framed wings enclosing the entrance forecourt had been erected. But much more was to happen in the meanwhile.

Lever had for some time been planning greatly to enlarge the house. The garden designer T. H. Mawson, who was engaged at Thornton Manor from 1905, claimed that the extent of the gardens persuaded Lever that the house was too small. Whether or not this was the case, there is a drawing dated 1908 by E. P. Mawson, architect son of the garden designer, for a new garden front. Although this scheme was not carried out, it is remarkably similar to the new front which was built by Lomax-Simpson in 1912-14. Shortly before his death Lomax-Simpson denied having seen the Mawson drawing, which suggests that he was closely directed by Lever himself. The new garden front completely changed the balance of the house. The old Douglas and Fordham elevation was obliterated, and in its place was built a large symmetrical E-plan front in free Jacobean style. More chaste and polished than all the previous work, it provided a new sense of cohesion to the collection of buildings it adjoined.

Most of the interiors date also from this ambitious remodelling. If, in spite of the regular garden front, the exterior seems something of a jumble, the interior is purposely eclectic. As with all Lever's houses, Thornton Manor was primarily a museum, a place to house his ever expanding collections of paintings, furniture and porcelain. He believed in an historical approach to interiors, with the style of each room suiting the objects with which it was furnished. As he wrote to Mawson in 1910, 'I feel that in the course of centuries we have gradually gained experience in the type of architecture suitable for each room. For instance, I prefer Georgian dining rooms as the rooms in which to give large dinners; for small dining rooms I prefer Tudor. For drawing rooms I prefer what is called the Adams style; for entrance halls the Georgian.

118. The garden front and gatehouse, Thornton Manor, by Lomax Simpson.

For a large room such as a music room, I prefer the period which I should call the Inigo Jones type of the Renaissance'. This approach would have been anathema to progressive designers following the Arts and Crafts tradition, but for many Edwardian interior decorators it was standard practice. At Thornton Manor there are two halls. The outer hall survives from the Douglas and Fordham house and has a rather too fiddly Adamesque ceiling. The inner hall, which was created by the addition of the new garden front, is similar in style but the detail is more correctly Georgian. Lever's intense national pride led him to collect largely English decorative arts, but between the two halls he included a French drawing room as a setting for his Boulle and Empire furniture. The walls are lined with unpolished *boiseries*, inlaid and finely carved with trophies and musical instruments. In the two wings of the garden front are the library and Adams Room. The library is Jacobean and has a plaster ceiling modelled on that of the state room in the Old Palace at Bromley-by-Bow, but with the texture of icing sugar. It is furnished more like a sitting room, with no books in evidence, but they do exist, stored in narrow book-stacks to each side of the doorway. The spacious Adams Room is in Lever's preferred style for drawing rooms, with the Adam device of a carpet echoing the design of the ceiling above. By contrast the early Georgian-style dining room is dark, sombre and formal. Heavily carved unpolished walnut panelling frames tapestries of Rococo subjects after designs by Teniers.

174

119. The French drawing room, Thornton Manor.

120. The music room at Thornton Manor, 1903.

The most interesting bedroom is Lever's own. All his life he slept in the open air, and at Thornton Manor he had a platform for his bed and a marble bath constructed in the angle of two roof slopes sheltered only by a glass canopy. In winter he was known to have awoken in the morning with a sprinkling of snow on the counterpane. The rooms on the entrance and garden fronts were all formed by the remodelling of the house in 1912-14. The most spectacular interior however is earlier. This is J. J. Talbot's music room which lies at the other end of the house. From the exterior this was expressed as a two-storey building to match the Douglas and Forham house. On the inside it is a single space and the upper level windows illuminate a wide glazed tunnel vault, leaving the walls free for the display of large paintings. The room was closely modelled on Norman Shaw's picture gallery built nearby at Dawpool for the shipowner T. H. Ismay in 1882-6, and it seems likely on the basis of this that Lever knew exactly what he wanted. The main difference from Dawpool is the position of the chimneypiece. At Thornton Manor this is on the side wall rather than at the end but, with its great marble organ gallery, it provides the same gargantuan focus. Reporting on a staff party in 1908, Lever Bros. magazine *Progress* commented, 'The new music room ... is indeed a magnificent apartment ... the beautifully panelled room, with its lofty ceiling, its carpet as soft as velvet, its commanding gallery, beneath which is a "cosy corner" ... the artistic masterpieces which grace the walls, the rare and antique china and choice bric-à-brac, the superb furniture – everything betokened comfort, beauty and happiness'. Contemporary photographs by Bedford Lemere show the room filled with furniture arranged in conversation groups and the walls flanked by commodes supporting rows of oriental pots. But in spite of the grandeur of its design and the brilliance of its contents, the room seemed even then oddly forbidding. Partly the deadening effect of top lighting, and partly the museum-like character of its displays, this impression must also reflect the nature of its restless patron. For the energy and self discipline of Lever's régime did not permit contemplation or idle pleasure.

In a letter to Mawson, Lever wrote, 'I am afraid I do not want a garden so much for rest as for promenades and walks. I have tried sitting down in the retreats and garden shelters, but I cannot rest in them 2 minutes, but on the contrary, I can walk about for a couple of hours at a time along the long stretch of walk I have made in the centre. One central feature is easily carried in mind and easily walked round, but a number of them, and a number of breaks and levels, I find irritating and annoying. This desire on my part to arrange promenades will explain a good deal of the planning I have done at Thornton'. Indeed much of the garden planning was done by Lever who only employed Mawson from 1905. Mawson admired his client's outlook, and their collaboration in the design of the gardens at Thornton as well as at Rivington and The Hill, Hampstead, two other houses, was a great source of satisfaction to Lever. The layout at Thornton is based around 'one central feature', a long straight path which runs from the house past a number of different elements: a pleached lime avenue, a rose pergola supported on reinforced concrete columns, a loggia, a clipped yew hedge, until it reaches the rose garden with its complex arrangement of circular beds connected by paths and steps. Beyond lie woodland walks and a 20-acre ornamental lake. Like the house which was used regularly for Lever Bros. staff parties and management dinners, the grounds were opened for garden parties and summer picnics for the children of the Port Sunlight workers.

Lever's philanthropy directed all his interests. He believed strongly in the enjoyment of beautiful things, and thought art should be available to everyone. So he established a number of museums during his life, and the greatest of these is the Lady Lever Art Gallery at Port Sunlight. Begun in 1914 as a memorial to his wife, this was to accommodate much of his huge collection, including a large part of the contents of Thornton Manor. Without the highlights provided by the great paintings and furniture, some of the rooms at Thornton Manor now seem unfriendly and contrived, and it is difficult to judge the architectural success of the house. In the gloomy shadows of the dining room or the chill light of the music room one is reminded of those pictures by Orchardson of unspoken domestic strife and empty solitude. Such morbid preoccupation however was never a feature of Lever's eventful life. In spite of the failure of some of his later business ventures, the collecting continued right up to his death in 1925 and, if the building now occupied by his grandson the 3rd Viscount is no longer a treasure house, its original contents can be more widely admired in the public gallery three miles away at Port Sunlight.

Studio xlviii, 140; T. H. Mawson, *The Art and Craft of Garden Marking*, 1926, 36, 48; T. H. Mawson, *The Life and Work of an English Landscape Architect*, 1927, 116, 208; Viscount Leverhulme, *Viscount Leverhulme*, 1927, 100, 290; *Ches Life* August/September 1950; *Country Heritage* 94; N. Cooper, *The Opulent Eye*, 1976, 201; Royal Academy, *Lord Leverhulme* 1980, 182; *CL* clxxii, 18, 110, clxxviii, 602; RIBA, Lomax-Simpson drawings.

TILSTONE LODGE, *Tilstone Fearnall*

568 612

Described by Webb around 1623 as 'the lofty pile of that sweet and delicate seat', Tilstone Hall was built around 1600 by Thomas Wilbraham of Woodhey. Now only a crumbling ruined gatehouse remains, standing neglected up a lane to a farm; on one face is an arched entrance and a pedimented mullioned window and on the other are fluted columns, recalling those at the family's other seat of Woodhey, nearby. Tilstone Hall was damaged during the Civil War and abandoned in favour of Woodhey, which was rebuilt around 1690 by Lady Elizabeth Wilbraham. The Cheshire estates passed to her daughter Grace, wife of Lionel Tollemache, 2nd Earl of Dysart. Helmingham in Suffolk was their principal seat and their grandson brought Ham House, Surrey into the family. Neither Woodhey nor Tilstone can have been of much interest in comparison, so although the estates were still farmed, the houses were not maintained. They were demolished in the 1730s and '40s.

121.   Tilstone Lodge from the south-west.

In 1821 a new house was begun at Tilstone Fearnall near a pool on the heath about one-third of a mile from the site of the old Hall. Earlier that year the 6th Earl of Dysart had died childless and his estates had been divided. Ham House and the earldom went to his elder sister Louisa, but the Suffolk and Cheshire estates passed through the younger sister Jane, wife of

178

Captain John Delap Halliday, to their son Admiral John Richard Delap Halliday. He had pursued a distinguished naval career, owned a house in London next door to Apsley House, and another house in Brighton. The Delap side had brought a profitable estate in Antigua. But as soon as he succeeded to the Cheshire estates he decided to build there, changing his surname to Tollemache. 'I intend the house for an occasional Residence to receive my tenants and for shooting and hunting', he wrote in December 1822 when the house was under construction. His predecessor, the 6th Earl of Dysart, had rented Calveley from the Bromleys for his occasional visits to Cheshire. But this was not enough for the Admiral, who perhaps felt that the estates would benefit from greater personal attention.

Despite his apparent wealth, the Admiral was at pains not to spend too much money on his new house, insisting to his agent in December 1822 'that the work may be very well done, but plain, strong and economically'. He had been tempted to build a larger house to accommodate his family of 12 children and in 1825, when the house was nearing completion, his son John put into his father's head the 'notion of extending the habitable part of this House to taking in the stables'. The Admiral decided against it: 'It cannot be made comfortable to receive my Family without the expenditure of a sum of money which could put me to real inconvenience. It does very well as a hunting Box in its present state and only as such is it really wanted . . . The Stables in my judgement do very well where they are, therefore I will not alter them until the Estate can afford to build good ones detached from the house'. All the letters quoted here are in the Dorfold papers at the John Rylands Library. The Tollemaches conducted their Cheshire affairs through the Nantwich firm of Tomkinson and Welby; the Tomkinsons had bought Dorfold from the Wilbrahams in the 18th century. During Admiral Tollemache's absence the Tomkinsons supervised the work at Tilstone Lodge, and the close relationship between the two families culminated in the marriage of the Admiral's second son Wilbraham Tollemache with Anne Tomkinson in 1844.

Letters in the same collection show that the architect of Tilstone Lodge was Thomas Harrison of Chester. On 22 July 1821 Harrison directed an assistant to 'attend to Admiral Halliday's House – I have sent the plan of the chamber floor and the elevations which I promised . . . A section and plans of the roof are making and will be sent on'. Harrison's 'Account for the Plans and Drawings of Tilstone Lodge' was requested on 16 February 1824 but neither the account nor the drawings have survived.

The house is pleasantly spacious but not grand. Its simplicity and harmony of proportion are so understated that in the absence of proof one would not suspect it was by Harrison; there is no hint of antique severity. The two storeys are stuccoed and scored to imitate ashlar, with sash windows and hardly any classical detail except for the unfluted Doric order and plain entablature of the porte cochère (now somewhat altered). This is in the centre of the west-facing entrance front, otherwise flat and smooth. The side facing south across the lake ends in a graceful shallow curve with a pretty cast-iron trellised verandah sheltering the drawing room and forming a balcony for the bedroom above. At the south-east corner is an orangery, originally fully glazed but now converted into a billiard room. It was added in the late 19th century and its arched windows and pedestrian detailing look fussy against the purity of Harrison's design. To the north is Harrison's service block which links with two long ranges enclosing a narrow court. The irregularity and lack of style of this section suggests that it was part of the older farm buildings onto which the house is said to have been built.

Inside is a roomy entrance hall with a top-lit staircase (altered in the late 19th century) and light and airy reception rooms. These have their Neo-classical cornices and reeded doorcases but no trace of the marble chimneypieces mentioned in the records. Construction began in June 1821, but Admiral Tollemache wanted to 'proceed by degrees towards the completion' so that the interiors were not decorated until mid-1825 and only in April 1826 was Dowbiggin of Mount Street, London asked to supply furniture for the principal rooms. 'I must positively have the place finished lawns and everything else this autumn', wrote the Admiral's son in April 1826. The lawns were probably laid out by the landscape gardener John Webb. In August 1821 Tomkinson wrote to his agent at Tilstone that 'Mr. Webb who lays out grounds has been at Oulton and spends this day with Colonel Egerton at Tarporley [Eaton Banks i.e. Arderne]. They propose going to Tilstone Lodge in the Morning and to fix the situation of the Out Buildings ... find out whether Mr. Webb has received any letter or Order from Admiral Halliday if not he should on no account give an opinion as it may offend both the Admiral and Mr. Harrison'. If Webb was consulted over the outbuildings, which are extensive, he may well have designed the park, which is characteristic of his style. The grounds take advantage of the existing pool, enlarged to a lake and, despite the flat countryside, are amongst the most beautiful in Cheshire, with clumps of trees, a flower garden and more recent yew hedges and herbaceous borders.

The Admiral's final contribution to the estate was the chapel of St Jude facing the park entrance across the main road from Tarporley. An early work by the Nantwich architect George Latham, it is an aisleless box with lancet windows, in a naive Commissioners' Gothic style, built in 1836 and consecrated in 1837, the year the Admiral died. He was succeeded by his son John, who had earlier tried to persuade his father to build a larger house. John, later 1st Lord Tollemache, was able to realise his ambition for a grandiose family seat in place of the comfortable but informal stucco house. After he had erected Peckforton Castle, Tilstone Lodge became the residence of his eldest son.

O ii, 9, 278, iii, 380; T i, 124; E. D. H. Tollemache, *The Tollemaches of Helmingham and Ham*, 1949, 136; *Ches Life* June 1959; JRL, Roundell of Dorfold papers.

TIRLEY GARTH, *Willington*

545 664

From the windows of Tirley Garth it is possible to see Peckforton Castle, the extravagant stronghold built by John Tollemache in 1844-50. Tirley Garth was erected 60 years later, and two houses of greater contrast can scarcely be imagined. Yet both are inspired by the same romantic spirit, interpreting in different ways the vision of an idealised medieval England. For the early Victorians, George Holland Ackers at Great Moreton or Tollemache at Peckforton, this meant an ostentatious display of strength and vigour; the Edwardians preferred a quieter approach. For Tirley Garth is a product of the Arts and Crafts movement, whose architects, reacting against the pretentious character of much modern design and the harshness of machine-made goods, turned to natural materials and a revival of traditional craftsmanship.

Originally named Tirley Court, the house was built for Bryan Leesmith, a director of the chemical firm Brunner Mond, later I.C.I. He chose as his architect C. E. Mallows. Mallows was known principally as a perspectivist, whose drawings were frequently included in the Royal Academy exhibitions, but not many of his own schemes were executed. His obituary commented that 'few prominent living architects have been less favoured by fortune or have received less assistance from extraneous influences exercised on their behalf by highly placed friends'. In the 29 years from 1886 when he set up in practice to his death in 1915, Tirley Garth was his largest project: it shows him to have been an architect of exceptional sensitivity.

During the six-year period of construction at Tirley Garth, Mallows had three different clients. Inevitably the plans changed many times and some of these changes can be traced from drawings which survive at the R.I.B.A. Drawings Collection. It is clear that the idea of a cloistered entrance courtyard or garth was to be the central feature of the house from its inception, but many alternatives were tried for the treatment of the exterior. Construction com-

122. Tirley Garth from the garden.

menced in 1907, the builder being William Wood of Hartford, and things appear to have gone smoothly at first. Drawings exhibited at the Royal Academy in 1908 show rearrangements and refinements, then in 1909 there was a major departure. The range on the north side of the garth was to be greatly enlarged to provide a winter garden and an immensely long T-shaped conservatory, together with a grand stable and garage court. This scheme however was never realised, for by 1911 Leesmith, who had presumably outstretched his finances, was negotiating for his company to take over the venture. Work stopped abruptly and in March 1912 the unfinished house was sold to Brunner Mond. It has been suggested that Brunner's son, another director of the company, intended to occupy the house, but in October of that year it was leased to R. H. Prestwich, a Manchester businessman. Fortunately for Mallows, Prestwich wished to finish the house without departing from the original concept.

Prestwich ran the family textile firm S. & J. Prestwich of Pandora Mills, Farnworth, north of Manchester. The firm supplied waterproof yarn for the famous Burberry overcoats, and Prestwich himself later became the chairman of Burberry's. The Prestwiches were an artistic and enlightened family, members of that group of newly rich industrialists which exerted a powerful and liberalising influence on Manchester's intellectual and cultural life at the turn of the century. Miss Irene Prestwich, the daughter who later inherited the lease of the house, wrote, 'We had lived in Manchester amongst the families of businessmen. It was a society that had retained good manners and thought for others, and had musical and artistic interests. Now we found ourselves amongst people absorbed in hunting, bridge parties, race meetings and beautiful gardens, with little time for the obligations and amenities of a quieter social life'. But it was the possibility of creating and enjoying a beautiful garden which drew them particularly to Tirley Garth, and in their inherited architect they found a sympathetic spirit. For Mallows regarded the design and layout of the garden to be as important as that of the house, and perhaps his greatest success is the manner in which the geometry of the house is carried outside into a series of brilliantly related garden spaces. The final garden design is the joint creation of Mallows and the celebrated landscape architect T. H. Mawson, who recalled self-importantly in his autobiography that Prestwich was one of a number of Manchester industrialists for whom he was laying out gardens in a spirit of friendly rivalry. It is clear that Mallows' conception of the garden had been formulated at an early stage. Drawings of 1907 show a series of terraces on the south side of the house leading to formal avenues, and in an article he wrote for *The Builder* in the following year he described the way in which he sought to integrate house and garden. In 1909 he provided *The Studio* with illustrations for a series of articles entitled 'Architectural Gardening' which included several perspectives of Tirley Garth. Nevertheless Mawson was probably responsible for the final layout, for the geometry of the orchard and the design of the terracing betray his hand. It is on the east side that the garden is at its most architectural, where a series of interlocking circles and semi-circles are penetrated by a strong axis.

The deliberate geometry is apparent too in the design of the house, and particularly in the progress from the outside to the inside through a number of contrasting spaces. From the open circular forecourt, visitors are drawn in beneath a low arch to the enchanting enclosed garth with its round pool and fountain, and then via the shady cloister to the rooms on the south wing. The courtyard plan had been developed by Lutyens in such houses as Overstrand Hall and Deanery Gardens, and had also been used on a smaller scale by W. E. Tower at nearby Portal. Unlike Lutyens, however, Mallows was not concerned with grand architectural gestures. The materials, roughcast with local sandstone for dressings, cause the building to sit comfortably in the gentle Cheshire landscape. Externally the house is enlivened by contrasts of rhythm and scale. The entrance elevation is a studied essay in asymmetry, its bold massing showing traces of Mackintosh and Voysey. The garden elevation however is symmetrical and, with its forceful modelling and gabled skyline, is more reminiscent of the Old English style of Norman Shaw or of his pupil Lethaby's first house, Avon Tyrell in Hampshire.

Inside, the feeling is of a house designed for family use, with a comfortable two-storey living hall facing south and the other main rooms to each side. The hall is a beautiful space, overlooked by galleries, and dominated by a huge semi-circular bay window. The fireplace is set within a broad inglenook, whilst another small ingle with window seat and built-in cupboards is tucked in beside the bay. The curious roof trusses with their twin braces are the result of a modification, for an early perspective drawing of the hall shows it with the upper brace only. But a later drawing with the two braces confirms that Mallows himself introduced the change, presumably for decorative, not structural reasons. The quality of craftsmanship throughout the house is

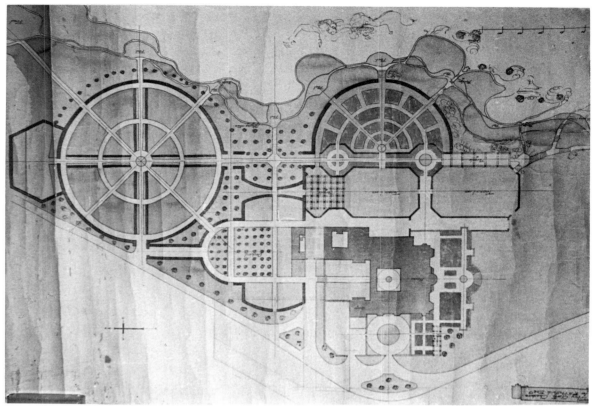

123. Garden plan by Mallows for Tirley Garth.

124. The entrance court, Tirley Garth.

125. The Great Hall, Tirley Garth.

126. Domed lobby and corridor, Tirley Garth.

characteristic of the best of the Arts and Crafts movement, and shows the continued care which Mallows exercised in spite of the difficulties of the commission. Alongside the hall and looking out into the garth is a wide corridor divided into bays by stone arches. It runs the length of the house and links two carefully proportioned lobbies surmounted by saucer domes. Off the eastern lobby is the dining room; the western one gives access to the white panelled drawing room. On the first floor there is also a corridor, separated from the hall gallery by a heavy oak screen with leaded windows. At the end is Mr. and Mrs. Prestwich's former bedroom retaining their original furniture, solid Edwardian pieces, comfortable and unostentatious. The hall is similarly furnished, and it is hard to believe that this is not still the home of a well-to-do family. For by the time that her father died in 1940, Irene Prestwich had decided that her mission in life was to establish at Tirley Garth a spiritual base for Moral Re-Armament, and in 1949 she used the capital left to her to buy the estate from I.C.I. It is now the property of a trust which runs it as a conference centre for the movement but, unlike so many institutional buildings, it is maintained in an exemplary manner. The family rooms have remained virtually unaltered, the gardens have been kept in their original form largely by the voluntary effort of those staying at the house, and any necessary new building has been designed and sited with unusual care and sensitivity.

Academy Architecture 1907 ii, 76, 1908 i, 40, 1912 ii, 54, 1915 i, 30; *Studio* xlii, 122, xlvi, 127; *BN* xciv, 104, 176, ciii, 903; *B* cviii, 437; T. H. Mawson, *The Life and Work of an English Landscape Gardener*, 1927, 208; Irene Prestwich, *A Personal Memoir*, 1971; *CL* clxxi, 702; RIBA Mallows drawings; Tirley Garth, Mallows drawings.

See also plate X, facing page 159.

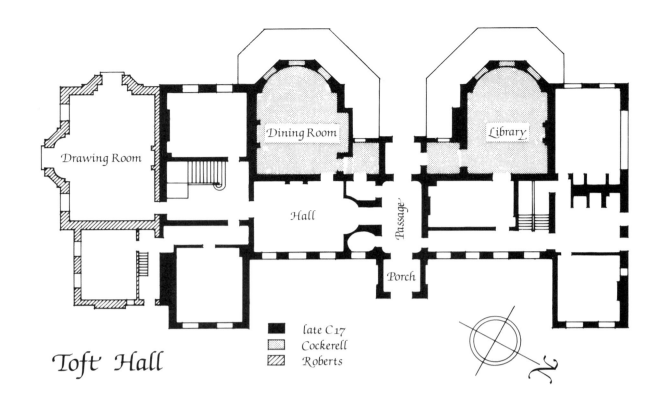

Toft Hall

Drawing Room

Dining Room

Library

Hall

Passage

Porch

■ late C17
▦ Cockerell
▨ Roberts

N

127.   The garden front of Toft Hall, *c.*1900, with additions by Cockerell and Roberts.

TOFT HALL, Toft

753 763

There is a striking view of Toft Hall from the Holmes Chapel Road, a long low house with a tall central tower set at the end of an ancient double avenue of oak and chestnut. The Hall was built of brick in the late 17th century to an extremely old-fashioned layout, perhaps that of the house which preceded it. Certainly many of the roof timbers were re-used from an earlier building. The plan was H-shaped with a central two-storey projecting porch. This led into a passage with the Great Hall on the left and family rooms in the cross wing at the upper end. Though it has since been altered, and the character of the rooms changed, the layout still remains roughly the same. The house was probably erected for George Leycester whose family had held the manor of Toft since the early 15th century. On his death in 1707 it passed to his son Ralph who planted a series of allées, of which the avenue is but the remains.

Major improvements took place in the early 19th century for another Ralph Leycester, who inherited the estate on the death of his brother George in April 1809. Ralph's grand-daughter Charlotte later recorded in a book of family notes, 'My grandfather . . . went out when very young to India where he made a comfortable fortune, though not one of the very large ones which used at that time to be shaken from the Pagoda tree'. With this fortune he had first bought a house in Surrey, but a letter written by him in June 1809 shows that he wasted no time in taking advantage of his inheritance: 'Ralph [his son] went with Mr. Cockerell . . . to Toft – Mr. C. has devised alterations which are approved by my brother Oswald and Ralph – it will make the house a very good one and I am perfectly satisfied with the Plan'. Mr. C. was Samuel Pepys Cockerell, an interesting and original architect whose most famous building is Sezincote, the eccentric Indian-style house in Gloucestershire erected for his brother Sir Charles. Sir Charles Cockerell made a large fortune in the East India Company and would perhaps have been known to Ralph Leycester. Cockerell's work at Toft however was not so exotic: his task was to enlarge and modernise the house on a limited budget. The plan at this time was still the basic H with the projecting porch. Cockerell's solution was to insert two extra reception rooms, a library and dining rooms into the angles of the cross wings on the garden side, linking them by a lead-covered canopy. The whole exterior was then faced in stucco to give it a rather plain Regency appearance (the hood moulds over the windows were not added until 1835 when many of the sashes were repaired). But he did introduce an odd note with the twin towers, one built over the entrance porch and another at the centre of the garden front. These curious vertical features, based on the towers of grand Jacobean houses, though without the usual ogee tops, give the Hall its distinctive gawky appearance. Building accounts show that the works were carried out between 1810 and 1813. Payments were made to Bernasconi for stucco work and to John Webb for remodelling the park to include a serpentine lake. The final bill was £30,399.

In 1850 there was another major extension, a new wing added by Henry Roberts for Ralph Gerard Leycester. Roberts, designer of Fishmongers' Hall, London, was an architect known chiefly as a pioneer of working-class housing. Though he carried out some minor country house work, he was probably commissioned at Toft through distant family connections with the Leycesters. He provided a new drawing room as part of a two-storey extension attached to one of the cross-wings. Externally it is stuccoed like the rest of the house, but it is more self-consciously Jacobean, with tall chimneys and a profusion of small gables. The interior is by contrast classical, with some touches of the Greek revival style which he had used at Fishmongers' Hall.

A service wing was also added during the 19th century, but this has now been demolished. In its place there is a flimsy crescent-shaped modern extension projecting onto the garden side. Toft remained in the Leycester family until 1977, but it has recently been extensively remodelled as offices. Due to the ravages of death-watch beetle and dry rot, much of the archaeological evidence of the history of the house has been destroyed, but the park, which remains in the family's possession, is being replanted.

O i, 506; T ii, 54; *Ches Life* July/August 1955; J. S. Curl, *The Life and Work of Henry Roberts*, 1983, 48; JRL and family collection, Leycester papers.

VALE ROYAL ABBEY, *Whitegate*

638 698 *House open to the public. (Privately owned)*

Vale Royal Abbey was once the largest Cistercian monastery in England and a place of enormous power and importance. After the Dissolution it became one of the county's principal seats. Today nothing remains of the abbey church, and the house, a clumsy classical stone block with rambling red brick wings, gives little idea of its former status. But it has recently become clear that the present building is substantially a conversion of the old monastic quarters, and it is now possible to reconstruct the basic form of the abbey complex.

According to the Ledger Book of the abbey, the story begins with the shipwreck of Prince Edward, the son of Henry III, probably during a cross channel voyage in 1263. There was a great storm and the Prince vowed to the Virgin that if saved he would found an abbey. The vow was accepted and the vessel was miraculously brought to shore. During the Barons' Wars which followed, the Prince, held hostage by Simon de Montfort, was well treated by the Cistercian monks of Dore Abbey near Hereford. It was this kindness which induced him to select them for his promised foundation. At first a site was proposed at Darnhall, but this proved unsuitable and an alternative was found four miles away which King Edward (as he had then become) named Vale Royal. It is not a spectacular site, but like all Cistercian settlements stands in a fertile valley remote from any large towns. Edward himself, en route for his Welsh campaigns in 1277, laid the foundation stone and decreed 'there shall be no monastery more royal than this one, in liberties, wealth and honour, throughout the whole world'.

Building commenced on an ambitious scale: in the first three years there were over one hundred and fifty skilled masons at work under the direction of Walter de Hereford, an important royal master mason, who later supervised the building of Caernarvon Castle. Edward instructed that the revenues of the county of Chester should pay for the abbey, and a royal clerk was appointed chamberlain of Chester and custodian of the works at Vale Royal. During the 1280s however less money became available as part of the county revenue began to be diverted to suppressing the Welsh revolts, and, occupied with other matters, in time the King lost interest. In 1290 Walter was informed that 'the King has ceased to concern himself with the works of that church and henceforth will have nothing more to do with them', and in 1301 the abbot recorded that no workmen had been employed for 10 years. The church was far from complete when Edward died in 1307 and, though the monks moved into the abbey in 1330, the Ledger Book shows that in 1336 the cloisters, chapter house and refectory had not been built, and the vaulting, roof and decoration of the church had still to be completed. It was not until 1353 when Abbot Thomas secured the patronage of the Black Prince who agreed to complete the project that money once again started to pour in.

The form of the abbey church is known only from the excavations carried out in 1911, 1912 and 1958. These show that it was originally an immense 420 feet in length with the standard Cistercian layout of nave, aisles and transepts. The east end however takes the form of a chevet with ambulatory and radiating chapels. This design is unique in England, and was based on that of Toledo Cathedral. It was the work of William of Helpeston, an outstanding designer, master mason to the Black Prince for Chester and North Wales, and was begun in 1359. All that now remains of the church above ground is the so-called nun's grave, a collection of pier bases and the head of a churchyard cross erected as an incongruous ensemble in the 19th century. It marks the approximate position of the high altar.

At the time of the Dissolution Vale Royal was very prosperous, but the abbots were unpopular

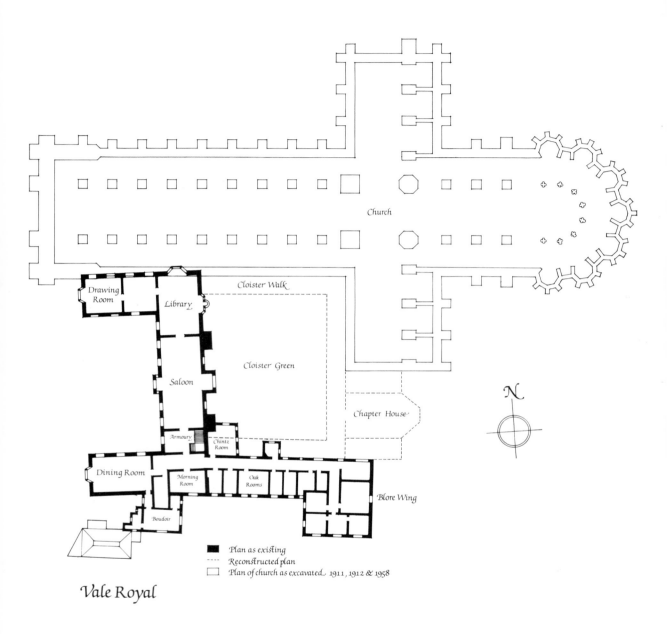

Church

Cloister Walk

Drawing
Room

Library

Cloister Green

Saloon

Chapter House

Armoury

Chintz
Room

Dining Room

Morning
Room

Oak
Rooms

Blore Wing

Boudoir

N

■ Plan as existing
--- Reconstructed plan
□ Plan of church as excavated 1911, 1912 & 1958

Vale Royal

with the local squirearchy and there would have been little sorrow at its suppression in 1539. The King's agent who organised the confiscation was Thomas Holcroft, to whom the major part of the lands were granted in 1542 for a payment of £450. But the Vale Royal estate continued in his family for only two generations and in 1616 it was sold for £9,000 to Mary, Lady Cholmondeley, widow of Sir Hugh Cholmondeley and heiress of Christopher Holford of Holford Hall. It remained with the Cholmondeleys, afterwards Earls of Delamere, until 1947. Thomas

Holcroft demolished the abbey church, but he kept most of the cloister ranges. The church stood to the left of the present house, its west end stretching some eighty-five feet out beyond the main front. As can be seen from the plan, this front was the west cloister range of the abbey, with the cloister green enclosed behind it. But here there is a puzzle, for in regular Cistercian plans the cloister green normally fills the whole rectangle between south transept and west end of the nave. At Vale Royal it joined the nave only half way along its length. The answer is probably that the church had been truncated by the time this range was built. It is known that there was a major collapse in a storm in October 1360 when the nave was blown down 'from the wall at the west end to the bell-tower before the gates of the choir' and piers fell 'like trees uprooted by the winds'. Funds were not forthcoming to rebuild, and eventually permission was sought from Richard II to curtail the nave. The west range was built in the 14th century, for the end gable of a roof structure of this date survives. The rest of the roof, though modified, is also monastic and dates from the late 15th century.

Also puzzling is the monastic function of this large range. The west cloister was normally used for the lay brothers' dormitory, and in the 14th century this would certainly have been the case. But by the 15th century when the new roof structure was built, lay brothers were no longer employed in Cistercian houses, and existing west ranges had often to be put to alternative uses. The uniformity of construction along the roof of the whole range suggests a monks' dormitory or refectory, but most likely it was a new abbot's lodgings over a cellarium. It was common at this time for abbots to build themselves lavish mansions. This is what happened at Cleve Abbey, Somerset and Hailes, Gloucestershire. It was also probably the arrangement at the other Cistercian foundation in Cheshire, Combermere Abbey, and certainly at the Augustinian Norton Priory. The adjoining south range too is formed out of the monastic buildings which enclosed the cloister green. These were the monastic kitchen and refectory, originally timber-framed with a stone ground floor but faced in brick in 1860. The eastern end was most likely the monks' dormitory; in 1833 it was rebuilt on the original foundations as a service wing. The kitchen was built as an open hall with a decorative roof structure on false hammerbeams. The refectory was at first floor level and has an elaborate roof dated by dendrochronology to 1470-5, though its unfinished state suggests that the room was never completed. A cloister walk followed the perimeter of the green and on the west side ran under the existing main building, for the arched openings now lighting the present entrance passage, although remodelled, are the original cloister windows. The chimney stacks which break up the cloister were not added until the late 16th century. The two missing sides of the cloister, north and east, are shown in an engraving of about 1774 as garden walls in picturesque decay.

The result of Thomas Holcroft's remodelling can be seen in the view of 1616, the year Vale Royal was acquired by Mary Lady Cholmondeley. This shows the west range with an external staircase and two projecting wings of unequal length built onto each side of the main front. The staircase led up to a screens passage flanked on the left by a Great Hall and on the right by a Great Chamber. The drawing shows a bay window which would have lit the dais of the hall, and on the roof a cupola serving as a lantern (the remains are still visible in the roof). It had become a very sizeable house and Lady Cholmondeley's standing was enhanced by a visit to Vale Royal in 1617 by James I.

By the 18th century the house had become old-fashioned and inconvenient, and the exterior was remodelled; the wall surface was broken up by giant pilasters, and huge sash windows with stone architraves and keystones were inserted in place of the earlier oriels. (Two of these sash windows remain in the east wall of the main block, although bricked up on the inside.) Surprisingly the external staircase was retained. Internally, in order to provide a grand entrance hall, the Great Hall, passage and Great Chamber were opened up into one long space with Gothick arcades at each end. The two wings projecting west from the main front were probably not completed until later for, in 1796 according to Lysons, the southern one (which had been

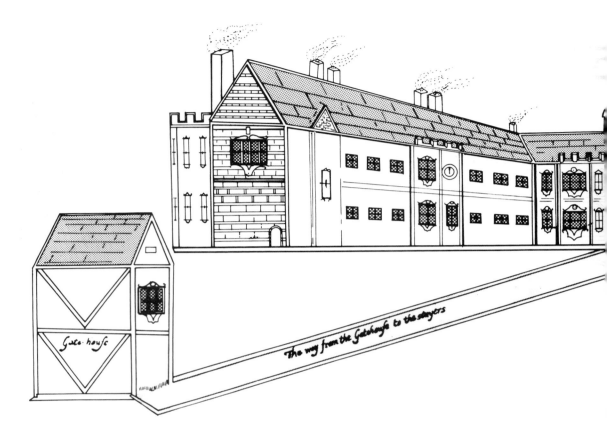

The way from the Gatehouse to the sawyers

Gate-house

destroyed in the Civil War) was rebuilt. This work was carried out for Thomas Cholmondeley, later 1st Lord Delamere, who held the estate from 1779 until his death in 1855.

His enthusiasm for improving the house and its grounds is reflected in the pocket book kept by his wife Henrietta which records building projects at Vale Royal between 1810 and 1848. The first entry of 1811 is the removal of the external steps and their replacement by an internal staircase with a vaulted corridor. The porch was re-erected at ground level. This was part of a scheme to improve the main reception rooms on the first floor which included blocking the arcades at each end to form an armoury, into which the new staircase rose, and a library. New chimneypieces were installed in the central saloon. Next came the construction of the large mullioned bay windows, the one over the porch and those at the ends of the two projecting wings. These bays are an early example of Tudor revivalism and all later alterations followed this style. The great sashes of the saloon were torn out in 1830 and replaced with timber cross windows, and 17th-century armorial glass originally from Utkinton Hall (and now in the Burrell collection) was installed. Major building works followed in 1833 to the design of Edward Blore. The old south-east wing of the house, still timber-framed, was taken down and rebuilt on the existing plan as service rooms in harsh red brick. Though Blore had a reputation as a reliable architect who kept costs under control, there was clearly reluctance to accept his fees, for it is recorded in the pocket book that the new wing cost £4,695 'including Mr. Blore's heavy charge of £127.15.0d. for plans etc.' Then in 1835 the saloon was elaborately redecorated.

128. West front of Vale Royal, based on a drawing of 1616.

The coats of arms of the Cholmondeley family which adorn the ceiling had first been painted in 1824 in 'neutral tints'. Now they were blazoned in heraldic colours and all the mouldings gilded.

The treatment of the other main rooms was carried out for Hugh Cholmondeley, the 2nd Baron. His architect was the young John Douglas who was yet to develop the Old English style for which he is noted. At Vale Royal he was content to reproduce Blore's Tudor style and on the exterior it is difficult to tell where Blore's work ends and Douglas's begins. Douglas recased the central south range in 1860 to link with Blore's south-east wing. This was until then timber-framed. It contains the King's Room and Oak Room in which there is 17th-century panelling and crude relief carvings of the foundation of the abbey and the visits of Henry VII and James I. In 1861 the south-west wing was added. In designing this Douglas tried to balance the composition of the south elevation, but its busy grouping of gables and spindly tower relates awkwardly to the long horizontal lines of the symmetrical west front. At about the same time the dining room was altered. This is a large room occupying the whole of the south projecting wing. It was first converted in 1821 and painted, like the saloon, with coats of arms. Douglas redecorated it and installed the spectacular mid-18th-century Palladian doorcase. As no records were kept of the 2nd Baron's improvements, the source of this item is not known, but its quality far outshines any of the *in situ* work at Vale Royal. The last major room to be refitted was the library. Into this also were installed woodcarvings: a 17th-century doorcase, and a chimneypiece

129.   West front of Vale Royal, *c*.1910.

130.   South front of Vale Royal, *c*.1910, showing the Blore wing with the Douglas extension on the left.

131. Palladian doorcase in the dining room at Vale Royal.

132. The saloon at Vale Royal, *c.*1910.

which until recently included a 16th-century German relief of the Annunciation in the style of Tilman Riemenschneider. These alterations were probably made in 1877 for this is the date of the pretty oriel window built out on the east side overlooking the 'nun's grave'.

A delightful account of the house written by Mrs. Mary Hopkirk describes the period when her grandfather Robert Dempster leased it from 1907 until his death in 1925. The house was taken fully furnished, complete with suits of armour, family portraits, servants and big game hunting trophies. Most famous of the paintings is the double portrait, now in the Tate Gallery, of the Cholmondeley sisters in ruffs, lying side by side in bed with their babies. Dempster cared deeply for the house and encouraged the excavations by Basil Pendleton which established the layout of the abbey church. He also made extensive improvements to the gardens under the direction of the architect L. Rome Guthrie. This period was the swansong of Vale Royal. After Dempster's death in 1925, the 4th Baron occupied the house for a brief period, but in 1928 the huge estate was sold piecemeal. After the war the house was purchased by Cheshire County Council for use as its police headquarters, but the scheme was soon abandoned and from 1947 to 1976 there was little care or maintenance. In recent years the decline has been halted but, in spite of some first-aid work, the future still looks uncertain.

Lysons ii, 814; O ii, 147; T i, 95; B. Pendleton, *Notes on the Cistercian Abbey of Vale Royal*, 1912; *RSLC* 1914, 68 *The Ledger Book of Vale Royal Abbey*; *Ches Life* July 1977; *VCH* iii, 156; CRO DBC/Acc 2309 Account Book; RCHM Typescript report 1977; M. Hopkirk, *Vale Royal Abbey*, ed. G. Holland 1980, typescript at CRO.

WINNINGTON HALL, *Northwich*

645 747

133. Winnington Hall with the alkali works.

Winnington Hall presents a strange sight. What was once a substantial country house within a large wooded park is now stranded amongst the towering structures of I.C.I.'s alkali works. That the house has survived at all is because John Brunner and Ludwig Mond, the founders of I.C.I., who acquired the estate in 1872 for their soda manufacturing enterprise, could not secure suitable houses locally, and so decided to restore and occupy it themselves. The building divided naturally between them, for it is in effect two houses joined together, one timber-framed and modest in scale, and the other of stone, elegant and sophisticated.

The timber-framed part dates from the late 16th or early 17th century, built for a younger son of the Warburtons of Warburton and Arley. It is a broad low house of two regular storeys, with a range of five equal gables along the front. A study of the roof timbers shows that there were originally just three gables on the entrance side. The two outer wings were added for Thomas Warburton, whose wife Anne, daughter of Sir Robert Williams of Penrhyn and Cochwillan, became in 1684 a joint heir to the Penrhyn estates near Bangor. This increased affluence may well have encouraged expansion. A service wing built of brick on the north side of the original house belongs to the early 18th century, and was most likely carried out for Thomas's son General Hugh Warburton. It is the next phase of extensions however which altered the character of the house so completely and brought to it architectural distinction.

General Hugh Warburton had only a daughter, Anne Susanna. In 1765 as heir presumptive to Winnington and half the Penrhyn estate, she made a clever marriage to a promising young politician, Richard Pennant, heir to the other half of Penrhyn. With the opening of the huge slate quarries at Nant Ffrancon, his family had become immensely wealthy, and his plans for Winnington were ambitious. There are no surviving drawings or documents relating to the work carried out, but it is accepted that the architect was either James or Samuel Wyatt. James has been favoured by Wyatt scholars on stylistic grounds, though Samuel has it on the basis of other evidence, for it is known that one of his close associates, John Cooper, worked at Winnington. Samuel designed alterations for the Bagots of Blithfield Hall in Staffordshire in 1769-70 where Cooper's family was in service. In 1776-9 Cooper was employed by Samuel as assistant at Baron Hill in Anglesey. Cooper began a practice of his own in 1779, designing Bodorgan Hall, also on Anglesey, for Owen Meyrick. A detailed correspondence with Meyrick survives at Bodorgan and includes reference to Cooper's employment as a carpenter at Winnington in 1775, and to his close relations with Samuel Wyatt. The fact that the two Wyatt brothers were running entirely separate practices by 1775 points conclusively to Samuel as the architect for Winnington.

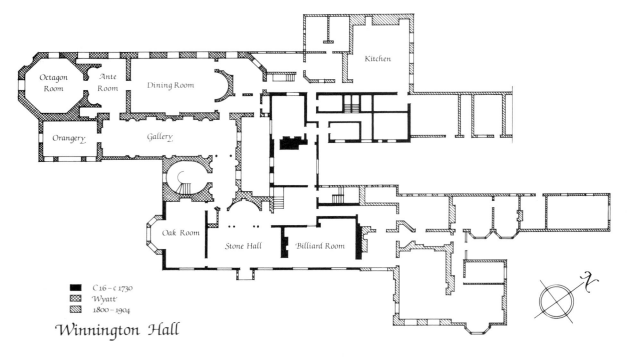

Winnington Hall

The Wyatt wing provided the house with a new focus and a new identity. A deep L-shaped two-storey block was added to the back of the original house. Within was a fashionable new suite of rooms comprising dining room, octagon room and orangery, reached by a spacious gallery lit by lunettes. The severe ashlar exterior with regularly-spaced tall sash windows and Coadestone plaques dominates the older vernacular house. But there are reasons to believe that this wing was merely the initial stage of a complete rebuilding. The junction of old and new is unresolved. No conscious attempt was made by Wyatt to relate the scale of the new building to the existing house. The external wall enclosing the staircase which stands at the junction was never faced in stone, and the blank areas of stone below the gallery lunettes suggest that this was intended to be within a lightwell. The strikingly handsome gallery providing circulation to the new rooms of the house is reached unceremoniously from a corner of the low entrance hall, formed by Wyatt within the old house seemingly as an afterthought. Very different is the grand formal approach to Doddington. It is odd also that a house which includes an orangery, an octagon and a gallery lacks a drawing room. It is hard to say however what form a complete rebuilding would have taken. Perhaps it was intended that a matching wing would be built in place of the old house. At all events the dissatisfaction later felt about the appearance of the old part led to its being roughcast and castellated in the early years of the 19th century in a vain attempt to make it harmonise better.

By 1782 Pennant had embarked on a major remodelling of his other seat, Penrhyn

134. Winnington Hall in 1866, showing the timber-framed block covered in roughcast.

Castle, designed by Samuel Wyatt in the Gothic style. Perhaps this caused him to lose interest in the plans for Winnington and have the job finished off prematurely. Finally he abandoned the matter altogether, and in the *Morning Chronicle* of 19 November 1807 there appeared an advertisement offering the whole estate for sale. It was bought in 1809 by Lord Stanley of Alderley, ostensibly for his son Edward, then aged seven. But the Hall at Alderley had burned down 30 years before and, as the family was still living in temporary accommodation on the Alderley estate, he installed his wife at Winnington, whilst he spent long periods in London. In 1817 they returned to Alderley where rebuilding had commenced, and let Winnington fall into disrepair. 'The plaything has lost its charm', wrote Lady Stanley, 'it is no longer new, and so now, like a child with a gilt cuckoo, I enjoy pulling it to pieces, as the only satisfaction it can give.' Their son Edward did not live at Winnington until 1842, and then only briefly, for in 1850 he succeeded to Alderley Park. He too seems to have neglected the house, his wife recording when they left that it was in a deplorable state, 'enough to give one the utmost melancholy'. It was therefore fortunate that the house then took on a new lease of life as a Girls' Academy under the direction of the Misses Bell who rented it from Lord Stanley. A regular visitor during the Bell régime was John Ruskin. On his first visit in 1859 he wrote to his father, 'This is such a nice place that I am going to stay till Monday: an enormous old-fashioned house – full of galleries and up and down stairs – but with magnificently large rooms where wanted'. In Miss Bell he found a sympathetic ear for his ideas on morals and education, but it was probably being surrounded by adolescent girls 'all healthy and happy as can be' which delighted him most; he enjoyed talking with them and playing hide and seek in the attics.

During the Stanley ownership, Brunner and Mond had been negotiating to buy land near Winsford, but in this they were thwarted by Lord Delamere who went to great lengths to prevent any soda works being erected near his Vale Royal estate. Consequently they turned to Winnington, aware that the 3rd Lord Stanley, who was notoriously short of money, had offered the Winnington estate of 600 acres for sale two years earlier without securing any bids. Lord Stanley's condition was that they should buy the whole estate including the Hall and woodland, which they did for the bargain price of £16,108. At first the new owners' inclination was to demolish the house, but there were obvious advantages in living on the premises, and in July 1873 Brunner wrote to a friend, 'I have had the roughcast stripped off the Old Hall and you will be charmed with the appearance of the oak framing now visible. It is worth a special journey to see it'. In fact much of the timberwork had to be replaced, and the attic floor in the gables was abandoned and its windows blocked. Some £2,000 was spent on repairs to the old house alone. The two families co-existed at Winnington during the formative years of the new company, the Brunners in the old house, the Monds in the Wyatt wing, but domestic disagreements led to the Brunners moving out in 1891. After the First World War the two halves were amalgamated as the Winnington Hall Club for company staff, and the building was restored under the direction of Darcy Braddell. An architect with a reputation for sensitive renovation of country houses, Braddell had already altered Melchet Court, the Monds' country house in Hampshire. He was an excellent choice, and the elegant appearance of the Winnington interiors today is largely the result of his work.

The entrance is via the Stone Hall, perhaps the hall and screens passage of the old house, now a low-ceilinged space dressed up by Wyatt in the Neo-classical style. The contrast of scale on entering the spacious gallery is dramatic. This combines the function of a central hall and a corridor, and is one of Wyatt's most successful interiors, a refinement of an unexecuted design which he had already prepared for Blithfield Hall. The main part is divided into four vaulted bays, and within the vaults are delicately glazed lunettes through which fall strong shafts of light. Below are oval medallions of Neo-classical figures, similar to those in the saloon at Heaton Hall, and niches containing black basalt vases. The niches were doubtless intended for candelabra as shown in the Blithfield scheme, but the vases, an idea of Braddell, who had them made specially by Wedgwood from 18th-century moulds, are an admirable substitute. At the end of the gallery is the orangery, a strange room to have included within the body of the house. The slender glazing bars to the huge windows are cast-iron, a detail pioneered by Samuel Wyatt, and perhaps used for the first time at Winnington. From the gallery a semi-circular apsed anteroom connects with the dining room and octagon room. Within the latter is some of the best decorative work, particularly a fine Neo-classical fireplace, a delicate plaster ceiling, and a frieze of winged gryphons, a motif repeated on the doorcases. The walls of this room were lined with 18th-century Chinese wallpaper, carefully retained by Braddell but unfortunately removed

135. The gallery at Winnington Hall in 1923, restored by Braddell.

136. Ceiling of the octagon room at Winnington Hall, 1923.

since. The dining room has an apsidal end containing the original curved sideboard, and other Wyatt sidetables are still in use within the house.

The staircase hall is off the shorter arm of the gallery. It is oval in plan and contains a modest stone staircase, perhaps, like Doddington, intended to be one of a pair had the house been built larger. On the first floor is one fine suite of Wyatt rooms, the octagon bedroom and an adjacent dressing room in which Ruskin reputedly slept. After the Winnington Hall Club took over, the bedrooms were used for visitors to the works, and Braddell designed furniture for the octagon bedroom, modelling it on the Garrick bedroom suite at the Victoria and Albert Museum. The bed and wardrobe, painted to imitate Chinese lacquer, are now stored in another room which alone preserves a Baroque fireplace, perhaps from the older part of the house.

137. The poultry house at Winnington Hall, late 19th century.

The 1807 notice of sale provides a description of the estate at that time. The land amounted to 640 acres, and included cottages, farms, an ice-house, dovecote and greenhouses. The stabling 'for fifty horses' which stood at the rear of the house was demolished by Brunner and Mond in 1875, and no record of it survives. There are photographs however of a remarkable poultry house of the early 1780s by Samuel Wyatt. A contemporary description tells us that this provided every comfort and convenience for some 600 hens, 'At one o'clock a bell rings, and the beautiful gate in the centre is opened. The poultry being then mostly walking in the paddock, and knowing by the sound of the bell that their repast is ready for them, fly and run from all corners, and rush in at the gate, everyone striving to get the first share in the scramble'. The hen house had a long facade with a tall centrepiece and square end pavilions connected by cast-iron columns. The unusual facing material was thin slates from the Penrhyn quarry, closely jointed and painted to resemble ashlar. A similar structure designed by John Cooper exists at Bodorgan Hall, but at Winnington, after conversion to a cottage, the hen house was demolished. The 'beautiful gate' had been moved during the Stanley ownership to Alderley Park where it still stands. The lodges to the estate existed until recently, but even these have now gone, and there is no trace of a pair of back-to-back cottages by Lewis Wyatt which were published in a book of architectural designs for Lord Penrhyn in 1800. Lord Penrhyn's advertisement of 1807 already drew attention to a 'most valuable Mineral, which, if attended to, far exceeds the value of this place as a residence'. With the later foundation at Winnington of one of the world's largest multinational companies, it is surprising that the residence has survived at all.

R. Beatson, *Communications to the Board of Agriculture*, 1797 i, 39; Lewis Wyatt, *Collections of Architectural Designs on Lord Penrhyn's Estates*, 1800; O ii, 204; T i, 105; *CL* liv, 314; A. S. Irvine, *A History of Winnington Hall*, 1951; J. M. Cohen, *The Life of Ludwig Mond*, 1956; Van Akin Burd, *The Winnington Letters of John Ruskin*, 1969; S. E. Koss, *Sir John Brunner*, 1970; *Transactions of the Anglesey Antiquarian Society*, 1983, 41; J. M. Robinson, *Georgian Model Farms*, 1983, 104, 145.

138. Woodhey chapel.

139. South front of Woodhey Hall: a drawing of 1837 copying an earlier view.

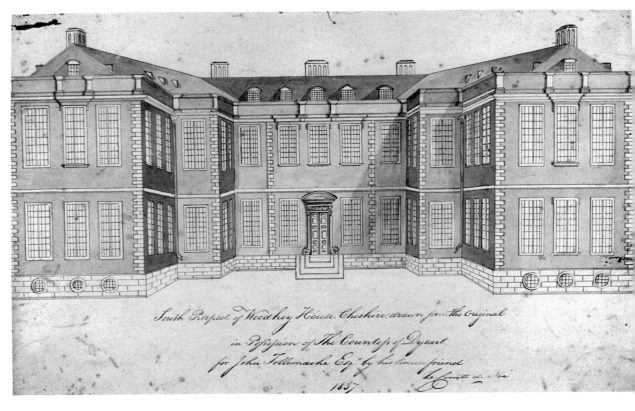

South Prospect of Woodhey House, Cheshire, drawn from the Original
in Possession of The Countess of Dysart.
for John Tollemache Esq.: by his sincere friend
1837.

WOODHEY HALL, *Faddiley (demolished)*

573 528 *Chapel open to the public. (Privately owned)*

Down a muddy track in the middle of a field stands Woodhey chapel, lone survivor of a vanished house of considerable grandeur. Woodhey Hall was built by Lady Wilbraham around 1690, and the chapel was added soon afterwards. The Hall replaced an earlier house assumed to have been of about 1600 from the fragments of it incorporated into the chapel. Lady Wilbraham was an indefatigable builder for she was also responsible for the new house and chapel at Weston Park, Staffordshire. Daughter and heiress of Edward Mitton of Weston, she married Sir Thomas Wilbraham of Woodhey. The chapel which she built at her Cheshire house demonstrates both her personal interest in architecture and the low-church bias of her religion.

The Wilbraham tradition of piety was of long standing. William Wilbraham's will of 1534 left money for 'a well disposed priest to sing for me . . . 20 years at my chapel of Woodhay', presumably referring to the domestic chapel of an even earlier Hall. At Rode Hall there is a book recording all the sermons preached in different local churches before members of the Wilbraham family between 1659 and 1661, showing that they regularly heard well-known Protestant divines. Sir Thomas, Elizabeth's husband, is known to have employed chaplains who had been expelled from the established church and in 1703, when Lady Wilbraham endowed the chapel at Woodhey, she stipulated 'someone of the reformed or protestant Religion 'or Communion opposed to popery'. His stipend was to be withheld if he showed any Romish leanings.

Lady Wilbraham's interest in architecture is evident from her copy, kept at Weston, of Palladio, the English translation of 1663 by Godfrey Richards. On the flyleaves are her manuscript notes and memoranda about building activities at Weston and Woodhey, listing prices for building materials, comparing estimates from different tradesmen and noting the rates paid by her friends. Lady Wilbraham was familiar with all the practical details of building, and perhaps was her own architect, for there is a family resemblance between the two houses. The appearance of Woodhey is known from later drawings of the front and side elevations, and the south front of Weston is substantially as she left it. Both are competently designed houses in the Carolean manner of brick with long and short stone quoins, tall windows and hipped roofs behind emphatic horizontal parapets. Both have circular windows, at Woodhey in the basement, and at Weston in the curved pediments of the attic storey.

The progress of the work at Woodhey can be deduced from Lady Wilbraham's jottings. In 1689 she noted 'the prices agreed with Allixander Webdall for his worke att Woodhey'. This was to include 'luthern windows' (dormers) and the floors were to be 'as well as ye best Parlor at Weston'. In 1690 she noted the comparative prices of brickwork from Mr. Taler, Mr. Russell, Mr. Webdall, the Londoners, Mr. Web (perhaps Thomas Webb of Middlewich, designer of Erdigg near Wrexham in 1683), and William Smith (perhaps of Warwick). Materials from the old house were re-used, for 'the servants Halle at Woodhey is to be wanscote w^h ye old Wainscote formerly in ye best Halle' and in November 1691 she obtained prices for painting the wainscot in various types of wood-graining and marbling from painters in London, Nantwich and Derby: she chose the man from Nantwich. The house was completed by 1692, the year her husband died. The chapel memoranda cover the period from 1697 to 1699. Her care to obtain good quality materials is evident from the notes on the price of bricks from the Woodhey kiln in 1697. 'Clarke ye Brick Maker is to hav 6^s 1000 for makeing thereof, but if any of them brewse bad he is to have nothing for such.' The following year 'Middleton the Slayter' gave prices for laying 'ye best blew slate' which had to be carried to the site from Chester. In October 1699 she wrote to Lord Dysart that the new chapel had been opened.

It is a small brick box with a hipped slate roof, stone quoins and stone surrounds to the arched and circular windows. In the east wall is a stone plaque with a weathered inscription and a lozenge with Lady Wilbraham's arms. The chapel is entered from doors facing each other in the side walls. Within, the pews are also ranged opposite each other as in an Oxbridge college. At the east end is a tall pulpit, simply carved with vertical swags of fruit, and between the east windows is a similarly carved panel crudely lettered with the Ten Commandments. Lit by tall arched casement windows, their small panes re-using much old glass, the interior is plain and austere, without starkness; the walls are whitewashed, the half-panelling and pews are stained dark, and a Victorian chequered tile floor replaces the original flags of 'ye best stone'. At the west end is a raised gallery, lit by the circular windows over the side doors. This is the family pew overlooking the nave and here Lady Wilbraham sat on one of the pair of straight-backed oak benches, warmed from corner fireplaces. Behind, concealed by a latticed canework screen, sat the servants. The family pew was entered from the back, communicating directly with the house. There is no stair for internal access between the pew and the chapel floor. It was simply a preaching box and the family never took communion here. For the sacraments they went to Acton. This explains the lack of an altar at Woodhey; all that was necessary was the pulpit and the reading pew in the north-east corner. The arrangements were very different at the high church chapel of Cholmondeley not far away.

Outside the chapel at the west end is a curious arrangement of steps, a raised earth walk and a loggia at the level of the family pew. When Lady Wilbraham's house was demolished and the chapel became an isolated building, a surviving fragment of the earlier Hall was moved to form a porch for the family pew entrance. This is the triple-arched loggia with fluted columns and a decorated frieze. It may have been an entrance or even part of a long open gallery of the type found in Jacobean houses. The loggia connects with a raised causeway possibly covering foundations of the house, and to the south is a high brick wall perhaps originally enclosing a formal garden. The exact position of the house is not known, nor which part of it joined on to the chapel. Some distance to the west is a substantial diapered brick range of the 17th century called a barn on an estate map of 1767 but originally a block of domestic offices. Behind it are later farm buildings and a Victorian farmhouse with the characteristic octagonal glazing of Peckforton estate farms. It is approached between the re-erected stone gate-piers of the Carolean Hall.

The Woodhey estate became a Tollemache property through the marriage of Lady Wilbraham's daughter, but the family left Cheshire and the house was demolished in the 1730s and '40s. The chapel was kept, served from Acton and Baddiley when the family ceased to appoint chaplains. In 1744 household accounts refer to its poor condition and to repairs, and the estate was still farmed by the family. The chapel was repaired again in 1926 and, when the estate later changed hands, the chapel was conveyed to the Woodhey Chapel Trust, formed by Sir Randle Baker Wilbraham of Rode whose death in 1979 is commemorated by a tablet on the porch. He did not live to see the excellent restoration completed for the Trust in 1981 by the Manchester architect Donald Buttress. Sensitive and unobtrusive in his repair work, he made one addition of his own design, a beautiful chandelier of oak and cast brass, a 20th-century contribution of which one hopes Lady Wilbraham, with her stern faith, would have approved.

O iii, 381; *CL* clxxiii, 578; CRO DTW/Acc 2225, Estate Map; Weston Park, Annotated copy of Palladio.

WYTHENSHAWE HALL, *Wythenshawe*

816 898 House and park open to the public. (Manchester City Council)

Wythenshawe Hall began as a half-timbered house of the same type as Litle Moreton, but its outward appearance today is largely a product of the 20th century. Just how little 16th-century work is left is apparent if the present entrance front is compared with the view of it in 1826 by J. C. Buckler, showing the nucleus of the present house coated in warm pink stucco, with sash windows replacing most of the wooden mullioned lattices. The only elements recorded by Buckler still there are the heavy oak studded door, most of the upper windows, and the lower portions of the big oak bressumers below the central gables, carved with scrollwork, armorials and pendants. Some of the existing details including the upper parts of the bressumers were carved in the 19th century, but the stucco was not removed until 1947. Because no views of the original timbering survived and what was left had decayed, most of the entrance front was rebuilt in imitation of timber framing but with new boards planted on the surface. The quatrefoil frieze and some of the close-studding appear to reflect an authentic pattern whereas the herringbone framing looks decidedly odd, probably an invention of the restorers.

Despite the alterations the early form of the house is still discernible, an H plan facing east with a central Great Hall open to the roof. Henry Taylor, writing in 1884, concluded from the evidence of internal timbers revealed by the removal of a plaster ceiling that there had been a spere-truss at the north end of the Great Hall. The house was rebuilt by Robert Tatton after a fire, according to a note on a deed of 1530; reconstruction must have taken place before 1579, when he died. The fire probably destroyed the Great Hall roof, and Robert Tatton would have inserted a floor to make the present two-storeyed central block containing a Hall and a Great Chamber above (now the dining room and the withdrawing room). He may well have built the house higher than before for the cross wings are lower than the centre.

Inside the house, surprisingly little of Robert Tatton's time is left. One of the principal features is the old main staircase off the upper end of the Hall, almost unrecognisable as its lower levels have been boxed in. Sixteenth-century timber studding is visible right at the top on the way to a small bedroom spuriously known as the Cromwell Room (Wythenshawe's connections with the Civil War are real enough but have been romantically embroidered). This contains the only original Elizabethan fireplace left in the house. Also of early date is the illusionistic painted panelling and the frieze of Renaissance grotesques discovered beneath the oak panelling on one wall of the Great Chamber. The frieze, more finely painted than contemporary decoration in other Cheshire houses, includes the arms of Robert Tatton and his wife Dorothy Booth of Dunham Massey in a form which points to a date of around 1570. The early 17th-century wall panelling, inlaid in a variety of intricate fret patterns, is the finest feature of the house and gives this room a luxurious character. There is also a large interior porch in front of the north doorway, similar to one of 1599 at Montacute in Somerset. Unfortunately, the ceiling was replaced in the 19th century in the neo-Elizabethan style, flat and lifeless compared to the original, part of which survives in the window bays. There is similar original plaster decoration and inlay in the withdrawing room at Bramall.

An inventory taken in 1643 after the Hall had been captured by the Parliamentarians shows that the house was part of a group of estate buildings including a chapel and a gatehouse, all within the moat, which is still recognisable from a dip in the ground a short distance in front of the house. More puzzling is the mention in the inventory of a Long Gallery. Its original position could have been along the west side behind the Great Hall but all traces have vanished, for a

140. Entrance front of Wythenshawe Hall: a watercolour by J. C. Buckler, 1926.

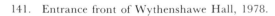

141. Entrance front of Wythenshawe Hall, 1978.

three-storey west wing of brick with sash windows was built there in the mid-18th century, most likely after the marriage in 1746 of William Tatton of Wythenshawe with Hester Egerton, heiress and sister of John Egerton of Tatton. Until 1806 the Tatton Park and Wythenshawe Hall estates were united in one family and the main architectural energies went into the rebuilding of Tatton. The estates were separated again in 1806 on the death of William Egerton.

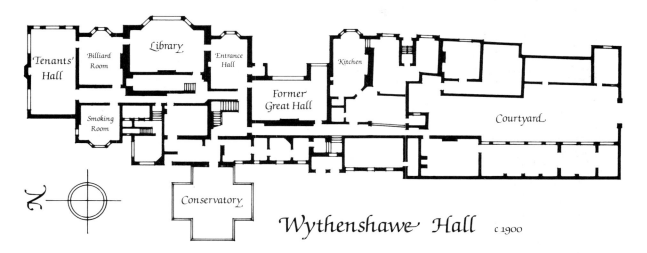

Wythenshawe Hall c 1900

Wythenshawe passed to the younger son Thomas William Tatton, who by Royal licence assumed the surname and arms of Tatton. At this period the house was coated in stucco and extended. The south end was turned into service quarters, the old staircase becoming the back stairs, and farther south a new U-shaped service wing was built round a courtyard. At the north a dining room was created from the screens passage and the Hall by removing the spere-truss. The porch, formerly leading straight on into the screens passage, was blocked and made to turn to the right into the space formerly occupied by the kitchen; this became the entrance hall. Behind it a new top-lit staircase hall was built. Farther north, a new wing was added containing a library and bedrooms above. The plaster ceilings suggest, if not the hand, then at least the influence of Lewis Wyatt who from 1807 was working for T. W. Tatton's brother at Tatton Park; the Gillow bookcases in the library at Wythenshawe are very similar to those in the library at Tatton. The Wythenshawe bookcases have recently been restored, and a version of the original red flock wallpaper hung to recreate the character of the room in the early 19th century, smaller and cosier than at Tatton. Evidence for the dating of these improvements comes from the documentation of the furniture in the Gillow archive. As early as 1797 a billiard table was ordered but most of the work seems to be after 1806; the library was not fitted up until 1813, the date of a drawing for the bookcases.

In 1827 T. W. Tatton died and was succeeded by his son and namesake who continued to alter the house. Wholesale remodelling was contemplated, for a set of drawings by Edward Blore kept at the Hall propose turning the back of the house into a new entrance front in the neo-Tudor style. But the scheme was not executed. Instead superficial Tudor trimmings were added to the exterior, including mullioned latticed windows, castellated bays, tall chimneys and a turret to house the bell which was confiscated during the Civil War by Colonel Robert Dukinfield and returned in 1828 by his descendant, Francis Dukinfield Astley. Inside the house T. W. Tatton's work was more drastic. The panelled dining room, the Great Chamber ceiling, the fireplaces and the brightly-coloured armorial glass are all Victorian; they have the unfortunate effect of removing from the principal apartments much of their original character. An inscription on the dining room ceiling states the room was restored in 1871-2; it was probably at this period that the pikes and other weapons were brought out and displayed as trophies of the Civil War. The house was extended to the north in 1862 by a billiard room and a smoking room, and in 1879 by the large half-timbered Tenants' Hall. Similar half timbering was allowed to creep over all the principal gables, and fancy barge boards were carved for the central block. Within, the library was redecorated in the aesthetic style of the 1880s.

R. H. G. Tatton succeeded in 1924 but two years later the Hall and the park were bought by Lord and Lady Simon and presented to the City of Manchester for public use; the rest of the estate was compulsorily purchased by the City for an ambitious and originally well-landscaped housing scheme designed by Barry Parker and Raymond Unwin. The Hall became a museum and its domestic character was eroded. After the war, decay on a large scale led to much demolition and reconstruction; between 1947 and 1952 the Georgian west wing, the early 19th-century service court and the Victorian conservatory were all taken down, the rendering on the entrance front was removed and the front entirely rebuilt. Lino, cream paint and strip lights arrived inside. Further renewal of rotted timbers had to be carried out between 1978 and 1983. The future looks brighter; restoration of the interior is proceeding, and though parts of the Hall are still neglected, the principal rooms are being carefully furnished and nursed back to life.

O iii, 608; T ii, 104; Taylor 139-41; W. H. Shercliffe, *Wythenshawe to 1926*, 1974, 23-4; MCRL Archives Dept., Henry Taylor papers; Wythenshawe Hall, Blore drawings.

Part Two

Abbeyfield, Sandbach
746 604

A neglected looking house, now roughcast but probably originally stuccoed, built *c.* 1800-10 for John Ford, the grounds laid out by Webb. The name comes from a nearby field once owned by the abbey of Dieulacres in Staffordshire. The house is in a very plain classical style, asymmetrical, with a good cast iron verandah on the garden side.
O iii, 100; T i, 142.

Abbots Moss Hall, Sandiway
592 683

A solid red brick early 19th-century house hidden in the Abbots Moss woods. It is said to have been built as a dower house for Vale Royal, for the 1st Lord Delamere. The entrance front has nine bays divided irregularly by pilaster strips. The principal rooms are along the garden front overlooking a small mere. At the centre of the house is a top-lit hall with an Edwardian staircase.

Aldersey Hall, Aldersey (demolished)
460 561

A plain block-like house of stucco with classical interiors. It was built in 1805 to replace the earlier house of the Aldersey family but was demolished *c.* 1958. A housing estate now occupies the site in the middle of derelict parkland and all that remains are two pairs of gate-piers, two lodges and a section of the walled garden with a gate dated 1901.
O ii, 739; T i, 39; Pike 1904, 27.

Alvaston Hall, Nantwich
665 546

Formerly the home of W. Massey but rebuilt in 1896-7 for Arthur Knowles, a wealthy businessman, and designed by Edward Salomons and A. Steinthal of Manchester. It is a picturesque, many-gabled house in a hard version of Norman Shaw's Old English style, of brick and half timber. Inside is a two-storey living hall lit by a large window of pale stained glass leaded in small scale patterns. A staircase of Anglo-Japanese design leads to a gallery. Off the hall are panelled rooms in the Queen Anne or Early Georgian styles. Now a hotel.
B lxxii, 360; Pike 1904, 84.

Antrobus Hall, Mobberley
801 790

An endearing small brick house of the early 18th century built for John Antrobus of the Knutsford family of Dissenters. It has a front garden enclosed by brick walls and rusticated gate-piers with cottage loaf tops. The house has a narrow frontage of five bays with cross windows and is not quite symmetrical. A path from the gate leads to the front door with its knocker dated 1709. To the left is a lower brick wing of *c.* 1760.
Stephen Murray, *Mobberley Records*, 1946-8, mss. at Altrincham Library.

Appleton Hall, Appleton (demolished)
622 844

A plain but substantial Regency style house with a curved bow and canopy built *c.* 1830 by Thomas Lyon on land originally owned by the Warburtons of Arley. It was demolished in the 1960s. Now there remains only a garden wall and a ruined Gothic lodge with a tablet inscribed *1860 TL.*
O i, 616; T ii, 81.

142.   Arderne Hall from the north-west, just prior to demolition in 1958.

143.   The billiard room at Arrowe Hall, late 19th century.

Arderne Hall, Tarporley
563 630

The present house, built in 1966 for John Lilley by the Liverpool architect David Brock, is composed of two interlocking drums three storeys in height, which afford spectacular views to the Peckforton Hills. The Hall stands on the foundations of a Victorian house demolished in 1958, a building no less progressive for its date. Designed by the Manchester church architect Joseph Crowther, it was a large Gothic house of brick erected in 1863 for George Baillie Arden Hamilton at a cost of £17,500. All that remains of Crowther's work is the hexagonal sandstone lodge on the Tarporley road just north of Portal. The sham ruin north of the Hall was built in 1835-45 for General Richard Egerton, a tenant of Eaton Banks, a previous house on the site. General Egerton is also known to have consulted John Webb on landscaping the park.
O ii, 239; *Ches Life* October 1936; CRO Dar/B/11, DAR/L/5; JRL, Roundell of Dorfold papers.

Arrowe Hall, Woodchurch
272 861

A stone house built in 1835 for J. R. Shaw, a Liverpool merchant, in a thin neo-Tudor style, and extended by John Cunningham of Liverpool. The skyline is busy with exaggeratedly steep gables, chimneys, castellations and a gabled three-storey tower. A billiard room and conservatory were added in 1876. In the late 19th century Captain Otho Shaw crammed the house with suits of armour, weapons and hunting trophies including in the billiard room a large case containing two wrestling tigers. There is a fancy lodge of 1856 and the gates are amusingly decorated with arrows. The Hall is now used for the handicapped and the grounds are a public park.
O ii, 527; T i, 82.

Ashfield Hall, Neston (demolished)
293 793

A handsome Neo-classical house with a giant Ionic portico and a central top-lit staircase hall. It was built in 1820-1 for Joseph Hayes Lyon whose family had profited from the development of Parkgate. There is a sketch design for the stables in the neo-Tudor style and an estimate for the stables signed by John and Edward Haycock 1819. The house is also likely to have been by the Haycocks as its appearance, known from Twycross, resembles their Shropshire houses. Ashfield was badly treated by the army in the Second World War and in 1958 was taken down to a height of one storey. It is now used as a barn.
T i, 61; CRO DHL/30 DD.

Ashley Hall, Ashley
768 849

Ashley Hall is chiefly famous for the Cheshire gentlemen who met there in 1715 to consider whether to support the Stuarts or the Hanoverians. They opted for the latter and to commemorate this in 1720 they commissioned the set of portraits now at Tatton, taken there in 1860 when Lord Egerton bought the Ashley estate. The portraits include the owner, Thomas Assheton. The Hall was partially demolished in 1972; the remaining section includes a 16th-century chimney stack, some timber framing and a window with Gothick glazing bars reset from the demolished range. The latter had some interesting interiors with 17th-century panelling and 18th-century Gothick plasterwork. A 17th-century carriage house and later stables line the approach.
O i, 556; *JCAS* xv, 5.

Ashton Hayes, Ashton
521 700

A seven-bay neo-Georgian house built in 1957 for Mrs. Violet Johnson, incorporating features of a large stuccoed house of 1780 which had been demolished. The latter was built for the Worthingtons but was bought in 1809 by Booth Grey, grandson of the 4th Earl of Stamford.
O ii, 335; T i, 125.

Astle Hall, Chelford
812 739

An irregular fragment of three storeys in white painted brick with gables and cross windows, overlooking a lake, with a park and a pretty *cottage orné* lodge. What survives may be a service wing as it bears little

resemblance to old views which show a regular Neo-classical house of the late 18th or early 19th century, probably a rebuilding for Thomas Parker who died in 1840.
O iii, 714; T ii, 113.

Aston Hall, Aston-by-Sutton (demolished)
551 780

Built in 1668 by Sir Willoughby Aston to replace an earlier house. Ormerod described the new one as sumptuous; it was a tall classical brick house with twin hipped roofs and a raised central attic. The grounds were improved by Repton whose 'Red Book' of 1793 was commissioned when Samuel Wyatt was advising on alterations. The Hall was demolished in 1938. There remains a brick dovecote of 1696, a Georgian dower house with a plain classical brick front, two lodges, one by Wyatt, and extensive walled gardens.
O i, 720; T ii; Pike 1904, 68.

144. Aston Park.

Aston Park, Aston-by-Budworth
677 782

A handsome five-bay house, formerly part of the Arley estate, with a semi-circular hooded doorcase dated 1715. Between the sash windows on the first floor is brick diapering in heart and diamond patterns. Inside, a broad central corridor serves four rooms of equal size. At the rear are two staircases: one is showy with twisted balusters, the other is a spiral within a timber-framed sleeve.

Backford Hall, Backford
398 718

An overdecorated neo-Elizabethan house of 1863 designed by John Cunningham in bright red brick with plenty of diaperwork and much showy ornamental stonework, curly gables, twisty chimneys, obelisks and fancy window surrounds. A large central porch leads to the interior, also lavishly and indiscriminately detailed; there is a top-lit galleried staircase hall with an inlaid marble floor and stained glass windows. The plainer stable block in diapered brick bears the date 1853. The house was built for Lt.-Col. Edward

Holt Glegg and replaced a brick mansion, which in its turn replaced the 16th-century Hall of the Birkenhead family. The grounds were laid out by John Webb. Now Council offices.
O ii, 366; T i, 74.

Baddiley Hall, Baddiley
605 504

Formerly a half-timbered house owned by the Mainwarings of Peover, whose tombs are in the little church nearby. The manor was sold after Sir Henry Mainwaring's death in 1797, by which time the house had been rebuilt as the present Baddiley Hall, a modest Georgian brick manor house, hardly more than a farmhouse.
O iii, 457.

Barrowmore Hall, Great Barrow (demolished)
475 690

A large house designed in 1881 by John Douglas for H. Lyle Smith, a Liverpool grain merchant. It was Douglas's best domestic work, of Ruabon brick and terracotta, richly ornamented with cusped panelling and diaper patterns. As in his earlier house, Oakmere, the skyline was dominated by a huge castellated tower. The house was destroyed during the Second World War and a hospital is now built on the site. The park and a lodge dated 1881 remain. Nearby is **Greysfield**, built in 1878 and shortly afterwards enlarged for Lyle Smith's partner Edward Paul.
BN xli, 494; H. Muthesius, *The English House*, 1904-5, English edition 1979, 33, 87.

Beeston Towers, Beeston
558 592

An extravaganza in the Cheshire half-timbered style like a bad dream of Little Moreton Hall. It was built for a timber merchant John Naylor of Warrington in 1886. There are three storeys, each jettied out, with carving and patterned timberwork. On the top floor are overlarge windows with decorative leading, and above this is a cupola with a pointed top. The plainer stables, of the early 19th century, belong to a former house, and the service wing is also simpler, though this too has applied half timbering and metalwork. It is now a hotel and restaurant, with unsympathetic flat roofed extensions.
Pike 1904, 42.

Betchton Hall, Betchton
794 591

Originally a timber-framed house, substantially rebuilt in brick in the 18th century and extended in the early years of the nineteenth. The service areas and a single casement window at the rear are all that remain of the Old Hall. Of the 18th-century rebuilding the main external feature is the central recessed bay of the side elevation, perhaps originally the entrance front. The present entrance front and the projecting wings of the side elevation are part of the later extension. The plain seven-bay front has an undersized doorway and a grander window above, the latter probably re-used from the 18th-century house. In the drawing room is a crisply carved late 18th-century fireplace brought in the 1960s from Faringdon House, Berkshire. The 18th-century rebuilding was for Richard Jackson, Prebendary of Chester, and the later work for Richard Galley. The initials of his son John Galley Day Jackson are carved high on the brickwork with the date 1839, the year of his death.
O iii, 298; J. P. Earwaker, *History of Sandbach*, 1890, 150.

Bexton Hall, Bexton
747 770

An attractive square symmetrical house of the late 17th century, probably built by the Daniel family. It is of brick with wooden cross windows and a steeply hipped roof with a flat viewing platform in the centre, originally having a cupola. There are five bays, the outer two projecting under small hipped gables, and the two storeys are raised up on a high basement with steps up to the front door. In front is a square walled garden.
O i, 509.

145. Bexton Hall before the removal of the cupola.

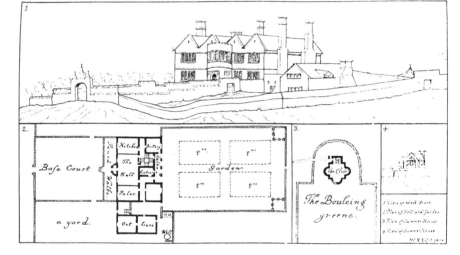

146. Bidston Hall, after a drawing of 1665.

147. The entrance front, Birtles Hall.

Bidston Hall, Bidston

287 903

A small stone house above the village, built *c.* 1620 for William Stanley, 6th Earl of Derby, probably as a hunting lodge for the Stanleys' deer park on Bidston Hill. The house is entered from a square walled forecourt with a crested gateway. In the centre of the facade is a curved bay with a porch, a glazed first floor and a scalloped parapet; all the detail is broad and heavy. At the back is a loggia with squat Tuscan columns. A drawing of 1665 shows a more balanced composition; instead of the flat skyline there were four gables to the roof. Also shown is a walled formal garden at the rear (fragments of angle pavilions remain) and a bowling green with a little summer house. Restored in the 1960s by Max Faulkner.
O ii, 360, 468; *THSLAC* lxxxviii, 61.

Birtles Hall, Over Alderley

858 747

A severe Neo-classical house built *c.* 1819 for Robert Hibbert who acquired the Birtles estate in 1791. It is faced with huge fine-jointed blocks of ashlar, now smoke-blackened, surmounted by a top-heavy cornice and balustrade. In September 1938 a fire consumed the interior. The owners, Mr. and Mrs. D. G. Norton, engaged the Manchester Arts and Crafts architect James Henry Sellers to reconstruct it. Sellers chose to paraphrase the original interiors rather than to restore them, so whilst the layout and proportion of the rooms were retained, the detail was greatly simplified. In the staircase hall, where the stone staircase survived, his sources are historical; in the reception rooms he produced an austere *moderne* look, designed as a setting for the elegant furniture he supplied for the house. Though simple and rectilinear in form, the furniture is luxuriously enriched with veneers and geometrical inlays, a characteristic reflected in the fireplaces of the house where plain timber surrounds enclose flat slabs of exquisite coloured marbles. Nearby is the small church of St Catherine, built as a private chapel by Thomas Hibbert in 1840. From the outside it looks unremarkable, but inside it displays the taste of a romantic antiquarian collector. The church is crammed with ecclesiastical ornament: Flemish glass of the 16th century, panelling, a carved pulpit dated 1696, sections of choir stalls and 17th-century furniture. To the south is the Old Hall, a fragment of the previous seat, built by the Swettenhams in the early 1700s.
O iii, 711; T ii, 117; *Ches Life* March/April 1958.

Blackden Manor, Goostrey

785 697

A timber-framed house with a twin-gabled entrance front rebuilt in brick. The house was built for the Kinsey family and probably dates from the early 17th century. It was much restored in 1920 by the architect James Henry Sellers who added new wings at the rear forming a courtyard where some original timbering is exposed. A window pane in the dining room has the engraved date 1675 and the big brick barn is dated 1709.
O iii, 139; *Ches Life* April/May 1953.

Bonis Hall, Prestbury

903 790

The seat of the Pigots until 1746 when sold to Charles Legh of Adlington. The Hall was remodelled in the early 19th century with an attractive curved bow and used by the Leghs as a dower house. In the early 20th century it was pebbledashed and shallow castellations were added. Now offices with modern extensions. Nearby is an earlier Adlington dower house, the timber-framed **Mill House**, on an E plan and dated 1603 over the porch. It was built by Sir Urian Legh, son of Thomas Legh of Adlington. The herringbone bracing on the entrance front remains, but the sides and rear have been partly replaced in brick and stone.
O iii, 668.

Booths Hall, Knutsford

766 780

A Georgian house of 1745 built for Peter Legh, but completely remodelled around the 1860s by Edward Habershon for John Pennington Legh. It stands close to the old moated site of an extensive courtyard house. The new Hall of 1745 was a plain brick box, enlarged in the early 19th century by the addition of

a two-storey wing. The Victorian recasing is in an Italianate style with bright red bricks, a heavy stone balustraded parapet, large plate glass windows and a ponderous stone porch resting on six pairs of coupled columns. At the side is a first floor conservatory and a bellcote with an onion dome. Much of the manor was sold at the turn of the century to wealthy Manchester businessmen who established the smaller surrounding estates; the beautiful setting has recently been spoiled by a large office complex built in the park. Across the main road a tall 18th-century rusticated pedestal supporting an urn marks the site of a former domestic chapel.
Aikin 424; O i, 498; T ii, 66; Pike 1904, 43.

148.   Bostock Hall from the south-east, before 1875.

Bostock Hall, Bostock Green
675 684

A large brick house, by 'Wyatt' according to Twycross, but since much altered and enlarged. It has an early Georgian core but was totally rebuilt in 1775 for Edward Tomkinson. Samuel Wyatt may have been involved as there is excellent characteristic plasterwork within. The house is L-shaped in plan with two main fronts, the entrance front with a tall central bow, and the garden front with two bows flanking a Venetian window, and a Diocletian window above. In 1792 Bostock was bought by the France family of Liverpool who lived there until 1950. John Webb made proposals for altering the house in 1826, but they were not carried out; he may have had a hand in the park. The house was extensively remodelled in the mid-19th century by the addition of a new cast-iron main staircase, an enlarged service wing and an Italianate porch. However, much of the stone balustrading, lunettes and other fancy external decoration is later, possibly even Edwardian. Vast red brick extensions were added in 1875 for Lt.-Col. Charles Hosken France Hayhurst, in a free mixture of Queen Anne and Gothic, with many gables, turrets and spires. Inside the house has been decorated in a succession of styles, Neo-classical, Pompeian and Italianate, but there is a great deal of mechanical Queen Anne work of the 1870s and '80s. The former dining room has exuberant *fin-de-siècle* decoration with painted trelliswork and peacocks, but also an excellent Neo-classical marble chimneypiece with large maidens. Between 1950 and 1980 the house was used as a school by Manchester Corporation, but is now privately owned.

O iii, 257; T i, 138; *Ches Life* August/September 1935; CRO DGN/1732.

Brackenwood, Higher Bebington (demolished)
317 840

A tall, gabled Tudor-style house built of local Storeton stone. It was an early work by Aston Webb with big mullioned windows and touches of Queen Anne-style decoration, and was designed for his brother-in-law J. J. Evans, a Liverpool chemical manufacturer. A drawing was shown at the Royal Academy in 1883. The house has been demolished but the Lower Lodge and the stables survive, the latter now as a golf club house.

BN xlv, 246, xlvii, 88; Pike 1904, 47.

Bradwall Hall, Bradwall Green (demolished)
750 633

Bradwall Hall was the ancient brick gabled house of the Bradwall and Venables families. In 1802 the estate was purchased by Dr. John Latham of Congleton, an eminent London physician, who rebuilt the Hall in a plain late Georgian style with cast-iron verandahs. It fell vacant in the 1920s and became ruinous soon after. The park, which was designed by John Webb, survives.

O iii, 114; T i, 131.

Brimstage Hall, Brimstage
305 827

A farmhouse built onto the remains of a medieval moated fortified tower house, the only one in Cheshire besides that at Doddington. The tower, which has been reduced in height, has a rib-vaulted room on the ground floor and a tall angle turret housing a staircase and garderobes. In style the building is late 14th or early 15th century, which fits in with the date 1398, when Sir Hugh Hulse and Margery his wife obtained a licence to build an oratory at Brimstage. Carved on the bosses of the vaulted room are fishes, commonly a Christian symbol, but this room was not necessarily the oratory. Vaulted rooms are customary in tower houses, and there may have been a detached chapel nearby.

149. The tower house at Brimstage Hall.

O ii, 434; Mortimer, 211; *THSLC* xlvii, 250.

Broxton Old Hall, Broxton
487 533

A large rambling black and white mansion of 1873 designed by John Douglas for Sir Philip de Grey Egerton as a dower house for Oulton Park. A timber-framed house of the 1590s built for Thomas Dod was incorporated, and the present central gables of the entrance elevation are an exact copy of the original front. Some fragments of this earlier house survive inside, as well as re-used 17th-century panelling and a good Jacobean doorcase. Carefully remodelled and extended in 1987-8 by The Carnell Green Partnership for Malcolm Walker.

O ii, 676; *BN* 16 May 1873, 558; Douglas i, 7; *Ches Life* August 1937, September 1963.

Bruntwood Hall, Cheadle
860 871

A large Gothic house of rock-faced sandstone with a tall castellated tower dated 1861, built for the Douglas family. It is asymmetrical, somewhat grim of aspect and mechanical in detail. The extensions, more fanciful and varied in silhouette, include a conservatory with a pitched roof and conical turret, a linking glazed corridor with tiles, mosaics and stained glass, and a billiard room dated 1893 for James Platt. The park is now public and the house offices.

Buglawton Hall, Buglawton
886 645

A castellated house added to variously and somewhat incoherently. The nucleus is of the 16th century, of brick on a stone plinth with half timbering visible within, but it was extended several times, and stuccoed and castellated in the early 19th century, probably for Samuel Pearson, a silk manufacturer who bought it in 1823. A service wing and a billiard room with interior decoration in the style of George Faulkner Armitage were added in the late 19th century. Within the 18th-century stable block there was until recently a good medieval timber roof, shamefully and needlessly replaced in steel by Manchester Corporation which now runs the house as a school. Nearby is **Crossley Hall**, a late 16th-century timber-framed house, once the Hall of a subordinate manor.
O iii, 41; T i, 143.

Bulkeley Hall, Bulkeley
523 538

An unsophisticated mid-Georgian house of brick built for Thomas Bulkeley. It is rectangular, with a symmetrical entrance front of seven bays and three storeys, a block cornice and a hipped roof. The doorcase, with simple semi-circular columns, is too small for its position in such a big facade.
O ii, 651; *Ches Life* May/June 1957.

Bulkeley, The Grange
534 541

A large Victorian house of the kind once regarded as a monstrosity, heavily detailed, with steep roofs, high chimneys and gables with applied half timbering. It is in a park with substantial farm buildings. Bulkeley Old Hall was a timber-framed house of *c*. 1600 built by Thomas Brassey. His descendant and namesake, the great railway contractor, replaced it with The Grange probably in the 1860s. The architect may have been Edward Habershon who designed Normanhurst, Surrey, built 1867 in a heavy French château style for Brassey's son Thomas.
O ii, 651; A. Helps, *Life and Labours of Mr. Brassey*, 1872, 20.

Burton Hall, Burton
508 638

An ingeniously devised small brick manor house built probably for John Werden a Chester lawyer, who bought the estate *c*. 1600. Described by Webb in the 1620s as a 'fair and fine conceitedly built house', it is a country reflection of the banquet houses and pleasure buildings erected for the Elizabethan court. It has a square plan and tall symmetrical elevations, each rising to a single gable. Windows are stacked one above another right up to the apex. In the later 17th century the interior was altered to form four rooms of equal size on each floor and a new staircase with twisted balusters was installed. The house stands behind a walled forecourt with an axial gateway.
O ii, 8, 329.

Burton Manor, Burton, Wirral
315 742

A large Edwardian house built for Henry Neville Gladstone, third son of the Prime Minister, and a successful Liverpool businessman. He bought the Burton estate in 1903 from the Congreve family which had established a seat there in 1805. His architect was Sir Charles Nicholson, who recased the earlier

150. Burton Hall.

151. The music room at Burton Manor, 1912.

house in local sandstone, extending it to provide grander accommodation and larger service quarters. On the garden elevations he was constrained by the existing pattern of fenestration, but the entrance facade with its bold centrepiece was new. Over the arched entrance is the Gladstone coat of arms, incorporating a negro's head, a reminder that the family wealth was based on slavery. The inner hall, lit from a small fountain court, leads to a series of reception rooms overlooking the western terrace. At the centre of the house is the large music room, a tall space like a medieval Great Hall, but in the neo-Georgian style. The interiors are spatially adventurous, but decoratively insipid; Gladstone himself complained of the final result. The large gardens are the work of T. H. Mawson and the architect A. Beresford Pite. Pite's schemes for an orangery, pavilions and terracing were only partially realised, but Mawson created a series of parterres, lily pools, borders, and a woodland walk making use of the old ice-house as a grotto. In the village street are cottages designed for Gladstone by Nicholson's friend H. S. Goodhart-Rendel, Mrs. Gladstone's nephew, and nearby is the vicarage by Nicholson himself. In 1926 the estate was sold for development, and in 1948 the house became a residential college.

O ii, 555; T i, 72; *CL* xxxii, 490; Macartney ii 1909, 143; P. H. W. Booth, *Burton Manor*, 1978; RIBA, Pite drawings.

Butley Hall, Prestbury
901 773

Rebuilt in 1777 by Peter Downes, owner of the Shrigley and Worth estates, who made it his principal home. The main front has seven bays and three storeys in coursed stone, with a central pedimented doorcase and rainwater heads dated 1777. To each side are wings containing Venetian windows. At the rear can be seen the three-storey gabled front of the former 17th-century house. Now divided into flats, its grounds developed for housing.

O iii, 668.

Caldy Manor, Caldy
226 854

A rambling picturesque red sandstone neo-Tudor house of 17th-century origin, bought in 1832 by R. W. Barton, a Manchester merchant. Improvements were carried out for him and his son, who employed W. & J. Hay on additions in 1864. Internal plasterwork in the main block is dated 1877. The main front faces the gardens, but behind is an irregular courtyard separated from the village street only by a stone wall, over which can be seen a cluster of gables, turrets, oriels, and a clock tower with a tall timber flèche. This was originally a bell-tower designed by C. E. Kempe, who was employed by Barton's widow Elizabeth to build a chapel in 1882. Some of Kempe's fittings are now in the village church, designed as a school in 1868 for Elizabeth Barton by G. E. Street. A 'Wrenaissance'-style hall, a billiard room and new entrance front were formed in 1906-7 by Guy Dawber. Recently marred by conversion into several dwellings.

O ii, 490; Macartney ii 1909, 60.

Calveley Hall, Alpraham (demolished)
605 593

The half-timbered Old Hall, surrounded by a wall with arrow slits, was demolished *c.* 1800, but it seems that the Davenport family had long since moved to another timber house which had been encased in brick and then, in the 19th century, half timbered again. When this house was demolished earlier this century, panelling from it was salvaged. Some is at Rookery Hall, Worleston, and some was used to line the smoke room of the Ellerman liner, *City of Durban*. A Georgian carved wood fireplace was also saved and is now in the state dressing room at Capesthorne, another Davenport house. Nothing remains on site, apart from a lodge, a school and other estate buildings.

O ii, 284; T i, 116.

Calveley Hall, Milton Green
454 587

A late 17th-century house concealed behind a later plain stuccoed facade. The passage from the front door leads to an exceptionally broad staircase. It appears to be squeezed into position, but probably originally descended into the middle of a central hall, and the ground floor rooms were later rebuilt round it. The staircase has double twisted balusters, but the newels are big open spirals with square tops decorated with carved coats of arms and surmounted by baskets of fruit. The quality of the carving and the classical detail suggest a provincial craftsman of the Restoration period. The staircase leads up to two unexpectedly grand apartments which occupy all five bays of the front. The larger, entered by double doors, is handsomely panelled throughout with bolection-moulded wainscoting. At one end is an extremely fine carved overmantel with the Calveley arms, three calves, flanked by pendant swags of fruit hanging from bows of ribbon. The arms, lozenge shaped for a widow, are those of the last Lady Calveley, Mary, second wife of Sir Hugh. She is known to have erected a domestic chapel in 1690 and died in 1705. Her arms are also seen on the left hand newel post of the stair, corresponding to those of Sir Hugh's first wife on the right hand post. From the upstairs room another pair of double doors leads to a smaller chamber formerly hung with tapestries above a panelled dado. These were removed to Lyme Park for, after Lady Calveley's death, the estate passed to the Leghs of Lyme by the marriage of one of Sir Hugh's sisters. O ii, 724, 769.

152. Carden Park, c.1900.

Carden Park, Clutton (demolished)
462 540
   An attractive Jacobean house, large and symmetrical, busily half-timbered, with two big outer gables and between them five smaller ones. The house was entered centrally through a loggia of three arches. There were many ogee Gothick windows and other evidence of the early 19th-century restoration for John Hurlestone Leche. The house was built by the Leches who lived there until it was destroyed by fire in 1912. All that survives is an ice-house, the stables, and the lodges, all early 19th century. The Carden Lodge is in the form of a grand classical triumphal arch with giant detached Ionic columns and a big attic.

223

The Clutton Lodge is less grand but more idiosyncratic, formed by two very chaste little French Neo-classical pepperpots each with a low dome and a terracotta urn on top. The plan of each is a concave sided square with the corners cut off. The gate-piers have pointed tops and good railings, but the gates themselves, attributed to the Davies brothers, have gone.
O ii, 701; T i, 27; FM ii, 373, vi, 318.

Carlett Park, Eastham (demolished)
362 812
An ugly brick mansion of 1859-60 by T. H. Wyatt for John Torr. It was vaguely Tudor in style but above the porch was a three-storey tower with a tall French pavilion roof. A chapel was built for Revd. W. E. Torr in 1884-5 to the design of John Douglas. The chapel, a small Gothic building with lancets and a corner turret, survives, but the house has been replaced by a multi-storey slab of concrete and glass. Now a College of Further Education.
O ii, 406; RIBA, T. H. Wyatt drawing.

Checkley Hall, Checkley
733 462
An attractive five-bay symmetrical brick house built 1694 by the Delves family of Doddington to replace a timber-framed Hall. Originally with a hipped roof as at Weston Hall, the attic was rebuilt and the house now has two and a half storeys, with sash windows on the ground floor, but still cross windows above. In front is a walled forecourt entered through stone gate-piers with ball finials.
O iii, 514.

Chelford, The Manor House
820 743
A complex timber-framed building dating from the early 17th century, with many later additions. The earliest part is the former hall with two pairs of crucks, divided later into two floors. A three-storey section bears the inscription *John Brooke Ecc 2 II Mary 1671* and, within, the verse from Ecclesiastes has been written out on a beam, 'When thou hast eaten and art full then shalt thou thank the Lord thy God'. There are extensive additions of the 19th and early 20th centuries, the latter for Col. Dixon of Astle Hall. Alongside is a late 16th-century tithe barn.
Ches Life August/September 1952.

Chorlton Hall, Backford
408 718
A U-shaped neo-Tudor house, the remodelling in 1846-7 of an early 19th-century building. The sash windows with glazing bars are re-used from the earlier house, but the hood moulds and shaped gables are part of the remodelling. On the outer bays are handsome stucco Gothic armorial reliefs of the Wicksted family who carried out the Tudorisation, including the motto *In Veritate Victoria*. Originally the property of the Stanleys of Hooton, two antiquaries owned it in later years. William Nicholls, F.S.A., Deputy Registrar of the Archdeaconry of Chester, and correspondent of Lysons' *Magna Britannia*, bought it in 1799 and presumably built the earlier house. His wife sold it in 1811 to George Ormerod, author of one of the chief sources of this book, the monumental *History of Cheshire*. It took him just nine years to write, most of it in this house which he sold to the Wicksteds of Nantwich in 1823.
O ii, 376; T. Hess & D. Watkin, *A History of Chorlton Hall*, 1979.

Chorlton Hall, Malpas
467 482
A 17th-century house with Tudor-style additions of the second quarter of the 19th century. A door on the stables, presumably removed from the Hall, is dated 1661 with an illegible inscription, perhaps that read by Ormerod as 'in the time of George Mainwaring 1660'. The entrance front has three gables of equal height and a central porch. By 1805 the house belonged to John Bennion, according to an estate map at the Hall which shows the house with a slightly different arrangement; but the entrance front appears to be of the 17th century despite the pebbledash cladding. The additions are in red sandstone with taller and steeper roofs. The interiors are all of the early 19th century. Nearby is the site of **Chorlton Old Hall**, a

moated half-timbered house, now demolished; and also the building now called **Chorlton Old Hall**, an E-plan brick farmhouse with shaped gables (one wing demolished). It was built in 1666 by Owen Clutton, whose family's arms are at base of the staircase.
O ii 665; T i, 41.

Christleton Old Hall, Christleton
442 658

An early 17th-century timber-framed house, built by a branch of the Egerton family and encased in harsh red brick for Revd. Lionel Garnett about 1870 when in use as the rectory. Its chief interest is inside where there is much good Jacobean plasterwork and panelling. In the hall is a chimneypiece with perspective panels, one with a unicorn, one with an eagle in a tree. The Pillar Room beyond has two pairs of carved mahogany balusters supporting a central beam. On the first floor is the main chamber, now the library, with a strapwork ceiling. In the north garden wall is a set of six early 18th-century bread ovens. Nearby in the village is **Christleton Hall**, a tall Georgian brick house of *c.* 1750 built for Townsend Ince, and now used as a law college.
O ii, 780; T i, 43; *Ches Life* March/April 1948.

Churton Hall, Churton
419 564

A half-timbered house built by the Barnston family and bearing their arms and crest in stucco. There is a loose painted board carrying the inscription *WB 1569 EB*. The plan is an E, with projecting gables of different design at either end and a porch placed to one side. Heavily restored 1978-80.
O ii, 746.

Claughton Manor, Birkenhead (demolished)
303 893

A small but lavish Italian palazzo-style villa of 1864 built for the industrial entrepreneur Sir William Jackson M.P., and designed by Charles Reed (later Verelst) of Liverpool. The exterior, of stone, had a very heavy classical cornice, a semicircular entrance portico and short low wings at each side. Inside, the rooms were magnificently decorated using coloured marbles, scagliola, mosaic floors, ornate plasterwork and gilding. The house was set in a park laid out by Paxton and commanded views of the Dee and the Mersey. Reed designed many villas in the area for Jackson *c.* 1843, and Paxton created Birkenhead Park, of which Jackson was the chief promoter.
T i, 86; Pike 1911, 69; C. G. Mott, *Reminiscences of Birkenhead*, 1900, 46.

Clonterbrook House, Swettenham
821 673

A small manor house of brick with five bays of wooden cross windows and a decorative string course. The lintel over the door bears the dates *JKL 1697* for Jeffery and Katherine Lockett, who married in 1679, and *DEL 1949* for Derek and Elizabeth Lockett, who bought the house in 1939 (it had left the ownership of the Lockett family in 1769). They restored it in 1949 using panelling from Bowood and Bryn-y-Pys. The shippon, damaged in an air raid in 1941, was rebuilt as a music room with a stage flanked by Ionic columns from Grassendale House, Liverpool, another Lockett property.
Ches Life September 1959.

Cogshall Hall, Comberbach
632 780

A plain squarish classical brick house built *c.* 1830 for Peter Jackson. The entrance front has five bays with a single storey Ionic portico, and there is a smaller portico on the east front. The interior has a staircase hall with detached columns and good plasterwork. In the drawing room is a fireplace with full-length dancing maidens. At the rear is an unfortunate suburban-style domestic wing and a large brick stable court with a cupola and a pedimented centrepiece.
O i, 656.

Colshaw Hall, Peover Superior
783 744

A restrained neo-Tudor style mansion of red brick with stone dressings by Douglas and Minshull, built for J. G. Peel in 1903. A drawing was exhibited at the Royal Academy in 1905. The entrance front is at the centre of an irregular three-sided courtyard. The house was altered and extended in 1907 by Percy Worthington.

Academy Architecture xxviii, 35, 45; Massey.

153. Compstall Hall: detail of lithograph from Twycross, 1850.

Compstall Hall, Compstall
962 909

A substantial Grecian-style house of ashlar with a long cast-iron balcony on one side and a single-storey porch, now altered. Originally called Green Hill, it was built on a hillside with views of the Peaks for George Andrew, whose family established the industrial community in the village, starting a calico printing works in 1819, and building workers' housing and community institutions, many of which survive. The house, since altered and enlarged, was designed by John Day and Goldsmith, and is typical of many simple Grecian villas built in the manufacturing areas outside Manchester in the early 19th century.

T ii, 130; R. E. Thelwall, *The Andrews and Compstall*, 1972.

Crabwall Hall, Mollington
384 695

Originally a gabled stone house built in the early 17th century by the Gamul family; it had been demolished by 1817. The present Hall consists of a modest brick cottage refronted in the early 19th century giving it the appearance of a toy fort. It is symmetrical, with a straight parapet, castellated octagonal corner turrets, a cental porch and a Gothic arched entrance. The windows, beneath square hood moulds and heavy stone lintels, have delicate cast-iron tracery with cusped arches. In the rear walls are 18th-century sashes. Extended in 1987 as a luxury hotel.

O ii, 577; *Ches Life* October/November 1950.

Crag Hall, Wildboarclough
988 688

A robust stone house of 1815 built for George Palfreyman who established a large textile printing works at Wildboarclough. It stands in a steeply wooded garden surrounded by moorland. In the centre of the five-bay front is an Ionic porch, and above it a window with classical entablature. The house has been extended to each side by large curved bows. With its slightly clumsy proportions it has an imposing air of millstone grit solidity.

O iii, 769; B. S. Beeken, *Crag Works, Wildboardclough*, nd.

Cranage Hall, Cranage
750 683

An Elizabethan-style mansion of 1828-9 by Lewis Wyatt for Lawrence Armistead, and very similar to the same architect's Eaton Hall, Eaton-by-Congleton. except that Cranage is smaller and lower. Both are not quite symmetrical and a trifle dull and heavy in their exceptionally early use of the neo-Elizabethan style. Cranage is of brick in varied diaper patterns, with stone, now much blackened, for dressings, including a parapet and mullioned windows. The plan is long and narrow and, apart from a pronounced attic above

the grand entrance porch, the skyline is flat. Now part of a hospital and surrounded by bland landscaping and modern buildings.
O iii, 128; T i, 144.

Crewe Hill, Farndon
421 527

A rambling stuccoed house of the early 19th century, enlarged from a farmouse for the Barnstons of Churton Hall. Inside is a marvellously eccentric creation: a galleried Great Hall, not large but crammed with a display of early Victorian antiquarianism. There is heavy oak furniture and dark stained woodcarving, all wildly fantastic, including bulbous balusters on the door panels, and a ceiling studded with bosses. Some of the carving is Jacobean, reputedly from Forest House, the Barnstons' Chester residence; other pieces like the fireplace supported on atlantes are 19th century. On the walls, amongst the family portraits, are halberds, swords, armour from the Civil War and the tattered colours of Queen Isabella of Spain. Some items are mementoes of Major Roger Barnston who was mortally wounded, aged 31, leading an assault at the relief of Lucknow, and is commemorated in the obelisk on the Farndon to Churton road.
O ii, 745; T i, 37; F. Latham, *Farndon*, 1981.

Crewood Hall, Crowton
567 762

The 16th-century house of the Gerrards, and, originally timber-framed, though Webb's *Itinerary*, *c*. 1623, already described it as 'a fair brick house'. It is U-shaped, with a hall between two cross wings. On the left of the hall is a porch dated 1638, with exposed timbering in the upper storey, which was built by Gilbert Gerrard and bears his arms. The Hall was remodelled and encased in brick in the 19th century.
O ii, 11, 128; A. W. Waterworth, *Crewood Hall*, 1970.

154. The Great Hall, Crewe Hill.

Daresbury Hall, Daresbury
585 825

A fine mid-Georgian house of brick built for George Heron in 1759 probably by the same architect as Hefferston Grange. It has three storeys and seven bays, the central three projecting below a pediment. At the centre is a good pedimented doorcase on scroll consoles. A vertical emphasis is given by the close spacing of the central part, the flat stone surrounds to the windows, and above all by the four broad bands of stone quoins. By the stables are additions built for the Spastics Society which has used it as a home since 1960.
O i, 735; T ii, 76; *Ches Life* March/April 1955.

Davenham Hall, Davenham
663 707

A very good stuccoed Neo-classical house built for Thomas Ravenscroft to replace the half-timbered Davenham Lodge. It must date from shortly before 1795, when Ravenscroft died and the estate was acquired by William Harper of Liverpool. The entrance front is symmetrical, with a pediment and a wide porch of six Tuscan columns. The interiors are especially fine. The entrance hall has bold Grecian plasterwork and a severe black marble chimneypiece. To the left, the drawing room has more delicate

155.   The entrance front of Daresbury Hall.

plaster decoration in the Wyatt style and a marble chimneypiece with dancing figures. The chief feature is the central staircase hall lit from a shallow dome; in the pendentives is fan-shaped plasterwork in the Wyatt manner. The staircase has an elegant wrought-iron balustrade, and rises to the first floor landing where there is a screen of four Doric columns with a correct and well proportioned entablature. In 1980 the house was restored for use as a nursing home.
O iii, 238; T i, 148.

Dawpool, Thurstaston (demolished)
246 844

A palatial mansion in red sandstone by Richard Norman Shaw 1882-6 for T. H. Ismay, a Liverpool shipowner, for whom Shaw also designed the White Star building in Liverpool. Dawpool was a hard, forbidding house in a spare Tudor style. It was asymmetrically planned, with gables, bays and big areas of mullioned windows, but lacked charm. A principal feature of the interior was the large barrel-vaulted gallery, the model for the music room at nearby Thornton Manor. Dawpool had a short life: the Ismays moved out in 1907 and the house was demolished in 1927. The stables, built in 1892, and the lodge survive. Parts of the house were re-used elsewhere, including the Kingsland Dance Hall, Birkenhead (dining room fireplace), *Imperial Hotel*, Llandudno (doors), and Portmeirion (picture gallery fireplace).
A. Saint, *Richard Norman Shaw*, 1976, 261.

Delamere Manor, Cuddington
584 712

A neo-Georgian brick house on a spectacular hill site. The garden front has symmetrical curved bay

228

156. The staircase hall, Davenham Hall.

157. The picture gallery at Dawpool, 1896.

windows and a verandah looking on to lawns which sweep down to Cuddington Mere. It was designed by Charles Saxon for Captain G. H. Wilbraham in 1938 to replace **Delamere House**, demolished the previous year. This was a chaste stone house designed by Samuel Wyatt for George Wilbraham in 1784, and had typical Wyatt features: a central two-storey domed bow, windows set in shallow stone arches, and Coadestone reliefs.

O ii, 136; T i, 112; Pike 1904, 31; *Ches Life* October 1936, September/October 1957; CRO, Wilbraham family diary.

Denna Hall, Ness
300 749

Originally called Denwall Hall, and near the site of the medieval Denwall Hospital for the poor and shipwrecked. It is on the windswept Dee estuary and shelters behind a high sandstone wall. Formerly a small building, it was enlarged in the early 19th century with bays, verandahs and balconies for Charles Stanley, younger brother of Sir Thomas Stanley of Hooton. It was later further enlarged and pebbledashed.

O ii, 542; Pike 1911, 63; *Ches Life* July 1959.

Denton Hall, Chonar Farm, Wilmslow
857 796

Not a Cheshire house, but a house moved to Cheshire. Denton Hall was an important late 15th-century quadrangular Lancashire mansion, built for the Holland family. Part was demolished in 1895 and fire destroyed the hall range in 1930. The fragment which survives was in 1979 rescued from the line of a motorway by Frank Smith and re-erected to house a collection of vintage automobiles. It is timber framed, though clad in 19th-century brickwork, and contains good carved posts, two with green men and foliage in the spandrels. On the outside only the pierced quatrefoils and carved tie beam of the gable hint at anything of interest within.

Taylor, 110; *Archaeological Journal* cxxvii, 156; RCHM Denton Hall report, 1979; *Country Houses of Greater Manchester*, ed. J. S. F. Walker and A. S. Tindall, 1985, 36, 165.

Duddon Old Hall, Duddon
516 647

A late 16th- or early 17th-century house, partly brick and partly timber-framed. There are additions, perhaps of the late 18th century, and an outbuilding dated 1665. The main part consists of a hall and cross wing, the latter with a highly decorated black and white gable end. It was much restored early this century: a photograph published by Ould in 1904 shows it just before restoration. In the cross wing on the first floor is the main chamber, wainscoted and open to the roof.

P & O, pl. lxxvi; CRO DAR/B/79.

Dukenfield Hall, Mobberley
793 797

A charming small manor house up a tree-lined drive and fronted by a walled garden with stone gatepiers. Though it looks like a symmetrical brick building with a central hall, gabled porch and two gabled cross wings, it is an enlargement of a small cruck-framed house of the late 16th or early 17th century, entered at one end. When it was faced with brick in the late 17th century, it was made to look symmetrical by adding more to one side than the other. At the same time, the cross wings were built and the roof heightened, as can be seen where the crucks have been cut off at the top and cambered trusses and queen posts put in. In the dining room there is a plaster ceiling in a countrified Restoration style dominated by a large oval laurel wreath, similar to a ceiling in a house in King Street, Knutsford. Originally known as Podmore House, the Hall received its present name when Sarah Parker brought it in marriage to Sir Charles Dukinfield in 1718 with her Over Tabley and Mobberley estates.

O iii, 818; *Ches Life* March 1963.

Dukinfield Hall, Dukinfield (demolished)
935 971

A rambling gabled house consisting of a half-timbered hall with jettied cross wings, partly refronted in brick with stone quoins *c.* 1700. Attached to the house was a domestic chapel built in stone in a crude

158. Dukenfield Hall, Mobberley.

Jacobean Gothic style with a hammerbeam roof, but dating back to 1398 when John de Dokenfield was granted a licence to build an oratory. In 1873 a new Congregational Chapel was built, incorporating the old Hall chapel. Farther up the hill, overlooking the River Tame, was **Dukinfield Lodge**, designed for himself by the portrait painter, architect and adventurer John Dukinfield Astley, known as 'Beau Astley'. After marrying the rich widow Lady Dukinfield Daniell in 1759 and rebuilding Over Tabley Hall on the Daniell estate near Knutsford, he inherited the Dukinfield estate on the death of her daughter in 1771 (she had died in 1762). His fashionable new seat was castellated, with a Gothick loggia, a saloon, a great octagon room with painted windows, a hothouse and an open bath with a dressing room. According to photographs taken just prior to demolition, it lacked refinement, and had been extended in the early 19th century by a brick wing with a bowed end. Astley also built roads, bridges, an inn, an iron foundry, and a model village with a circus of brick houses for the factory workers. The Lodge was demolished in 1949, the Hall in 1951, and the chapel is now a ruin.

Aikin, 452; O iii, 814; *Connoisseur* clxxii, 256; *Country Houses of Greater Manchester*, ed. J. S. F. Walker and A. S. Tindall, 1985, 39, 165.

Dutton Hall, Dutton (demolished)
593 776

This exceptionally fine example of a timber-framed Hall, built 1539-42, admired by Fletcher Moss and Parkinson and Ould, and sketched by W. R. Lethaby, was purchased in 1926 by Cheshire County Council and sold to a demolition contractor. However, fragments were incorporated into the restoration of another half-timbered house, Homestall, Ashurstwood near East Grinstead, renamed Dutton Homestall, now Stoke Brunswick School. The work was carried out for J. A. Dewar. The rebuilt Great Hall retains its lengthy

231

159. The porch at Dutton Hall c.1900, before resiting.

160. The garden front of Eaton Hall, Eaton-by-Congleton, just prior to demolition in 1980.

inscription running round the inside, commemorating the Dutton Hall lawsuit, won by Sir Piers Dutton, builder of the house, after which he was confirmed as rightful heir. The porch, richly carved with coats of arms, grotesque heads and arabesque ornament, was rebuilt with its inscription and the date 1541. The bell in the inner courtyard at Dutton Homestall is another Cheshire relic, and came from Norton Priory. O i, 653; FM i, 6; P & O, 38, pl. xcv; *BN* 14 April 1911; F. H. Crossley, *Cheshire*, 1949, 343.

Eaton Hall, Eaton-by-Congleton (demolished)
863 655

Eaton Hall, a small Georgian box, was in the early 19th century purchased by the Antrobus family of Congleton. In 1813 the architect S. P. Cockerell (who had designed the Congleton Guildhall) drew up an unexecuted scheme to enlarge the house and remodel the park for Sir Edmund Antrobus, a partner in Coutts Bank. But Eaton was not enlarged until 1827, one year after it had been inherited by Edmund's nephew, Gibbs Crawford Antrobus, formerly a member of Wellington's diplomatic staff. He obtained alternative schemes from Lewis Wyatt and from Thomas Lee, formerly Wyatt's clerk of works, but it was Wyatt's scheme which was preferred. Antrobus first wanted to enlarge the existing house, but was persuaded to accept a new building on a different site and in the Elizabethan style; Mrs. Antrobus wrote that she was 'glad to find . . . that the style of Architecture you gave us is not so much more expensive than the Grecian'. It was, like Cranage, a very early example of the Elizabethan revival, but was still basically a classical house in Elizabethan dress. The entrance front was irregular, with towers, shaped gables and an attic over the porch, but the garden front made no attempt to disguise its basic symmetry. The details were plain and heavy, with very large stone mullioned windows, and mostly conventional classical interiors. In the 20th century the grounds were sold for sand quarrying. Excavations took place only a few feet from the house, so that, just prior to its demolition in 1981, the building teetered on the edge of a huge abyss. Wyatt's stable block dated 1831 survives nearby.
O i, 657, iii, 563; T ii, 102; *Ches Life* January/February 1952; Robinson, 150, 247; CRO, Eaton Hall drawings.

Egerton Hall, Egerton (demolished)
516 506

The fragmentary remains of a 14th-century chapel are all that is left of the moated Hall built by the Egertons and demolished in 1760. The domestic chapel dates back to 1360 when Philip de Egerton was granted a licence to celebrate divine service there. Though Ormerod describes the chapel as a ruin, it was restored in 1819 by Sir John Grey Egerton of Oulton, but again fell into disrepair.
O ii, 627.

Endon Hall, Bollington
936 765

A Tudor-style house of local stone built beneath the Kerridge Hill for William Clayton who developed the Endon Quarry. It was begun in the 1830s and enlarged 20 years later. The stables, which are more remarkable than the house, are castellated and surmounted by an open bellcote. In the park is a large icehouse of *c.* 1840.

Frankby Hall, Frankby
243 865

A small, rather weak castellated mansion of red sandstone, designed by William Culshaw and built 1846-7 for Sir Thomas Royden, shipowner and M.P. It was converted to two cemetery chapels in 1938-9. On the main front is a central oriel over the door, flanked by turrets, and on either side were two storeys of mullioned Tudor windows, now replaced by tall Perpendicular windows lighting the chapels.

Fulshaw Hall, Wilmslow
844 801

A symmetrical H-plan brick house with a central hall and two cross wings, built in 1684 for Samuel Finney, a merchant who later emigrated to Pennsylvania and became a member of the state's first Council. Although greatly enlarged, the form of the original house is clear from the west front: twin ball-finialled gables, stone mullioned windows, and heavy rusticated quoins. The east front was similar, but in 1735 the cross wings were extended and a service wing built for Samuel Finney II, who ruined himself in the process and disappeared to America. His son Samuel III, miniaturist to Queen Charlotte, restored the house in 1765. Major additions in red Accrington brick in the Jacobean style were carried out for Richard Lingard Monk in 1886. His arms, dated 1893, are carved on the chimneypiece in the former hall, and most of the interior features are of this period. Fine landscaped grounds are being obliterated for a huge office complex which takes in the adjoining property, **Harefield House**, a heavy classical brick mansion erected for George Fox in 1849.

O iii, 603; R. Scott, *Fulshall Hall and Harefield House*, 1976; R. Scott, *The Families and Estate of Fulshaw*, 1981; CCRO Finney family manuscript, Earwaker collection.

161.   The Great Hall, Gawsworth Old Rectory.

Gawsworth New Hall, Gawsworth
892 699

A new house begun in 1707 by Lord Mohun to replace the dilapidated Gawsworth Hall, but left uncompleted in 1712 following his death in a duel fought with his cousin the Duke of Hamilton. Probably intended to form a quadrangle, the house is U-shaped, with one immensely long side of 16 regular bays and two shorter sides. It is oddly plain and institutional in character, the only decorative feature being the fine Corinthian doorcase supporting the arms of the 1st Earl of Harrington, designed by Sir Hubert Worthington for Captain R. G. Peel and dated 1914. Behind the Hall is New Barn Farm, which includes a huge model barn built by the Earl of Harrington *c.* 1745, and described in 1757 as 'the finest farmhouse and offices in England'.

R. Richards, *The Manor of Gawsworth*, 1957; J. M. Robinson, *Georgian Model Farms*, 1983, 71, 122.

Gawsworth Old Rectory, Gawsworth
890 698

Though built as a rectory, this late medieval timber-framed building has all the characteristics of a small Cheshire manor house, and survives in more original condition than the nearby Old Hall. It was built for George Baguley, parish priest of Gawsworth from 1470-97, and consists of a long narrow range built of close-studded framing (the jettied two-storey porch and the bay window date from the 19th century). The original shafted oak door opens into the screens passage where three service doorways survive. The Great Hall roof is supported on a central queen-post truss with a carved boss, and on the back wall is a tall cusped three-light Gothic window like one in the Great Chamber at Bramall. The house was restored by William Hall, rector from 1724-69, as recorded on the overmantel in the solar. Neglected in the 19th century, it was again restored in 1873-4 for Revd. Henry Augustus Stanhope by Norman Shaw, who removed a set of clumsy stairs inserted in the hall, and added a wing of brick and half timber containing a dining room and staircase.

Ches Life June/July 1952; R. Richards, *The Manor of Gawsworth*, 1957; A. Saint, *Richard Norman Shaw*, 1977, 148.

Gayton Hall, Gayton
273 804

A 17th-century house refaced in the early 18th century by the Glegg family. At the rear are gables and cross windows, but the front is a handsome design of nine bays, the central three projecting slightly, all of brick with stone bands, quoins and parapet. The central doorcase has an open scroll pediment and fluted Ionic columns; unfortunately this is not used as the entrance, and a projecting porch two bays to

the right spoils the symmetry. Inside are two Jacobean staircases. North of the house is an octagonal brick dovecote dated 1663 containing nesting boxes for 1,000 birds.
O ii, 518; T i, 58; *Ches Life* August 1936.

Goyt Hall, Bredbury
923 902

A timber-framed house built *c.* 1570 for Randal Davenport, whose initials are carved on the middle two gables. It has two big projecting gables and two smaller ones in the re-entrant angles, one of these containing the porch. The big outer gable on the right has been rebuilt in brick.
O iii, 822; R. Hunter, *History of Bredbury and Romiley*, 1974.

Grafton Hall, Tilston (demolished)
450 513

Built in 1613 by Sir Peter Warburton, Grafton was a large and stately house on an E-plan with three gables and pyramid capped towers at either end. In the drawing room there was excellent panelling and a plaster frieze with animal heads. The Hall was restored and extended in 1883 for a branch of the Stanleys of Alderley by the London architect John Birch, who also designed a stable block. Mostly demolished in 1963.
O ii, 704; Douglas i, 43; *B* xlv, 146.

Greenbank, Chester
410 646

A very grand stucco house of two storeys with a seven-bay front, the central three bays with a raised parapet, giant pilasters and garlanded panels above the very tall windows. The garden elevation is perplexingly of three storeys, each one lower than those on the entrance side. The interior has good plasterwork and an impressive staircase hall with columns and a Neo-classical balustrade. The house was built in 1820 for John Swarbreck Rogers, a Chester glove manufacturer who was Mayor of Chester 1821-2. From 1907 it was occupied by Peter Jones, an Ellesmere Port industrialist, connoisseur and patron of the arts. He filled it with his collection of 18th-century furniture, and commissioned work from architects and craftsmen. The gatehouse and front door are neo-Georgian designs by C. H. Reilly; the fanlight is lettered *EPJ 1820-1923 MJ*, giving the date of the house and of the restoration. In front is a Victorian stone wall, formerly carrying gates and railings by the Birmingham Guild. Now restored and converted for Chester College of Further Education.
Pike 1904, 41; CCRO, Deeds of Greenbank.

Hallwood, Halton
542 808

The house of Sir John Chesshyre, prime sergeant to George II, remodelled *c.* 1710 and surprisingly modest for so wealthy a man. The stables are grander; the enlargement of a late medieval building, they form a long narrow stone range with irregularly spaced giant pilasters, two pedimented doorways, and first floor oval windows. The house is of rough stone, to which a five-bay brick front was added with a broad pediment across the whole facade. The interiors are more impressive and include pedimented doorcases and a carved oak staircase with fluted Corinthian newels. Plans dated 1798 to reface the house in Neo-classical style for Thomas Brooke, son of Sir Richard Brooke of Norton Priory, were not carried out. Now the *Tricorn Inn*, a seedy public house.
O i, 711; Axon, *Cheshire Gleanings*, 1884, 75; CRO DBN/C/9C/5.

Halton Grange, Runcorn
519 822

An ornate and overscaled villa in the Italianate style, designed 1853-6 by Charles Reed of Liverpool for Thomas Johnson, a soap and alkali manufacturer. It has a belvedere tower, overhanging eaves, balconies and heavy stucco enrichments of a nouveau-riche character. Inside is opulent plasterwork and a double height staircase hall with an elaborate Minton tile floor, marbled columns and a cantilevered staircase. On the landing hang *The Continence of Scipio* and *Sophonisba*, two vast and brilliantly coloured paintings by the Italian Rococo artist Andrea Casali, in William Kent frames. The paintings are from

162. The entrance front of Grafton Hall just prior to demolition in 1963.

163. The staircase hall at Greenbank, c.1920.

Kent's Wanstead House and were recorded at Eaton Hall in 1824. Halton Grange became the property of another soap manufacturer in 1871, but since 1933 has been Runcorn Town Hall. There is a tall glass office block of 1965 attached, and the grounds are a public park.

Hampton Hall, Malpas
508 491

A puzzling and ambitious house, perhaps never completed. The earliest section is the close-studded timber-framed range of three gables which forms the main block. This comprises a central hall with rooms to each side, and is dated 1591 on the back of the massive courtyard door. Adjoining the gabled front is an elaborate 17th-century timber-framed porch. This mixes classical motifs – scrolls, modillions and pediment, with the old decoration – balusters and studded door. Behind the porch runs a long south wing in several stages. It has a huge chimney of glazed diaper-patterned bricks, and beyond is a section built of massive ashlar blocks, perhaps originally a separate building. Inside is a small panelled room with a 17th-century chimneypiece framing a painted panel of a man on horseback in a fantastic landscape. In an adjoining room is another Jacobean chimneypiece with an arcaded overmantel decorated with gryphons and grotesque figures holding orbs. The house was built for the Bromley family, but in the 18th century passed to the Dods and became a farm, which it remains. The present owners have restored and furnished it in a solid and traditional farmhouse manner.
O ii, 641.

Hankelow Hall, Hankelow
668 463

An individual early Georgian brick house of 10 bays built for Gabriel Wettenhall and altered for his son Nathaniel in 1755-7. The three storeys are surmounted by an immensely tall parapet with ball finials resting on thin pilaster strips. The alterations of 1755 were by the architect William Baker of nearby Highfields. He remodelled the ground floor, replacing the five windows to each side of the centre by two larger ones. On the death of Nathaniel Wettenhall it passed to Edward Tomkinson who rebuilt Bostock. In this century it has suffered neglect and is now empty and becoming ruinous.
O iii, 477; T ii, 19; Oswald, 124.

Harden Hall, Bredbury
919 933

A ruined Elizabethan house, built in 1597 for Ralph and Ellen Arderne of Alvanley. It was a tall stone house with three stepped gables, those in the centre and on the right projecting to form the hall porch and hall bay respectively. The hall, which was reached by an external staircase, was lit by big mullioned windows, with cusped windows in the attics. At the back another square bay projected from the dais end of the hall, and in the centre, rising above the roofline, was an octagonal tower with conical top containing a staircase. Inside there was panelling and decorative plasterwork, and a collection of portraits, some from Utkinton Hall, but 'none of them good ones' (Aikin). There was also a detached half-timbered jettied building, probably a gatehouse. The Hall was abandoned during the 19th century and today very little remains. Amongst the ruins are two incongruous suburban houses, made up from the outbuildings flanking the Hall.
Aikin, 448; O iii, 822; Heginbotham ii, 144; Taylor, 142; MCRL, Henry Taylor mss.

Hare Hill, Over Alderley
875 767 *Garden open to the public. (National Trust)*

A plain red brick box with a shallow hipped roof erected *c.* 1800 for William Hibbert of Birtles Hall. The most notable feature is the slightly later ironwork verandah with chinoiserie supports and a tented glass roof continuous on two sides.
O iii, 584.

Harrytown Hall, Bredbury
931 907

Originally a stone house on the E plan with three projecting gables and a central entrance, it looks Jacobean but is dated 1671 over the door. It has been much altered. A brick cross wing was built in 1760 by John Bruckshaw replacing one of the stone gables. In the early 19th century the house was given the

164.   Harden Hall, *c.*1900.

'olden time' treatment with a vengeance. Huge Tudor-style mullioned windows were put into the front, and the inside was decorated with Gothic tracery like icing sugar. At the rear, another wing was added in 1864 in Victorian Gothic style. The detached chapel is dated 1864. Latterly a convent, now flats.
O iii, 823; T ii, 118; Pike 1904, 105.

Hartford Manor, Hartford
645 725
   A five-bay ashlar house with a stucco wing attached. At the front is a central curved bay, and before this is an unfluted Tuscan porch with pronounced entasis and triglyphs. The porch may be an addition. The house is said to have been refronted *c.* 1820 for John Marshall, a salt manufacturer, but the core is earlier. Inside the entrance hall are three 18th-century doorcases with good carving. Now the offices of North West Gas.
Pike 1904, 115.

Haslington Hall, Haslington
748 560
   A large timber-framed house, the home of the Vernon family until 1700. The core is a late 15th-century Great Hall from which remain the collared roof with cusped wind braces, now in the attic, and the arches of the screens passage. It was refaced and enlarged in the late 16th century by the addition of the two cross wings with their showy timber framing, probably for Sir Thomas Vernon. Ormerod says that the present Hall is one side of a quadrangular building, but there is no clear evidence to support this view. On the east side is a large 17th-century brick service wing. 20th-century extensions, half-timbered in imitation of the original, confuse the earlier form of the house, but the new entrance gable and the rear bay window

are skilful additions built for Col. Humphrey Watts who restored the house in the 1920s.
O iii, 319; P & O, pl. xcix; FM vii, 107; *Ches Life* May 1955, January 1957.

Hassall Hall, Hassall
770 573

An H-plan house of the 17th century refronted in the early 19th century, and now presenting a somewhat mixed appearance. The front is stuccoed, with the remains of square hood moulds over the windows. At the centre is a doorcase with a broken pediment on columns, and a Gothic fanlight. The garden is surrounded by a brick wall with a gazebo in one corner.
O iii, 296

Haughton Hall, Haughton
588 564

Rebuilt in 1891-4 by J. F. Doyle of Liverpool for the shipowner Ralph Brocklebank, owner of a large art collection. Doyle, who worked for other members of the family, was a protégé of Norman Shaw, and had worked with Shaw for T. H. Ismay, another Liverpool shipowner. Haughton, unlike Ismay's forbidding Dawpool, adopts Shaw's Old English manner of picturesque massing, tall chimneys and varied materials. However the main house was altered *c.* 1950; it was reduced from three storeys to two, the tile hanging was removed, and it was roughcast. The garden front has three big curved bays, a much simplified version of the original busily variegated design. Doyle's intentions can be more fully appreciated from the attractive complex of outbuildings which preserve their red brick, tile hangings and clay tile roofs, particularly the stable court with its nicely asymmetrical entrance and pagoda roof with tiny louvred dormers. Within the attractive gardens is a glass-house with an onion dome.
Ches Life November/December 1954.

Hawthorne Hall, Wilmslow
843 813

Originally a timber-framed yeoman house of *c.* 1610 built for John Latham of Irlam, but refaced in brick and extensively improved for John Leigh in 1698. The framing, still visible in the gables within the roof and in an internal wall, shows how the house was increased in width. The improved house was conservative, probably because of the constraints of re-using the old structure: the rows of stone flagged gables, the crudely carved parapets, the mullioned windows and cross passage plan, one room deep, were old fashioned for 1698. But an up-to-date feature was the central glazed cupola, provided for viewing the large formal gardens which are recorded on an engraving. The grounds are now lost to suburban housing, but in the house, which is used as offices, the main panelled interiors are retained as period furnished rooms, and a modest extension is concealed behind mellow brick garden walls.
O iii, 545, 592; Earwaker i, 129; H. Hodson, *A Portrait of Wilmslow*, 1974, 100; Broster album, private collection.

Heawood Hall, Nether Alderley
837 757

A complicated and disjointed-looking house, the core late 17th-century, but the most striking feature a tall early 18th-century wing with rusticated quoins, forming a five-bay garden front. The main front, formerly of stone with mullioned windows, was refaced in 1899 in brick with twin stuccoed gables. Built by the Hollinshead family, but in the 19th century part of the Alderley estate.
O iii, 567; Pike 1904, 121.

Hefferston Grange, Weaverham
604 735

A brick house of 1741 with similar detailing to the slightly later Daresbury Hall, 1759. It was built for Philip Henry Warburton, distantly descended from the Warburtons of Arley. The house is of two storeys, with stone quoins of even length making broad vertical bands, and a good classical stone doorcase with a curved pediment on scroll brackets; the entrance is in the recessed centre of a seven-bay front. In the 1770s it was inherited by Nicholas Ashton of Woolton, Lancs., who enlarged it in Neo-classical style. On the left facade are later cast-iron balconies, and an entrance on the right side, later still, is dated *1876 RHAE*. Now in the grounds of The Grange Hospital, it has been shamefully neglected.
O ii, 174.

165.   Hawthorne Hall, *c.*1900.

Henshall Hall, Mossley, Congleton (demolished)
877 622

A large house in debased Gothic style built in diapered brick with patterned roofs by the Macclesfield architect James Stevens for J. H. Williamson of Tunstall in 1873-7. The porch, which was flanked by big plate glass windows, led to a huge central staircase hall lit from above, with a ceiling much like that of Stevens' Council Chamber for the Macclesfield Town Hall. A music room in red brick and a fine conservatory with rocks and a waterfall were added later. The house was demolished in 1975 and its grounds are now a drab housing estate.

BA 21 December 1877, 304; Pike 1904, 44.

The Hermitage, Holmes Chapel
766 682

A rambling, irregular house of red brick with sash windows, the product of many alterations. It was originally a stone house of the 16th century built for the Winningtons. In 1702 the estate was purchased by Thomas Hall of Cranage who added a taller symmetrical brick house with a shell-canopied doorway and a hipped roof. In the late 19th and early 20th centuries it was variously extended round a courtyard. Additions included a brick tower, canted bays overlooking the garden and an Arts and Crafts roughcast extension with a curved bay window. The 16th-century wing was demolished in 1949 when A. C. Fairclough converted the rest into three dwellings.

O iii, 129; *Ches Life* October/November 1949; CRO Map DDX 329.

Highfields, Audlem
675 410

A half-timbered house with a plain front of three equal gables, the central one recessed. Inside are attractively old fashioned oak-panelled rooms and, unusually, two late 17th-century staircases with twisted balusters, one a double spiral. The earliest secure date is 1615, carved on one of the fireplaces, with the initials WD for William Dod, whose house this was. The plan is symmetrical, with a central hall entered axially; but the porch is Victorian and the off-centre door to the drawing room behind the hall may be a survival of an earlier screens passage arrangement. The drawing room, half-timbered but of lighter construction than the rest of the house, is supposed to have been added in the 18th century by the architect William Baker, who married Jane Dod in 1736 and lived here until his death in 1771. But a 17th-century date is more probable for it is unlikely that half timbering survived so late, particularly as Baker was a classical architect; his best known work, the Butter Market at Ludlow, is in a rusticated James Gibbs style. He also repaired and surveyed local houses such as Dorfold and Hankelow. Highfields was stuccoed in the early 19th century but its somewhat regularised appearance dates from the 1880s when the Bakers sold the house and the new owners removed the stucco, adding a service wing, brick chimneys and other features. Continuity was restored when the Bakers returned in 1944.

Oswald, 109; J. B. Baker, *Highfields, Audlem* guidebook, 1982.

High Legh Halls, High Legh (demolished)
702 839

There were two Halls here, East Hall and West Hall, very close to one another, lived in by distinct branches of the Leghs. The **West Hall** (Egerton Leigh) was a half-timbered building, and Ormerod's

166. The entrance front at Highfields.

engraving shows it in 1814 as a gabled house of some pretension. Shortly after 1814 it was enlarged or rebuilt in brick. At the same time Thomas Harrison of Chester built a new chapel with an Ionic front. The chapel, burnt down in 1891, has had its remaining fragments incorporated into the parish church. The Hall was demolished in 1935. The **East Hall** (Cornwall Legh) was the larger building, erected in 1581 for Thomas Legh who in the same year built a chapel, since enlarged, and then restored by Butterfield. The house had a fanciful tall tower with spires. In 1780 Henry Cornwall Legh inherited the estate, demolished the Elizabethan house, and in 1782 had a Georgian brick house built by John Hope of Liverpool. Henry's son George employed William Wilkins to build stables and a coach house, and the Hall, by now called High Legh Hall, was stuccoed. Repton drew up a 'Red Book' in 1791. He built the surviving brick lodge with fancy bargeboards, and landscaped the park, now almost completely obliterated. With Nash he later planned a picturesque village on the green at the park entrance, but this was never built. In 1833 James Hakewill added a dining room to the house and built another lodge, which remains together with a school house, both of stone in an Italianate style. The Hall was demolished in 1963 and the land developed for suburban-type housing.

O i, 449, 460; T ii, 71; Pike 1904, 29; *Ches Life* December 1949, January 1950; N. Temple, *John Nash and the Village Picturesque*, 1979.

Hinderton Hall, Neston
305 784

An early work by Alfred Waterhouse built in 1856 for Christopher Bushell, a Liverpool wine merchant. The main block is roughly square, of rock-faced sandstone, its outline broken by tall gables and steeply pitched roofs of patterned slate, and the entrance is marked by a thin corner tower. The reception rooms are grouped informally around a generous two-storey entrance-cum-staircase hall, an early example of this popular Victorian plan. 20th-century extensions were built for Sir Percy Bates, chairman of Cunard. The original stable block and three lodges in matching style survive.

B xvii, 42; J. Fawcett ed., *Seven Victorian Architects*, 1976, 106.

Hockenhull Hall, Tarvin
485 661

Built for Hugh Whishaw, a gentleman of Chester, who bought the estate from the Hockenhulls in 1713; the back of the Hall is irregular and may incorporate parts of an earlier house. Hockenhull is classical, of brick with a giant order of Ionic pilasters and a recessed centre, deriving from the work of Francis Smith of Warwick. But in the early 19th century, the original parapet and heavy cornice must have been replaced by the present overhanging roof, resulting in 'an oddly unbalanced appearance. The form of the central doorway, also the interrupted entablature and giant order, are similar to those at Buntingsdale, Shropshire, a much grander and more assured house designed *c.* 1730 by Smith. Whoever built Hockenhull may have known or worked at Buntingsdale. Hockenhull is now entered from a side porch dating, like the roof, from the early 19th century, and little remains of the original interior.

O ii, 317.

Holford Hall, Plumley
709 755

A very pretty fragment of a much larger moated timber house rebuilt for Mary Cholmondeley (née Holford) after the death of her husband Sir Hugh Cholmondeley in 1601. There is a fine double arched stone bridge and opposite it a timber-framed block originally the centre of a U-shaped range with a forecourt facing the moat. The house has three storeys jettied out, with two broad gables set close together, and is decorated with much carving and patterned timberwork. On the left a wing has been demolished, leaving exposed a wall of timber framing with brick infill, recently rebuilt; on the right projects a modern brick structure replacing a wing which according to old photographs was close studded and so probably earlier than what survives. It had continuous glazing on the first floor, and below was an open loggia of fluted timber columns. This part was shamefully pulled down in the 1880s. Mary Cholmondeley lived at Holford before moving to Vale Royal in 1616.

O i, 672; *THSLC* lxvi, 255; *BA* xi, 164; N. G. Philips, *Views of the Old Halls of Lancashire and Cheshire*, 1893, 119.

167.　The former entrance front at Hockenhull Hall.

168.　Holford Hall, *c.*1880.

Hollin Hall, Bollington
934 770

A coarsely detailed Gothic revival house of *c.* 1870 for Joseph Brook jnr., built of rock-faced stone in a mixture of Tudor and Jacobean styles with castellations and a tower. The elaborate entrance hall, modelled on that at Abney, has a heavily carved Imperial staircase approached through three Gothic arches on octagonal scagliola columns. Now a hotel. Nearby is **Hollin Old Hall**, an early 17th-century core enlarged in the 18th century for Richard Broster; the cellar contains a large slab reading 'This must stand here for ever, Richard Broster 1757'. The Old Hall was remodelled *c.* 1870.
O iii, 702.

Hollingworth Hall, Hollingworth (demolished)
003 978

A stone house in the vernacular style of the Pennine region. It was built in the 17th century, but was said to incorporate older work, and consisted of a central block and cross wings. It was the ancient seat of the Hollingworth family who sold it in 1734. About one hundred years later it was repurchased by Captain Robert de Hollyngworthe who was probably responsible for rebuilding the porch, re-using an older coat of arms said to have survived from a gatehouse. The Hall was sold again in 1866 and finally demolished in 1944 by the Manchester Corporation Waterworks Committee, despite local protests.
O iii, 870; T. Middleton, *Annals of Hyde*, 1899, 224.

Hoole Hall, Chester
430 680

A small 18th-century country house with extensive 19th-century additions. The nucleus probably dates from soon after 1757 when the estate was purchased by Revd. John Baldwin. It is a miniature astylar Palladian villa of brick with stucco dressings. The centrepiece is enclosed by quoins, and above is a broken pediment enriched by a stucco coat of arms. The additions include a stucco garden front and a large and elaborate cast-iron conservatory, carried out for the Hamilton family. The Reverend's son Thomas Baldwin made an early balloon flight from the grounds in 1785. Derelict until recently, the house has been converted into a hotel, swamped by car parks and new bedroom wings. Nearby was **Hoole House**, famous for its rockery created by Lady Broughton. Beyond a flower garden rose fantastic tall and jagged heaps of rock chosen for their shape and colouring and planted with trees; the design was based on a small model of the Savoy mountains and the Chamonix valley. The house, built *c.* 1760 for William Hamilton and extended by Thomas Harrison, has been demolished and the gardens are now occupied by housing.
O ii, 813; T i, 46; *Gardeners' Magazine* xiv, 353.

Hooton Hall, Childer Thornton (demolished)
370 776

Designed in 1778 by Samuel Wyatt for Sir William Stanley, to replace the earlier courtyard house, half-timbered with a stone wing and tower dating back to 1486 when the Stanleys received a licence to crenellate. The earliest of Wyatt's villa-type houses, Hooton was a simple two-storey structure on a rusticated basement. On the garden front was a central domed bow flanked by tripartite windows. In 1802 Repton produced a landscape scheme for Sir Thomas Stanley. About 1850 Hooton was bought by R. C. Naylor, a wealthy Liverpool banker, who in 1854 employed James K. Colling to remodel the house in a grandiloquent Italianate style. He transformed Wyatt's quiet entrance front by adding a ground floor porch, and over it a row of giant detached columns with a heavy entablature supporting statues, after the manner of C. R. Cockerell. The house was much extended with wings, a chapel and a tower 100 feet high containing a smoking room. Inside he made a magnificent arched and colonnaded sculpture gallery with rich plasterwork. The gardens were laid out by W. A. Nesfield. For Naylor, Colling also designed the Albany, Liverpool, and the remarkable church on the Hooton estate, St Paul's, a large ornate Rundbogenstil building in polychromatic stone, completely at odds with Wyatt's lodges which survive in its shadow. The house was used as a military hospital in the First World War, and was demolished *c.* 1935.
W. Watts, *The Seats of the Nobility and Gentry*, 1780, pl. xxiii; O ii, 415; T i, 51; *Civil Engineer & Architects' Journal*, 1854 xvii, 20.

169. The gallery, Hooton Hall, c.1900.

Hulme Hall, Allostock

725 724

A moated house across a fine medieval bridge of two stone arches with triangular buttresses between them. The house, now a farm dominated by a silo, was the ancient home of the Grosvenors and the Shakerleys: it has been encased in brick but within are a 17th-century staircase and medieval timbers. O iii, 153.

Ince Manor, Ince

450 767

The remains of a moated grange belonging to the Benedictine Abbey of St Werburgh, Chester, comprising hall and lodgings, two separate ranges of stone around a courtyard. Both date from the 13th century, the time of the abbey's greatest prosperity, though much later medieval work is evident. The hall has four tall mullioned and transomed windows on the east side, facing the road. These were inserted after the Dissolution, but the elliptical arches above were probably built to support a battlemented parapet, perhaps following the licence to crenellate granted in 1398. The entrance is from the courtyard through an arched doorway protected by arrowslits, and within the thickness of the wall is a passage and a staircase which led to a solar at the upper end of the hall. The passage is roofed with Caernarvon arches, so called because of their first recorded use at Caernarvon Castle in 1283-1301. Masons engaged on abbey buildings were also used in the construction of the King's Welsh castles, and in 1277 Edward himself visited Ince. The lodgings probably formed four separate chambers providing sleeping quarters for the monks or lay brothers working on the manor lands. There are two floors, the upper one as shown on the Buck engraving of 1727 reached by an external staircase. At the Dissolution Ince Manor became the property of St Werburgh's

245

Cathedral, but in 1547 it was granted to Sir Richard Cotton of Combermere. The hall was altered to suit secular use, but the lodgings seem not to have changed until they were converted into cottages in the 18th century. Both buildings, still in private hands, are now ruinous and stand in the shadow of the Stanlow Oil Refinery.

O ii, 13; P. Thompson, *Ince Manor*, n.d.; C. Platt, *The Monastic Grange in Medieval England*, 1969, 210.

Ingersley Hall, Rainow
946 774

A T-shaped house in a harsh moorland setting built *c.* 1775 for John Gaskell. Extensions were erected at each end of the main west front in 1833 for John Upton Gaskell; a smart Grecian-style entrance facade to the north, and at the south a top-heavy Tuscan doorcase, probably removed from the centre of the original 18th-century west front. In the 19th century the family bred horses, and at the side of the house are extensive stable yards set behind a handsome coach house with Mannerist-style rustication. The hall is now a religious retreat overlooking Kerridge Hill and White Nancy, the beehive-shaped folly built in 1817 by the Gaskells to commemorate Waterloo.

O iii, 771.

Inglewood, Ledsham
347 758

A large comfortable house in late Arts and Crafts style dated 1915 and built for F. H. Fox, a Liverpool marine insurance millionaire. It is mostly half-timbered, with tall diapered brick chimneys, a jumble of half-hipped Lakeland slate roofs, leaded windows and finely carved stone dressings. A central projecting stone porch has the date and arms. On the side elevation is an open timber balcony with a view south over terracing and Old English formal gardens. High mellowed brick walls enclose the west gardens, and decorative wrought-iron gates lead to planted avenues and a lake. Now a training centre.

170. Ince Manor: entrance to the Great Hall from the courtyard.

Irby Hall, Irby
254 855

A picturesque timber-framed hall with gabled cross wings, on the site of a moated manor house of St Werburgh's Abbey. It was probably built in the late 16th or early 17th century for John Harpur, or for Thomas Leigh who acquired it from him in 1602. In 1888 it was straightened out and refaced with a hard new red sandstone ground floor and regular timbering above; just how much it had lost is seen in the photograph prior to restoration illustrated by Irvine. It was further modernised in 1971.

O ii, 510; Mortimer, 266; Irvine, 32.

Jodrell Hall, Jodrell Bank
796 702

A plain brick Georgian house built for the Jodrell family in 1779. It has three storeys and five bays with a central pediment enclosing a circular window. On the left is a lower service wing, and set back to the right a small Jacobean revival wing, an inappropriately scaled and fussy addition by John Douglas, who also added a stone porch dated 1885. At the house (now Terra Nova School) is a drawing in a rough style, dated 1779, probably the work of the builder.

Ches Life September 1955.

246

171. The south front of Inglewood.

172. Kerfield House.

173. Langley Hall.

Kerfield House, Knutsford

770 770

This suave neo-Georgian house was until 1912 a plain yellow brick High Victorian villa called Beechwood. It was transformed by Percy Worthington for a Manchester businessman, Lt.-Col. Sydney Goldschmidt, as a setting for his furniture collection. The villa was recased in mellow red brick, hiding the roofs behind a parapet, and adding a new drawing room to convert the L-shaped plan into a square. The symmetrical entrance front of five bays has at its centre a fine carved timber doorcase with Composite pilasters and a fanlight. The interior was remodelled around a spacious staircase hall. To the left is the dining room which has an early 18th-century fireplace. On the right are two adjoining rooms which can be combined by sliding back panels in the connecting wall, the morning room panelled in oak, and the drawing room with pedimented doorcases decorated with rams' heads.

CL lxv, 181; Macartney v 1913, 40.

Langley Hall, Langley

937 716

A well proportioned classical house of rubble stone with an unusually tall hipped roof. The entrance front has seven bays of sash windows, a central doorway and fine shell porch containing a cartouche with a carved face and the inscription *MAC 1696* for M. Clowes and his wife. Inside is a wide oak staircase (lacking its original balusters) reached via a flagged entrance hall. To the left is a room with bolection-moulded panelling. The Hall has recently been rescued from dereliction and now forms three dwellings.

O iii, 763.

Lawton Hall, Church Lawton

823 556

A large and puzzling 18th-century house on high ground overlooking a lake. The puzzling aspects are first the awkwardness of the plan, basically a double pile but with an extremely narrow service passage between the two principal rooms, and second the centrepieces of the two main fronts. Whilst the sides are of two-and-a-half storeys, the centres are of two, each higher, and their treatment relates oddly to the composition as a whole. These must be the result of alterations made soon after the house was built, for the inconvenience of the interior defies logical planning. The entrance front has a pedimented centrepiece with a grand Tuscan doorway and a tall arched window above. The projecting porch to one side is a mid-19th-century addition. On the garden side there is at the centre a wide canted bay with a ground floor Venetian window and blank roundels above. Inside are only two main rooms, one in the centre of each front: the entrance hall, later converted into a dining room, and behind it the saloon. Both have splendid Rococo decoration, somewhat the worse for wear. In the former is a ceiling with plasterwork similar to Belmont Hall, and walls with framed panels incorporating hunting devices. In the saloon are doorcases and a fireplace in the manner of William Kent. The study, formerly a small dining room to the left of the entrance hall, is lined with 17th-century oak panelling with a pronounced frieze of linked arcading, all painted white. A good Jacobean stone fireplace with chunky classical detail is surmounted by a quite separate overmantel, both perhaps re-used from the old Hall on a nearby moated site. The house was probably built for Robert Lawton who held the estate from 1736-70. The wings were added in the 1830s for his grandson Charles, and in the grounds is a memorial of 1853 with a poem written by his wife Mariana 'On the death of a Bullfinch that sang God Save the Queen when bidden to do so'. Lawton Hall is now empty and badly in need of repair.

O iii, 15; T i, 145.

Lea Hall, Wimboldsley

680 640

A charming little house, a brick box of the early 18th century, set in a flat landscape. It is symmetrical, of five bays with a big hipped roof and a viewing platform on top. The railing of the platform and the chimneys are Victorian, but many original features survive such as the panelled rooms on the first floor, the small-paned windows and the fine external doorcase with a scrolly pediment. There are two rusticated gatepiers set to one side as at Langley Hall. The Hall was built for the Lowndes family, though the arms over the door are those of Joseph Verdin who owned it during the 19th century. Now in ruinous condition.

O iii, 218.

174.   The entrance front of Lawton Hall.

Leasowe Castle, Wallasey

265 908

On the bleak north shore of the Wirral, overlooking the sea, stands Leasowe Castle, originally built in 1593 for Ferdinando, 5th Earl of Derby, as a 'standing' for watching races. (Webb records a racecourse here in 1608.) The building then consisted of an octagonal stone tower. Shortly afterwards four square turrets were attached, each capped by three gables and ball finials, making a geometrical conceit of the kind enjoyed by the Elizabethans. A blocked window on what was the outside of the original tower, now concealed by additions, still remains with the Stanley emblem, the legs of Man, but the date of 1593 recorded there is not visible. In 1818 John Foster snr. of Liverpool transformed Leasowe into a picturesque castellated mansion for Mrs. L. W. Boode, the widow of a West India planter. Foster hid the original structure by building a four-storey tower, flanked by diagonally set lower blocks, all castellated, to make a symmetrical entrance front, extending it to the left with a long loggia terminating in another tower. Boode's daughter married Sir Edward Cust, Master of Ceremonies to Queen Victoria, and a military historian. He further enlarged the house and decorated it in an eccentric antiquarian manner, installing panelling from the Star Chamber at Westminster, purchased when the old Exchequer was demolished in 1836. The present Star Chamber room however is largely a pastiche, as the panelling was removed when Cust sold the estate in 1893. Cust also built an entertaining staircase which has in the balustrade to each step a tablet with the name of a decisive British battle, the name of the sovereign in whose reign it was fought, and the name of the British and enemy generals in command. The stair runs from Blenheim to

Sebastopol. Cust's gate-piers survive with dogs bearing his punning motto Qui Cust Odit Caveat. In 1893 the house became a hotel, and then a convalescent home, and there are ugly additions employing thinly applied half timbering and unsympathetic red brick. From 1970 it lay empty, but now it is once again a hotel.
O ii, 473; Mortimer, 294; T i, 55; *Ches Life* February 1966.

Legh Hall, Mottram St Andrew
885 782
A symmetrical brick Georgian house probably built for William Brocklehurst of Macclesfield who bought the estate from the Massies in the mid-18th century. It has sash windows with keystones and broad architraves, and a modillion cornice. At the left is an early 19th-century extension with a shallow bow. Adjacent is **Legh Old Hall**, an H-plan house of the late 16th century with later alterations. It is of stone, but the interior suggests it was originally timber-framed.
O iii, 697.

Limefield, Bollington
936 782
A smooth ashlar-faced house in the Grecian style built *c.* 1830 for Joseph Brook snr. The stables are of rougher stone with Gibbs surrounds to the windows. Nearby is **Rock Bank House**, a stone villa in the Tudor Gothic style built *c.* 1843 for Brooks's brother-in-law Martin Swindells. The two families were jointly involved in running the huge Clarence Mill.
Wilmslow Historical Society, *Cotton Town: Bollington and the Swindells Family*, 1973.

Littleton Hall, Littleton
440 667
A small stucco house in flat parkland designed by Benjamin Gummow for Thomas Dixon in 1806. It has a canted bay running up the centre and a verandah, but has since been much altered with irregular additions.
O ii, 784; T i, 43.

Lower Carden Hall, Tilston
460 523
A half-timbered house on a T-shaped plan consisting of a hall and a south cross wing. The hall was refronted in the 17th century, and probably at this time it was divided horizontally, but crown-posts in the bedrooms indicate a 15th-century date. The front gable of the cross wing is of the mid-16th century. It has double jettying, a huge bressumer and busy close-set diagonal bracing. The Hall belonged to the Leches of Carden and was restored in 1899 for Sir John Leche. Some of the features of this date including finials and bargeboards are seen elsewhere on Carden estate buildings.
O ii, 701; P & O, pl. lxxvii; *Ches Life* December 1959.

Lower Huxley Hall, Huxley
497 623
A moated house reached across a stone bridge surmounted by a Jacobean arched gateway gaily embellished with scrolls and finials. The lower part of the bridge is medieval, as too is the right-hand wing of the house, its timbering replaced in the 18th century by brick facing. This wing housed the original Great Hall, of which the arched braced trusses of the roof survive, but a floor was inserted in the 16th century, and in the 17th the staircase took the place of the screens passage. Like Little Moreton it was originally a courtyard house, but only two sides now survive. The main block facing the gateway is Jacobean and provided on the ground floor a new hall with two projecting bays. At the centre is an armorial tablet with two crests, one the Wrights of Bickley and Stretton, the other unidentified, but not of a Cheshire family. It may not be original to the house, for the builder of the new range was either Joshua Clive, the owner in 1600, or Thomas Wilbraham of Nantwich who married Clive's daughter Rachel in 1619. Thomas was the nephew of Ralph Wilbraham who in 1616 built Dorfold Hall which has a similar layout.
O ii, 591, 801.

175.   Lower Huxley Hall from across the moat.

Lower Kinnerton Hall (Bridge Farmhouse), Lower Kinnerton
341 621

An E-plan house erected beside the brook which divides Cheshire from Wales. It is dated 1685 and bears the initials *TTET*. Built of brick with stone dressings, it has strikingly tall Dutch gables, three on the entrance front and one facing the road. These have huge reverse-curved scrolls supporting pediments, a 17th-century vogue derived originally from two houses in Holborn drawn in 1619 by John Smythson. At the rear is a 19th-century wing with Gothick glazing and a fine cobbled courtyard.
O ii, 852.

Lyme Green Hall, Sutton
915 707

An 18th-century house of coursed rough stone with ashlar keystones, voussoirs and long and short quoins. On one side is a large extension of the early 20th century in an exaggerated Lutyens-like version of the same style with bigger quoins, keystones and voussoirs, and big scrolly chimneys. The extension forms an open courtyard and is flanked by two low pavilions, one an orangery. The hopper heads and balconies bear the monogram *JBS* for J. Bradley Smale, a Macclesfield silk manufacturer. Now a nursing home.

Lymm Hall, Lymm
685 871

A moated house built in the 17th century for the Domvilles. It has an E-shaped stone front with mullioned windows, stepped gables on the wings and in the centre a single storey porch surmounted by a balustrade, but not all this is original. Of the 17th century is the recessed centre and the porch; unlike the wings this section has a plinth and a moulded string course, and the two big mullioned windows flanking the porch are much more weathered than the others. Then perhaps in the 18th or early 19th century the wings were added; a watercolour view kept at the house shows them with flat parapets and sash windows. Finally *c.* 1840 the stepped gables and the other mullioned windows were installed making the symmetrical neo-Jacobean front depicted by Twycross. He also shows the irregular garden elevation of *c.* 1840. Both fronts are virtually unchanged, but there is a service wing to one side and behind it facing the garden is a late Victorian addition. The moat in front of the house, although drained, is still there, and also the stone bridge, now widened. Beyond is a stone range with boat-shaped gable ends, irregular fenestration and a parapet like that on the Hall porch. Called the Moat House, it was probably not a domestic range as there is no original chimney. Behind it is a cobbled yard and 19th-century outbuildings incorporating three older datestones. The earliest is *WSD 1700* for William and Susanna Domville who may have built the Hall. Next is *TTM 1779* for Thomas and Mary Taylor: Thomas's father, who died in 1778, inherited Lymm through the female line of the Domvilles. Last is *W&SEB* for the Battersbys who improved the house in the 19th century. In the garden is an ice-house and two cock-pits. Edward Kemp designed the rose garden, now overgrown.

O i, 580; T ii, 77; E. Kemp, *How to lay out a Garden*, 1864; *Ches Life* November 1935.

Manley Knoll, Manley
513 726

A mellow Arts and Crafts house idyllically sited overlooking a terraced garden with views of the Cheshire plain. The house was designed in 1912 for Llewellyn Jones in a mixture of materials and styles. The entrance front is of brick with canted bays and a scrolled flat canopy in the early Georgian style, a little like Philip Webb; there is Voysey-type roughcast, and the garden front has four big half-timbered gables all with different Cheshire patterns using untarred beams. The terraces are laid out in semi-formal style, with yew hedges enclosing different spaces. After the war the house was purchased by the Demetriades family who made a spectacular woodland garden in the adjoining quarry. In 1922 the Manchester architect James Henry Sellers transformed the interior and supplied quantities of suave neo-Georgian furniture.

Marbury Hall, Comberbach (demolished)
651 765

See main entry on Belmont Hall. Two rusticated gate piers and a section of the walled garden are all that now remain.

Marbury Hall, Marbury near Whitchurch
561 451

On the opposite bank of Marbury Mere from the church, Marbury Hall is a Regency house of white stucco with twin curved bows. It was built in 1810 for the Poole family who moved here from **Marley Hall**, a half-timbered house now rebuilt. There is a pretty lodge of sandstone with playful cusped decoration.

T ii, 17.

Marple Hall, Marple (demolished)
943 893

A timber-framed house built in the 15th century for the Vernons and bought by the Bradshawes in 1606. It was enlarged and encased in red sandstone for Col. Henry Bradshawe, the parliamentarian commander, whose younger brother was the regicide John Bradshawe. The north entrance was dated 1658 and the stables with stepped gables and clock tower 1669. The south front had four gables, a central tower with a cupola, and mullioned windows. Sashes were introduced on one side of the front in the 18th century. The interiors included good stained glass in the hall, panelled rooms and some Rococo and Gothick detail. The family in 1761 became the Bradshawe-Isherwoods, and in the 20th century the novelist Christopher Isherwood spent school holidays at Marple. Much of the furniture was sold in 1929; the Hall was neglected and after 1953 it was abandoned. Isherwood inherited it in 1940 whilst in America but never liked it and passed it on to his brother who lived at another house on the estate, **Wyberslegh Hall**, a farmhouse which in the 19th century had been turned into a castellated eye-catcher. Wyberslegh is now derelict and of Marple, demolished in 1956, only the stone plinth and the 1658 datestone remain on a hillside overlooking the river Goyt.

O iii, 842; T ii, 108; *Ches Life* April 1954; C. Isherwood, *Kathleen and Frank*, 1971.

176. Marbury Hall, Comberbach, *c*.1900.

177. The stables at Marple Hall, *c*.1880.

178.   Marton Hall, *c*.1880.

Marton Hall, Marton (demolished)
848 674

A good almost symmetrical timber-framed house on an H plan with gabled cross wings and a central gable on the entrance side. In the centre was a large hall and on the left a room with a carved chimneypiece inlaid with the arms of the Davenports of Marton. In 1904 Edward Ould described the house as 'charming in design and colour with roof of sea-weed green, and creamy walls, with the pink blush of brickwork showing through the worn plaster' and regretted that 'the inevitable restoration is imminent, and, truth to tell, the rain comes in through the lovely roof and the precious walls'. He was right; it was demolished and replaced by a farmhouse soon afterwards. A fireplace is now at Capesthorne.
O iii, 725; FM i, 73; P&O, 34, pls. lxxxviii, lxxxix.

Meadowlands, Mere
715 831

An Arts and Crafts house in roughcast and red brick designed in 1903 by the architect Frank Dunkerley for his brother William Dunkerley and his wife Amy; their initials and the date are on the stables and the hall fireplace. A nursery wing was added in 1907. The house is dominated by strikingly large gables with an overhanging stone roof. The rooms are freely planned to take advantage of the sunlight, though the lobby, hall and staircase are cramped. Near the road is a miniature stable court with a polygonal tower on one side. The gardens are by T. H. Mawson. Now a training college.
R. J. Gain, *Frank Dunkerley* (unpublished thesis), 1983; Mawson archive.

Mellor Hall, Mellor

985 893

A two-storey symmetrical late 17th-century stone house on a hillside. It corresponds to the classical Restoration type, but with crude, provincial detailing: cross windows on the ground floor (the first floor has sashes), flat unmoulded strings, keystones, quoins and a hipped roof of graded stone slates. The door has a bolection surround, scroll brackets at the top, and above is an astonishingly tall double scroll open pediment housing a later Royal coat of arms. The house is attached at the back to a lower building with gables, one of which carries a tablet *IC 1691*. The same initials with the dates 1688 and 1692 on outbuildings are those of James Chetham who bought Mellor in 1686.

Mere Old Hall, Mere

724 816

The Mere family were Royalists in the Civil War and had to sell their estates. They were bought in 1652 by Peter Brooke, a younger son of the Brookes of Norton, who rebuilt the house 'very handsomely' according to Sir Peter Leycester. In 1756 an advantageous marriage was made between another Peter Brooke and Frances, heiress and daughter of James Langford of Antigua. A series of views at the Hall chart its growth. In the early 18th century it was a substantial brick house of eleven bays by nine with rusticated quoins and a heavy parapet. Later a two-storey domed bow was added as a central entrance porch, and later still the front was extended with polygonal pavilions. But at some stage, perhaps in the late 19th century, the house was truncated and remodelled so that it is difficult to relate what is left to the evidence of the views. What remains is an L-shaped house, Regency in character, probably the left-hand section of the main front and part of the side. The domed bow and the pavilions have gone. The house has markedly projecting eaves and is stuccoed (though Ormerod described it as brick). The finest original survival is the tall staircase hall hung with portraits. There is an elegant latticed iron balustrade and two big delicate semi-circular fanlight overdoors, both curiously blocked. Upstairs is a room with a coved ceiling and walls lined with excellent mahogany library bookcases of the early 19th century clearly designed for another room, and a marble chimneypiece carved with heads wreathed in vines, perhaps from the original dining room. On the ground floor much of the decoration is Edwardian in the 'Adams' style, and there are tiles and stained glass of the 1880s in the entrance hall. Amongst the family pictures are sporting paintings, including one of Kilton, a favourite horse who gave his name to a nearby inn. In 1834 the Lichfield architect Thomas Johnson designed a new house for Peter Langford Brooke and the family moved there across the road. **Mere New Hall** was a very fancy Elizabethan affair of diapered red brick, large and symmetrical with a porte cochère, many turrets and shaped gables. Finding the New Hall too large, the family returnd to the old house in 1914; the New Hall was sold and turned into a country club. Most of it was destroyed by fire in the 1970s, but there remains a gatehouse, stables, clock tower, and a fragment of the house with a very unsympathetic modern extension. It is now full of golf-playing Manchester businessmen.

O i, 464; T ii, 67; APSD; *Ches Life* September 1964.

Mere Hall, Bidston

295 877

A vast and heavy neo-Jacobean pile of red brick with red sandstone dressings and a red tiled roof, built around 1880 for Sir John Gray Hill, an eminent maritime lawyer. The architect was Edmund Kirby of Liverpool. It has many gables and dormers, mullioned windows with leaded lights, and a tower with a conical top, all freely composed but without coherence. The interior in the Queen Anne taste is now divided up, but some features remain including a lobby with good panelling. The house was extended in a similar style, and more recently a modern block has been added. Surrounding this house on Bidston Hill are other large detached houses in leafy gardens built by Liverpool magnates, but Mere Hall is the tallest and showiest, and one of the first.

Pike 1904, 57.

Middlewich Manor, Middlewich

698 653

Originally a brick house of *c.* 1800, encased in ashlar *c.* 1840 with a broad semi-circular Ionic porch placed at the centre of the main front, probably for William Court. In the 1870s the pair of windows to each side of the centrepiece was replaced by full height canted bays. Now a nursing home approached through a modern housing estate.

T i, 151.

Mobberley New Hall, Mobberley
797 797

A stone house in a dull neo-Elizabethan style, built in 1848 for Major Blakiston who in that year married one of the Wrights of Mobberley Old Hall. The entrance front is symmetrical with shaped gables, oriel windows and a Gothic porch. On the left is a billiard room extension designed by Corson and Aitken in 1870 for W. J. Harter. The garden front has later alterations.

O i, 420; Stephen Murray, *Mobberley Records*, 1946-8, mss. at Altrincham Library; Massey.

Mobberley Old Hall, Mobberley
793 797

A moated 17th-century house in two parts. At the rear is a low brick range with mullioned windows and a single gable, built in 1612 for Robert Robinson, son of a Yorkshire wool merchant. This is the remains of the 'fine contrived new house of brick' noted by Webb *c*. 1623. It is now the service wing to a later 17th-century block also of brick but taller and grander with stone quoins, string courses and a two-storey bay. This part was probably erected for Laurence Wright of Offerton, for whom the barn, dated 1686, was built. The Hall has no proper entrance front; the front door is in the gable end of the later block. Though the doorway itself is neo-Tudor, the gable end has Georgian windows and an oculus and dates from the 18th century, suggesting either that the house has been truncated or that it was intended to have been larger. The interior, old-fashioned and traditionally furnished, is charmingly rambling and incoherent, particularly the rear part, with many changes of level. There is a small panelled entrance hall and a fine mid-18th-century staircase. Both the atmospheric study, lit by the ground floor bay window, and the drawing room over it, have good 17th-century panelling and angle fireplaces. One of the outbuildings has been furnished as an old pharmacy to house a remarkable collection of drug jars. In the extensive gardens part of the moat survives and the line of the rest of it is marked by a yew hedge of great antiquity running alongside the main road.

O i, 409, 420, iii, 696; *Ches Life* March/April 1949.

Mollington Hall, Mollington (demolished)
386 702

A symmetrical Georgian house of 1756-7 built for Thomas Hunt to replace an older Hall. The new house was a plain but handsome rectangular block of seven bays, in brick with a central classical doorcase. Improvements were made in the 19th century for John Fielden whose motto and crest is on the railway bridge and station nearby. In 1897 the house was bought by T. Gibbons Frost whose initials are on the surviving lodge of 1907. The Hall was demolished in 1938 and a housing estate now occupies the park. The ice house survives.

O ii, 381; T i, 80; *JCAS* xli, 63.

Moseley Hall, Knutsford
767 773

A house in a heavy neo-Tudor style built for Charles Benton in 1890-1 by Paul Ogden of Manchester and extended in 1901. It consists of a brick ground floor with half timbering above and a tall cluster of gables and chimneys. The plan is symmetrical and cross-shaped, with a roomy south-facing living hall and an ingenious top-lit staircase leading to a gallery supported on fat timber balusters. The oak panelled reception rooms are decorated in mixed Jacobean and Arts and Crafts styles. Originally called The Terrace, in 1918 it was bought and renamed by John Davies, formerly of Moseley Hall, Cheadle, another Victorian black and white house (now demolished).

Macartney iv 1911, 137.

Moss Hall, Audlem
655 441

This half-timbered farmhouse dated 1616 over the porch was once a prosperous gentry house built for

179. Moss Hall, *c*.1900.

180. Mottram Old Hall.

Hugh Massy. The appealingly crooked E-shaped facade has four big gables and a narrower one in the centre. The closely set timbering is relieved by richly carved brackets and moulded bressumers. Originally the window lights were grouped to form T-shapes. On the ground floor is the Hall and over it the Great Chamber. More remarkable are the two rooms on the left with robust classical detail, stone fireplaces and 17th-century painted coats of arms on the overmantels, very like the painted wooden tablets by the Randle Holme family of heraldic artists, so common in Cheshire churches. The arms of Massy impaling Cotton refer to the marriage of Hugh Massy's son William (d. 1668) to Dorothy, daughter of Sir George Cotton of Combermere.
O iii, 468.

Mottram Old Hall, Mottram-in-Longendale
994 964

A handsome ashlar Greek Revival house refronting an earlier Hall: there are mullioned windows and a 17th-century doorway on one side. The new facade is symmetrical with five bays, a central pediment, a single storey porch and a smart cast-iron balcony and railings. Inside is a fine classical staircase hall. The lodge has austere grooved rustication on the sides and a good Doric portico, but is marred by a Victorian Tudor extension and poor recent additions. The stables are of the earlier period, though the round windows and hammered rustication are later. The Old Hall was owned by a collateral line of the Hollingworths of Hollingworth Hall, but was sold c. 1800 to Samuel Hadfield who was responsible for remodelling it. From 1861 it was lived in by the Gothic revival architect E. H. Shellard. Nearby was **Hill End**, built in 1827 for George Sidebottom and inherited by John Chapman, M.P., a local industrialist. This was a smaller, plainer ashlar house in the Grecian style and may have been by the same architect. It was demolished after 1936.
O iii, 870; T ii, 126; Pike 1904, 67.

Newton Hall, Hyde
942 958

The ancient home of the de Newtons, and one of the earliest surviving timber-framed structures in Cheshire. It is in a bleak industrial area and was saved from destruction by William Kenyon and Sons, who had it re-erected 1969-70 following the medieval sequence of construction, but incorporating one glazed section for viewing. There survive one timber-framed long wall and three cruck frames. The plan is boat-shaped, showing the influence of Scandinavia (see Baguley Hall), and, according to carbon dating, the timbers are of c. 1380.
AMS xviii, 65.

Newton Hall, Mobberley
803 797

A 17th-century house of brick on a stone plinth and with stone quoins, built for Francis Newton between 1634 when he bought the estate and 1676 when he died. It is now all rendered apart from the quoins. The front facing the road has three gables with 19th-century bargeboards and the entrance was formerly at the centre. On the roadside are two rusticated gate-piers; there must have been another pair on the entrance axis.
Stephen Murray, *Mobberley Records*, 1946-8, mss. at Altrincham Library.

Norcliffe Hall, Styal
829 835

A large Tudor-style mansion of 1831 by the Lichfield architect Thomas Johnson for Robert Hyde Greg, whose family formerly lived at Quarry Bank House next to Styal Mill. Of orange brick with stone dressings, it is a picturesque assembly of irregular gables and tall octagonal chimneys. A four-stage tower and billiard room were added in 1860 in matching style. Inside is a mixture of heavy Tudor and classical details, including a staircase hall lit by tall mullioned windows with armorial glass. In the fine landscaped grounds is a miniature version of Stonehenge erected in the mid-19th century.
O iii, 591; APSD.

Norley Hall, Norley

565 730

An irregular house in the Tudor style, rendered, with hood moulds, gables, tall chimneys and a large two-storey bay window prominent on the garden side. The entrance porch has a decorative pierced parapet, coarse detailing and luridly coloured glass. Built *c.* 1500 on the site of an earlier house of the Hall family, Norley was enlarged in 1697 for John Hall and rebuilt in 1782 for William Hall; its present neo-Tudor appearance dates from *c.* 1845 when it was enlarged for Samuel Woodhouse, one of a Liverpool family with estates in Marsala. His architect was Alfred Bowyer Clayton who exhibited a drawing for it at the Liverpool Academy in 1845.

O ii, 143; T i, 127.

Normans Hall, Prestbury

888 763

An L-shaped house, the south range a 16th-century timber-framed hall and parlour with a decorative gable, and the larger east range a sensitive addition in brick of 1921 by the London architect Henry Boddington for H. B. Crook.

Ches Life June 1956; Massey.

181. Norton Priory, showing the Victorian porch to the Norman undercroft.

Norton Priory, Runcorn (demolished)

548 831 *Site open to the public. (Norton Priory Museum)*

The 12th-century Augustinian Priory was acquired at the Dissolution by Vice-Admiral Sir Richard Brooke who demolished most of it but remodelled for his own use the abbot's quarters, with their vaulted undercroft. A big Palladian house was built on the site in the 1730s or '40s, later remodelled by James Wyatt for another Sir Richard Brooke before his death in 1781. The new piano nobile, reached by a grand external double staircase, was built over the undercroft. In the middle of the 19th century the importance of the medieval remains was realised and a feature made of them; the external stair was demolished in

1868 and a new ground floor porch built so that the house was entered via the undercroft. From the 18th century onwards encroaching industry threatened to eat away at the estate; the Brookes fought against canals crossing their land, then later against railways and chemical fumes. In 1928 the family gave up and left, the house was demolished and the stone was used to build a sulphuric acid plant. But the medieval work was kept and is now the centrepiece of a museum. What remains is the Victorian porch, inside which is a fine Romanesque doorway with nook shafts and zig-zag decoration, a Victorian replica made to balance it, a vaulted undercroft, and a remarkable stone statue of St Christopher 11 feet high, formerly a devotional object for travellers fording the Mersey at low tide. In the grounds are a Wyatt summerhouse and a rustic tea-house of 1829.
O i, 680; Neale 1829; T ii, 44; *Archaeological Journal* cxxiii, 68; *Norton Priory* guidebook, 1975; *VCH*, 165.

North Rode, Manor House
892 671

A stuccoed house of 1838-40 built for John Smith Daintry of the Macclesfield banking and silk family, and replacing an earlier house destroyed by fire. It has shallow hipped roofs with overhanging eaves, and Gothick sashes, some later replaced with groups of tall plate-glass windows. The classical porch is a Victorian replacement for a Gothick porch with clustered shafts now re-erected as a free-standing garden folly. The mixture continues inside with Gothick shutter cases, a central top-lit staircase hall and a panelled Jacobean-style room. A wooden model of the house shows the large service wing of 1878, now demolished. The house is beautifully situated overlooking a mere.
O iii, 737; T ii, 124; *Ches Life* April/May 1956.

Oakmere, Sandiway
589 704

182. Oakmere Hall.

One of the earliest houses of John Douglas, built in 1867 for John Higson, a Liverpool merchant, who never lived in it. Its bold massing and picturesque outline are best seen from a distance. The irregular north and west garden elevations are punctuated by a series of French Gothic motifs, a massive tower with a pavilion roof, circular angle turrets and steep pointed dormers. The entrance is marked by a porte cochère supporting another tower. In spite of the range of features used, the wall surfaces of rock-faced sandstone are harsh and the carving mechanical; more sympathetic is the later 19th-century extension to the entrance front, presumably also by Douglas. Inside is a Great Hall reaching right up to the roof, a dramatic space with a gallery, and a bridge which crosses the staircase. Now a convalescent home.
Girouard, 185.

Oakwood Hall, Romiley (demolished)
943 902

A Tudor revival house by the architect Edward Walters, more renowned for his palazzo-style banks and warehouses in Manchester. It was designed for Ormerod Heyworth whose cotton gassing works of 1833-7, Oakwood Mill, is nearby. The house was demolished recently, apart from the ground floor of coursed rubble with the datestone *1845 OH*. The Hall had a prominent tower and stood on a steep bank with terraced gardens overlooking the river Goyt. The lodge and low octagonal gatepiers survive.
T ii, 129.

Ollerton Hall, Ollerton

785 760

The nucleus of this residence is 17th century, of brick, on an H-plan, with twin-gabled cross wings and small-paned windows, still visible at the rear. It was built for one of the Bigelow family, descendants of the Baguleys of Baguley Hall, perhaps William Bigelow who is recorded as owning land at Ollerton in 1666. A plaque in the small central gable over the entrance is lettered *THP 1728* for Thomas Hubert Potts. Later the house was stuccoed and various rambling extensions added. To the north-west is **Ollerton Grange**, a freely composed neo-Tudor house of bright red brick built by the Manchester architect John Brooke for Cyril Lowcock in 1901. The entrance elevation with a profusion of shaped gables, mullioned windows and tall diagonally set chimneys is composed around an octagonal tower with an ogee cap. O ii, 174.

Oughtrington Hall, Oughtrington

695 870

Built *c.* 1810 by Trafford Trafford whose family held the Oughtrington estate from the 15th century. The Hall is a plain Neo-classical house of brick with stone dressings, later stuccoed. At the centre is a wide canted bay and a porch of paired Tuscan columns. To each side is a tripartite window within a blank segmental arch. In 1862 the house was bought by G. C. Dewhurst, a Manchester cotton manufacturer who enlarged the service wing and built the large St Peter's church nearby to the design of Slater and Carpenter. It is said by Ormerod that the main lodge and entrance gates were designed by Thomas Harrison, but on stylistic grounds this seems unlikely. More like Harrison's work is the house itself, but it too lacks sufficient distinction. It is now a school. O i, 587; T ii, 60.

Oulton Park, Little Budworth (demolished)

590 648

Now famous as a motor racing circuit insensitively imposed on the landscape park of William Emes and John Webb, Oulton was a Baroque mansion rebuilt for John Egerton in 1716 to replace a Tudor house destroyed by fire. The new building had 15 bays with a grand Corinthian centrepiece and a pediment filled with carved trophies. A drawing in the Broster album at Tatton Park records a dome, though if built this did not survive to be photographed. The side elevations had curved pediments and the end bays of the front had gabled panels in an Artisan Mannerist style which suggests links with the Worcester school of architects. Within was an imposing double height entrance hall with Corinthian pilasters and a groined plaster vault. Lewis Wyatt altered the interior *c.* 1816-26 adding stables and a terrace, and placing Neo-classical urns on the parapet. The house was burned down in 1926. Farm buildings, garden walls and a pair of wrought iron gates remain, together with a lodge designed by Joseph Turner of Whitchurch *c.* 1775 in the form of a stucco arch with screen walls. There is also a Gothic monument of 1846 to Captain J. F. Egerton of the Bengal Horse Artillery, designed by Scott and Moffat. The gates and gatepiers of 1725 at Malpas church were moved there from Oulton in 1773. O ii, 219; T i, 106; *CL* xxiii, 774; *Ches Life* November 1934; J. Lees-Milne, *English Country Houses, Baroque*, 1970, 283.

Over Tabley Hall, Tabley Superior

719 799

An amusing but gawkily proportioned Georgian Gothick facade with sashes and spiky pinnacles stuck on to a plain earlier house, a remodelling of the old Over Tabley Hall, built for the Daniell family; nearby a 17th-century outbuilding survives with stone plinth, quoins and mullioned windows. This piece of scenery, now marooned near motorway exit roads, is the work of John Astley, portrait painter and architect, who built it on the estate settled on him by the rich Lady Dukinfield Daniell whom he married in 1759. The facade dates from before 1771 when he transferred his attentions to his new Gothick house on the Dukinfield Hall estate. O i, 476.

183.   Oulton Park, 1908.

Overton Hall, Malpas
471 483

The nucleus of this once moated house is the late 16th-century timber-framed hall and screens passage built by the Alports, now divided into two floors. In the present upper rooms trusses and wind braces are visible, and on the exterior there is crude herringbone bracing on the first floor, which was probably once jettied. The big stone external chimney of the hall fireplace is partially obscured by the symmetrical villa front built on to the hall by the Gregsons in the early 19th century. The hall is now a comfortable farmhouse.

O ii, 668; *Ches Life* October 1972.

Pole Bank Hall, Woodley
946 932

A square brick house with a pediment and a single storey stone porch supported on two pairs of Ionic columns. On the garden side a big curved bow overlooks terraced gardens. It was built for Samuel Ashton, owner of Apethorn Mills, Hyde. Samuel's son Thomas lived here until 1831 when he was murdered by men in the pay of trades union activists. Now an old people's home.

A. Lock, *Hyde in Old Photographs*, 1981.

Poole Hall, Ellesmere Port (demolished)
394 785

A picturesque early 16th-century manor house overlooking the Mersey, built for Thomas Poole, Seneschal of Birkenhead Priory, who died in 1547, and later enlarged. The earlier part consisted of a jumble of stone and timber-framed gables with a two-storey castellated porch leading to the Great Hall. On the first floor was a panelled room with carved portrait heads in low relief, knot designs and armorials including those of Thomas Poole and his wife Mary Talbot. The style of the panelling was similar to that still existing at Smithills Hall, Lancashire, of the 1530s. The fireplace in the Great Hall was dated 1574; the stone east front was probably added at the same time in a more regular style. It had striking octagonal turrets with three storeys of windows, and pointed roofs. In the 1930s the Hall was bought by Bowaters who demolished it to expand their paper works.

O ii, 422, 437; Irvine, 18; *Manchester Guardian*, 8 June 1937; R. Glasgow, *The Hardwares of Cheshire*, 1948, 36.

Poole Hall, Nantwich
646 552

A compact house of brick and stone built for William Massey of Chester between 1812 when he inherited the estate from the Elcocke family and 1817, the date of his marriage. The park was laid out by John Webb. The house is plain externally, but the interior, in the Lewis Wyatt manner, is of sufficient quality to be by one of Wyatt's associates. At the centre of the severe entrance front is a semi-circular Ionic porch with a broad doorcase and fanlight like an Irish Georgian house. Within are a set of elegantly proportioned rooms with exceptionally fine plasterwork. The central top-lit hall has a stone cantilever staircase and

184. The drawing room at Poole Hall.

marble floor. In the dining room is a shallow curved alcove with its original mahogany sideboard en suite with the dining table. The drawing room has a tunnel-vaulted ceiling and at one end a screen of Corinthian columns. The marble fireplace is supported on herms in the form of Grecian maidens. In the study, which was panelled in 1907, are pieces of 16th-century glass, perhaps from the old Hall. They include the arms of Thomas Gamul of Buerton who married Elena Poole, members of the Longford family of Longford Hall, Derbyshire, and the Masseys, together with scenes of soldiers displaying weapons and traders selling cakes and fruit.

O iii, 352; T i, 21; *Ches Life* April 1961.

Poulton Hall, Poulton Lancelyn
335 817

The home of the Lancelyn family (later Lancelyn Green) since the 11th century, Poulton is a modest 17th-century manor house since altered externally so as to look more like a Victorian villa. The castle on a nearby site was destroyed in the Wars of the Roses and replaced by the Old Hall which in turn was succeeded by the present house built by Richard Greene, who inherited in 1653. Of brick and stone, it was originally similar in style to the surviving brewhouse. The quoins, hipped roof and some small-paned dormer windows remain from this period. A library wing was added in the early 18th century, and broader sash windows were introduced. In the early 19th century the house was stuccoed, given a symmetrical entrance front with a Doric porch, and Regency features such as the curved bows facing the garden. A Victorian service wing and a billiard room extension of 1883 were added and shortly afterwards the stucco was covered in roughcast. The ground floor rooms are decorated with curios, arranged with theatrical flair. From the hall a 17th-century staircase with twisted balusters leads up to a perfect example of a scholar's domestic library, added for Rev. Thomas Green, Rector of Woodchurch, who came to live here on his brother's death in 1711. It is a low-ceilinged, book-lined room and, like a miniature Oxbridge college library, it is divided into alcoves, three on either side. In two of them are sash windows, each lighting built-in reading desks. Besides the 18th-century library of theological, scientific and literary subjects, the room houses a distinguished collection of Victorian children's books formed by the late Roger Lancelyn Green who himself wrote over sixty books here. His son Richard, a leading Conan Doyle scholar, has reconstructed in one of the attics Sherlock Holmes's study at 221B Baker Street, furnished with an eye for authentic detail.

O ii, 440; T i, 64; R. Lancelyn Green, *Poulton Lancelyn, the story of an ancestral home*, 1948; *Ches Life* December 1955, January 1956, March 1968.

Poynton Hall (demolished)
935 844

A serpentine lake, remnants of a park and two small lodges on the busy London Road are all that survive of the seat of the Warrens. The 16th-century timber-framed Hall was extended with a Jacobean entrance tower and a forecourt bounded by castellated angle towers; an early Georgian red brick wing was also added. Then in the 1750s Sir George Warren built a new large classical mansion on another site. This was an L-shaped house with two wings connected by a tall octagonal staircase tower surmounted by a lantern. He laid out the park with lakes and planting in the manner of Brown and around 1775 the remains of the old Hall buildings were formed into an eyecatcher called **The Towers** and dressed up with a castellated gateway like a toy fort, 'a sad attempt at something Gothic', according to Lord Torrington. In 1826 the estate passed to the Vernons of Sudbury Hall, Derbyshire, who soon after demolished the Hall and in 1869 enlarged The Towers with a haphazard arrangement of castellated projections and conservatories, as the principal house on the estate. This too was pulled down in 1935. The Vernons' main interest in Poynton was the exploitation of the estate for coal mining, and the extensive network of tramways, inclines and industrial buildings which they created can still be found amongst the suburban sprawl.

Revd. J. Watson, *Memoirs of the Ancient Earls of Warren*, 1782 ii, 130, 162; O iii, 685; T ii, 85; Neale 1829; Torrington ii, 180; Harris, 206; CRO, Plans of Vernon estates DVE/10/8.

Puddington Old Hall, Puddington
326 733

The ancient property of the Masseys, a leading Jacobite family. The Hall, formerly moated, overlooks the Dee estuary, close to the Welsh border. What remains is three sides of a quadrangular timber-framed

185. The library at Poulton Hall.

186. Poynton Old Hall before 1775, from a painting by Thomas Stringer.

house, now roughcast and quite altered on the outer faces, but with an internal courtyard displaying timbering of the late 15th century. The original plan of the house is obscure, but on the south side of the courtyard is an open gallery and cloister, a simpler version of that which existed at Agecroft Hall, Lancashire, now re-erected at New Richmond, Virginia. Inside the north-west corner (the Priest's House flat) are three early trusses indicating that this was formerly a Great Hall or a solar open to the roof. The Priest's House within the north range is named after Saint John Plessington, tutor to the Massey children, who was seized at Puddington following the Popish plot and hanged at Chester Castle in 1679. In 1760 John Stanley (who assumed the name Massey) built **Puddington New Hall** immediately to the north but it was largely destroyed by fire in 1867. Only the two matching brick wings of eight bays each survive; these were originally joined by a central block facing across the estuary. Following the destruction of the New Hall, the Stanleys enlarged a shooting box to form another house, **Puddington Hall**, south of the Old Hall. This was taken down in 1904 and rebuilt in sandstone in a free Tudor style. The south lodge with its gate-piers dates from the earlier rebuilding, the roughcast north lodge from the same period.
O ii, 560; Irvine, 20.

187.   The garden front of Ramsdell Hall, seen across the Macclesfield Canal.

Ramsdell Hall, Scholar Green
843 581

An appealingly quirky house comprising a central block with long side wings. A good view of it can be obtained from the Macclesfield Canal. The central part, dating from the mid 18th century, is of brick, three storeys high and L-shaped. The inner corner of the L is canted to contain the entrance, a handsome

Venetian doorcase on shafted columns, with Gothick glazing. On the garden front are Venetian windows, a small pediment and a profusion of ball finials. The wings, probably added around 1768 when new planting was carried out on the estate, extend the garden front by some 100 feet and were built largely for show. The architect for both phases could be William Baker who designed the nearby Astbury Rectory in 1757-8. This shares with Ramsdell an exaggerated tallness, a parapet heavy with ball finials, and side wings. The angled plan produces an unusual interior. The dining room is octagonal and the hall hexagonal, though their 18th-century character has been altered. In the drawing room is a good Rococo ceiling. At the entrance to the grounds is a splendid pair of tall rusticated gate-piers supporting noble eagles bearing shields with a boar's head crest, probably an Edwardian addition. The gate-piers were acquired in the late 1950s by a local businessman Stanley Harrison whose initials appear in the wrought iron gates.
Ches Life July/August 1954; Oswald, 126.

Ravenscroft Hall, Middlewich
704 677

A plain stucco house of 1837 built for William T. Buchanan in place of a Jacobean Hall, and later extended. The nucleus is a two-storey five-bay block with tall windows, trellises, overhanging eaves and an Ionic porch. The additions include an Italianate belvedere tower in yellow brick (now partially stuccoed), probably of 1852 when the Moss family bought the Hall, and extensions with two-storey canted bays and a single storey octagonal room, perhaps a game larder. Some of the rebuilding took place in 1877, the date on the drawing room fireplace. Until then there existed a fine Jacobean ceiling with a female figure in plaster holding a caduceus and a cornucopia, signifying peace and plenty, recorded by John Douglas in 1872.
O iii, 207; T i, 150; Douglas ii, pl. 52.

Reaseheath Hall, Nantwich
646 540

A Wilbraham house, purchased in 1722 by the Tomkinsons of Dorfold and in 1878 rebuilt in a busy gabled Queen Anne style in hot red brick with much decoratively moulded brickwork and Jacobean detail. It was enlarged in 1892. It is irregular except for the entrance front which is entered through a stone porch in the simpler Tudor style of *c.* 1830, perhaps kept from the previous house. Inside is a half-panelled staircase hall and gallery, and a large window with armorial glass. Now the Cheshire Agricultural College.
O iii, 357, 481; A. Lamberton, *Reaseheath*, 1984.

Ridley Hall, Bulkeley (demolished)
547 548

Now a fragment, forlornly incorporated into farm buildings, Ridley Hall was once one of the county's great houses. Originally the seat of the Ridley family, about the middle of the 15th century it became the property of the wealthy Sir William Stanley, brother of the first Earl of Derby. Stanley rebuilt Holt Castle, and set up his son and daughter with new houses at Tatton and Sutton Weaver. At Ridley, according to Leland, he 'made of a poor old place the finest gentleman's house of all Cheshire'. He was beheaded in 1495 for his connection with the pretender to the throne Perkin Warbeck, and his estates were confiscated by the crown. In 1514 Ridley was granted to Sir Ralph Egerton, whose family became one of the richest and most powerful in Cheshire in the 16th century. His architectural patronage can be seen in the exquisite Ridley chapel of 1527 at Bunbury church. Webb described Ridley *c.* 1623 as 'a stately house and a great demesne', though at this time the family fortune was being dissipated by gambling. The form of Ridley Hall is not known, nor the relative extent of the Stanley and Egerton contributions. What now remains is a massive stone gateway, and its scale gives some indication of the likely size of the Hall. The gatehouse has a flattened arch on responds and is perhaps early 16th century. Over it, set into a later brick wall, is a very weathered stone relief, probably Elizabethan, showing a coat of arms of many quarterings, including the three Egerton arrows surmounted by the Egerton crest of a hand holding a sword. Flanking the arms are crude demi-figure herms, and beside these are men blowing horns and little kneeling dogs, supported on scrolls. On the inner face of the courtyard is a similar arch but no carving, and between, on the underside of the chamber above the gatehouse, is an ancient timber ceiling. The gateway now forms the entrance to a large cobbled farmyard with later brick ranges to each side. Ormerod described another feature, the

former Ridley courthouse called the Star Chamber after its carved star shapes inside, but this is no longer there. Ridley resisted a Royalist attack in the Civil War, but in 1700 the Hall, no longer Egerton property, was burned down by a servant accidentally setting fire to a chest of flax.
Leland v, 23; O ii, 8, 298.

188. The ruins of Rocksavage: an engraving after de Wint, 1818.

Rocksavage, Runcorn (demolished)
526 799

An Elizabethan house, now ruinous, built 1565-8 by Sir John Savage to replace his ancient seat of Clifton Hall nearby. Rocksavage stood proudly on a hillside overlooking the river Weaver, an area now badly scarred by industry and motorways. The house was quadrangular, entered through a gateway flanked by octagonal towers like the slightly later Brereton, built by Savage's son-in-law. James I stayed at Rocksavage in 1617 en route for Halton Castle and Chester. Behind the ruins, farther up the hill, is a very grand block of domestic offices, truncated and surrounded by farm buildings. Now called **Clifton Hall**, it dates from the early 18th century during the brief period when the estate came into the Barrymore family. This may be the work of the architect Henry Sephton who worked at Halton: it was originally a symmetrical U-shaped range of brick with giant stone pilasters, cross windows, a classical doorcase with broken pediment and a steeply hipped roof. One end of the U no longer exists. Shortly afterwards the house was brought by marriage into the Cholmondeley family, and then left to fall into decay.
Aikin, 415; O i, 711, 717, 408; CRO Rev. J. Greswell, *An Account of Runcorn and its environs*, 1803; CRO DCH/ H/516-7, Rocksavage Estate Plans.

The Rookery, Tattenhall
485 587

A big rambling house in the revived Cheshire vernacular with much decorative timbering and a large sandstone chimneystack. Originally the property of the Orton family, it was reconstructed for F. W. Wignall of Tate & Lyle, and is dated 1909 on the hopperheads. The interior is panelled and includes a large drawing room with an inglenook and, facing the garden, a dining room in Restoration style with heavy plasterwork featuring Liver birds on the ceiling. There is a formal garden with clipped yews and a pretty pepperpot-shaped lodge with a pyramid thatched roof and eyebrow dormers. Now a nursing home.
F. Latham, *Tattenhall*, 1978, 80.

Rookery Hall, Worleston
659 560

Originally a plain late Georgian brick house belonging to William Hilton Cooke of Chester, a Jamaica sugar planter. In 1867 the estate was bought by Baron William von Schroder, a merchant banker. His late 19th-century alterations made it more grandiose, with ashlar cladding and vaguely Elizabethan details. Of two storeys, it has a Corinthian porch, mullioned windows and a steep Loire-style pavilion roof over a corner tower. The nouveau-riche air suits its present use as a luxurious restaurant and hotel, complete with circular baths and gold-plated taps. The interior re-uses panelling from Calveley Hall.

Sandbach Old Hall, Sandbach
758 607

A large black and white house with the date 1656 and the monogram TB in a gable. The timbering of the front with close-studding and baluster motifs is largely 19th century as the house was much restored by Lord Crewe in 1887, but original framing infilled with brick remains at the rear. Inside are some Jacobean fireplaces and an oak baluster staircase, but none of these is *in situ*. Now a hotel.
O iii, 98.

Sharston Hall, Northenden (demolished)
834 886

A three-storey brick house of five bays with stone quoins, built for the Worthingtons in 1701. It had a good Ionic doorcase with an open pediment and a florid shield bearing the family arms. A large Jacobean-style wing with a belvedere was added in the1870s. The estate was acquired by Manchester City Council in 1927, a road was built past the front door and the Hall deteriorated. Seriously vandalised in the 1970s, it was scandalously neglected until 1984 when the Council demolished it as a dangerous structure. A poor replica has since been built as an office block on an adjacent site.
O iii, 612; *Manchester Notes and Queries*, 1896-8, 50.

189.   Shotwick Hall.

Shotwick Hall, Shotwick
337 721

A small brick house of 1662, old-fashioned for its date, on an E-shaped plan with three gables and a square walled front garden with axial gate-piers. The detail is vernacular, with brick nogging as seen on other houses in the village and windows with wooden mullions, renewed but using much old glass. There are wooden arched heads on the doors and the staircase has simple plaster relief decoration and flat wooden balusters of a type common in Cheshire. Over a fireplace are the arms of Shotwick quartered with Hockenhull and *IEH 1662* commemorating the marriage of Robert de Hockenhull to Alice de Shotwick in the reign of Edward I, and the building of the present hall for Joseph Hockenhull and his wife Elizabeth. The house was used with considerable artist's licence as the setting for a murder in Mrs. Linnaeus Banks' novel *God's Providence House* of 1865.

O ii, 563; *THSLC* lxvii, 67.

Shotwick Park, Saughall
358 703

A large house by John Douglas built of brick with red sandstone dressings and red tiled roofs, in a simple Tudor style with little decoration, but a characteristically varied roofline. It was built for Horace Trelawney in 1872 (the date is on the weathervane), sold in 1906 and altered in 1907 for Thorneycroft Vernon, whose coat of arms is seen over the entrance and elsewhere. Like Oakmere, Douglas's house of only five years earlier, Shotwick is an effective composition from a distance, but close to, the detailing is dull. Now a nursing home.

BA xi, 36.

Shrigley Hall, Pott Shrigley
943 798

An impressive Regency house of stone erected on the edge of moorland for William Turner, a mill owner from Blackburn who acquired the Shrigley estate in 1818. His architect was Thomas Emett snr., a member of a family of Preston timber merchants. The broad entrance front has a central pediment and Ionic portico; on each end bay is a tripartite window beneath a shallow arch in the Wyatt manner. The principal rooms, which all face west for the fine views, lie on either side of a grand entrance hall, formerly open to a high dome and skylight. Unfortunately the Imperial staircase has been removed from this space and a floor inserted below the dome. The house has good Neo-classical plasterwork, mostly in the Lewis Wyatt style, but the pattern of twisted vines in the dome is particularly original. The Salesian Mission, which ran the house for over fifty years as a school, made the changes to the interior and added an attic floor in place of the open stone balustrade. They also built the church dedicated to St John Bosco, its strikingly tall silhouette dominating the house. The church was designed by Philip Tilden, a late Arts and Crafts architect, and built alongside the house in 1936. Its simple geometry of octagonal nave imposed upon a Greek cross achieves great spatial complexity. From the angles project corner chapels connected by round arches, a design described by Tilden as like a sitting hen 'with its chapels tucked around her, each separate in their lives yet attached to the living body by protective mother love'. In the absence of funds, the architect himself painted the Stations of the Cross and the altarpiece, but the recent departure of the Salesians has meant the removal of the fittings. After a period of disuse the house is to become a hotel and there are plans to reinstate the staircase; the church faces a new life as a health club.

O iii, 772; T ii, 114; W. A. Abram, *History of Blackburn*, 1877, 228, 404; *Builder* clxviii, 492; P. Tilden, *True Remembrances*, 1954, 142; RIBA S6/3 drawing of the church.

Somerford Park, Somerford (demolished)
814 651

An 18th-century house enlarged in several stages. The nucleus dated from *c.* 1720 when Peter Shakerley moved here from Hulme Hall, Allostock. He also had the chapel built after a quarrel with the Rector of Astbury; it is dated 1725, a simple preaching box of chequered brick with stone quoins and arched openings. Shakerley vowed never to go to Astbury church again and is buried outside his chapel. The Hall was extended during the course of the 18th century by T. F. Pritchard, and towards 1800 was enlarged by Lawrence Robinson of Middleton, Lancashire, who had been associated with several members of the Wyatt family. At right angles to the nine-bay earlier house he added a rectangular block with canted ends and a two-storey domed bow. A matching block was built at the other end. The additions were for C. W. J.

190. Shrigley Hall and chapel.

191. Somerford Park.

Shakerley, between 1790 and 1797. His grandson, Sir Charles Watkin Shakerley, further enlarged the house, employing Salvin, who added a heavy Italianate porch. The Hall was demolished in 1927 and now only the chapel, an icehouse and part of the stables remain. The park was laid out in the early 19th century by Davenport and Webb but is now mostly farmland.

O iii, 58, 152; T i, 128; R. Richards, *Old Cheshire Churches*, 1973, 856; *Vanishing Houses of England*, Save Britain's Heritage, 1982, 15.

Somerford Booths Hall, Somerford Booths

830 656

A moated house of 1612 built for Edmund Swetenham. It was improved in 1817 for Clement Swetenham by John Webb the landscape gardener and architect, who also worked at Somerford Park nearby. The improvements included a large square mullioned and castellated bay window in the middle of the south front. The house is a dull composition, small and roughcast, with gables and Tudor-style windows with square hoodmoulds. Now offices.

O iii, 560; T ii, 101.

Soss Moss Hall, Nether Alderley

828 759

A modest H-plan half-timbered house built for Thomas Wyche and dated on a massive stone chimney 1583. Duplication of timbers at the inner angles suggests that the house was built in two stages, hall and west cross wing first, and east wing with chimney later; but half-cut mortices in the tie beam of the roof truss at the junction indicate that the decision to extend was made before the first phase was completed. Only one gable retains its original magpie timbering. The huge chimney on the east end serves three stone fireplaces and contains a closet with garderobes. The kitchen was used between 1835 and 1940 as Nether Alderley Methodist Chapel.

O ii, 568; *THSLC* i, 12.

Staley Hall, Stalybridge

976 997

A gaunt Pennine vernacular house built in the late 16th century for the Booth family, later Earls of Stamford. Originally timber framed, it was clad in millstone grit soon after completion. The facade has five gables, stepping back to the centre with the porch at one side. Dilapidated in the 1880s, it was used as a farmhouse at least until the 1930s, but is now a roofless ruin, the stone blackened by industrial pollution. It stands under an electricity pylon overlooking a landscape of cooling towers in the moorland valley below.

O iii; *Ashton Reporter Pictorial*, 1931.

Stanthorne Hall, Middlewich

682 666

A tall brick house of three bays with a Tuscan doorcase built 1804-7 for Richard Dutton who bought the estate from the Leicesters of Tabley. Inside is a graceful staircase hall, and the main rooms have suave fireplaces of black marble.

O iii, 262.

Storeton Hall, Storeton

306 843

Now a farm, but built of the ruins of an important house erected *c.* 1360 for the Stanleys, ancestors of the Earls of Derby. Until about 1480 when they built Hooton Hall, Storeton was their principal residence. It was H-shaped, with a Great Hall in the centre, facing east, cross wings at either end, and a forecourt between. Nothing remains of the kitchen wing to the south, but the two-storey north wing survives. On the upper floor, over the withdrawing room, are the remains of the solar fireplace and a blocked Gothic window, though the roofline has been changed. On the ground floor are buttresses and an attached smaller block, formerly the chapel. The front wall of the hall, with blocked openings, still stands, but it now confusingly forms the rear wall of a long farm range running across the former forecourt. The stone comes from the noted local quarry.

O ii, 445; *THSLC* xlix, 47.

Stretton Hall, Stretton
447 527

A chaste symmetrical Georgian brick house erected *c.* 1763 for John Leche, son of the rector of Tilston. It has a central block of two storeys over a basement, and two single storey wings. The doorway is raised up above a pair of curved steps at the centre of a wide canted bay. There is a touch of grandeur in the entrance hall with its screen of scagliola columns, but the fine Neo-classical fireplace is a later replacement; only in the bedrooms do original Rococo fireplaces survive. After 1785 Stretton became a secondary house to the Carden estate, but in 1912 the Jacobean Carden Hall was destroyed by fire. Sir John Leche moved to Stretton and created the gardens with their radiating avenues and yew hedges raised on stone blocks taken from the base of Carden Hall. The stables, 17th-century in date, belong to an earlier house on the site and have recently been extended to house a helicopter. Nearby are two 17th-century brick houses with shaped gables, **Stretton Old Hall** and **Stretton Lower Hall**, the latter formerly moated, and dated on a fireplace *JHL 1660*, perhaps for one of the Leches of Carden.
Harrison & Co., *Picturesque Views*, 1788; O ii, 711; *Ches Life* April/May 1950.

192. Stretton Hall.

Sutton Hall, Sutton
925 715

A house of the 16th or 17th century, since much altered, most recently as a hotel. It is U-shaped, with irregular gables, that on the left of stone, and on the right timber-framed with a jetty supported on carved wooden figures, one representing a warrior in scale armour. In the centre between the gabled wings is the former Great Hall, now the dining room, and to its left the original entrance passage. Sash windows with

Gothick glazing were inserted in the early 19th century. Behind the house across a courtyard is a small stone chapel with the chaplain's house attached, and a lych gate and burial ground, all most likely of the 16th century. The chapel was used for Catholic worship in the 17th century. It later fell into disuse but was restored in 1950.

O iii, 761; *Ches Life* July/August 1958.

Sutton Hall, Sutton Weaver
544 792

Hidden inside the brick walls of an ordinary looking farmhouse is one of the most important and least known late medieval timber-framed houses in Cheshire, dating from the late 15th century and probably once much bigger. It now consists of two large and handsome apartments one above the other, both divided by later partitions. The ground floor room has a flat ceiling supported by heavy richly-moulded beams which rest on ribbed uprights carved with narrow colonettes and polygonal capitals in the perpendicular style. The Great Chamber above has a magnificent open timber roof supported on the continuation of the upright posts from below, though on this floor the colonettes and capitals are even more elaborate. The main roof trusses are big cambered tie beams, each joined to the short collar above by a row of vertical posts, forming an open screen like a mullioned window. All the members are finely moulded making an interior of great richness, enhanced by quatrefoil windbracing on the underside of the roof. There are traces

193. The Great Chamber at Sutton Hall, Sutton Weaver.

of the former screens passage in one of the side walls of the first floor, and in each room is a big 16th-century stone fireplace. In an upper chamber a stone chimneybreast is painted in colours with armorials and classical grotesques of the late 16th century. In the Middle Ages Sutton was the principal seat of the Duttons, who changed their name to Warburton in the 13th century when they acquired the manor of that name. In 1469 Sir Piers Warburton built a new seat at Arley, and Sutton became the residence of his son and heir John. The work at Sutton may date from 1485, when John married Jane, daughter of Sir William Stanley of Ridley. Stanley's wealth lay behind the building of his son's house, the Old Hall at Tatton, and also financed the work at Sutton Weaver. The roof at Tatton is similar in type to that at Sutton. Closer in overall form as well as roof structure to Sutton, is the south wing at Bramall, where the ground floor has a flat ceiling of moulded beams and over it is a big chamber with an open roof; but the woodwork at Sutton is of much finer quality than either Bramall or Tatton. The high degree of elaboration and craftsmanship is closer to contemporary church roofs in Cheshire than to any other domestic work.
O i, 569, 572, 730; Hanshall, 407.

Swettenham Hall, Swettenham `
810 665

A 17th-century house remodelled in the early 19th century with stucco, canted bays and a castellated entrance front. Some of the outbuildings date from the 17th century: a coat of arms and a plaque inscribed *TFS 1696* for Thomas Swettenham and his wife Frances is on the stables, a handsome range of brick with stone quoins and mullioned windows. There is a small Victorian Gothic chapel dated 1852 in the grounds.
O iii, 73; T i, 133; *Ches Life* February/March 1953.

Swineyard Hall, High Legh
678 838

A 16th-century moated house built by a branch of the Leghs of High Legh. At one end of the house the moat is filled with water and a half-timbered gable survives, jettied, with lozenge patterns and simple studding below. The other end, including the corresponding gable, has been roughcast, with square hood moulds.
O i, 463.

Tattenhall Hall, Tattenhall
486 582

A Jacobean house erected before 1622 for Richard Bostock. It has an irregular plan, with a central part containing the hall recessed between two gables. Though stylistically the gables are similar, different window and floor heights suggest that they have been conceived separately. The screens passage is entered from what is now the rear, and the front entrance is in a re-entrant angle of the larger gable, as at Dorfold. The house is of brick, an early example for Cheshire, and all the windows have stone mullions, some unusually large in size. Used as a farmhouse by the early 18th century, it was bought and restored by Robert Barbour of Bolesworth in 1856. He erected the gate-piers and the model farm buildings in 1860 to the design of James Harrison of Chester.
O ii, 591, 718; F. Latham, *Tattenhall*, 1978, 80.

Thelwall Hall, Thelwall
655 877

A good Georgian house of brick, probably built for Thomas Pickering after 1747, the date he succeeded to the estate of his father, an eminent barrister. The house originally had seven bays with a central pediment, and it was entered on the piano nobile from an external double staircase. It has since been much altered with bay windows and other extensions. Now the Chaigeley School.
O i, 746; T ii, 72.

Thorncliffe Hall, Hollingworth
002 967

A stone house in a simple neo-Jacobean style with three very big and fancy shaped gables on the main front. It was originally built for the Bretland family in the 17th century, and eventually passed to the architect Edwin Hugh Shellard who was probably responsible for remodelling it. He married in 1850 and is recorded as living at Thorncliffe from 1852-63.

O iii, 870.

Thornton House, Thornton Hough

304 812

Built for Joseph Hirst, Yorkshire woollen manufacturer and improving landlord of the village, and then rebuilt in the Old English style in 1895 by Grayson and Ould for James Darcy Lever, Lord Leverhulme's brother and junior partner. This is an attractive and freely grouped design combining stone and timber in a picturesque, busy composition of gables, tall chimneys and Tudor windows. The black and white entrance gable is based on the now demolished Darcy Lever Hall, Lancashire. The plan is L-shaped, set around two sides of a forecourt. The house was skilfully extended on one side by J. Lomax Simpson in 1906. Also in the village but nearer to Thornton Manor are **Copley**, a playful Tudor-Gothic house in rock-faced stone with a lodge dated 1867 and a square tower modelled on Brimstage Hall; and **Hesketh Grange** of 1894, designed for Lord Leverhulme's father and sisters by Grayson and Ould.

Royal Academy, *Lord Leverhulme*, 1980, 183, 186.

Thornycroft Hall, Siddington

865 712

The home of the Thornycroft family, built in the mid-18th century and remodelled in the 1830s. Now a barrack-like, oddly proportioned stucco house with a single storey Ionic porch; on the garden side is a bow window and balcony overlooking two lakes. Behind the house is an 18th-century stable block with a cupola. Now a seminary.

O iii, 731; T ii, 112; White's *Directory of Cheshire*, 1860.

Thurstaston Hall, Thurstaston

247 841

A house of eccentric charm in a sleepy Wirral backwater where it forms a pretty group with the village green and J. L. Pearson's church, built for T. H. Ismay of nearby Dawpool, now demolished. Thurstaston Hall was built on a moated site for the de Roedelants, who were granted the manor after the Conquest, and was extended by their descendants the Whitmores and the Gleggs. The elements of its U-shaped front run chronologically from right to left. First is a 14th-century stone wing of two storeys with a timber roof structure. This was probably the cross wing to a Great Hall on the site of the central part of the house. Secondly the central part itself, rebuilt in the late 17th century in brick and stone. The entrance front is a countrified attempt at the Restoration style. It has an oversized parapet, quoins, urns and a classical doorcase with a stone armorial tablet leaning perilously out of an open pediment. Inside is a big symmetrical entrance hall and several rooms with good bolection-moulded panelling. Thirdly, echoing the medieval wing is a neo-Tudor dining room and service wing of 1836 added for John Baskervyle Glegg. There are also the remains of a medieval chapel and a stone wing dated 1680 but in a different style from the entrance front. At the back is a chaotic maze of steps, closets, passageways and service rooms, all miraculously unimproved.

O ii, 506; Mortimer, 264; T i, 70; *THSLC* lxxv, 1; *Ches Life* August/September 1949.

Torkington Lodge, Hazel Grove

927 868

A plain house of brick with twin pediments, heavily moulded, and a porch with thin paired columns. It was built c. 1820 for Orford Holte to replace a large mansion of the early 18th century erected for the Leghs of Booths. The house is now owned by Stockport Borough Council and the park is open to the public.

O iii, 837, 929.

Trafford Hall, Wimbolds Trafford

451 721

A tall sturdy Georgian brick house of five bays built in 1756 for George Edward Gerrard. On the left side of the entrance front is a later single storey pavilion, linked by a service wing and a screen wall with

194.   The gateway and entrance front, Thurstaston Hall.

rusticated gate-piers, an arrangement probably once mirrored on the right. At the rear is a plain ballroom added in the early 19th century. Inside is a spacious hall and a fine staircase with twisted balusters, marked on the south elevation by a Venetian window. Alterations have reduced the interest of the interior, but a handsome carved doorcase with a frieze of oak leaves survives in one first floor room. There is a Gothick lodge of the 1840s west of the house.
O ii, 35; T i, 120.

Tushingham Hall, Tushingham
530 451

A remodelling of a moated farmhouse for Daniel Vawdrey who purchased it in 1814. It is in a plain neo-Tudor style, stuccoed, with mullioned windows, square hood moulds and a triple-arched porch. Inside is a late 17th-century staircase from Dearnford Hall near Whitchurch. There is fine parkland and gardens, a lake, and part of the original moat. A brick lodge with a rustic timber porch is dated 1867 with the names of Theodosia and Benjamin Vawdrey, Daniel's son.
O ii, 654.

Twemlow Hall, Twemlow Green
783 685

A 17th-century brick house with a symmetrical five-bay front, much altered in 1810 for William Bache

277

Booth. Formerly moated, it stands on the edge of a steep hill overlooking the Dane Valley. Recently modernised.

O iii, 136; T i, 139.

Tytherington Old Hall, Macclesfield

913 760

A timber-framed L-shaped house built for the Worths. One cross wing survives, fronted by a big jettied gable of the late 16th century. At the other end of the building is close studding, perhaps the remains of an earlier 16th-century cross wing to the hall. In the early 19th century a new stone house was built on to the east side. This extension has recently been demolished together with a group of barns, one with cruck frames, set round a duck pond. The surrounding land has been developed as a massive housing estate and the Hall, shamefully neglected, is at last being restored. But it has outlived **Tytherington House**, a large Italianate mansion built in the 19th century for a branch of the Brocklehurst family, Macclesfield silk manufacturers and bankers. The house was demolished for a housing estate in the 1960s. Nearby is **Hurdsfield House**, another Brocklehurst residence, now a clinic hemmed in by Council housing.

O iii, 700; T ii, 123.

Upton Manor, Upton, Wirral

269 888

A showy Italianate villa designed by John Cunningham in 1857 for the ship-owner William Inman. Though not large, it speaks new money. It is built of ashlar with pronounced quoins, a projecting cornice, and a balustraded portico with coupled Doric columns. There is a tall belvedere tower with balconies and arched windows, and an extension in the same style but on a more generous scale. This was added before 1875 and has two large bays overlooking terraced gardens. The interior is very splendid, with a galleried hall and domed roof light; the staircase was reconstructed in 1911. Recently a school, now a nursing home.

O ii, 483.

Utkinton Hall, Utkinton

553 647

The ancient seat of the Done family, hereditary Foresters of Delamere, Utkinton is now a rambling untidy farmhouse and much of the original courtyard house has been taken down. The long range running at right angles to the road was probably the Great Hall block, and preserves its original studded oak door. Inside the hall, now divided into two storeys, is a free-standing octagonal wooden post on a stone base, running up both floors to support the roof. The Done line terminated in 1629 with the death of Sir John Done, whose daughter married Sir John Crewe. The Crewes had a chapel consecrated in 1635 but the house was plundered of its plate and jewels by the Royalists in 1644. The frontage to the road was built *c.* 1700 for Sir John Crewe in a rustic Queen Anne style of brick with stone quoins and cross windows, all set upon an earlier basement. Many of the windows are now blocked and the once magnificent tall brick gate-piers are crumbling and ruinous. The stained glass and the staircase were removed to Tarporley Rectory in the 18th century. The glass then went to Vale Royal and is now in the Burrell Collection, Glasgow.

O ii, 248, 251; *JCAS* xv, 142; *The Genealogist*, xxxviii, 1921-2; FM i, 20.

Walton Hall, Higher Walton

600 849 *House and park open to the public. (Warrington Borough Council)*

A large dull Elizabethan revival house of brick and stone built in 1836 for Gilbert Greenall, M.P., grandson of the founder of the Wilderspool brewery. The Hall, freely planned, with gables, turrets, oriels and bay windows, has been much reduced; the tops of some of the stepped gables have been removed and a billiard room tower of 1870 has been demolished, as has most of the service wing, though the clock tower remains. The interior is plain except for the Imperial staircase with a good panelled and carved timber ceiling. In one room is a marble overmantel of 1871 by the local sculptor Warrington Wood showing Diana hunting. The house is used by Warrington Museum and the grounds are a public park. Nearby was

195.   Utkinton Hall.

Walton Lea, a classical mansion of 1863 designed by Edward Walters of Manchester for the Warrington industrialist John Crosfield (demolished *c.* 1930).
O i, 737; T ii, 75; *TCLAS* lxxi, 117; J. N. Slater, *A Brewer's Tale*, 1980.

Weaver Hall, Darnhall
669 643
   An early 17th-century H-plan house substantially rebuilt in the early 18th century, probably as a result of severe subsidence which occurred here in 1713; it was remodelled in 1847. The house was the seat of the Stanleys before they acquired the Alderley estate.
O ii, 210.

Weston Hall, Weston
732 515
   A five-bay Restoration house of brick, with massive well-proportioned stone dressings. There are two main storeys, sashed and raised up on a basement with steps up to the entrance. The roofline is heavy, with a tall hipped roof, dormers and high chimneys. The date 1677 is given in brick numerals. The manor belonged to the Delves family of Doddington who built the similar Checkley Hall.
O iii, 510.

196. Wettenhall Hall: a drawing by John Douglas, 1872.

Wettenhall Hall, Wettenhall (demolished)
623 626

A good brick house reflecting the style known as Artisan Mannerism. It had three shaped gables surmounted by pediments and matching two-storey bay windows with pierced stone parapets. In the centre was a big pedimented doorcase with a Tuscan order and a rusticated arch. The house was dated 1635 over the central first floor window. At this period the manor was sold by John Brereton to Roger Wilbraham of Dorfold. Though it is not recorded which of these built the Hall, the Wilbrahams had London connections and Artisan Mannerism was a London masons' style. The appearance of the house is known from John Douglas' drawings; it was demolished about 1930.
O ii, 194; Douglas i, 24.

Whatcroft Hall, Davenham
681 699

A modest Georgian brick house built in 1780 and enlarged in 1807 by James Topping, a barrister, who added a new front and an exotic looking ogee dome on an octagonal drum. This is over the centre of the house and contains a circular cantilevered stone staircase with a delicate trellis balustrade, Gothick windows and plaster fan vaulting. The stair connects the different floor levels of the two parts of the house: the earlier portion faces the garden whilst the taller addition forms the entrance front. The house was later roughcast and extended with bay windows, a loggia and a service wing, all removed in 1938 when it was remodelled and reduced for Mrs. F. F. Stirling. On an island in an ornamental moat is a circular Gothick summerhouse lined with shells by the daughters of Mr. Topping.
O iii, 260; Pike 1904, 119; *Ches Life* March/April 1954.

Whirley Hall, Henbury
876 746

A brick house of three storeys with two shaped gables, each containing oval windows. There is a stone in the roof dated 1599 probably taken from the timber-framed house formerly adjoining. The present house appears to be of the late 17th century and has been much altered, particularly in the 18th century. In the

197.   Whirley Hall, *c*.1900.

198.   The entrance front, Willaston Old Hall.

1950s the house was restored and the windows regularised, thus giving the facade a more conventional character than before. Low wings were added on either side for a drawing room and kitchen.
Ches Life June 1961.

Willaston Old Hall, Willaston
330 777

A modestly sized manor house with three tall gables peering over a clipped yew hedge close by the village green. The house is built plainly of brick with dressings, plinth and mullioned windows of red sandstone. It probably dates from the early 17th century, despite the date-stone over the door inscribed HB 1558. This was carved in the 19th century, presumably copying the date which Ormerod recorded in 1819 as recently discovered on a chimneypiece. But the house has a symmetrical plan with a central hall and one room to each side; 1558 is too early for such an arrangement. The HB stands for Hugh Bennet; the will of Hugh Bennet jnr., dated 1615, refers to his 'house in Willinston' and the inventory attached to it suggests a substantial household, whilst his father, also Hugh Bennet, is not recorded as living here. On the first floor is an angle fireplace with pargetting gaily painted with the Bennet arms, flowers, fruit, lion masks and cherubs' heads all of the late 17th century; the fireplace was installed between 1663 and 1673, the dates of Hearth Tax returns. Described by Ormerod as 'moss grown and ruinous', the Hall was let to farmers until 1920 when the Bennets sold it. It has recently been restored.
O ii, 544; E. C. Bryan, *The Bennets of Willaston Old Hall*, n.d.

Willaston Hall, Wistaston
674 526

A two-and-a-half storey brick house of *c.* 1700 built for John Bayley and refronted for him in 1737. Symmetrical lower wings were added to each side in 1833 and 1838. The gabled rear elevation shows the original house. The new front was erected without increasing the height of the roof, so that gabled dormers are concealed behind a tall parapet surmounted by urns. Tripartite windows were inserted on the ground floor when the 19th-century wings were added, and the date 1737 is on the rainwater pipes moved from the sides of the main block at the same time. Inside, the best room, to the right of the entrance, is of 1737. It is panelled, with a deep modillion cornice and a large carved chimneypiece in a provincial version of the style of William Kent. Two homely maidens, Night and Day, one with eyes closed, the other open, each with one hand cupping an ample breast, support the mantel, and in the centre is the head of Apollo within a sunburst.
O iii, 487; White's *Directory of Cheshire*, 1860; *Ches Life* June 1937, June 1970.

Willington Hall, Willington
533 660

An early house by George Latham of Nantwich, on the strength of which he gained the commission for Arley Hall. Willington was built in 1829 for Major W. Tomkinson and is in the Jacobean style of diapered brick with shaped gables, in the manner of the old family seat of Dorfold Hall. The east front was added in 1878 for James Tomkinson, though its towers have since been removed. A Tuscan porch was attached in 1955.
O ii, 338; T i, 122; Pike 1904; Latham letters at Arley Hall, letter of 10 February 1830; CRO DTM.

Willot Hall, Prestbury
888 803

A good late medieval hall house built for the Willots of Foxtwist, and encased in stone in the 17th century for Henry Malbon or his son Samuel. It consists of a Great Hall, originally entered on the right, and a two-storey cross wing on the left. Later in the 17th century a brick service wing of two-and-a-half storeys was added, set back behind the screens passage. The house was sensitively restored and extended in 1933-9 for Harry Hyde-Parker by Thomas Worthington & Sons. The entrance was moved to the cross wing and the hall was re-opened to the roof, its great arch-braced tiebeams and crown posts largely renewed. A new screen and minstrel's gallery were made up of old timbers. The restoration was incomplete at the outbreak of war, and the house is untouched since that time, attractively weathered and old fashioned.
O iii, 668.

199. Willot Hall, *c.*1920.

200. Woodbank.

Withington Hall, Withington (demolished)

811 723

Two houses joined at 45 degrees to one another: a modest brick structure of the mid-18th century with a hipped roof, and a grander stuccoed house built *c*. 1795 for John Baskervyle Glegg. The latter part was in the manner of Samuel Wyatt with a semi-circular bow at the centre of the entrance front and interiors with Neo-classical plasterwork. The house was demolished in 1963 and replaced with a modest colour-washed brick house for Mr. E. A. Crosby. A mid-18th-century octagonal dovecote and a stable block dated 1797 remain. In the garden is a remarkable Roman sarcophagus of the early 3rd century showing the Three Graces with figures of a man and his wife at each end, brought to Withington from Italy in the 19th century.

O iii, 718; T ii, 99; *Ches Life* November/December 1953.

Woodbank, Stockport

914 904

A small, crisply cut neo-Grecian box of a house built in 1812 for Peter Marsland, a Stockport mill owner who moved out of the town because his former house was attacked by Luddites. Woodbank was designed by Thomas Harrison and relies on nicety of proportion and smooth ashlar surfaces, now much blackened, with very little enrichment. The entrance front, only three bays wide, has a semi-circular Ionic porch, a favourite Harrison motif. On the rear facade pairs of chaste Ionic half-columns are placed between windows. Alongside is a lower service block. The house is on the villa plan with rooms arranged around a narrow top-lit staircase hall within which climbs a cantilevered stair with a wrought-iron balustrade. The entrance hall has a coffered tunnel vault ceiling. In both these rooms are plaster reliefs after Canova brought from Errwood Hall, Derbyshire in 1930. The library has a built-in clock and barometer by Whitehursts of Derby. Sold in 1929, Woodbank was opened as a museum between 1930 and 1948 but is now used as offices by the local authority and has an unloved municipal look. The grounds are a public park. Beneath a patch of wasteland in a nearby housing estate is the family vault where Peter Marsland, a Unitarian, lies buried.

T ii, 127; Heginbotham ii, 48, 149, 348.

Wrenbury Hall, Wrenbury

599 486

The home of the Starkey family, whose monuments by John Bacon jnr. grace the parish church. The Hall dates back to the 17th century and has a twisted baluster staircase. Ormerod called it a large white building with gables but it was rebuilt in stone after a fire *c*. 1914. It is in a regular Elizabethan style with four stepped gables and a central porch. After a period of institutional use it is now a private house again.

O iii, 395; T ii, 22; Pike 1904, 33.

INDEX

Clonterbrook House, 225
Clowes, M., 248
Clutton, Owen, 224
Cockerell: Sir Charles, 187; S. P., 187, 233
Cogshall Hall, 225
Cole, William, 35-8, 169
Colling, J. K., 244
Colshaw Hall, 226
Combermere, 1st Viscount, 63-4
Combermere Abbey, 7, 48, 60-5, 191
Compstall Hall, 7, 226
Compton Hall, J., 84-6
Comyn Ching, 152
Congreve family, 220
Conseiglio, Francesco, 125
Cornwall Legh, *see* Legh of High Legh
Cooke, William Hilton, 268
Cooper, John, 198, 202
Copley, 276
Corson and Aitken, 256
Cotes, Francis, 164
Cotman, John Sell, 122
Cotton family, 246
Court, William, 255
Crabwall Hall, 226
Crace, J. G., 8, 11, 12-14
Crag Hall, 226
Cranage Hall, 8, 226-7, 233
Crawshawbooth, Lancashire, 143-4
Creswick, Benjamin, 146, 148
Crewe: of Crewe, 35, 66-71, 79, 269; of Utkinton, 278
Crewe Hall, 1, 6, 23, 25, 56, 66-71
Crewe Hill, 227
Crewood Hall, 227
Crook, H. B., 259
Crosby, E. A., 284
Crosfield, John, 279
Crossley family, 65
Crossley Hall, 220
Crowther, J. S., 8, 213
Cubitt and Co., 71
Culshaw, William, 233
Cunningham, John, 7, 214, 278
Curzon, Robert, 165
Cust, Sir Edward, 249

Dahl, Michael, 81
Daintry, John Smith, 260
Dale, Richard, 119
Danesfield, Buckinghamshire, 115
Daniel family, 215
Daniell family, 261
Danyers, Sir Thomas, 123
Darbyshire, Alfred, 127
Darcy Lever Hall, Lancashire, 276
Daresbury Hall, 227, 239
Dauntsey Park, Chippenham, 160
Davenham Hall, 7, 227
Davenport: of Bramall, 39, 42, 51; of

Calveley, 222; of Capesthorne, 48, 51; of Chorley, 57; of Goyt, 235; of Marton, 254
Davenport Bromley, Revd. Walter, 51
Davies Brothers, 87, 224
Davies, John, 256
Davison, T. Raffles, 148
Dawber, Guy, 222
Dawpool, 9, 176, 228, 239
Day, John, and Goldsmith, 7, 226
Dearnford Hall, Whitchurch, 277
Delamer of Dunham Massey, 81
Delamere of Vale Royal, 190-6, 200, 211
Delamere House, 230
Delamere Manor, 9, 228-30
Delves of Doddington, 7, 75, 224, 279
de Delves, John, 72
Demetriades family, 252
Dempster, Robert, 196
Denna Hall, 230
Dennys, John, 94-5, 160
Denton Hall, 230
Denwall Hospital, 230
Derby, Ferdinando, 5th Earl of, 249
Detroit Institute of Arts, 45
Dewar, J. A., 231
Dewhurst, G. C., 261
van Diest, Adrian, 81
Dieulacres, Staffordshire, 211
Disley parish church, 127
Dixon of Astle, 224
Dixon, Thomas, 250
Dod: of Broxton, 219; of Edge, 97-8; of Hampton, 237; of Highfields, 241
Doddington Hall, 1, 5, 7, 72-6, 167, 199, 202, 224
Domville family, 251-2
Done family, 278
Dore Abbey, Hereford, 189
Dorfold Hall, 6, 48, 77-80, 137, 241, 250, 282
Douglas: family, 220; John, 5, 8, 27, 94, 115, 193, 219, 246, 260, 267, 270, 280
Douglas and Fordham, 173, 174
Douglas and Minshull, 226
Dowbiggin of London, 134, 179
Downes, Peter, 222
Doyle, J. F., 9, 239
Duchy of Lancaster, 71
Duddon Old Hall, 230
Dukenfield Hall, 230
Dukinfield, Col. Robert, 209
Dukinfield Hall, 230-1, 261
Dukinfield Lodge, 231
Dunham Massey Hall, 19, 81-6
Dunkerley, Frank, 254
Dutton: Sir Piers, 233; Richard, 272
Dutton of Sutton, 275
Dutton Hall, 231-3
van Dyck, Anthony, 139

Eaton Banks, Tarporley, 180, 213
Eaton Hall: Chester, 1, 3, 5, 8, 36, 38, 64,

287

Harpur, John, 246
Harrington, Earls of, 101, 234
Harris, John, 82, 83, 84
Harrison: James, 36, 275; Stanley, 267;
    Thomas, 7, 35, 79, 165, 179-80, 242, 244,
    261, 284
Harrytown Hall, 237-8
Harter, W. J., 256
Hartford Manor, 238
Harthill church, 36
Haslington Hall, 238
Hassall Hall, 239
Hatfield House, Hertfordshire, 68
Haughton Hall, 9, 239
Hawkstone, Shropshire, 35, 167
Hawthorne Hall, 239
Hay, W. & J., 222
Haycock, John and Edward, 213
Heaton Hall, Lancashire, 72, 74, 157, 200
Heawood Hall, 239
Hefferston Grange, 227, 239
Helmingham Hall, Suffolk, 134, 178
Helpeston, William of, 189
Henbury Hall, 9, 111-14
Henshall Hall, 240
de Hereford, Walter, 189
Hermitage, The, 240
Heron, George, 227
Hesketh Grange, 276
Heyworth, Ormerod, 260
Hibbert: of Birtles, 217; of Hare Hill, 237
High Legh Halls, 4, 241-2
Highfields, 237, 241
Higson, John, 260
Hill, The, Hampstead, 176
Hill: Sir John Gray, 255; Samuel, 167
Hill Bark, 5, 9, 115-18
Hill End, 258
Hinderton Hall, 242
Hiorne Brothers, 155, 158
Hirst, Joseph, 276
Hobart, Sir Henry, 79
Hockenhull family, 270
Hockenhull Hall, 7, 242
Hodkinson, Edward, 159-60
Holcroft, Thomas, 189-91
Holford Hall, 242
Holland of Denton, 230
Holland, Graham, 157
Hollin Hall, 244
Hollin Old Hall, 244
Hollingworth family, 244, 258
Hollingworth Hall, 244
Hollinshead family, 239
Holmes, Sherlock, 264
Holt Castle, 166, 267
Holte family, 47
Holte, Orford, 276
Hondford family, 107
Hoole Hall, 244
Hoole House, 244

Hooton Hall, 7, 9, 224, 244, 272
Hope, John, 82, 155-7, 242
Hopkirk, Mary, 196
Horne, Herbert, 146-8
Hough End Hall, 171
Houghton, Lord, 71
Houghton Hall, Norfolk, 53
Howard, John, 47
Hudson: Robert, 115; Thomas, 155
Hughes, John, 25
Hulme Hall, 245, 270
Hulse, Sir Hugh, 219
Hunt, Thomas, 256
Hurdsfield House, 278
Hyde-Parker, Harry, 282

I.C.I., 22, 181, 197
Image, Selwyn, 146-8
Ince, Townsend, 225
Ince Blundell Hall, Lancashire, 130
Ince Manor, 245-6
Ingersley Hall, 246
Inglewood, 5, 246
Inman, William, 278
Irby Hall, 246
Isherwood, Christopher, 252
Ismay, T. H., 176, 228, 239, 276

Jackson: Peter, 225; Richard, 215; Sir
    William, 225
James I, 66, 77, 191, 268
James II, 123
Jodrell family, 246
Jodrell Bank, 48
Jodrell Hall, 246
Johnson: James, 48, 50; Dr. Samuel, 63;
    Thomas, 235; Thomas (architect), 8, 255,
    258; Mrs. Violet, 213
Jones: Llewellyn, 252; Peter, 235
Joubert, Amedée, 127

Kauffman, Angelica, 34
Kedleston Hall, Derbyshire, 74
Keele Hall, Staffordshire, 48
Kelly, Felix, 111-13
Kemp, Edward, 252
Kempe, C. E., 144, 222
Kent, William, 235
Kenyon, William & Sons, 258
Kerfield House, 9, 150, 248
Kerridge, 5
Kilndown, Christ Church, 24
Kip, J., 81-2
Kirby, Edmund, 27, 255
Knowles, Arthur, 211
Knutsford, Sessions House, 165
Knyff, Leonard, 81

Lancelyn family, 264
Langford Brooke, Peter, 255
Langley, Batty, 111
Langley Hall, 248

Reilly, C. H., 235
Reindeer Inn, Banbury, 71
Repton, Humphry, 71, 155, 158, 167, 169, 214, 242, 244
Richards, Raymond, 101-2
Richardson, C. J., 25, 68
Ridley Hall, 6, 166, 267-8
Ripley, Abbot Simon, 159
Rivers, Earl, 31
Rivington, Lancashire, 176
Robartes, Lady Isabella, 17
Roberts, Henry, 187
Robinson: Lawrence, 7, 270; Robert, 256
Rock Bank House, 250
Rocksavage, 5, 6, 45, 268
Rode Hall, 9, 155-8, 205
de Roedelant family, 276
Rogers, John Swarbreck, 235
Romaine Walker, R. H., 115
Rome Guthrie, L., 196
Romney, George, 164
Rookery, The, Tattenhall, 268
Rookery Hall, Worleston, 222, 268
Rose Corner, Tattenhall, 38
Rossi, Charles, 87
Royal Academy, 12, 72, 152, 181, 219, 226
Royden: Sir Ernest, 116; Sir Thomas, 233
Rubens, Peter Paul, 92
Rufford Old Hall, Lancashire, 15, 17
Runcorn Town Hall, 237
Ruskin, John, 200, 202

Saighton Grange, 5, 95, 159-60
Salesian Mission, 270
Salford Art Gallery, 11
Salomons & Steinthal, 211
Salutation, The, Sandwich, 152
Salviati & Co., 51
Salvin, Anthony, 8, 24-5, 31, 48, 51, 132-4, 272
Samwell, William, 7, 87-9
Sandbach Old Hall, 269
Savage family, 15, 45, 268
Saxon, Charles, 230
Scarisbrick Hall, Lancashire, 101
Schmalz, Herbert J., 42
von Schroder, Baron William, 268
Scott, George Gilbert, 157
Scott & Moffat, 261
Sellers, James Henry, 9, 217, 252
Sephton: Daniel, 19, 130; Henry, 130, 268
Sezincote, Gloucestershire, 187
Shakerley: of Hulme, 245; of Somerford, 270-2
Sharston Hall, 269
Shaw: family, 213; John, 12, 84; R. Norman, 9, 176, 228, 234, 239
Shellard, E. H., 258, 276
Shields, Frederic, 92
Shillito, Daniel, 164
Shotwick Hall, 7, 270
Shotwick Park, 270
Shrigley and Hunt, 146-147

Shrigley Park, 270
Sidebottom, George, 258
Skidmore of Coventry, 92
Slater and Carpenter, 261
Smale, J. Bradley, 251
Smirke, Sir Robert, 56
Smith: Bernard, 17; Francis, 7, 48, 242; Frank, 230; H. Lyle, 215; William, 48, 52, 205
Smith Barry family, 31, 34
Smithills Hall, Bolton, 30, 263
Snyders, Frans, 92
Somerford Booths Hall, 272
Somerford Park, 4, 7, 9, 270-2
Somerset House, London, 123
Soss Moss Hall, 57, 272
South Mimms, Hertfordshire, 118
Staley Hall, 272
Stamford, Earls of, 81-6
Stand Old Hall, Lancashire, 30
Stanhope, Revd. Henry Augustus, 234
Stanhope House, Bromborough, 101
Stanley: of Alderley, 7, 20, 22, 57, 199-200, 202, 235; Earls of Derby, 217; of Hooton, 224, 230, 244; of Puddington, 266; of Storeton, 272; of Weaver, 279
Stanley, Sir William, 166, 267-8, 275
Stanlow Oil Refinery, 245
Stanthorne Hall, 272
Stanyan, Edward, 79
Starkey family, 284
Stevens, James, 240
Stirling, Mrs. F. F., 280
Stockport: Borough Council, 11, 39, 123, 276, 284; St Mary's church, 8, 19, 128, 129-30; St Peter's church, 128, 129
Stoke Brunswick School, 231
Stokes, G. H., 169
Stokesay Castle, Shropshire, 173
Stoneleigh Abbey, Warwickshire, 45
Storeton Hall, 5, 272
Strafford, *see* Wentworth, Thomas
Strawberry Hill, Twickenham, 53, 92
Street, G. E., 25, 222
Stretton: Hall, 273; Lower Hall, 273; Old Hall, 273
Stringer, Thomas, 265
Sudbury Hall, Derbyshire, 84
Sutton Hall: Sutton, 273-4; Sutton Weaver, 39, 166-7, 267, 274-5
Swakeleys, Middlesex, 137
Swetenham of Somerford Booths, 270
Swettenham: of Birtles, 217; of Swettenham, 275
Swettenham Hall, 5, 275
Swindells, Martin, 250
Swinyard Hall, 275

Tabley House, 5, 7, 161-5
Tabley Old Hall, 7, 30, 161
Talbot, J. J., 173, 176
Tamworth Castle, Staffordshire, 142
Tarporley: Hunt Club, 3; Rectory, 278

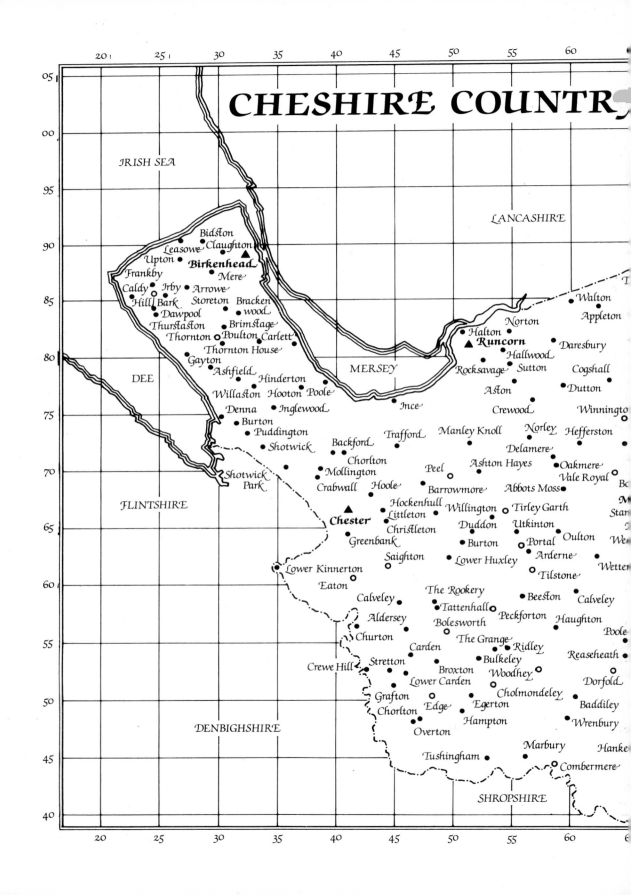

CHESHIRE COUNTRY

IRISH SEA

LANCASHIRE

Bidston
Leasowe · Claughton
Upton ·
Frankby · **Birkenhead** ▲
Caldy · Irby · Mere
Hill Bark · Arrowe
Dawpool · Storeton · Bracken
Thurstaston · Brimstage · wood
Thornton · Poulton · Carlett
Thornton House
Gayton
Ashfield
Hinderton
Willaston · Hooton · Poole
Denna · Inglewood
Burton
Puddington
Shotwick

Walton
Appleton
Norton
Halton · Daresbury
Runcorn ▲
Hallwood
Rocksavage · Sutton · Cogshall
Aston · Dutton
Crewood · Winningto
Manley Knoll · Norley · Hefferston
Trafford · Delamere
Backford · Ashton Hayes · Oakmere
Chorlton · Peel · Vale Royal
Mollington · Abbots Moss
Crabwall · Hoole · Barrowmore
Hockenhull · Willington · Tirley Garth
Littleton · Duddon · Utkinton
Chester ▲ · Christleton · Portal · Oulton
Greenbank · Burton · Arderne
Saighton · Lower Huxley · Tilstone
Lower Kinnerton
Eaton
Calveley · The Rookery · Beeston · Calveley
Aldersey · Tattenhall · Peckforton · Haughton
Bolesworth · Poole
Churton · The Grange · Ridley · Reaseheath
Carden · Bulkeley · Woodhey · Dorfold
Stretton · Broxton · Cholmondeley · Baddiley
Crewe Hill · Lower Carden · Egerton · Wrenbury
Grafton · Edge · Hampton · Hanke
Chorlton · Overton · Marbury
Tushingham · Combermere

DEE

MERSEY

Ince

FLINTSHIRE

DENBIGHSHIRE

SHROPSHIRE